Programming in Objective-C

Programming in Objective-C

Stephen G. Kochan

DEVELOPER'S
LIBRARY

Sams Publishing, 800 East 96th Street, Indianapolis, Indiana 46240

Programming in Objective-C

International Standard Book Number: 0-672-32586-1

Library of Congress Catalog Card Number: 2003092538

Printed in the United States of America

First Printing: *November 2003*

Second printing with corrections: *March 2004*

08 09 10 11 12   14 13 12 11

Trademarks

Warning and Disclaimer

Bulk Sales

Sams Publishing offers excellent discounts on this book when ordered in quantity for bulk purchases or special sales. For more information, please contact

U.S. Corporate and Government Sales
1-800-382-3419
corpsales@pearsontechgroup.com

For sales outside of the United States, please contact

International Sales
international@pearsontechgroup.com

Acquisitions Editor
Kathryn Mohr

Development Editor
Scott Meyers

Managing Editor
Charlotte Clapp

Project Editor
George E. Nedeff

Indexer
Johnna Dinse

Proofreader
Eileen Dennie

Technical Editor
Mike Trent
Jack Purdum

Team Coordinator
Vanessa Evans

Interior Designer
Gary Adair

Cover Designer
Alan Clements

Page Layout
Stacey Richwine-DeRome

❖

To Ve, and, in loving memory, to Roy

❖

Contents At a Glance

Table of Contents

About the Author

Stephen Kochan is the author and coauthor of several bestselling titles on the C language, including *Programming in C, Programming in ANSI C*, and *Topics in C Programming*, and several Unix titles, including *Exploring the Unix System* and *Unix Shell Programming*. He has been programming on Macintosh computers since the introduction of the first Mac in 1984 and wrote *Programming C for the Mac* as part of the Apple Press Library.

About the Technical Reviewers

Michael Trent has been programming in Objective-C since 1997 and programming Macs since well before that. He is a regular contributor to Steven Frank's www.cocoadev.com Web site, technical reviewer for numerous books and magazine articles, and occasional dabbler in Mac OS X open source projects. Currently, he is using Objective-C and Apple Computer's Cocoa frameworks to build professional video applications for Mac OS X. Michael holds a bachelor of science degree in computer science and a bachelor of arts degree in music from Beloit College of Beloit, Wisconsin. He lives in Santa Clara, California, with his lovely wife Angela.

Jack Purdum teaches in the Department of Computer Technology at Purdue University. He received his B.A. degree from Muskingum College and his M.A. and Ph.D. degrees from Ohio State University. He is a bestselling author of more than a dozen programming books and was president of a software firm that specialized in compilers and other programming tools.

We Want to Hear from You

As the reader of this book, you are our most important critic and commentator. We value your opinion and want to know what we're doing right, what we could do better, what areas you'd like to see us publish in, and any other words of wisdom you're willing to pass our way.

You can email or write me directly to let me know what you did or didn't like about this book—as well what we can do to make our books stronger.

Please note that I cannot help you with technical problems related to the topic of this book, and that due to the high volume of mail I receive, I might not be able to reply to every message.

When you write, please be sure to include this book's title and author, as well as your name and contact information. I will carefully review your comments and share them with the author and editors who worked on the book.

Email: devlib@samspublishing.com

Mail: Mark Taber
          Associate Publisher
          Sams Publishing
          800 East 96th Street
          Indianapolis, IN 46240 USA

Reader Services

For more information about this book or others from Sams Publishing, visit our Web site at www.samspublishing.com. Type the ISBN (excluding hyphens) or the title of the book in the Search box to find the book you're looking for.

Introduction

THE "C" PROGRAMMING LANGUAGE WAS PIONEERED by Dennis Ritchie at AT&T Bell Laboratories in the early 1970s. It was not until the late 1970s, however, that this programming language began to gain widespread popularity and support. This was because until that time C compilers were not readily available for commercial use outside of Bell Laboratories. Initially, C's growth in popularity was also spurred on in part by the equal, if not faster, growth in popularity of the Unix operating system, which was written almost entirely in C.

The Objective-C language was designed by Brad J. Cox in the early 1980s. The language was based on a language called SmallTalk-80. Objective-C was *layered* on top of the C language, meaning extensions were added to C to create a new programming language that enabled *objects* to be created and manipulated.

NeXT Software licensed the Objective-C language in 1988 and developed its libraries and a development environment called NEXTSTEP. In 1992, Objective-C support was added to the Free Software Foundation's GNU development environment. This software is in the public domain, which means anyone who wants to learn how to program in Objective-C can do so by downloading its tools at no charge.

In 1994 NeXT Computer and Sun Microsystems released a standardized specification of the NEXTSTEP system called OPENSTEP. The Free Software Foundation's implementation of OPENSTEP is called GNUStep. There's also a Linux version that includes the Linux kernel and the GNUStep development environment called, appropriately enough, LinuxSTEP.

On December 20, 1996, Apple Computer announced that it was acquiring NeXT Software and the NEXTSTEP/OPENSTEP environment became the basis for the next major release of Apple's operating system, OS X. Apple's version of this development environment was called Cocoa. With built-in support for the Objective-C language, coupled with development tools such as Project Builder (or its successor Xcode) and Interface Builder, a powerful development environment was created for application development on the OS X.

When contemplating writing a tutorial on Objective-C, a fundamental decision had to be made. As with all prior texts on Objective-C, I could write mine to assume the reader already knew how to write C programs. I could also teach the language from the perspective of using the rich library of routines, such as the Foundation and Application Kit frameworks. Some texts also take the approach of teaching how to use the development tools, like the Mac's Project Builder and Interface Builder.

I had several problems adopting this approach. First, learning the entire C language before learning Objective-C is wrong. C is a *procedural* language containing many features that are not necessary for programming in Objective-C, especially at the novice level. In fact, resorting to some of these features goes against the grain of adhering to a good object-oriented programming methodology. It's also not a good idea to teach all the details of a procedural language before learning an object-oriented one. This starts the programmer off in the wrong direction, and gives the wrong orientation and mindset for fostering a good object-oriented programming style. Just because Objective-C is an extension to the C language doesn't mean you have to learn C first!

So, I decided neither to teach C first nor to assume prior knowledge of the language. Instead, I decided to take the unconventional approach of teaching Objective-C and the underlying C language as a single integrated language, and from an object-oriented programming perspective. The purpose of this book is as its name implies: to teach you how to program in Objective-C. It makes few assumption about the platform you're running under, the development tools you have available, or the library of classes at your disposal. All that material can be learned elsewhere, after you've learned how to write programs in Objective-C. In fact, mastering that material will be much easier after you have a solid foundation on how to program in Objective-C. This book does not assume much, if any, previous programming experience. In fact, if you're a novice programmer, you should be able to learn Objective-C as your first programming language from this text.

This book teaches Objective-C by example. As each new feature of the language is presented, a small complete program example is usually provided to illustrate the feature. Just as a picture is worth a thousand words, so is a properly chosen program example. If you have access to an Objective-C compiler, you are strongly encouraged to run each program (all of which are available online) and compare the results obtained on your system to those shown in the text. By doing so, not only will you learn the language and its syntax, but you will also become familiar with the process of compiling and running Objective-C programs.

This book is divided into two logical parts. Part I, "The Objective-C Language," teaches the essentials of the language. Part II, "The Foundation Framework," teaches how to use the rich assortment of predefined classes that form the Foundation framework.

A *framework* is a set of classes and routines that have been logically grouped together to make developing programs easier. Much of the power of programming in Objective-C rests on the extensive frameworks that are available. The Foundation framework has been implemented across many different systems, including Unix (and its variants such as Linux and Solaris), Windows (under a Unix layer such as CygWin or MinGW), and Mac OS X. By using the classes in the Foundation framework, you can take advantage of a powerful assortment of built-in classes and develop your programs more quickly and in a more portable manner.

Chapter 2, "Programming in Objective-C," begins by teaching you how to write your first program in Objective-C. Special attention is given to how to enter, compile, and run Objective-C programs on Mac OS X and on Windows and non-Mac Unix systems using the GNU gcc compiler.

Because developing graphical user interfaces (GUIs) is not taught in this book, a method was needed to get input and produce output. Most of the examples in this text are command-line driven, so they take input from the keyboard and produce their output in a window, perhaps a Terminal window under Unix or Mac OS X, or an MS-DOS window under Windows.

Chapter 3, "Classes, Objects, and Methods," covers the fundamentals of object-oriented programming. Some terminology is introduced here, but it's kept to a minimum. The mechanism for defining a class is introduced in the chapter, and the means for sending messages to instances or objects are also covered. Instructors and seasoned Objective-C programmers will notice that I use *static* typing for declaring objects. I think this is the best way for the student to get started, from the perspective of allowing the compiler to catch more errors, making the programs more self-documenting, and encouraging the new programmer to explicitly declare her data types when they are known. As a result, the notion of the id type and its power is not fully explored until Chapter 9, "Polymorphism, Dynamic Typing, and Dynamic Binding."

Chapter 4, "Data Types and Expressions," describes the basic Objective-C data types and how to use them in your programs.

Chapter 5, "Program Looping," introduces the three looping statements you can use in your programs: for, while, and do.

Making decisions is fundamental to any computer programming language. Chapter 6, "Making Decisions," covers the Objective-C language's if and switch statements in detail.

Chapter 7, "More on Classes," delves more deeply into working with classes and objects. Details about methods, multiple arguments to methods, and local variables are discussed here.

Chapter 8, "Inheritance," introduces the key concept of *inheritance*. This feature makes the development of programs easier because you can take advantage of what comes from above. Inheritance and the notion of subclasses make modifying and extending existing class definitions easy.

Chapter 9 discusses three fundamental characteristics of the Objective-C language. Polymorphism, dynamic typing, and dynamic binding are the key concepts covered here.

Chapters 10–13 round out the discussion of the Objective-C language, covering issues such as initialization of objects, protocols, categories, the preprocessor, and some of the underlying C features, including functions, arrays, structures, and pointers. These underlying features are often unnecessary (and often best avoided) when first developing object-oriented applications. It's recommended you skim Chapter 13, "Underlying C Features," the first time through the text and return to it only as necessary to learn more about a particular feature of the language.

Part II begins with Chapter 14, "Introduction to the Foundation Framework," which gives an introduction to the Foundation framework and its root object called NSObject.

Important features of the Foundation framework are covered in Chapters 15–19. These include working with number and string objects, collections, working with the file system, memory management, and copying and archiving objects.

By the time you're done with Part II, you will be able to develop fairly sophisticated programs in Objective-C that work with the Foundation framework.

Because object-oriented parlance involves a fair amount of terminology, Appendix A, "Glossary," provides definitions of some common terms.

Appendix B, "Objective-C Language Summary," gives a summary of the Objective-C language and is provided for your quick reference.

In Appendix C, "Foundation Framework Headers," a brief summary of the Foundation framework header files is provided. This list will give you a quick idea of the types of capabilities that are offered by this framework.

Appendix D, "Fraction and Address Book Examples," gives the source code listing for three classes that are developed and used extensively throughout this text. One class is for working with fractions. The other two enable you to define an address book and perform various operations with it.

After you've learned how to write Objective-C programs, you can go in several directions. You might want to lean more about the underlying C programming language, or you may want to start writing Cocoa programs to run on Mac OS X. In any case, the resources listed in Appendix E, "Resources," will guide you in the right direction.

All the program examples in this book were run on Mac OS X Version 10.2.6 as well as using GNUStep base version 1.6.0 under MinGW on a Windows XP system. The text teaches you how to write Objective-C programs that are portable and independent of any particular operating system and machine architecture.

There are several people I would like to acknowledge for their help in the preparation of this text. First, I want to thank Tony Iannino and Steven Levy for reviewing the manuscript. I am also grateful to Mike Gaines for providing his input.

I'd also like to thank my technical editors, Jack Purdum and Mike Trent. Mike provided the most thorough review of any book I've ever written. Not only did he point out some weaknesses, but he was also generous enough to offer his suggestions as well. Because of Mike's comments, I changed my approach to teaching memory management and tried to make sure that every program example in this book is "leak-free."

From Sams Publishing I'd like to thank my editor Kathryn Mohr for, well, just for *everything*. It was a pleasure working with Katie on this book and I am sorry that I won't get a chance to work with her again at Sams. Also from Sams I'd like to thank Scott Meyers for his help and for taking over where Katie left off.

Catherine Babin supplied the cover photograph and provided me with many wonderful pictures from which to choose. Having the cover art from a friend makes the book even more special.

My children showed an incredible amount of maturity and patience while I pulled this book together over their summer vacation. To Gregory, Linda, and Julia, I love you!

Stephen G. Kochan
August 2003

I

The Objective-C Language

2

Programming in Objective-C

IN THIS CHAPTER WE'LL DIVE RIGHT IN and show you how to write your first Objective-C program. You won't work with objects just yet; that is the topic of the next chapter. We want you to understand the steps involved in keying in a program and compiling and running it. Special attention is given to this process under Windows and on a Macintosh computer.

To begin, let's pick a rather simple example—a program that displays the phrase `Programming is fun.` on your screen. Without further ado, here is an Objective-C program to accomplish this task.

Program 2.1

```
// First program example
#import <stdio.h>

int main (int argc, const char *argv[])
{
  printf ("Programming is fun.\n");

  return 0;
}
```

Before we go into a detailed explanation of this program, let's learn the steps involved in compiling and running it. You first need to enter the lines from Program 2.1 into a text file. Then, you need to issue the right commands to compile and execute it. Let's examine how to go about doing that in detail.

Compiling and Running Programs on the Mac

If you're using Mac OS X, you have two choices. You can either compile and run your program using the GNU Objective-C compiler in a Terminal window, or you can use Project Builder[1]. Let's go through the sequence of steps using either method. Then, you can decide how you want to work with your programs throughout the rest of this book.

1. These tools should be preinstalled on all Macs that came with OS X. If you separately installed OS X, then make sure you install the Developer Tools as well.

Compiling Programs in a Terminal Window

The first step is to start the Terminal application on your Mac. The Terminal application is located in the Applications folder, stored under Utilities. Its icon is shown in Figure 2.1.

Terminal

Figure 2.1   Terminal program icon.

Start the Terminal application, and you'll see a window that looks like Figure 2.2.

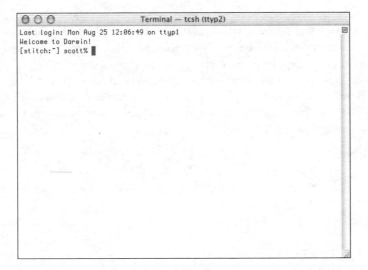

Figure 2.2   Terminal window.

Commands are typed after the $ (or % depending on how your Terminal application is configured) on each line. If you're familiar with using Unix, this will be straightforward.

First, you need to enter the lines from Program 2.1 into a file. You can begin by creating a directory in which to store your program examples. Then, you must run a text editor, such as vi or emacs, to enter your program:

```
sh-2.05a$ mkdir MySrc     Create a directory to store programs in
sh-2.05a$ cd MySrc        Change to the new directory
sh-2.05a$ vi main.m       Start up a text editor to enter program
   . .
```

In the previous example and throughout the remainder of this text, commands entered by you, the user, are indicated in boldface.

For Objective-C files, you can choose any name you want; just make sure the last two characters are `.m`. This is done out of convention, so that the compiler knows you have an Objective-C program. Other commonly used filename suffixes are shown in Table 2.1.

Table 2.1 **Common Filename Suffixes**

Extension	Meaning
`.c`	C language source file
`.cc`, `.cpp`	C++ language source file
`.h`	Header file
`.m`	Objective-C source file
`.mm`	Objective-C++ source file
`.pl`	Perl source file
`.o`	Object (compiled) file

After you've entered your program into a file, you can use the GNU Objective-C compiler, which is called `gcc`, to compile and link your program. The general format of the `gcc` command is

```
gcc files -o progname -l objc
```

Here, `files` is the list of files to be compiled. In our example, we have only one such file and we're calling it `main.m`. `progname` is the name of the file that will contain the executable if the program compiles without any errors. The rest of the line contains information about linking your program. The option

```
-l objc
```

says to link with the Objective-C runtime library called `objc`. Just remember to use this option at the end of each line.

Let's call the program `prog1`; here then is the command line to compile your first Objective-C program:

```
sh-2.05a$ gcc main.m -o prog1 -l objc   Compile main.m & call it prog1
sh-2.05a$
```

The return of the command prompt without any messages means that no errors were found in the program. Now you can subsequently execute the program by typing the name `prog1` at the command prompt:

```
sh-2.05a$ prog1          Execute prog1
sh: prog1: command not found
sh-2.05a$
```

This is the result you'll probably get unless you've used Terminal before. The fact is that the Unix shell (which is the application running your program) doesn't know where prog1 is located. We won't get into all the details here. You have two options: One is to precede the name of the program with the characters . / so that the shell knows to look in the current directory for the program to execute. The other is to add the directory in which your programs are stored (or just simply the current directory) to your PATH variable. Ask someone for help on how to do this if needed.

Let's take the first approach here:

```
sh-2.05a$ ./prog1          Execute prog1
Programming is fun.
sh-2.05a$
```

That's better! If you used Terminal to compile and execute your program, you can skip the next section. However, you might want to skim this section to learn how you can also use Project Builder to compile and run your programs.

Compiling and Running Programs Using Project Builder

Project Builder is a sophisticated application that allows you to easily type in, compile, debug, and execute programs. If you plan on doing serious application development on the Mac, learning how to use this powerful tool is worthwhile. We'll just get you started here. Later, we'll return to Project Builder and take you through the steps involved in developing a graphical application with it.

Note

As of the writing of this book, Apple was in the process of replacing Project Builder with an improved tool called Xcode. Notable interface differences do exist, but Xcode behaves very similarly and these instructions should work fine. That said, any big discrepancies will be pointed out.

First, Project Builder is located in the Developer folder inside a subfolder called Applications. Its icon is shown in Figure 2.3.

Project Builder

Figure 2.3   Project Builder icon.

Start Project Builder. Under the File menu, select New Project (see Figure 2.4).

Figure 2.4   Starting a new project.

A window will then appear, as shown in Figure 2.5.

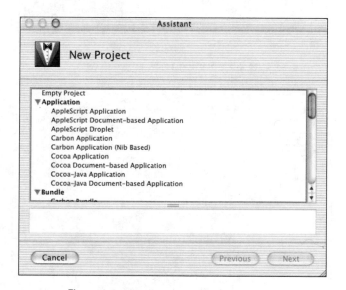

Figure 2.5   Starting a new project (cont'd).

Unfortunately, there is no project type that you can select here that describes precisely what you want to do, so select Cocoa Application. After highlighting Cocoa Application, click Next. This brings up a new window shown in Figure 2.6.

Let's call the first program `prog1`, so type that into the Project Name field. For the Location field, you can let the Mac choose where to store your project files, or you can type in a directory. By default, it stores the project in the directory `~/prog1/`, where the Unix notation `~` is used to specify the name of your Home directory.

The Next button changes to Finish; clicking it causes the Location field to be filled in, if you didn't fill it in yourself. It then closes the Assistant window, replacing it with the window that appears in Figure 2.7.

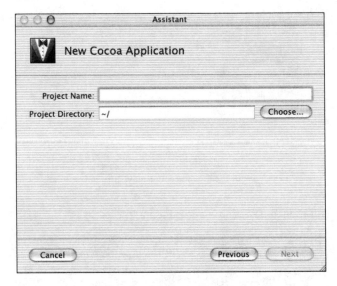

Figure 2.6   Starting a new project (cont'd).

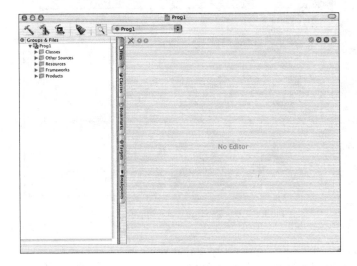

Figure 2.7   Project Builder file list window.

Now it's time to type in your first program, so under prog1 in the left side of the window, click Other Sources. This reveals the file main.m, as shown in Figure 2.8.

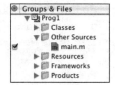

Figure 2.8   `main.m` file.

Highlight the file `main.m`. Your Project Builder window should now appear as shown in Figure 2.9.

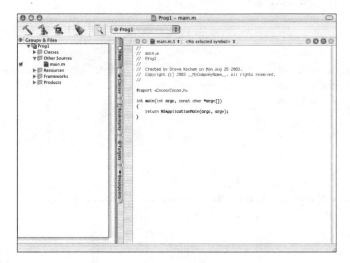

Figure 2.9   File `main.m` and edit window.

The right side of the window shows the file called `main.m` and contains the following lines:

```
//
// main.m
// prog1
//
// Created by Steve Kochan on Mon Aug 25 2003.
// Copyright (c) 2003 __MyCompanyName__. All rights reserved.
//

#import <Cocoa/Cocoa.h>

int main(int argc, const char *argv[])
{
  return NSApplicationMain(argc, argv);
}
```

You can edit your file inside this window. Project Builder has created a template file for you to use. Unfortunately, it's a little more than you need right now. Therefore, remove a couple of lines and continue. To make `main.m` look more like your first program, replace the line

```
#import <Cocoa/Cocoa.h>
```

with the line

```
#import <stdio.h>
```

and replace the line that reads

```
return NSApplicationMain(argc, argv);
```

with

```
return 0;
```

You can leave all the lines at the beginning of `main.m` that start with two slash characters (//). Those lines are *comments*, and we'll talk more about them shortly.

Your program in the edit window should now look like this:

```
//
// main.m
// prog1
//
// Created by Steve Kochan on Mon Aug 25 2003.
// Copyright (c) 2003 __MyCompanyName__. All rights reserved.
//

#import <stdio.h>

int main (int argc, const char *argv[])
{
  printf ("Programming is fun.\n");
  return 0;
}
```

Don't worry about all the colors shown for your text on your screen. Project Builder indicates values, reserved words, and so on using different colors.

Now it's time to compile and run your first program—in Project Builder terminology it's called *build* and run. You need to save your program first, however. This can be done by selecting Save from the File menu. If you try to compile and run your program without first saving your file, Project Builder asks whether you want to first save your program.

Under the Build menu, you can select either Build or Build and Run. Select the latter because that automatically runs the program if it builds without any errors. You can also activate Build and Run by clicking the 🔳 icon that appears in the toolbar.

A window labeled `Build: prog1 - (prog1)` appears first and details the build process. You'll see several text lines scrolling quickly through a small section of the window in the middle. Those are the actual command lines that are being executed to build your program example. In fact, Project Builder uses the same `gcc` compiler you used in the Terminal application window in the previous section.

If you made mistakes in your program, you'll see error messages listed during this step. In that case, go back, fix the errors, and repeat the process. After all the errors have been removed from the program, a new window appears; it's labeled `Run: prog1 - (prog1)`. This window contains the output from your program and should look similar to Figure 2.10. If this window does not automatically appear, go to the `main` menu bar and select Show Run Log from the `Debug` menu.

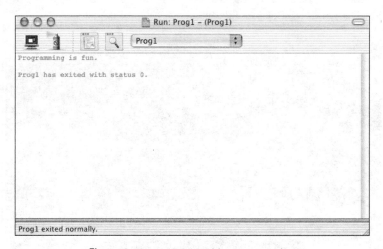

Figure 2.10   Project Builder Run window.

You're now done with the procedural part of compiling and running your first program with Project Builder (whew!). The following summarizes the steps involved in creating a new program with Project Builder:

1. Start the Project Builder application

2. If this is a new project, select File, New Project.

3. For the type of application, select Cocoa Application and click Next.

4. Select a name for your project, and optionally a directory to store your project files in. Click Finish.

5. Under Other Sources you will see the file `main.m`. Highlight that file. Type your program into the edit window on the right side of the screen.

6. Save the changes you've entered by selecting File, Save.

7. Build and run your application by selecting Build, Build and Run.

8. If you get any compiler errors or the output is not what you expected, make your changes to the program and repeat steps 6 and 7.

Compiling and Running Programs under Windows

If you're running Windows, you can download an Objective-C compiler that is part of the MinGW system from http://www.mingw.org, get an Objective-C compiler that runs under CygWin (http://www.cygwin.com/)[2], or ask your system administrator to locate or install a compiler for you.

Using the Objective-C compiler from MinGW is a good choice because the Objective-C compiler runs without any special software in a DOS-box under Windows. We'll go through the steps involved in compiling and running an Objective-C program under that environment. These steps are virtually identical to those outlined for compiling Objective-C programs using Terminal on the Mac.

We'll assume you have installed the MinGW system. Start the MS-DOS Prompt utility. You should see a window similar to Figure 2.11.

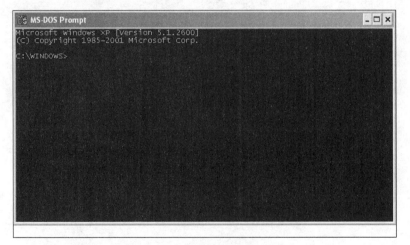

Figure 2.11   MS-DOS window.

(What appears on your window might appear slightly different, depending on which version of Windows you're running, for example.) You have to find where your Objective-C compiler is located. If you followed the standard installation procedures, it's located in the directory C:\MinGW\bin. To have the system find the Objective-C compiler (the next time you boot your system), you should add this directory to your PATH in your autoexec.bat file. You should add a line that looks something like this:

```
SET PATH=%PATH%;C:\MINGW\BIN
```

To type in your first program, you can use any editor you like; the built-in Windows editor edit will work just fine. Let's assume you have typed Program 2.1 into a file called main.m in a directory on your C: drive called mysrc. You can now use the

---

2. CygWin is a Unix environment that runs under Windows. The good news is that it's free. However, you should be aware that Objective-C support is *not* normally provided with the compiler that is distributed with CygWin.

Objective-C compiler that comes with MinGW to compile and link your program. The general format of the command to do this is

```
gcc files -o progname -l objc
```

where `files` is the list of files to be compiled. In this example, you have only one such file, called `main.m`. `progname` is the name of the file that will contain the executable program if the compiler detects no errors. The rest of the line contains information about linking your program. The option

```
-l objc
```

says to link with the Objective-C runtime library called `objc`. Just remember to use this option at the end of each line.

If you call your program `prog1`, the command line to compile your first Objective-C program would be as follows:

```
C:\mysrc> gcc main.m -o prog1 -l objc    Compile main.m call it prog1
main.m:1:2: warning: #import is obsolete, use an #ifndef wrapper in the header
file
C:\mysrc>
```

In the previous example and throughout the remainder of this text, the commands entered by the user are indicated in boldface.

The compiler issues a warning message that has to do with the `#import` statement that appears in the program. You should ignore this message.

The return of the command prompt after the warning message means that no errors were found in the program. You can subsequently execute the program by typing the name `prog1` at the command prompt, like so:

```
C:\mysrc> prog1           Execute prog1
Programming is fun.       Program output
C:\mysrc>
```

Line-by-Line Explanation of Your First Program

Now that you are familiar with the steps involved in compiling and running Objective-C programs, let's take a closer look at this first program. Here it is again.

Program 2.1
___

```
// First program example
#import <stdio.h>

int main (int argc, const char *argv[])
{
  printf ("Programming is fun.\n");
  return 0;
}
```
___

In Objective-C, lowercase and uppercase letters are distinct. Also, Objective-C does not care where on the line you begin typing—you can begin typing your statement at any position on the line. This fact can be used to your advantage in developing programs that are easier to read.

Comments

The first line of the program

```
// First program example
```

introduces the concept of the *comment*. A comment statement is used in a program to document a program and enhance its readability. Comments serve to tell the reader of the program—be it the programmer or someone else whose responsibility it is to maintain the program—just what the programmer had in mind when she wrote a particular program or a particular sequence of statements.

You can insert comments into an Objective-C program in two ways. One is by using two consecutive slash characters (//). Any characters that follow these slashes up to the end of the line are ignored by the compiler.

A comment can also be initiated by the two characters / and *. This marks the beginning of the comment, and these types of comments have to be terminated. To end the comment, the characters * and / are used, once again without any embedded spaces. All characters included between the opening /* and the closing */ are treated as part of the comment statement and are ignored by the Objective-C compiler. This form of comment is often used when comments span many lines of code, such as in the following:

```
/*
  This file implements a class called Fraction, which
  represents fractional numbers. Methods allow manipulation of
  fractions, such as addition, subtraction, etc.

  For more information, consult the document:
    /usr/docs/classes/fractions.pdf
*/
```

Which style of comment you use is entirely up to you. Just note that you can't nest the /* style comments.

You should get into the habit of inserting comment statements in the program as the program is being written or typed into the computer. There are three good reasons for this. First, documenting the program while the particular program logic is still fresh in your mind is far easier than going back and rethinking the logic after the program has been completed. Second, by inserting comments into the program at such an early stage of the game, you can reap the benefits of the comments during the debug phase, when program logic errors are isolated and debugged. A comment can not only help you (and others) read through the program, but can also help point the way to the source of the logic mistake. Finally, I have yet to discover a programmer who actually enjoys documenting a program. In fact, after you have finished debugging your program, you will probably not relish the idea of going back to the program to insert comments. Inserting comments while developing the program makes this sometimes tedious task a bit easier to handle.

The next line of Program 2.1 that reads

```
#import <stdio.h>
```

tells the compiler to locate and process a file named `stdio.h`, which is a system file—that is, not a file you created. `#import` says to import or include the information from that file into the program, exactly as if the contents of the file were typed into the program at that point. You imported the file `stdio.h` because it has information about the `printf` output routine used later in the program.

In Program 2.1, the line that reads

```
int main (int argc, const char *argv[])
```

specifies that the name of the program is `main`, which is a special name that indicates precisely where the program is to begin execution. The reserved word `int` that precedes `main` specifies the type of value `main` returns, which is an integer (more about that soon). We will ignore what appears between the open and closed parentheses for now. These have to do with what are known as *command-line arguments*, a topic we address in Chapter 13, "Underlying C Language Features."

Now that you have identified `main` to the system, you are ready to specify precisely what this routine is to perform. This is done by enclosing all the program *statements* of the routine within a pair of curly braces. In the simplest case, a statement is just an expression that is terminated with a semicolon. All the program statements included between the braces will be taken as part of the `main` routine by the system. Program 2.1 has two statements. The first statement specifies that a routine named `printf` is to be invoked, or *called*. The parameter, or *argument*, to be passed or handed to the `printf` routine is the following string of characters:

```
"Programming is fun.\n"
```

The `printf` routine is a function in the Objective-C library that simply prints or displays its argument (or arguments, as you will see shortly) on the screen. The last two characters in the string, namely the backslash (\) and the letter n, are known collectively as the *newline* character. A newline character tells the system to do precisely what its name implies—go to a new line. Any characters to be printed after the newline character then appear on the next line of the terminal or display. In fact, the newline character is very similar in concept to the carriage return key on a typewriter.

All program statements in Objective-C must be terminated by a semicolon (;). This is why a semicolon appears immediately following the closed parenthesis of the `printf` call.

The second program statement in `main`

```
return 0;
```

says to terminate execution of `main` and to send back, or *return*, a status value of 0. By convention, 0 means that the program ended normally. Any nonzero value typically means some problem occurred—for example perhaps a file that was needed by the program couldn't be located.

If you're using Project Builder and you glance back to your Run window (refer to Figure 2.10), you'll recall that after the line of output from printf, the following was displayed:

```
prog1 has exited with status 0.
```

You should understand what that message means now.

Now that we have finished discussing your first program, let's modify it to also display the phrase "And programming in Objective-C is even more fun." This can be done by simply adding another call to the printf routine, as shown in Program 2.2. Remember that every Objective-C program statement must be terminated by a semicolon.

Program 2.2

```
#import <stdio.h>

int main (int argc, const char *argv[])
{
  printf ("Programming is fun.\n");
  printf ("Programming in Objective-C is even more fun.\n");

  return 0;
}
```

If you type in Program 2.2 and then compile and execute it, you can expect the following output at your terminal.

Program 2.2 **Output**

```
Programming is fun.
Programming in Objective-C is even more fun.
```

As you will see from the next program example, you don't need to make a separate call to the printf routine for each line of output. Study the program listed in Program 2.3 and try to predict the results before examining the output (no cheating, now!).

Program 2.3

```
#import <stdio.h>

int main (int argc, const char *argv[])
{
  printf ("Testing...\n..1\n...2\n....3\n");
  return 0;
}
```

Program 2.3   **Output**

```
Testing...
..1
...2
....3
```

Displaying the Values of Variables

Not only can simple phrases be displayed with printf, but the values of *variables* and the results of computations can be displayed as well. Program 2.4 uses the printf routine to display the results of adding two numbers, namely 50 and 25.

Program 2.4

```
#import <stdio.h>

int main (int argc, const char *argv[])
{
    int sum;

    sum = 50 + 25;
    printf ("The sum of 50 and 25 is %i\n", sum);
    return 0;
}
```

Program 2.4   **Output**

```
The sum of 50 and 25 is 75
```

The first program statement inside main defines the variable sum to be of type integer. All program variables must be defined before they are used in a program. The definition of a variable specifies to the Objective-C compiler how it will be used by the program. This information is needed by the compiler to generate the correct instructions to store and retrieve values into and out of the variable. A variable defined as type int can be used to hold only integral values—that is, values without decimal places. Examples of integral values are 3, 5, −20, and 0. Numbers with decimal places, such as 2.14, 2.455, and 27.0, are known as *floating point* numbers and are real numbers.

The integer variable sum is used to store the result of the addition of the two integers 50 and 25. We have intentionally left a blank line following the definition of this variable to visually separate the variable declarations of the routine from the program statements; this is strictly a matter of style. Sometimes the addition of a single blank line in a program can help make the program more readable.

The program statement

```
sum = 50 + 25;
```

reads as it would in most other programming languages: The number 50 is added (as indicated by the plus sign) to the number 25, and the result is stored (as indicated by the assignment operator, the equal sign) into the variable sum.

The printf routine call in Program 2.4 now has two arguments enclosed within the parentheses. These arguments are separated by a comma. The first argument to the printf routine is always the character string to be displayed. However, along with the display of the character string, you often might want to have the value of certain program variables displayed as well. In this case, you want to have the value of the variable sum displayed at the terminal after the characters are displayed:

```
The sum of 50 and 25 is
```

The percent character inside the first argument is a special character recognized by the printf function. The character that immediately follows the percent sign specifies what type of value is to be displayed at that point. In the previous program, the letter i is recognized by the printf routine as signifying that an integer value is to be displayed.

Whenever the printf routine finds the %i characters inside a character string, it automatically displays the value of the next argument to the routine. Because sum is the next argument to printf, its value is automatically displayed after the characters The sum of 50 and 25 is are displayed.

Now try to predict the output from Program 2.5.

Program 2.5

```
#import <stdio.h>

int main (int argc, const char *argv[])
{
    int value1, value2, sum;

    value1 = 50;
    value2 = 25;
    sum = value1 + value2;

    printf ("The sum of %i and %i is %i\n", value1, value2, sum);

    return 0;
}
```

Program 2.5 **Output**

```
The sum of 50 and 25 is 75
```

The first program statement inside main defines three variables called value1, value2, and sum all to be of type int. This statement could have equivalently been expressed using three separate statements as follows:

```
int value1;
int value2;
int sum;
```

After the three variables have been defined, the program assigns the value 50 to the variable value1 and then the value 25 to value2. The sum of these two variables is then computed and the result assigned to the variable sum.

The call to the printf routine now contains four arguments. Once again, the first argument, commonly called the *format string*, describes to the system how the remaining arguments are to be displayed. The value of value1 is to be displayed immediately following the display of the characters The sum of are displayed. Similarly, the values of value2 and sum are to be printed at the appropriate points as indicated by the next two occurrences of the %i characters in the format string.

This discussion concludes this introductory chapter on developing programs in Objective-C. By now, you should have a good feel as to what is involved in writing a program in Objective-C, and you should be able to develop a small program on your own. In the next chapter, you will begin to examine some of the finer intricacies of this powerful and flexible programming language. But first, try your hand at the exercises that follow to make sure you understand the concepts presented in this chapter.

Exercises

1. If you have access to an Objective-C compiler, type in and run the five programs presented in this chapter. Compare the output produced by each program with the output presented after each program.

2. Write a program that displays the following text:
   ```
   In Objective-C, lowercase letters are significant.
   main is where program execution begins.
   Open and closed braces enclose program statements in a routine.
   All program statements must be terminated by a semicolon.
   ```

3. What output would you expect from the following program?
   ```
   #import <stdio.h>

   int main (int argc, const char *argv[])
   {
       printf ("Testing...");
       printf ("....1");
       printf ("...2");
       printf ("..3");
       printf ("\n");
       return 0;
   }
   ```

4. Write a program that subtracts the value 15 from 87 and displays the result, together with an appropriate message.

5. Identify the syntactic errors in the following program. Then type in and run the corrected program to make sure you have identified all the mistakes:

```
#import <stdio.h>

int main (int argc, const char *argv[]);
(
    INT sum;
    /* COMPUTE RESULT //
    sum = 25 + 37 - 19
    / DISPLAY RESULTS /
    printf ('The answer is %i\n' sum);

    return 0;
}
```

6. What output would you expect from the following program?

```
#import <stdio.h>

main (int argc, const char *argv[]))
{
    int answer, result;

    answer = 100;
    result = answer - 10;

    printf ("The result is %i\n", result + 5);

    return 0;
}
```

3

Classes, Objects, and Methods

IN THIS CHAPTER YOU LEARN ABOUT SOME KEY CONCEPTS in object-oriented programming and start working with classes in Objective-C. You'll need to learn a little bit of terminology, and we'll keep it fairly informal. We'll also cover only some of the basic terms here because you can easily get overwhelmed. Refer to Appendix A, "Glossary," at the end of this book for more precise definitions of these terms.

What Is an Object, Anyway?

An *object* is a thing. Think about object-oriented programming as a thing and something you want to do to that thing. This is in contrast to a programming language such as C, known as a procedural programming language. In C, you typically think about what you want to do first and then you worry about the objects...almost the opposite from object-orientation.

Let's take an example from everyday life. Let's assume you own a car, which is obviously an object, and one that you own. You don't have just any car; you have a particular car that was manufactured in a factory, maybe in Detroit, maybe in Japan, or maybe someplace else. Your car has a vehicle identification number (VIN), which uniquely identifies that car.

In object-oriented parlance, your car is an *instance* of a car. And continuing with the terminology, car is the name of the class from which this instance was created. So, each time a new car is manufactured, a new instance from the class of cars is created, and each instance of the car is referred to as an object.

Your car might be silver, have a black interior, and be a convertible or hardtop, and so on. Additionally, you perform certain actions with your car. For example, you drive your car, fill it with gas, (hopefully) wash it, take it in for service, and so on. This is depicted in Table 3.1.

Table 3.1 **Actions on Objects**

Object	What You Do with It
Your car	Drive it
	Fill it with gas
	Wash it
	Service it

The actions listed in Table 3.1 can be done with your car, and they can also be done with other cars as well. For example, your sister drives her car, washes it, fills it with gas, and so on.

Instances and Methods

A unique occurrence of a class is an instance, and the actions that are performed on the instance are called *methods*. In some cases, a method can be applied to an instance of the class or to the class itself. For example, washing you car applies to an instance (in fact, all the methods listed in Table 3.1 would be considered instance methods). Finding out how many types of cars a manufacturer makes would apply to the class, so it would be a class method. Suppose you have two cars that came off the assembly line that are seemingly identical: They both have the same interior, same paint color, and so on. They might start out the same, but as each car is used by its respective owner, it acquires its own unique characteristics. For example, one car might end up with a scratch on it and the other might have more miles on it. Each instance or object contains not only information about its initial characteristics it acquired from the factory, but also its current character-istics. Those characteristics can change dynamically. As you drive your car, the gas tank becomes depleted, the car gets dirtier, and the tires get a little more worn.

Applying a method to an object can affect the *state* of that object. If your method is to "fill up my car with gas," after that method is performed your car's gas tank will be full. The method will have affected the state of the car's gas tank.

The key concepts here are that objects are unique representations from a class, and each object contains some information (data) that is typically private to that object. The methods provide the means of accessing and changing that data.

The Objective-C programming language has the following particular syntax for applying methods to classes and instances:

```
[ ClassOrInstance method ];
```

In this syntax, a left bracket is followed by the name of a class or instance of that class, which is followed by one or more spaces, which is followed by the method you want to perform. Finally, it is closed off with a right bracket and a terminating semicolon. When you ask a class or an instance to perform some action, you say that you are sending it a *message*; the recipient of that message is called the *receiver*. So, another way to look at the general format described previously is as follows:

```
[ receiver message ] ;
```

Let's go back to the previous list and write everything in this new syntax. Before you do that, though, you need to get your new car. Go to the factory for that, like so:

```
yourCar = [Car new];      get a new car
```

You send a message to the `Car` class (the receiver of the message) asking it to give you a new car. The resulting object (which represents your unique car), is then stored in the variable `yourCar`. From now on, `yourCar` can be used to refer to your instance of the car, which you got from the factory.

Because you went to the factory to get the car, the method new is called a *factory* or *class* method. The rest of the actions on your new car will be instance methods because they apply to your car. Here are some sample message expressions you might write for your car:

```
[yourCar prep];      get it ready for first-time use
[yourCar drive];     drive your car
[yourCar wash];      wash your car
[yourCar getGas];    put gas in your car if you need it
[yourCar service];   service your car

[yourCar topDown];   if it's a convertible
[yourCar topUp];
```

Your sister Sue can use the same methods for her own instance of a car:

```
[suesCar drive];
[suesCar wash];
[suesCar getGas];
```

This is one of the key concepts behind object-oriented programming (that is, applying the same methods to different objects), and you'll learn more about that later.

You probably won't need to work with cars in your programs. Your objects are likely to be computer-oriented things, such as windows, rectangles, pieces of text, or maybe even a calculator or a playlist of songs. And just like the methods used for your cars, your methods might look similar, as in the following:

```
[myWindow erase];              Clear the window
[myRect getArea];              Calculate the area of the rectangle
[userText spellCheck];         Spell check some text
[deskCalculator clearEntry];   Clear the last entry
[favoritePlaylist showSongs];  Show the songs in a playlist of favorites
```

An Objective-C Class for Working with Fractions

Now it's time to define an actual class in Objective-C and learn how to work with instances of the class.

Once again, you'll learn procedure first. As a result, the actual program examples might not seem very practical. We'll get into more practical stuff later.

Suppose you needed to write a program to work with fractions. Maybe you needed to deal with adding, subtracting, multiplying them, and so on. If you didn't know about classes, you might start with a simple program that looked like this:

Program 3.1

```
// Simple program to work with fractions
#import <stdio.h>

int main (int argc, char *argv[])
{
   int  numerator = 1;
   int  denominator = 3;
   printf ("The fraction is %i/%i\n", numerator, denominator);

   return 0;
}
```

Program 3.1 **Output**

```
The fraction is 1/3
```

In Program 3.1 the fraction is represented in terms of its numerator and denominator. The first two lines in main both declare the variables numerator and denominator as integers and assign them initial values of 1 and 3, respectively. This is equivalent to the following lines:

```
int numerator, denominator;

numerator = 1;
denominator = 3;
```

We represented the fraction 1/3 by storing 1 into the variable numerator and 3 into the variable denominator. If you needed to store a lot of fractions in your program, this could be cumbersome. Each time you wanted to refer to the fraction, you'd have to refer to the corresponding numerator and denominator. And performing operations on these fractions would be just as awkward.

It would be better if you could define a fraction as a single entity and collectively refer to its numerator and denominator with a single name, such as myFraction. You can do that in Objective-C, and it starts by defining a new class.

Program 3.2 duplicates the functionality of Program 3.1 using a new class called Fraction. Here, then, is the program followed by a detailed explanation of how it works.

Program 3.2

```
// Program to work with fractions - class version

#import <stdio.h>
#import <objc/Object.h>

//------- @interface section -------

@interface Fraction: Object
{
  int  numerator;
  int  denominator;
}

-(void)   print;
-(void)   setNumerator: (int) n;
-(void)   setDenominator: (int) d;

@end

//------- @implementation section -------


@implementation Fraction;
-(void) print
{
  printf (" %i/%i ", numerator, denominator);
}

-(void) setNumerator: (int) n
{
  numerator = n;
}

-(void) setDenominator: (int) d
{
  denominator = d;
}

@end

//------- program section -------


int main (int argc, char *argv[])
{
  Fraction  *myFraction;
```

Program 3.2   **Continued**

```
// Create an instance of a Fraction

myFraction = [Fraction alloc];
myFraction = [myFraction init];

// Set fraction to 1/3

[myFraction setNumerator: 1];
[myFraction setDenominator: 3];

// Display the fraction using the print method

printf ("The value of myFraction is:");
[myFraction print];
printf ("\n");
[myFraction free];

return 0;
}
```

Program 3.2   **Output**

```
The value of myFraction is: 1/3
```

As you can see from the comments in Program 3.2, the program is logically divided into three sections, as depicted in Figure 3.1:

- @interface section
- @implementation section
- program section

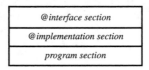

Figure 3.1   Program structure.

The @interface section describes the class, its data components, and its methods, whereas the @implementation section contains the actual code that implements these methods. Finally, the program section contains the program code to carry out the intended purpose of the program.

Each of these sections is a part of every Objective-C program, even though you might not need to write each section yourself. As you'll see, each section is typically put in its own file. For now, however, we'll keep it all together in a single file.

The @interface Section

When you define a new class, you have to do a few things. First, you have to tell the Objective-C compiler where the class came from. That is, you have to name its *parent* class. Second, you have to specify what type of data is to be stored in the objects of this class. That is, you have to describe the data that members of the class will contain. These members are called the *instance variables*. Finally, you need to define the type of operations, or *methods*, that can be used when working with objects from this class. This is all done in a special section of the program called the @interface section. The general format of this section looks like this:

```
@interface NewClassName: ParentClassName
{
   memberDeclarations;
}

methodDeclarations;
@end
```

By convention, class names begin with an uppercase letter, even though it's not required. This enables someone reading your program to distinguish class names from other types of variables by simply looking at the first character of the name. Let's take a short diversion to talk a little bit about forming names in Objective-C.

Choosing Names

In Chapter 2, "Programming in Objective-C," you used several variables to store integer values. For example, you used the variable sum in Program 2.4 to store the result of the addition of the two integers, 50 and 25.

The Objective-C language allows data types other than just integers to be stored in variables as well, provided the proper declaration for the variable is made before it is used in the program. Variables can be used to store floating-point numbers, characters, and even objects (or more precisely, references to objects).

The rules for forming names are quite simple: They must begin with a letter or underscore (_), and they can be followed by any combination of letters (upper- or lowercase), underscores, or the digits 0–9. The following is a list of valid names:

- sum
- pieceFlag
- i
- myRectangle
- numberOfMoves
- _sysFlag
- ChessPiece

On the other hand, the following names are not valid for the stated reasons:

- `sum$value`—$ is not a valid character.
- `piece flag`—Embedded spaces are not permitted.
- `3Spencer`—Names can't start with a number.
- `int`—This is a reserved word.

`int` cannot be used as a variable name because its use has a special meaning to the Objective C compiler. This use is known as a *reserved name* or *reserved word.* In general, any name that has special significance to the Objective-C compiler cannot be used as a variable name. Appendix B, "Objective-C Language Summary," provides a complete list of such reserved names.

You should always remember that upper- and lowercase letters are distinct in Objective-C. Therefore, the variable names `sum`, `Sum`, and `SUM` each refer to a different variable. As noted, when naming a class, start it with a capital letter. Instance variables, objects, and method names, on the other hand, typically begin with lowercase letters. To aid readability, capital letters are used inside names to indicate the start of a new word, as in the following examples:

`AddressBook`	This could be a class name.
`currentEntry`	This could be an object.
`current_entry`	Underscores are also used by some programmers as word separators.
`addNewEntry`	This could be a method name.

When deciding on a name, keep one recommendation in mind: Don't be lazy. Pick names that reflect the intended use of the variable or object. The reasons are obvious. Just as with the comment statement, meaningful names can dramatically increase the readability of a program and will pay off in the debug and documentation phases. In fact, the documentation task will probably be greatly reduced because the program will be more self-explanatory.

Here again is the `@interface` section from Program 3.2:

```
//------- @interface section -------

@interface Fraction: Object
{
  int  numerator;
  int  denominator;
}

-(void) print;
-(void) setNumerator: (int) n;
-(void) setDenominator: (int) d;

@end
```

The name of the new class (NewClassName) is Fraction, and its parent class is Object. (We'll talk in greater detail about parent classes in Chapter 8, "Inheritance.") The Object class is defined in the file objc/Object.h, which is why that file (along with stdio.h) is imported at the beginning of Program 3.2:

```
#import <objc/Object.h>
```

Instance Variables

The memberDeclarations section specifies what types of data are stored in a Fraction, as well as the names of those data types. As you can see, this section is enclosed inside its own set of curly braces. For your Fraction class, the declarations

```
int   numerator;
int   denominator;
```

say that a Fraction object has two integer members called numerator and denominator.

The members declared in this section are known as the instance variables. As you'll see, each time you create a new object, a new and unique set of instance variables also is created. Therefore, if you have two Fractions, one called fracA and another called fracB, each will have its own set of instance variables. That is, fracA and fracB each will have its own separate numerator and denominator. The Objective-C system automatically keeps track of this for you, which is one of the nicer things about working with objects.

Class and Instance Methods

You have to define methods to work with your Fractions. You'll need to be able to set the value of a fraction to a particular value. Because you won't have direct access to the internal representation of a fraction (in other words, direct access to its instance variables), you must write methods to set the numerator and denominator. You'll also write a method called print that will display the value of a fraction. Here's what the declaration for the print method looks like in the interface file:

```
-(void) print;
```

The leading minus sign (-) tells the Objective-C compiler that the method is an instance method. The only other option is a plus sign (+), which indicates a class method. A class method is one that performs some operation on the class itself, such as creating a new instance of the class. This is similar to manufacturing a new car, in that the car is the class and you want to create a new one—which would be a class method.

An instance method performs some operation on a particular instance of a class, such as setting its value, retrieving its value, displaying its value, and so on. Referring to the car example, after you have manufactured the car, you might need to fill it with gas. The operation of filling it with gas is performed on a particular car, so it would be analogous to an instance method.

Return Values

When you declare a new method, you have to tell the Objective-C compiler whether the method returns a value, and if it does, what type of value it returns. This is done by enclosing the return type in parentheses after the leading minus or plus sign. So, the declaration

```
-(int) getNumerator;
```

specifies that the instance method called `getNumerator` returns an integer value. Similarly, the line

```
-(double) getDoubleValue;
```

declares a method that returns a double precision value. (You'll learn more about this data type in Chapter 4, "Data Types and Expressions.")

A value is returned from a method using the Objective-C `return` statement, similar to the way in which we returned a value from `main` in previous program examples.

If the method returns no value, you indicate that using the type `void`, as in the following:

```
-(void) print;
```

This declares an instance method called `print` that returns no value. In such a case, you do not need to execute a `return` statement at the end of your method. Alternatively, you can execute a `return` without any specified value, as in the following:

```
return;
```

You don't need to specify a return type for your methods, although it's better programming practice if you do. If none is specified, `id` is the default. You'll learn more about the `id` data type in a later chapter. Basically, the `id` type can be used to refer to any type of object.

Method Arguments

Two other methods are declared in the `@interface` section from Program 3.2:

```
-(void) setNumerator: (int) n;
-(void) setDenominator: (int) d;
```

These are both instance methods that return no value. Each method takes an integer argument, which is indicated by the `(int)` in front of the argument name. In the case of `setNumerator`, the name of the argument is n. This name is arbitrary, and it is the name the method uses to refer to the argument. Therefore, the declaration of `setNumerator` specifies that one integer argument called n will be passed to the method and that no value is returned. This is similar for `setDenominator`, except the name of its argument is d.

Notice the syntax of the declaration for these methods. Each method name ends with a colon, which tells the Objective-C compiler that the method expects to see an argument. Next, the type of the argument is specified, enclosed in a set of parentheses, in much the same way the return type is specified for the method itself. Finally, the symbolic name to be used to identify that argument in the method is specified. The entire declaration is terminated with a semicolon. This syntax is depicted in Figure 3.2.

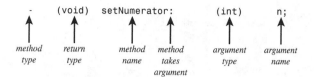

Figure 3.2   Declaring a method.

When a method takes an argument, you also append a colon to the method name when referring to the method. setNumerator: and setDenominator: would therefore be the correct way to identify these two methods—each of which takes a single argument. Also, the identification of the print method without a trailing colon indicates that this method does not take any arguments. In Chapter 7, "More on Classes," you'll see how methods that take more than one argument are identified.

The @implementation Section

As noted, the @implementation section contains the actual code for the methods you declared in the @interface section. Just as a point of terminology, you say that you *declare* the methods in the @interface section and that you *define* them (that is, give the actual code) in the @implementation section.

The general format for the @implementation section is as follows:

```
@implementation NewClassName;
 methodDefinitions;
@end
```

NewClassName is the same name that was used for the class in the @interface section. You can use the trailing colon followed by the parent class name, as we did in the @interface section:

```
@implementation Fraction: Object;
```

However, it's optional and typically not done.

The methodDefinitions part of the @implementation section contains the code for each method specified in the @interface section. Similar to the @interface section, each method's definition starts by identifying the type of method (class or instance), its return type, and its arguments and their types. However, instead of the line ending with a semicolon, the code for the method follows, enclosed inside a set of curly braces.

Here's the @implementation section from Program 3.2:

```
//------- @implementation section -------


@implementation Fraction;
-(void) print
```

```
{
  printf (" %i/%i ", numerator, denominator);
}

-(void) setNumerator: (int) n
{
  numerator = n;
}

-(void) setDenominator: (int) d
{
  denominator = d;
}

@end
```

The `print` method uses `printf` to display the values of the instance variables `numerator` and `denominator`. But to which numerator and denominator does this method refer? It refers to the instance variables contained in the object that is the receiver of the message. That's an important concept, and we'll return to it shortly.

The `setNumerator:` method takes the integer argument you called n and simply stores it in the instance variable `numerator`. Similarly, `setDenominator:` stores the value of its argument d in the instance variable `denominator`.

The Program Section

The `program` section contains the code to solve your particular problem, which can be spread out across many files, if necessary. Somewhere you must have a routine called `main`, as we've previously noted. That's where your program always begins execution. Here is the program section from Program 3.2:

```
//------- program section -------

int main (int argc, char *argv[])
{
  Fraction  *myFraction;

  // Create an instance of a Fraction

  myFraction = [Fraction alloc];
  myFraction = [myFraction init];

  // Set fraction to 1/3

  [myFraction setNumerator: 1];
  [myFraction setDenominator: 3];
```

```
// Display the fraction using the print method

printf ("The value of myFraction is:");
[myFraction print];
printf ("\n");

[myFraction free];

return 0;
}
```

Inside main you define a variable called myFraction with the following line:

```
Fraction *myFraction;
```

This line says that myFraction is an object of type Fraction; that is, myFraction is used to store values from your new Fraction class. The asterisk (*) in front of myFraction is required, but don't worry about its purpose now. Technically, it says that myFraction is actually a reference (or *pointer*) to a Fraction.

Now that you have an object to store a Fraction, you need to create one, just like you ask the factory to build you a new car. This is done with the following line:

```
myFraction = [Fraction alloc];
```

alloc is short for *allocate*. You want to allocate memory storage space for a new fraction. The expression

```
[Fraction alloc]
```

sends a message to your newly created Fraction class. You are asking the Fraction class to apply the alloc method, but you never defined an alloc method, so where did it come from? The method was inherited from a parent class. Chapter 8 deals with this topic in detail.

When you send the alloc message to a class, you get back a new instance of that class. In Program 3.2, the returned value is stored inside your variable myFraction. The alloc method is guaranteed to zero out all of an object's instance variables. However, that does not mean that the object has been properly initialized for use. You need to initialize an object after you allocate it.

This is done with the next statement in Program 3.2, that reads as follows:

```
myFraction = [myFraction init];
```

Again, you are using a method here that you didn't write yourself. The init method initializes the instance of a class. Note that you are sending the init message to myFraction. That is, you want to initialize a specific Fraction object here, so you don't send it to the class—you send it to an instance of the class. Make sure you understand this point before continuing.

The init method also returns a value, namely the initialized object. You take the return value and store it in your Fraction variable myFraction.

The two-line sequence of allocating a new instance of class and then initializing it is done so often in Objective-C that the two messages are typically combined, as follows:

```
myFraction = [[Fraction alloc] init];
```

The inner message expression

```
[Fraction alloc]
```

is evaluated first. As you know, the result of this message expression is the actual Fraction that is allocated. Instead of storing the result of the allocation in a variable as you did before, you directly apply the init method to it. So, again, first you allocate a new Fraction and then you initialize it. The result of the initialization is then assigned to the myFraction variable.

As a final shorthand technique, the allocation and initialization is often incorporated directly into the declaration line, as in the following:

```
Fraction *myFraction = [[Fraction alloc] init];
```

This coding style is used often throughout the remainder of this book, so it's important that you understand it.

Returning to Program 3.2, you are now ready to set the value of your fraction. The program lines

```
// Set fraction to 1/3

[myFraction setNumerator: 1];
[myFraction setDenominator: 3];
```

do just that. The first message statement sends the setNumerator: message to myFraction. The argument that is supplied is the value 1. Control is then sent to the setNumerator: method you defined for your Fraction class. The Objective-C system knows that it is the method from this class to use because it knows that myFraction is an object from the Fraction class.

Inside the setNumerator: method, the passed value of 1 is stored inside the variable n. The single program line in that method takes that value and stores it in the instance variable numerator. So, you have effectively set the numerator of myFraction to 1.

The message that invokes the setDenominator: method on myFraction follows next. The argument of 3 is assigned to the variable d inside the setDenominator: method. This value is then stored inside the denominator instance variable, thus completing the assignment of the value 1/3 to myFraction. Now you're ready to display the value of your fraction, which is done with the following lines of code from Program 3.2:

```
// display the fraction using the print method

printf ("The value of myFraction is:");
[myFraction print];
printf ("\n");
```

The first `printf` call simply displays the following text:

```
The value of myFraction is:
```

A newline is not appended to the end of the line so that the value of the fraction as displayed by the `print` method appears on the same line. The `print` method is invoked with the following message expression:

```
[myFraction print];
```

Inside the `print` method, the values of the instance variables `numerator` and `denominator` are displayed, separated by a slash character. The final `printf` call back in `main` simply displays a newline character.

The last message in the program,

```
[myFraction free];
```

frees the memory that was used for the `Fraction` object. This is a critical part of good programming style. Whenever you create a new object, you are asking for memory to be allocated for that object. Also, when you're done with the object, you are responsible for releasing the memory it uses. Although it's true that the memory will be released when your program terminates anyway, after you start developing more sophisticated applications, you can end up working with hundreds (or thousands) of objects that consume a lot of memory. Waiting for the program to terminate for the memory to be released is wasteful of memory, can slow your program's execution, and is not good programming style. So, get into the habit right now!

It seems as if you had to write a lot more code to duplicate in Program 3.2 what you did in Program 3.1. That's true for this simple example here; however, the ultimate goal in working with objects is to make your programs easier to write, maintain, and extend. You'll realize that later.

The last example in this chapter shows how you can work with more than one fraction in your program. In Program 3.3, you set one fraction to 2/3, set another to 3/7, and display them both.

Program 3.3

```
// Program to work with fractions - cont'd

#import <stdio.h>
#import <objc/Object.h>

//------- @interface section -------

@interface Fraction: Object
{
  int  numerator;
  int  denominator;
}
```

Program 3.3 **Continued**

```
-(void) print;
-(void) setNumerator: (int) n;
-(void) setDenominator: (int) d;


@end

//------- @implementation section -------


@implementation Fraction;
-(void) print
{
  printf (" %i/%i ", numerator, denominator);
}

-(void) setNumerator: (int) n
{
  numerator = n;
}

-(void) setDenominator: (int) d
{
  denominator = d;
}

@end

//------- program section -------

int main (int argc, char *argv[])
{
  Fraction   *frac1 = [[Fraction alloc] init];
  Fraction   *frac2 = [[Fraction alloc] init];

  // Set 1st fraction to 2/3

  [frac1 setNumerator: 2];
  [frac1 setDenominator: 3];

  // Set 2nd fraction to 3/7

  [frac2 setNumerator: 3];
  [frac2 setDenominator: 7];
```

Program 3.3   **Continued**

```
// Display the fractions

printf ("First fraction is:");
[frac1 print];
printf ("\n");

printf ("Second fraction is:");
[frac2 print];
printf ("\n");

[frac1 free];
[frac2 free];

return 0;
}
```

Program 3.3   **Output**

```
First fraction is: 2/3
Second fraction is: 3/7
```

The @interface and @implementation sections remain unchanged from Program 3.2. The program creates two Fraction objects called frac1 and frac2 and then assigns the value 2/3 to the first fraction and 3/7 to the second. Realize that, when the setNumerator: method is applied to frac1 to set its numerator to 2, the instance variable frac1 gets its instance variable numerator set to 2. Also, when frac2 uses the same method to set its numerator to 3, its distinct instance variable numerator is set to the value 3. Each time you create a new object, it gets its own distinct set of instance variables. This is depicted in Figure 3.3.

Figure 3.3   Unique instance variables.

Based on which object is getting sent the message, the correct instance variables are referenced. Therefore, in

```
[frac1 setNumerator: 2];
```

it is frac1's numerator that is referenced whenever setNumerator: uses the name numerator inside the method. That's because frac1 is the receiver of the message.

Accessing Instance Variables and Data Encapsulation

You've seen how the methods that deal with fractions can access the two instance variables `numerator` and `denominator` directly by name. In fact, an instance method can always directly access its instance variables. A class method can't, however, because it's dealing only with the class itself and not with any instances of the class (think about that for a second). But what if you wanted to access your instance variables from someplace else—for example, from inside your `main` routine? You can't do that directly because they are hidden. The fact that they are hidden from you is a key concept called *data encapsulation*. It enables someone writing class definitions to extend and modify his class definitions without worrying about whether programmers (that is, users of the class) are tinkering with the internal details of the class. Data encapsulation provides a nice layer of insulation between the programmer and the class developer.

You can access your instance variables in a clean way by writing special methods to retrieve their values. For example, you'll create two new methods called, appropriately enough, `numerator` and `denominator` to access the corresponding instance variables of the `Fraction` that is the receiver of the message. The result will be the corresponding integer value, which you will return. Here are the declarations for your two new methods:

```
-(int) numerator;
-(int) denominator;
```

And here are the definitions:

```
-(int) numerator
{
  return numerator;
}

-(int) denominator
{
  return denominator;
}
```

Note that the names of the methods and the instance variables they access are the same. There's no problem doing this; in fact, it is common practice. Program 3.4 tests your two new methods.

Program 3.4

```
// Program to access instance variables - cont'd

#import <stdio.h>
#import <objc/Object.h>
//------- @interface section -------
```

Program 3.4   **Continued**

```objc
@interface Fraction: Object
{
  int  numerator;
  int  denominator;
}

-(void) print;
-(void) setNumerator: (int) n;
-(void) setDenominator: (int) d;
-(int) numerator;
-(int) denominator;

@end

//------- @implementation section -------


@implementation Fraction;
-(void) print
{
  printf (" %i/%i ", numerator, denominator);
}

-(void) setNumerator: (int) n
{
  numerator = n;
}

-(void) setDenominator: (int) d
{
  denominator = d;
}

-(int) numerator
{
  return numerator;
}

-(int) denominator
{
  return denominator;
}

@end


//------- program section -------
```

Program 3.4 **Continued**

```
int main (int argc, char *argv[])
{
  Fraction  *myFraction = [[Fraction alloc] init];

  // Set fraction to 1/3

  [myFraction setNumerator: 1];
  [myFraction setDenominator: 3];

  // Display the fraction using our two new methods

  printf ("The value of myFraction is: %i/%i\n",
      [myFraction numerator], [myFraction denominator]);
  [myFraction free];

  return 0;
}
```

Program 3.4 **Output**

```
The value of myFraction is 1/3
```

The `printf` statement

```
printf ("The value of myFraction is: %i/%i\n",
  [myFraction numerator], [myFraction denominator]);
```

displays the results of sending two messages to `myFraction`: the first to retrieve the value of its `numerator`, and the second the value of its `denominator`.

Incidentally, methods that set the values of instance variables are often collectively referred to as *setters*, and methods used to retrieve the values of instance variables are called *getters*. For the `Fraction` class, `setNumerator:` and `setDenominator:` are the setters and `numerator` and `denominator` are the getters.

It should also be pointed out here that there is also a method called `new` that combines the actions of an `alloc` and `init`. So, the line

```
Fraction *myFraction = [Fraction new];
```

could be used to allocate and initialize a new `Fraction`. It's generally better to use the two-step allocation and initialization approach so you conceptually understand that two distinct events are occurring: You're first creating a new object and then you're initializing it.

Now you know how to define your own class, create objects or instances of that class, and send messages to those objects. We'll return to the `Fraction` class in later chapters.

You'll learn how to pass multiple arguments to your methods, how to divide your class definitions into separate files, and also about key concepts such as inheritance and dynamic binding. However, now it's time to learn more about data types and writing expressions in Objective-C. First, try the exercises that follow to test your understanding of the important points covered in this chapter.

Exercises

1. Which of the following are invalid names? Why?

   ```
   Int              playNextSong      6_05
   _calloc          Xx                alphaBetaRoutine
   clearScreen      _1312             z
   ReInitialize     _                 A$
   ```

2. Based on the example of the car in this chapter, think of an object you use every day. Identify a class for that object and write five actions you do with that object.

3. Given the list in exercise 2, use the following syntax:

   ```
   [instance method];
   ```

   to rewrite your list in this format.

4. Imagine that you owned a boat and a motorcycle in addition to a car. List the actions you would perform with each of these. Do you have any overlap between these actions?

5. Based on question 4, imagine you had a class called a Vehicle and an object called myVehicle that could be either a Car, a Motorcycle, or a Boat. What if you wrote the following:

   ```
   [myVehicle prep];
   [myVehicle getGas];
   [myVehicle service];
   ```

   Do you see any advantages of being able to apply an action to an object that could be from one of several classes?

6. In a procedural language such as C, you think about actions and then write code to perform the action on various objects. Referring to the car example, you might write a procedure in C to wash a vehicle and then inside that procedure write code to handle washing a car, washing a boat, washing a motorcycle, and so on. If you took that approach and then wanted to add a new vehicle type (see the previous exercise), do you see advantages or disadvantages to using this procedural approach over an object-oriented approach?

7. Define a class called Point that will hold a Cartesian coordinate (x, y), where x and y are integers. Define methods to individually set the x and y coordinates of a point and retrieve their values. Write an Objective-C program to implement your new class and test it.

Data Types and Expressions

IN THIS CHAPTER, WE WILL TAKE A LOOK at the basic data types and describe some fundamental rules for forming arithmetic expressions in Objective-C.

Data Types and Constants

You have already been exposed to the Objective-C basic data type int. As you will recall, a variable declared to be of type int can be used to contain integral values only—that is, values that do not contain decimal places.

The Objective-C programming language provides three other basic data types: float, double, and char. A variable declared to be of type float can be used for storing floating-point numbers (values containing decimal places). The double type is the same as type float, only with roughly twice the accuracy. Finally, the char data type can be used to store a single character, such as the letter *a*, the digit character *6*, or a semicolon (more on this later).

In Objective-C, any number, single character, or character string is known as a *constant*. For example, the number 58 represents a constant integer value. The character string "Programming in Objective-C is fun.\n" is an example of a constant character string. Expressions consisting entirely of constant values are called *constant expressions*. So, the expression

`128 + 7 - 17`

is a constant expression because each of the terms of the expression is a constant value. But if i were declared to be an integer variable, the expression

`128 + 7 - i`

would not represent a constant expression.

Type `int`

In Objective-C, an integer constant consists of a sequence of one or more digits. A minus sign preceding the sequence indicates that the value is negative. The values 158, –10, and 0 are all valid examples of integer constants. No embedded spaces are permitted between the digits, and values larger than 999 cannot be expressed using commas. (So, the value 12,000 is not a valid integer constant and must be written as 12000.)

Two special formats in Objective-C enable integer constants to be expressed in a base other than decimal (base 10). If the first digit of the integer value is a 0, the integer is taken as expressed in *octal* notation—that is in base 8. In that case, the remaining digits of the value must be valid base-8 digits and therefore must be 0–7. So, to express the value 50 in base-8 in Objective-C, which is equivalent to the value 40 in decimal, the notation 050 is used. Similarly, the octal constant 0177 represents the decimal value 127 ($1 \times 64 + 7 \times 8 + 7$). An integer value can be displayed at the terminal in octal notation by using the format characters %o in the format string of a `printf` statement. In such a case, the value is displayed in octal without a leading zero. The format character %#o does cause a leading zero to be displayed before an octal value.

If an integer constant is preceded by a zero and the letter *x* (either lowercase or uppercase), the value is taken as being expressed in hexadecimal (base-16) notation. Immediately following the letter *x* are the digits of the hexadecimal value, which can be composed of the digits 0–9 and the letters a–f (or A–F). The letters represent the values 10–15, respectively. So, to assign the hexadecimal value FFEF0D to an integer variable called `rgbColor`, the statement

```
rgbColor = 0xFFEF0D;
```

can be used. The format characters %x display a value in hexadecimal format without the leading 0x and with using lowercase letters a–f for hexidecimal digits. To display the value with the leading 0x, you use the format characters %#x, as in the following:

```
printf ("Color is %#x\n", rgbColor);
```

An uppercase X, as in %X or %#X, can be used to display the leading x and hexidecimal digits that follow using uppercase letters.

Storage Sizes and Ranges

Every value, whether it's a character, an integer, or a floating-point number, has a *range* of values associated with it. This range has to do with the amount of storage allocated to store a particular type of data. In general, that amount is not defined in the language; it typically depends on the computer you're running on and is therefore called *implementation* or *machine dependent*. For example, an integer can take up 32 bits on your computer, or perhaps it might be stored in 64. You should never write programs that make any assumptions about the size of your data types. You are, however, guaranteed that a minimum amount of storage will be set aside for each basic data type. For example, it's guaranteed that an integer value will be stored in a minimum of 32 bits of storage, which is the size of a word on many computers. However, once again, it's not guaranteed. See Table B.2 in Appendix B, "Objective-C Language Summary," for more information about data type sizes.

Type `float`

A variable declared to be of type `float` can be used for storing values containing decimal places. A floating-point constant is distinguished by the presence of a decimal point. You can omit digits before the decimal point or digits after the decimal point, but obviously you can't omit both. The values `3.`, `125.8`, and `-.0001` are all valid examples of floating-point constants. To display a floating-point value at the terminal, the `printf` conversion characters `%f` are used.

Floating-point constants can also be expressed in so-called *scientific notation*. The value `1.7e4` is a floating-point value expressed in this notation and represents the value 1.7×10^{-4}. The value before the letter `e` is known as the *mantissa*, whereas the value that follows is called the *exponent*. This exponent, which can be preceded by an optional plus or minus sign, represents the power of 10 by which the mantissa is to be multiplied. So, in the constant `2.25e-3`, the `2.25` is the value of the mantissa and `-3` is the value of the exponent. This constant represents the value 2.25×10^{-3}, or 0.00225. Incidentally, the letter `e`, which separates the mantissa from the exponent, can be written in either lowercase or uppercase.

To display a value in scientific notation, the format characters `%e` should be specified in the `printf` format string. The `printf` format characters `%g` can be used to let `printf` decide whether to display the floating-point value in normal floating-point notation or in scientific notation. This decision will be based on the value of the exponent: If it's less than -4 or greater than 5, `%e` (scientific notation) format is used; otherwise, `%f` format is used.

A *hexadecimal* floating constant consists of a leading `0x` or `0X`, followed by one or more decimal or hexadecimal digits, followed by a `p` or `P`, followed by an optionally signed binary exponent. For example, `0x0.3p10` represents the value $3/16 \times 2^{10} = 0.5$.

Type `double`

The type `double` is very similar to type `float`, but it is used whenever the range provided by a `float` variable is not sufficient. Variables declared to be of type `double` can store roughly twice as many significant digits as can a variable of type `float`. Most computers represent `double` values using 64 bits.

Unless told otherwise, all floating-point constants are taken as `double` values by the Objective-C compiler. To explicitly express a `float` constant, append either an `f` or `F` to the end of the number, like so:

```
12.5f
```

To display a `double` value, the format characters `%f`, `%e`, or `%g`, which are the same format characters used to display a `float` value, can be used.

Type `char`

A `char` variable can be used to store a single character[1]. A character constant is formed by enclosing the character within a pair of single quotation marks. So `'a'`, `';'`, and `'0'`

---

1. Appendix B discusses methods for storing characters from extended character sets, through special escape sequences, universal characters, and *wide* characters.

are all valid examples of character constants. The first constant represents the letter *a*, the second is a semicolon, and the third is the character zero—which is not the same as the number zero. Do not confuse a character constant, which is a single character enclosed in single quotes, with a character string, which is any number of characters enclosed in double quotes.

The character constant ' \n '—the newline character—is a valid character constant even though it seems to contradict the rule cited previously. The reason for this is that the backslash character is a special character in the Objective-C system and does not actually count as a character. In other words, the Objective-C compiler treats the character ' \n ' as a single character, even though it is actually formed by two characters. Other special characters are initiated with the backslash character. See Appendix B for a complete list. The format characters %c can be used in a printf call to display the value of a char variable at the terminal.

In Program 4.1, the basic Objective-C data types are used.

Program 4.1

```
#import <stdio.h>

int main (int argc, char *argv[])
{
    int    integerVar = 100;
    float  floatingVar = 331.79;
    double doubleVar = 8.44e+11;
    char   charVar = 'W';

    printf ("integerVar = %i\n", integerVar);
    printf ("floatingVar = %f\n", floatingVar);
    printf ("doubleVar = %e\n", doubleVar);
    printf ("doubleVar = %g\n", doubleVar);
    printf ("charVar = %c\n", charVar);

    return 0;
}
```

Program 4.1 **Output**

```
integerVar = 100
floatingVar = 331.790009
doubleVar = 8.440000e+11
doubleVar = 8.44e+11
charVar = W
```

In the second line of the program's output, you will notice that the value of 331.79, which is assigned to floatingVar, is actually displayed as 331.790009. In fact, the actual value displayed is dependent on the particular computer system you are using. The reason for this inaccuracy is the particular way in which numbers are internally represented inside the computer. You have probably come across the same type of inaccuracy when dealing with numbers on your pocket calculator. If you divide 1 by 3 on your calculator, you get the result .33333333, with perhaps some additional 3s tacked on at the end. The string of 3s is the calculator's approximation to one third. Theoretically, there should be an infinite number of 3s. But the calculator can hold only so many digits, thus the inherent inaccuracy of the machine. The same type of inaccuracy applies here: Certain floating-point values cannot be exactly represented inside the computer's memory.

Qualifiers: long, long long, short, unsigned, and signed

If the qualifier long is placed directly before the int declaration, the declared integer variable is of extended range on some computer systems. An example of a long int declaration might be

```
long int factorial;
```

This declares the variable factorial to be a long integer variable. As with floats and doubles, the particular accuracy of a long variable depends on your particular computer system. On many systems, an int and a long int both have the same range and either can be used to store integer values up to 32-bits wide ($2^{31} - 1$, or 2,147,483,647).

A constant value of type long int is formed by optionally appending the letter L (upper- or lowercase) onto the end of an integer constant. No spaces are permitted between the number and the L. So, the declaration

```
long int numberOfPoints = 131071100L;
```

declares the variable numberOfPoints to be of type long int with an initial value of 131,071,100.

To display the value of a long int using printf, the letter l is used as a modifier before the integer format characters i, o, and x. This means that the format characters %li can be used to display the value of a long int in decimal format, the characters %lo can display the value in octal format, and the characters %lx can display the value in hexadecimal format.

A long long integer data type can be used like so:

```
long long int maxAllowedStorage;
```

This declares the indicated variable to be of the specified extended accuracy, which is guaranteed to be at least 64 bits wide. Instead of a single letter *l*, two *l*s are used in the printf string to display long long integers, as in "%lli".

The long qualifier is also allowed in front of a double declaration, like so:

```
long double US_deficit_2004;
```

A `long double` constant is written as a floating constant with the letter l or L immediately following, like so:

`1.234e+7L`

To display a `long double`, the L modifier is used. So, `%Lf` would display a `long double` value in floating-point notation, `%Le` would display the same value in scientific notation, and `%Lg` would tell `printf` to choose between `%Lf` and `%Le`.

The qualifier `short`, when placed in front of the `int` declaration, tells the Objective-C compiler that the particular variable being declared is used to store fairly small integer values. The motivation for using `short` variables is primarily one of conserving memory space, which can be an issue in cases where the program needs a lot of memory and the amount of available memory is limited.

On some machines, a `short int` takes up half the amount of storage as a regular `int` variable does. In any case, you are guaranteed that the amount of space allocated for a `short int` will not be less than 16 bits.

There is no way to explicitly write a constant of type `short int` in Objective-C. To display a `short int` variable, place the letter h in front of any of the normal integer conversion characters: `%hi`, `%ho`, or `%hx`. Alternatively, you can use any of the integer conversion characters to display short `ints` because they can be converted into integers when they are passed as arguments to the `printf` routine.

The final qualifier that can be placed in front of an `int` variable is used when an integer variable will be used to store only positive numbers. The following

`unsigned int counter;`

declares to the compiler that the variable `counter` is used to contain only positive values. By restricting the use of an integer variable to the exclusive storage of positive integers, the accuracy of the integer variable is extended.

An `unsigned int` constant is formed by placing the letter u (or U) after the constant, like so:

`0x00ffU`

You can combine the letters u (or U) and l (or L) when writing an integer constant, so

`20000UL`

tells the compiler to treat the constant 20000 as `unsigned long`.

An integer constant that's not followed by any of the letters u, U, l, or L and that is too large to fit into a normal-sized `int` is treated as an `unsigned int` by the compiler. If it's too small to fit into an `unsigned int`, the compiler treats it as a `long int`. If it still can't fit inside a `long int`, the compiler makes it an `unsigned long int`.

When declaring variables to be of type `long int`, `short int`, or `unsigned int`, you can omit the keyword `int`. Therefore, the `unsigned` variable `counter` could have been equivalently declared as follows:

`unsigned counter;`

You can also declare `char` variables to be `unsigned`.

The `signed` qualifier can be used to explicitly tell the compiler that a particular variable is a signed quantity. Its use is primarily in front of the `char` declaration, and further discussion is beyond the scope of this book.

Type `id`

The `id` data type is used to store an object of any type. It is in a sense a generic object type. For example, the line

```
id    number;
```

declares `number` to be a variable of type `id`. Methods can be declared to return values of type `id`, like so:

```
-(id) newObject: (int) type;
```

This declares an instance method called `newObject` that takes a single integer argument called `type` and returns a value of type `id`. You should note that `id` is the default type for return and argument type declarations. So, the following

```
+allocInit;
```

declares a class method that returns a value of type `id`.

The `id` data type is an important data type used often in this book. It is mentioned in passing here for the sake of completeness. The `id` type is the basis for very important features in Objective-C know as *polymorphism* and *dynamic binding*, which are extensively discussed in Chapter 9, "Polymorphism, Dynamic Typing, and Dynamic Binding."

Table 4.1 summarizes the basic data types and qualifiers.

Table 4.1   **Basic Data Types**

Type	Constant Examples	`printf chars`
char	'a', '\n'	%c
short int	—	%hi, %hx, %ho
unsigned short int	—	%hu, %hx, %ho
int	12, -97, 0xFFE0, 0177	%i, %x, %o
unsigned int	12u, 100U, 0XFFu	%u, %x, %o
long int	12L, -2001, 0xffffL	%li, %lx, %lo
unsigned long int	12UL, 100ul, 0xffeeUL	%lu, %lx, %lo
long long int	0xe5e5e5e5LL, 500ll	%lli, %llx, &llo
unsigned long long int	12ull, 0xffeeULL	%llu, %llx, %llo
float	12.34f, 3.1e-5f, 0x1.5p10, 0x1P-1	%f, %e, %g, %a
double	12.34, 3.1e-5, 0x.1p3	%f, %e, %g, %a
long double	12.34l, 3.1e-5l	%Lf, $Le, %Lg
id	nil	%p

Arithmetic Expressions

In Objective-C, just as in virtually all programming languages, the plus sign (+) is used to add two values, the minus sign (-) is used to subtract two values, the asterisk (*) is used to multiply two values, and the slash (/) is used to divide two values. These operators are known as *binary* arithmetic operators because they operate on two values or terms.

You have seen how a simple operation such as addition can be performed in Objective-C. The following program further illustrates the operations of subtraction, multiplication, and division. The last two operations performed in the program introduce the notion that one operator can have a higher priority, or *precedence*, over another operator. In fact, each operator in Objective-C has a precedence associated with it. This precedence is used to determine how an expression that has more than one operator is evaluated: The operator with the higher precedence is evaluated first. Expressions containing operators of the same precedence are evaluated either from left to right or from right to left, depending on the operator. This is known as the *associative* property of an operator. Appendix B provides a complete list of operator precedences and their rules of association.

Program 4.2

```
// Illustrate the use of various arithmetic operators

#import <stdio.h>

int main (int argc, char *argv[])
{
  int a = 100;
  int b = 2;
  int c = 25;
  int d = 4;
  int result;

  result = a - b; // subtraction
  printf ("a - b = %i\n", result);

  result = b * c; // multiplication
  printf ("b * c = %i\n", result);

  result = a / c; // division
  printf ("a / c = %i\n", result);

  result = a + b * c; // precedence
  printf ("a + b * c = %i\n", result);

  printf ("a * b + c * d = %i\n", a * b + c * d);
  return 0;
}
```

Program 4.2   **Output**

```
a - b = 98
b * c = 50
a / c = 4
a + b * c = 150
a * b + c * d = 300
```

After declaring the integer variables a, b, c, d, and result, the program assigns the result of subtracting b from a to result and then displays its value with an appropriate printf call.

The next statement

```
result = b * c;
```

has the effect of multiplying the value of b by the value of c and storing the product in result. The result of the multiplication is then displayed using a printf call that should be familiar to you by now.

The next program statement introduces the division operator—the slash. The result of 4, as obtained by dividing 100 by 25, is displayed by the printf statement immediately following the division of a by c.

On some computer systems, attempting to divide a number by zero results in abnormal termination of the program. Even if the program does not terminate abnormally, the results obtained by such a division will be meaningless. In Chapter 6, "Making Decisions," you will see how you can check for division by zero before the division operation is performed. If it is determined that the divisor is zero, an appropriate action can be taken and the division operation averted.

The expression

```
a + b * c
```

does not produce the result of 2550 (102 × 25); rather, the result as displayed by the corresponding printf statement is shown as 150. This is because Objective-C, like most other programming languages, has rules for the order of evaluating multiple operations or terms in an expression. Evaluation of an expression generally proceeds from left to right. However, the operations of multiplication and division are given precedence over the operations of addition and subtraction. Therefore, the expression

```
a + b * c
```

is evaluated as

```
a + (b * c)
```

by the Objective-C system. (This is the same way this expression would be evaluated if you were to apply the basic rules of algebra.)

If you want to alter the order of evaluation of terms inside an expression, you can use parentheses. In fact, the expression listed previously is a perfectly valid Objective-C expression. Thus, the statement

```
result = a + (b * c);
```

could have been substituted in Program 4.2 to achieve identical results. However, if the expression

```
result = (a + b) * c;
```

were used instead, the value assigned to `result` would be 2550 because the value of a (100) would be added to the value of b (2) before multiplication by the value of Objective-C (25) would take place. Parentheses can also be nested, in which case evaluation of the expression proceeds outward from the innermost set of parentheses. Just be sure to have as many closed parentheses as you have open ones.

You will notice from the last statement in Program 4.2 that it is perfectly valid to give an expression as an argument to `printf` without having to first assign the result of the expression evaluation to a variable. The expression

```
a * b + c * d
```

is evaluated according to the rules stated previously as

```
(a * b) + (c * d)
```

or

```
(100 * 2) + (25 * 4)
```

The result of 300 is handed to the `printf` routine.

Integer Arithmetic and the Unary Minus Operator

Program 4.3 reinforces what we have just discussed and introduces the concept of integer arithmetic.

Program 4.3

```
// More arithmetic expressions
#import <stdio.h>
int main (int argc, char *argv[])
{
   int   a = 25;
   int   b = 2;
   int   result;
   float c = 25.0;
   float d = 2.0;
```

Program 4.3 **Continued**

```
printf ("6 + a / 5 * b = %i\n", 6 + a / 5 * b);
printf ("a / b * b = %i\n", a / b * b);
printf ("c / d * d = %f\n", c / d * d);
printf ("-a = %i\n", -a);

return 0;
}
```

Program 4.3 **Output**

```
6 + a / 5 * b = 16
a / b * b = 24
c / d * d = 25.000000
-a = -25
```

We inserted extra blank spaces between int and the declaration of a, b, and result in the first three statements to align the declaration of each variable. This helps make the program more readable. You also might have noticed in each program presented thus far that a blank space was placed around each operator. This, too, is not required and is done solely for aesthetic reasons. In general, you can add extra blank spaces just about anywhere that a single blank space is allowed. A few extra presses of the spacebar will prove worthwhile if the resulting program is easier to read.

The expression in the first printf call of Program 4.3 reinforces the notion of operator precedence. Evaluation of this expression proceeds as follows:

1. Because division has higher precedence than addition, the value of a (25) is divided by 5 first. This gives the intermediate result of 4.

2. Because multiplication also has higher precedence than addition, the intermediate result of 5 is next multiplied by 2, the value of b, giving a new intermediate result of 10.

3. Finally, the addition of 6 and 10 is performed, giving a final result of 16.

The second printf statement introduces a new twist. You would expect that dividing a by b and then multiplying by b would return the value of a, which has been set to 25. But this does not seem to be the case, as shown by the output display of 24. Did the computer lose a bit somewhere along the way? Very unlikely. The fact of the matter is that this expression was evaluated using integer arithmetic.

If you glance back at the declarations for the variables a and b, you will recall that they were both declared to be of type int. Whenever a term to be evaluated in an expression consists of two integers, the Objective-C system performs the operation using integer arithmetic. In such a case, all decimal portions of numbers are lost. Therefore, when the value of a is divided by the value of b, or 25 is divided by 2, you get an intermediate result of 12 and *not* 12.5 as you might expect. Multiplying this intermediate result by 2 gives the final result of 24, thus explaining the "lost" digit.

As can be seen from the next-to-last `printf` statement in Program 4.3, if you perform the same operation using floating-point values instead of integers, you obtain the expected result.

The decision of whether to use a `float` variable or an `int` variable should be made based on the variable's intended use. If you don't need any decimal places, use an integer variable. The resulting program will be more efficient—that is, it will execute more quickly on many computers. On the other hand, if you need the decimal place accuracy, the choice is clear. The only question you then must answer is whether to use a `float` or `double`. The answer to this question will depend on the desired accuracy of the numbers you are dealing with, as well as their magnitude.

In the last `printf` statement, the value of the variable a is negated by use of the unary minus operator. A *unary* operator is one that operates on a single value, as opposed to a binary operator, which operates on two values. The minus sign actually has a dual role: As a binary operator, it is used for subtracting two values; as a unary operator, it is used to negate a value.

The unary minus operator has higher precedence than all other arithmetic operators, except for the unary plus operator (+), which has the same precedence. So the expression

```
c = -a * b;
```

results in the multiplication of -a by b. Once again, in Appendix B you will find a table summarizing the various operators and their precedences.

The Modulus Operator

The last operator to be presented in this chapter is the modulus operator, which is symbolized by the percent sign (%). Try to determine how this operator works by analyzing the output from Program 4.4.

Program 4.4

```
// The modulus operator

#import <stdio.h>

int main (int argc, char *argv[])
{
    int a = 25, b = 5, c = 10, d = 7;

    printf ("a %% b = %i\n", a % b);
    printf ("a %% c = %i\n", a % c);
    printf ("a %% d = %i\n", a % d);
    printf ("a / d * d + a %% d = %i\n", a / d * d + a % d);

    return 0;
}
```

Program 4.4 **Output**

```
a % b = 0
a % c = 5
a % d = 4
a / d * d + a % d = 25
```

The first statement inside main defines and initializes the variables a, b, c, and d in a single statement.

As you know, printf uses the character that immediately follows the percent sign to determine how to print the next argument. However, if it is another percent sign that follows, the printf routine takes this as an indication that you really intend to display a percent sign and inserts one at the appropriate place in the program's output.

You are correct if you concluded that the function of the modulus operator % is to give the remainder of the first value divided by the second value. In the first example, the remainder, after 25 is divided by 5, is displayed as 0. If you divide 25 by 10, you get a remainder of 5, as verified by the second line of output. Dividing 25 by 7 gives a remainder of 4, as shown in the third output line.

Let's now turn our attention to the expression evaluated in the last statement. You will recall that any operations between two integer values in Objective-C are performed with integer arithmetic. Therefore, any remainder resulting from the division of two integer values is simply discarded. Dividing 25 by 7, as indicated by the expression a / d, gives an intermediate result of 3. Multiplying this value by the value of d, which is 7, produces the intermediate result of 21. Finally, adding the remainder of dividing a by d, as indicated by the expression a % d, leads to the final result of 25. It is no coincidence that this value is the same as the value of the variable a. In general, the expression

```
a / b * b + a % b
```

will always equal the value of a, assuming of course that a and b are both integer values. In fact, the modulus operator % is defined to work only with integer values.

As far as precedence is concerned, the modulus operator has equal precedence to the multiplication and division operators. This implies, of course, that an expression such as

```
table + value % TABLE_SIZE
```

will be evaluated as

```
table + (value % TABLE_SIZE)
```

Integer and Floating-Point Conversions

To effectively develop Objective-C programs, you must understand the rules used for the implicit conversion of floating-point and integer values in Objective-C. Program 4.5 demonstrates some of the simple conversions between numeric data types.

Program 4.5

```
// Basic conversions in Objective-C

#import <stdio.h>

int main (int argc, char *argv[])
{
    float   f1 = 123.125, f2;
    int     i1, i2 = -150;
    char    c = 'a';

    i1 = f1;    // floating to integer conversion
    printf ("%f assigned to an int produces %i\n", f1, i1);

    f1 = i2;    // integer to floating conversion
    printf ("%i assigned to a float produces %f\n", i2, f1);

    f1 = i2 / 100;    // integer divided by integer
    printf ("%i divided by 100 produces %f\n", i2, f1);

    f2 = i2 / 100.0;    // integer divided by a float
    printf ("%i divided by 100.0 produces %f\n", i2, f2);

    f2 = (float) i2 / 100;    // type cast operator
    printf ("(float) %i divided by 100 produces %f\n", i2, f2);

    return 0;
}
```

Program 4.5 **Output**

```
123.125000 assigned to an int produces 123
-150 assigned to a float produces -150.000000
-150 divided by 100 produces -1.000000
-150 divided by 100.0 produces -1.500000
(float) -150 divided by 100 produces -1.500000
```

Whenever a floating-point value is assigned to an integer variable in Objective-C, the decimal portion of the number gets truncated. So, when the value of f1 is assigned to i1 in the previous program, the number 123.125 is *truncated*, which means that only its integer portion, or 123, is stored in i1. The first line of the program's output verifies that this is the case.

Assigning an integer variable to a floating variable does not cause any change in the value of the number; the value is simply converted by the system and stored in the floating variable. The second line of the program's output verifies that the value of i2 (−150) was correctly converted and stored in the `float` variable f1.

The next two lines of the program's output illustrate two points that must be remembered when forming arithmetic expressions. The first has to do with integer arithmetic, which we have already discussed in this chapter. Whenever two operands in an expression are integers (and this applies to `short`, `unsigned`, and `long` integers as well), the operation is carried out under the rules of integer arithmetic. Therefore, any decimal portion resulting from a division operation is discarded, even if the result is assigned to a floating variable (as we did in the program). When the integer variable i2 is divided by the integer constant 100, the system performs the division as an integer division. The result of dividing −150 by 100, which is −1, is therefore the value that is stored in the `float` variable f1.

The next division performed in the previous program involves an integer variable and a floating-point constant. Any operation between two values in Objective-C is performed as a floating-point operation if either value is a floating-point variable or constant. Therefore, when the value of i2 is divided by 100.0, the system treats the division as a floating-point division and produces the result of −1.5, which is assigned to the `float` variable f1.

The Type Cast Operator

You've already seen how enclosing a type inside a set of parentheses is used to declare the return and argument types when declaring and defining methods. It serves a different purpose when used inside expressions.

The last division operation from Program 4.5 that reads

```
f2 = (float) i2 / 100;   // type cast operator
```

introduces the type cast operator. The type cast operator has the effect of converting the value of the variable i2 to type `float` for purposes of evaluation of the expression. In no way does this operator permanently affect the value of the variable i2; it is a unary operator that behaves like other unary operators. Because the expression -a has no permanent effect on the value of a, neither does the expression (float) a.

The type cast operator has a higher precedence than all the arithmetic operators except the unary minus and unary plus. Of course, if necessary, you can always use parentheses in an expression to force the terms to be evaluated in any desired order.

As another example of the use of the type cast operator, the expression

```
(int) 29.55 + (int) 21.99
```

is evaluated in Objective-C as

```
29 + 21
```

because the effect of casting a floating value to an integer is one of truncating the floating-point value. The expression

```
(float) 6 / (float) 4
```

produces a result of 1.5, as does the following expression:

```
(float) 6 / 4
```

The type cast operator is often used to coerce an object that is a generic `id` type into an object of a particular class. For example,

```
id    myNumber;
Fraction *myFraction;
    ...
myFraction = (Fraction *) myNumber;
```

takes the `id` variable `myNumber` and converts it into a `Fraction` object. The result of the conversion is assigned to the `Fraction` variable `myFraction`. You'll learn more about this in a later chapter.

Assignment Operators

The Objective-C language permits you to combine the arithmetic operators with the assignment operator using the following general format:

```
op=
```

In this format, *op* is any of the arithmetic operators, including +, -, *, /, and %. In addition, *op* can be any of the bit operators for shifting and masking, which is discussed later.

Consider this statement:

```
count += 10;
```

The effect of the so-called "plus equals" operator += is to add the expression on the right side of the operator to the expression on the left side of the operator and to store the result back into the variable on the left-hand side of the operator. So, the previous statement is equivalent to this statement:

```
count = count + 10;
```

The expression

```
counter -= 5
```

uses the "minus equals" assignment operator to subtract 5 from the value of `counter` and is equivalent to this expression:

```
counter = counter - 5
```

A slightly more involved expression is

```
a /= b + c
```

which divides a by whatever appears to the right of the equals sign—or by the sum of b and c—and stores the result in a. The addition is performed first because the addition operator has higher precedence than the assignment operator. In fact, all operators but the comma operator have higher precedence than the assignment operators, which all have the same precedence.

In this case, this expression is identical to the following:

```
a = a / (b + c)
```

The motivation for using assignment operators is threefold. First, the program statement becomes easier to write because what appears on the left side of the operator does not have to be repeated on the right side. Second, the resulting expression is usually easier to read. Third, the use of these operators can result in programs that execute more quickly because the compiler can sometimes generate less code to evaluate an expression.

A Calculator Class

It's time now to define a new class. We're going to make a Calculator class, which will be a simple four-function calculator you can use to add, multiply, subtract, and divide numbers. Similar to a regular calculator, this one must keep track of the running total, or what's usually called the *accumulator*. So, methods must let you set the accumulator to a specific value, clear it (or set it to zero), and retrieve its value when you're done. Program 4.6 includes the new class definition and a test program to try your calculator.

Program 4.6

```
// Implement a Calculator class

#import <objc/Object.h>
#import <stdio.h>

@interface Calculator: Object
{
    double accumulator;
}

// accumulator methods
-(void)  setAccumulator: (double) value;
-(void)  clear;
-(double) accumulator;

// arithmetic methods
-(void) add: (double) value;
-(void) subtract: (double) value;
-(void) multiply: (double) value;
-(void) divide: (double) value;
@end

@implementation Calculator;
-(void) setAccumulator: (double) value
{
        accumulator = value;
}

-(void) clear
{
```

Program 4.6 **Continued**

```
        accumulator = 0;
}

-(double) accumulator
{
        return accumulator;
}

-(void) add: (double) value
{
        accumulator += value;
}

-(void) subtract: (double) value
{
        accumulator -= value;
}

-(void) multiply: (double) value
{
        accumulator *= value;
}

-(void) divide: (double) value
{
        accumulator /= value;
}
@end

int main (int argc, char *argv[])
{
    Calculator *deskCalc;

    deskCalc = [[Calculator alloc] init];

    [deskCalc clear];
    [deskCalc setAccumulator: 100.0];
    [deskCalc add: 200.];
    [deskCalc divide: 15.0];
    [deskCalc subtract: 10.0];
    [deskCalc multiply: 5];
    printf ("The result is %g\n", [deskCalc accumulator]);
    [deskCalc free];

    return 0;
}
```

Program 4.6 **Output**

```
The result is 50
```

The `Calculator` class only has one instance variable, a `double` value that holds the value of the accumulator. The method definitions themselves are quite straightforward.

Notice the message that invokes the `multiply` method:

```
[deskCalc multiply: 5];
```

The argument to the method is an integer, yet the method expects a `double`. There is no problem here because numeric arguments to methods are automatically converted to match the type expected. A `double` is expected by `multiply:`, so the integer value 5 automatically is converted to a double precision floating value when the function is called. Even though this automatic conversion takes place, it's still better programming practice to supply the correct argument types when invoking methods.

Realize that unlike the `Fraction` class, where you might work with many different fractions, you might want to work with only a single `Calculator` object in your program. Yet it still makes sense to define a new class to make working with this object easy. At some point, you might want to add a graphical front end to your calculator so the user can actually click buttons on the screen like one of the calculator applications you probably have installed on your system.

In several of the exercises that follow, you'll see that one additional benefit of defining a `Calculator` class has to do with the ease of extending it.

Bit Operators

Various operators in the Objective-C language work with the particular bits inside a number. These operators are presented in Table 4.2.

Table 4.2 **Bit Operators**

Symbol	Operation
&	Bitwise AND
|	Bitwise inclusive-OR
^	Bitwise OR
~	Ones complement
<<	Left shift
>>	Right shift

All the operators listed in Table 4.2, with the exception of the ones complement operator (~), are binary operators and as such take two operands. Bit operations can be performed on any type of integer value but cannot be performed on floating-point values.

The Bitwise AND Operator

Bitwise ANDing is frequently used for masking operations. That is, this operator can be used to easily set specific bits of a data item to 0. For example, the statement

```
w3 = w1 & 3;
```

assigns to w3 the value of w1 bitwise ANDed with the constant 3. This has the effect of setting all the bits in w3, other than the rightmost two bits, to 0 and preserving the rightmost two bits from w1.

As with all binary arithmetic operators in C, the binary bit operators can also be used as assignment operators by adding an equal sign. The statement

```
word &= 15;
```

therefore performs the same function as the following:

```
word = word & 15;
```

Additionally, it has the effect of setting all but the rightmost four bits of word to 0.

When using constants in performing bitwise operations, it is usually more convenient to express the constants in either octal or hexadecimal notation.

The Bitwise Inclusive-OR Operator

When two values are bitwise inclusive-ORed in C, the binary representation of the two values is again compared bit by bit. This time, each bit that is a 1 in the first value *or* a 1 in the second value produces a 1 in the corresponding bit of the result.

The bitwise inclusive-OR operator is often used to combine several values together, where each value typically has only a single bit turned on in the value. For example, assuming that NSCaseInsensitiveSearch has the predefined value 1 and NSAnchoredSearch has the predefined value 8, the statement

```
searchOptions = NSCaseInsensitiveSearch | NSAnchoredSearch;
```

could be used to set the value for searchOptions to be the combination of the NSCaseInsensitiveSearch and NSAnchoredSearch options.

The Bitwise Exclusive-OR Operator

The bitwise exclusive-OR operator, which is often called the XOR operator, works as follows: For corresponding bits of the two operands, if either bit is a 1—but not both—the corresponding bit of the result is a 1; otherwise, it is a 0.

One interesting property of the exclusive-OR operator is that any value exclusive-ORed with itself produces 0. Another interesting trick with the exclusive-OR operator is to use it to exchange two values without using another memory location. Normally, you would interchange two integers, called i1 and i2, with a sequence of statements such as follows:

```
temp = i1;
i1 = i2;
i2 = temp;
```

(Assume in the previous sequence of statements that `temp` has been appropriately declared.) Using the exclusive-OR operator, you can exchange values without the need of the temporary storage location, like so:

```
i1 ^= i2;
i2 ^= i1;
i1 ^= i2;
```

It is left as an exercise for you to verify that the previous statements do, in fact, succeed in interchanging the values of `i1` and `i2`.

The Ones Complement Operator

The ones complement operator is a unary operator, and its effect is to simply "flip" the bits of its operand. Each bit of the operand that is a 1 is changed to a 0, and each bit that is a 0 is changed to a 1.

The Left Shift Operator

When a left shift operation is performed on a value, the bits contained in the value are literally shifted to the left. Associated with this operation is the number of places (bits) that the value is to be shifted. Bits that are shifted out through the high-order bit of the data item are lost, and 0s are always shifted in through the low-order bit of the value. So, if `w1` is equal to 3, the expression

```
w1 = w1 << 1;
```

which can also be expressed as

```
w1 <<= 1;
```

results in 3 being shifted one place to the left, which results in 6 being assigned to `w1`.

The operand on the left of the << operator is the value to be shifted, whereas the operand on the right is the number of bit positions the value is to be shifted by.

The Right Shift Operator

As implied from its name, the right shift operator (>>) shifts the bits of a value to the right. Bits shifted out of the low-order bit of the value are lost. Right shifting an unsigned value always results in 0s being shifted in on the left—that is, through the high-order bits. What is shifted in on the left for signed values depends on the sign of the value being shifted and also on how this operation is implemented on your computer. If the sign bit is 0 (meaning the value is positive), 0s are shifted in no matter what machine you have. However, if the sign bit is 1, on some machines 1s are shifted in and on others 0s are shifted in. This former type of operation is known as an *arithmetic* right shift, whereas the latter is known as a *logical* right shift.

It should be noted that the language does not produce a defined result if an attempt is made to shift a value to the left or right by an amount that is greater than or equal to the number of bits in the size of the data item. So, on a machine that represents integers in 32 bits, for example, shifting an integer to the left or right by 32 or more bits is not guaranteed to produce a defined result in your program. You should also note that if you shift a value by a negative amount, the result is also undefined.

Now it is time to show an actual program example that illustrates the use of the various bit operators (see Program 4.7).

Program 4.7

```
// Bitwise operators illustrated
#import <stdio.h>

int main (int argc, char *argv[])
{
    unsigned int w1 = 0xA0A0A0A0, w2 = 0xFFFF0000,
                 w3 = 0x00007777;

    printf ("%x %x %x\n", w1 & w2, w1 | w2, w1 ^ w2);
    printf ("%x %x %x\n", ~w1, ~w2, ~w3);
    printf ("%x %x %x\n", w1 ^ w1, w1 & ~w2, w1 | w2 | w3);
    printf ("%x %x\n", w1 | w2 & w3, w1 | w2 & ~w3);
    printf ("%x %x\n", ~(~w1 & ~w2), ~(~w1 | ~w2));

    w1 ^= w2;
    w2 ^= w1;
    w1 ^= w2;
    printf ("w1 = %x, w2 = %x\n", w1, w2);
    return 0;
}
```

Program 4.7 **Output**

```
a0a00000 ffffa0a0 5f5fa0a0
5f5f5f5f ffff ffff8888
0 a0a0 fffff7f7
a0a0a0a0 ffffa0a0
ffffa0a0 a0a00000
w1 = ffff0000, w2 = a0a0a0a0
fffe0000 a0a0a000 77770000
7fff8000 a0a0a0 0
```

You should work out each of the operations from Program 4.7 with a paper and pencil to verify that you understand how the results were obtained.

I should mention the precedence of the various operators here. The AND, OR, and exclusive-OR operators each have lower precedence than any of the arithmetic or relational operators but have higher precedence than the logical AND and logical OR operators. The bitwise AND is higher in precedence than the bitwise exclusive OR, which in turn is higher in precedence than the bitwise OR. The unary ones complement operator has higher precedence than *any* binary operator. For a summary of operator precedence, see Appendix B.

In the fourth `printf` call, it is important to remember that the bitwise AND operator has higher precedence than the bitwise OR because this fact influences the resulting value of the expression.

The fifth `printf` call illustrates DeMorgan's rule—namely that ~(~a & ~b) is equal to a | b, and that ~(~a | ~b) is equal to a & b. The sequence of statements that follows next in the program verifies that the exchange operation works as discussed in the section on the exclusive-OR operator.

Types: `_Bool`, `_Complex`, and `_Imaginary`

Before leaving this chapter, I should mention that there are three other types in the language called `_Bool`, for working with Boolean (that is, 0 or 1) values, and `_Complex` and `_Imaginary` for working with complex and imaginary numbers, respectively.

Support for `_Complex` and `_Imaginary` types is optional for a compiler[2]. For more information, look at the summary of data types in Appendix B.

Objective-C programmers tend to use the `BOOL` data type instead of `_Bool` for working with Boolean values in their programs. This "data type" is actually not a data type unto itself but is actually another name for the `char` data type. This is done with the language's special `typedef` keyword, which is described in Chapter 10, "More on Variables and Data Types."

Exercises

1. Which of the following are invalid constants. Why?

   ```
   123.456    0x10.5    0X0G1
   0001       0xFFFF    123L
   0Xab05     0L        -597.25
   123.5e2    .0001     +12
   98.6F      98.7U     17777s
   0996       -12E-12   07777
   1234uL     1.2Fe-7   15,000
   1.234L     197u      100U
   0XABCDEFL  0xabcu    +123
   ```

2. Write a program that converts 27° from degrees Fahrenheit (F) to degrees Celsius (C) using the following formula:
   $$C = (F - 32) / 1.8$$

---

2. As of this writing, the `gcc` compiler version 3.3 does not have full support for these data types.

3. What output would you expect from the following program?

```
#import <stdio.h>

int main (int argc, char *argv[])
{
    char c, d;

    c = 'd';
    d = c;
    printf ("d = %c\n", d);

    return 0;
}
```

4. Write a program to evaluate the polynomial shown here:
$$3x^3 - 5x^2 + 6$$
for $x = 2.55$

5. Write a program that evaluates the following expression and displays the results (remember to use exponential format to display the result):
$$(3.31 \times 10^{-8} \ x + 2.01 \times 10^{-7}) \ / \ (7.16 \times 10^{-6} + 2.01 \times 10^{-8})$$

6. *Complex* numbers are numbers that contain two components: a *real* and an *imaginary* part. If a is the real component, and b is the imaginary component, the notation
   $$a + b \ i$$
   is used to represent the number.

   Write an Objective-C program that defines a new class called Complex. Following the paradigm established for the Fraction class, define the following methods for your new class:

```
-(void) setReal: (double) a;
-(void) setImaginary: (double) b;
-(void) print;     // display as a + bi
-(double) real;
-(double) imaginary;
```

   Write a test program to test your new class and methods.

7. Suppose you are developing a library of routines to manipulate graphical objects. Start by defining a new class called Rectangle. For now, just keep track of the rectangle's width and height. Develop methods to set the rectangle's width and height, retrieve these values, and calculate the rectangle's area and perimeter. Assume that these rectangle objects describe rectangles on an integral grid, such as a computer screen. In that case, assume the width and height of the rectangle are integer values.

Here is the @interface section for the Rectangle class:

```
@interface Rectangle: Object
{
    int   width;
    int   height;
}

-(void) setWidth: (int) w;
-(void) setHeight: (int) h;
-(int) width;
-(int) height;
-(int) area;
-(int) perimeter;
@end
```

Write the @implementation section and a test program to test your new class and methods.

8. Modify the add:, subtract:, multiply:, and divide: methods from Program 4.6 to return the resulting value of the accumulator. Test the new methods.

9. After completing exercise 8, add the following methods to the Calculator class and test them:

```
-(double) changeSign;   // change sign of accumulator
-(double) reciprocal;   // 1/accumulator
-(double) xSquared;     // accumulator squared
```

10. Add a memory capability to the Calculator class from Program 4.6. Implement the following method declarations and test them:

```
-(double) memoryClear;      // clear memory
-(double) memoryStore;      // set memory to accumulator
-(double) memoryRecall;     // set accumulator to memory
-(double) memoryAdd;        // add accumulator to memory
-(double) memorySubtract;   // subtract accumulator from memory
```

5

Program Looping

IN OBJECTIVE-C YOU CAN REPEATEDLY execute a sequence of code in several ways. These looping capabilities are the subject of this chapter, and they consist of the following:

- The `for` statement
- The `while` statement
- The `do` statement

We'll start with a simple example: counting numbers.

If you were to arrange 15 marbles into the shape of a triangle, you would end up with an arrangement that might look something like this:

The first row of the triangle contains one marble, the second row contains two marbles, and so on. In general, the number of marbles required to form a triangle containing *n* rows would be the sum of the integers from 1 through *n*. This sum is known as a *triangular number*.

If you started at 1, the fourth triangular number would be the sum of the consecutive integers 1–4 (1 + 2 + 3 + 4), or 10.

Suppose you wanted to write a program that calculated and displayed the value of the eighth triangular number at the terminal. Obviously, you could easily calculate this number in your head, but for the sake of argument, let's assume you wanted to write a program in Objective-C to perform this task. Such a program is shown in Program 5.1.

The technique of Program 5.1 works fine for calculating relatively small triangular numbers, but what would happen if you needed to find the value of the 200th triangular number, for example? It certainly would be tedious to have to modify Program 5.1 to explicitly add up all the integers from 1 to 200. Luckily, there is an easier way.

Program 5.1

```
#import <stdio.h>

// Program to calculate the eighth triangular number

int main (int argc, char *argv[])
{
    int triangularNumber;

    triangularNumber = 1 + 2 + 3 + 4 + 5 + 6 + 7 + 8;

    printf ("The eighth triangular number is %i\n", triangularNumber);
    return 0;
}
```

Program 5.1   **Output**

```
The eighth triangular number is 36
```

One of the fundamental properties of a computer is its capability to repetitively execute a set of statements. These looping capabilities enable programmers to develop concise programs containing repetitive processes that could otherwise require thousands or even millions of program statements to perform. The Objective-C language contains three program statements for program looping.

The for Statement

Let's take a look at a program that uses the for statement. The purpose of Program 5.2 is to calculate the 200th triangular number. See whether you can determine how the for statement works.

Program 5.2

```
// Program to calculate the 200th triangular number
// Introduction of the for statement


#import <stdio.h>

int main (int argc, char *argv[])
{
    int n, triangularNumber;
```

Program 5.2   **Continued**

```
triangularNumber = 0;

for ( n = 1; n <= 200; n = n + 1 )
    triangularNumber += n;

printf ("The 200th triangular number is %i\n", triangularNumber);

return 0;
}
```

Program 5.2   **Output**

```
The 200th triangular number is 20100
```

Some explanation is owed for Program 5.2. The method employed to calculate the 200th triangular number is really the same as that used to calculate the 8th triangular number in the previous program—the integers from 1 to 200 are summed.

The variable `triangularNumber` is set equal to 0 before the for statement is reached. In general, you need to initialize all variables to some value (just like your objects) before you use them in your program. As you'll learn later, certain types of variables are given default initial values, but you should set them anyway.

The for statement provides the mechanism that enables you to avoid having to explicitly write each integer from 1 to 200. In a sense, this statement is used to generate these numbers for you.

The general format of the for statement is as follows:

```
for ( init_expression; loop_condition; loop_expression )
    program statement
```

The three expressions enclosed within the parentheses—init_expression, loop_condition, and loop_expression—set up the environment for the program loop. The *program statement* that immediately follows (which is, of course, terminated by a semicolon) can be any valid Objective-C program statement and constitutes the body of the loop. This statement is executed as many times as specified by the parameters set up in the for statement.

The first component of the for statement, labeled init_expression, is used to set the initial values before the loop begins. In Program 5.2, this portion of the for statement is used to set the initial value of n to 1. As you can see, an assignment is a valid form of an expression.

The second component of the for statement specifies the condition(s) necessary for the loop to continue. In other words, looping continues as long as this condition is satisfied. Once again referring to Program 5.2, the loop_condition of the for is specified by the following relational expression:

```
n <= 200
```

This expression can be read as "n less than or equal to 200." The "less than or equal to" operator (which is the less than character [<] followed immediately by the equal sign [=]) is only one of several relational operators provided in the Objective-C programming language. These operators are used to test specific conditions. The answer to the test is yes (or TRUE) if the condition is satisfied and no (or FALSE) if the condition is not satisfied.

Table 5.1 lists all the relational operators available in Objective-C.

Table 5.1 **Relational Operators**

Operator	Meaning	Example
==	Equal to	count == 10
!=	Not equal to	flag != DONE
<	Less than	a < b
<=	Less than or equal to	low <= high
>	Greater than	points > POINT_MAX
>=	Greater than or equal to	j >= 0

The relational operators have lower precedence than all arithmetic operators. This means, for example, that an expression such as

```
a < b + c
```

is evaluated as

```
a < (b + c)
```

This is as you would expect. It would be TRUE if the value of a were less than the value of b + c and FALSE otherwise.

Pay particular attention to the is equal to operator (==) and do not confuse its use with the assignment operator (=). The expression

```
a == 2
```

tests whether the value of a is equal to 2, whereas the expression

```
a = 2
```

assigns the value 2 to the variable a.

The choice of which relational operator to use depends on the particular test being made and in some instances on your particular preferences. For example, the relational expression

```
n <= 200
```

can be equivalently expressed as

```
n < 201
```

Returning to the previous example, the program statement that forms the body of the for loop—triangularNumber += n;—is repetitively executed *as* long as the result of the relational test is TRUE, or in this case, as long as the value of n is less than or equal to 200. This program statement has the effect of adding the value of n to the value of triangularNumber.

When the loop_condition is no longer satisfied, execution of the program continues with the program statement immediately following the for loop. In this program, execution continues with the printf statement after the loop has terminated.

The final component of the for statement contains an expression that is evaluated each time after the body of the loop is executed. In Program 5.2, this loop_expression adds 1 to the value of n. Therefore, the value of n is incremented by 1 each time after its value has been added into the value of triangularNumber, and it ranges in value from 1 through 201.

It is worth noting that the last value that n attains, namely 201, is not added into the value of triangularNumber because the loop is terminated as soon as the looping condition is no longer satisfied, or as soon as n equals 201.

In summary, execution of the for statement proceeds as follows:

1. The initial expression is evaluated first. This expression usually sets a variable that is used inside the loop, generally referred to as an *index* variable, to some initial value (such as 0 or 1).

2. The looping condition is evaluated. If the condition is not satisfied (the expression is FALSE), the loop is immediately terminated. Execution continues with the program statement that immediately follows the loop.

3. The program statement that constitutes the body of the loop is executed.

4. The looping expression is evaluated. This expression is generally used to change the value of the index variable, frequently by adding 1 to it or subtracting 1 from it.

5. Return to step 2.

Remember that the looping condition is evaluated immediately on entry into the loop, before the body of the loop has executed one time. Also, remember not to put a semicolon after the closed parenthesis at the end of the loop because this will immediately end the loop.

Program 5.2 actually generates all the first 200 triangular numbers on its way to its final goal, so it might be nice to generate a table of these numbers. To save space, however, let's assume that you want to print a table of just the first 10 triangular numbers. Program 5.3 performs this task.

Program 5.3

```
// Program to generate a table of triangular numbers

#import <stdio.h>

int main (int argc, char *argv[])
{
    int n, triangularNumber;
```

Program 5.3 **Continued**

```
printf ("TABLE OF TRIANGULAR NUMBERS\n\n");
printf (" n  Sum from 1 to n\n");
printf ("--- --------------\n");

triangularNumber = 0;

for ( n = 1; n <= 10; ++n ) {
      triangularNumber += n;
      printf (" %i         %i\n", n, triangularNumber);
}

return 0;
}
```

Program 5.3 **Output**

```
TABLE OF TRIANGULAR NUMBERS

 n  Sum from 1 to n
--- --------------
 1      1
 2      3
 3      6
 4      10
 5      15
 6      21
 7      28
 8      36
 9      45
10      55
```

In Program 5.3, the purpose of the first three `printf` statements is simply to provide a general heading and to label the columns of the output. Notice that the first `printf` statement contains two newline characters. As you would expect, this has the effect of not only advancing to the next line, but also inserting an extra blank line into the display.

After the appropriate headings have been displayed, the program calculates the first 10 triangular numbers. The variable n is used to count the current number whose sum from 1 to n you are computing, and the variable `triangularNumber` is used to store the value of triangular number n.

Execution of the `for` statement commences by setting the value of the variable n to 1. As mentioned earlier, the program statement immediately following the `for` statement constitutes the body of the program loop. But what happens if you want to repetitively execute not just a single program statement, but a group of program statements? This can be accomplished by enclosing all such program statements within a pair of braces. The system then treats this group, or *block*, of statements as a single entity. In general, any place in a Objective-C program that a single statement is permitted, a block of statements can be used, provided that you remember to enclose the block within a pair of braces.

Therefore, in Program 5.3, both the expression that adds n into the value of triangularNumber and the printf statement that immediately follows constitute the body of the program loop. Pay particular attention to the way the program statements are indented. At a quick glance, you can easily determine which statements form part of the for loop. You should also note that programmers use different coding styles; some prefer to type the loop this way:

```
for ( n = 1; n <= 10; ++n )
{
  triangularNumber += n;
  printf (" %i %i\n", n, triangularNumber);
}
```

Here, the opening brace is placed on the line following the for. This is strictly a matter of taste and has no effect on the program.

The next triangular number is calculated by simply adding the value of n to the previous triangular number. The first time through the for loop, the previous triangular number is 0, so the new value of triangularNumber when n is equal to 1 is simply the value of n, or 1. The values of n and triangularNumber are then displayed, with an appropriate number of blank spaces inserted in the format string to ensure that the values of the two variables line up under the appropriate column headings.

Because the body of the loop has now been executed, the looping expression is evaluated next. The expression in this for statement appears a bit strange, however. Surely, you must have made a typographical mistake and meant to insert n = n + 1 instead of this funny-looking expression:

```
++n
```

The fact of the matter is that ++n is actually a perfectly valid Objective-C expression. It introduces a new (and rather unique) operator in the Objective-C programming language—the *increment operator*. The function of the double plus sign, or the increment operator, is to add 1 to its operand. Addition by 1 is such a common operation in programs that a special operator was created solely for this purpose. Therefore, the expression ++n is equivalent to the expression n = n + 1. At first glance it might appear that n = n + 1 is more readable, but you will soon get used to the function of this operator and even learn to appreciate its succinctness.

Of course, no programming language that offers an increment operator to add 1 would be complete without a corresponding operator to subtract 1. As you would guess, the name of this operator is the *decrement operator*, and it is symbolized by the double minus sign. So, an expression in Objective-C that reads

```
bean_counter = bean_counter - 1
```

can be equivalently expressed using the decrement operator, like so:

```
--bean_counter
```

Some programmers prefer to put the ++ or -- after the variable name, as in n++ or bean_counter--. This is acceptable and is a matter of personal preference.

You might have noticed that the last line of output from Program 5.3 doesn't line up. This minor annoyance can be corrected by substituting the following printf statement in place of the corresponding statement from Program 5.3.

```
printf ("%2i %i\n", n, triangularNumber);
```

To verify that this change solves the problem, here is the output from the modified program (called Program 5.3A).

Program 5.3A **Output**

```
TABLE OF TRIANGULAR NUMBERS

 n  Sum from 1 to n
---  ---------------
 1      1
 2      3
 3      6
 4      10
 5      15
 6      21
 7      28
 8      36
 9      45
10      55
```

The primary change made to the printf statement is the inclusion of a field width specification. The characters %2i tell the printf routine that not only do you want to display the value of an integer at that particular point, but also that the size of the integer to be displayed should take up two columns in the display. Any integer that would normally take up less than two columns (that is, the integers 0–9) will be displayed with a leading space. This is known as *right justification*.

Thus, by using a field width specification of %2i, you guarantee that at least two columns will be used for displaying the value of n; you also ensure that the values of triangularNumber will be aligned.

If the value to be displayed requires more columns than are specified by the field width, printf simply ignores the field width specification and uses as many columns as are necessary to display the value.

Terminal Input

Program 5.2 calculates the 200th triangular number, and nothing more. What if you wanted to calculate the 50th or the 100th triangular number instead? Well, if that were the case, you would have to change the program so that the for loop would be executed the correct number of times. You would also have to change the `printf` statement to display the correct message.

An easier solution might be to somehow have the program ask you which triangular number you wanted to calculate. Then, after you had given your answer, the program could calculate the desired triangular number. Such a solution can be effected by using a routine called `scanf`. The `scanf` routine is similar in concept to the `printf` routine. Whereas the `printf` routine is used to display values at the terminal, the purpose of the `scanf` routine is to enable the programmer to type values into the program. Program 5.4 asks the user which triangular number should be calculated, calculates that number, and then displays the results.

Program 5.4

```
#import <stdio.h>

int main (int argc, char *argv[])
{
    int n, number, triangularNumber;

    printf ("What triangular number do you want? ");
    scanf ("%i", &number);

    triangularNumber = 0;

    for ( n = 1; n <= number; ++n )
        triangularNumber += n;

    printf ("Triangular number %i is %i\n", number, triangularNumber);

    return 0;
}
```

In the program output that follows, the number typed in by the user (100) is set in bolder type to distinguish it from the output displayed by the program.

Program 5.4 **Output**

```
What triangular number do you want? 100
Triangular number 100 is 5050
```

According to the output, the number 100 was typed in by the user. The program then calculated the 100th triangular number and displayed the result of 5050 at the terminal. The user could have just as easily typed in the number 10, or 30, if he wanted to calculate those particular triangular numbers.

The first `printf` statement in Program 5.4 is used to prompt the user to type in a number. Of course, it is always nice to remind the user what it is you want entered. After the message is printed, the `scanf` routine is called. The first argument to `scanf` is the format string, which is similar to the format string used by printf. In this case, the format string doesn't tell the system what types of values are to be displayed but rather what types of values are to be read in from the terminal. Like printf, the %i characters are used to specify an integer value.

The second argument to the scanf routine specifies where the value that is typed in by the user is to be stored. The & character before the variable number is necessary in this case. Don't worry about its function here, though. We will discuss this character, which is actually an operator, in great detail when we talk about pointers in Chapter 13.

Given the preceding discussion, you can now see that the scanf call from Program 5.4 specifies that an integer value is to be read from the terminal and stored into the variable number. This value represents the particular triangular number the user wants to have calculated.

After this number has been typed in (and the Enter key on the keyboard has been pressed to signal that typing of the number is completed), the program calculates the requested triangular number. This is done in the same way as in Program 5.2—the only difference being that, instead of using 200 as the limit, number is used as the limit.

After the desired triangular number has been calculated, the results are displayed and execution of the program is then complete.

Nested for Loops

Program 5.4 gives the user the flexibility to have the program calculate any triangular number that is desired. But suppose the user had a list of five triangular numbers to be calculated? In such a case, the user could simply execute the program five times, each time typing in the next triangular number from the list to be calculated.

Another way to accomplish the same goal, and a far more interesting method as far as learning about Objective-C is concerned, is to have the program handle the situation. This can best be accomplished by inserting a loop into the program to repeat the entire series of calculations five times. The for statement can be used to set up such a loop. The following program and its associated output illustrate this technique.

Program 5.5

```
#import <stdio.h>

int main (int argc, char *argv[])
{
  int n, number, triangularNumber, counter;

  for ( counter = 1; counter <= 5; ++counter ) {
        printf ("What triangular number do you want? ");
        scanf ("%i", &number);

        triangularNumber = 0;

        for ( n = 1; n <= number; ++n )
            triangularNumber += n;
```

Program 5.5 **Continued**

```
        printf ("Triangular number %i is %i\n\n", number, triangularNumber);

    }

  return 0;
}
```

Program 5.5 **Output**

```
What triangular number do you want? 12
Triangular number 12 is 78

What triangular number do you want? 25
Triangular number 25 is 325

What triangular number do you want? 50
Triangular number 50 is 1275

What triangular number do you want? 75
Triangular number 75 is 2850

What triangular number do you want? 83
Triangular number 83 is 3486
```

The program consists of two levels of for statements. The outermost for statement is as follows:

```
for ( counter = 1; counter <= 5; ++counter )
```

This specifies that the program loop is to be executed precisely five times. This can be seen because the value of counter is initially set to 1 and is incremented by 1 until it is no longer less than or equal to 5 (in other words, until it reaches 6).

Unlike the previous program examples, the variable counter is not used anywhere else within the program. Its function is solely as a loop counter in the for statement. Nevertheless, because it is a variable, it must be declared in the program.

The program loop actually consists of all the remaining program statements, as indicated by the braces. You might be able to more easily comprehend the way this program operates if you conceptualize it as follows:

```
For 5 times
{
   Get the number from the user.
   Calculate the requested triangular number.
   Display the results.
}
```

The portion of the loop referred to in the preceding as *Calculate the requested triangular number* actually consists of setting the value of the variable `triangularNumber` to 0 *plus the `for` loop that calculates the triangular number.* Thus, a `for` statement is actually contained within another `for` statement. This is perfectly valid in Objective-C, and nesting can continue even further to any desired level.

The proper use of indentation becomes even more critical when dealing with more sophisticated program constructs, such as nested `for` statements. At a quick glance, you can easily determine which statements are contained within each `for` statement.

`for` Loop Variants

Before leaving this discussion of the `for` loop, we should mention some of the syntactic variations that are permitted in forming this loop. When writing a `for` loop, you might discover that you have more than one variable that you want to initialize before the loop begins, or perhaps more than one expression that you want evaluated each time through the loop. You can include multiple expressions in any of the fields of the `for` loop, provided you separate such expressions by commas. For example, in the `for` statement that begins

```
for ( i = 0, j = 0; i < 10; ++i )
    . . .
```

the value of i is set to 0 and the value of j is set to 0 before the loop begins. The two expressions i = 0 and j = 0 are separated from each other by a comma, and both expressions are considered part of the `init_expression` field of the loop. As another example, the `for` loop that starts

```
for ( i = 0, j = 100; i < 10; ++i, j -= 10 )
    . . .
```

sets up two index variables: i and j, which initialize to 0 and 100, respectively, before the loop begins. Each time after the body of the loop is executed, the value of i is incremented by 1 and the value of j is decremented by 10.

Just as you might need to include more than one expression in a particular field of the `for` statement, you also might need to omit one or more fields from the statement. This can be done simply by omitting the desired field and marking its place with a semicolon. The most common application for the omission of a field in the `for` statement occurs when no initial expression needs to be evaluated. The `init_expression` field can simply be left blank in such a case, as long as the semicolon is still included, like so:

```
for ( ; j != 100; ++j )
    . . .
```

This statement might be used if j were already set to some initial value before the loop was entered.

A `for` loop that has its `looping_condition` field omitted effectively sets up an infinite loop—that is, a loop that theoretically will be executed forever. Such a loop can be used as long as some other means is used to exit from the loop (such as executing a `return`, `break`, or `goto` statement, as discussed later in this book).

You can also define variables as part of your initial expression inside a `for` loop[1]. This is done using the typical ways in which we've defined variables in the past. For example, the following can be used to set up a `for` loop with an integer variable `counter` both defined and initialized to the value 1, like so:

```
for ( int counter = 1; counter <= 5; ++counter )
```

The variable `counter` is only known throughout the execution of the `for` loop (it's called a *local* variable) and cannot be accessed outside the loop. As another example, the `for` loop

```
for ( int n = 1, triangularNumber = 0; n <= 200; n = n + 1 )
    triangularNumber += n;
```

defines two integer variables and sets their values accordingly.

The while **Statement**

The `while` statement further extends the Objective-C language's repertoire of looping capabilities. The syntax of this frequently used construct is as follows:

```
while ( expression )
    program statement
```

The *expression* specified inside the parentheses is evaluated. If the result of the *expression* evaluation is TRUE, the *program statement* that immediately follows is executed. After execution of this statement (or statements if enclosed in braces), *expression* is again evaluated. If the result of the evaluation is TRUE, the *program statement* is again executed. This process continues until *expression* finally evaluates FALSE, at which point the loop is terminated. Execution of the program then continues with the statement that follows *program statement*.

As an example of its use, the following program sets up a `while` loop, which merely counts from 1 to 5.

---

1. This is a feature added to the 1999 ANSI C Standard (sometimes referred to as C99). If you're using gcc and you get an error trying to use this feature, try adding the -std=c99 option to the gcc command line.

Program 5.6

```
// This program introduces the while statement

#import <stdio.h>

int main (int argc, char *argv[])
{
    int count = 1;

    while ( count <= 5 ) {
         printf ("%i\n", count);
         ++count;
    }
    return 0;
}
```

Program 5.6 **Output**

```
1
2
3
4
5
```

The program initially sets the value of count to 1; execution of the while loop then begins. Because the value of count is less than or equal to 5, the statement that immediately follows is executed. The braces serve to define both the printf statement and the statement that increments count as the body of the while loop. From the output of the program, you can see that this loop is executed five times or until the value of count reaches 5.

You might have realized from this program that you could have readily accomplished the same task by using a for statement. In fact, a for statement can always be translated into an equivalent while statement, and vice versa. For example, the general for statement

```
for ( init_expression; loop_condition; loop_expression )
    program statement
```

can be equivalently expressed in the form of a while statement, like so:

```
init_expression;
while ( loop_condition )
{
    program statement
    loop_expression;
}
```

When you become familiar with the use of the while statement, you will gain a better feel as to when it seems more logical to use a while statement and when to use a for statement. In general, a loop executed a predetermined number of times is a prime candidate for implementation as a for statement. Also, if the initial expression, looping expression, and looping condition all involve the same variable, the for statement is probably the right choice.

The next program provides another example of the use of the while statement. The program computes the greatest common divisor of two integer values. The greatest common divisor (we'll abbreviate it hereafter as gcd) of two integers is the largest integer value that evenly divides the two integers. For example, the gcd of 10 and 15 is 5 because 5 is the largest integer that evenly divides both 10 and 15.

A procedure, or algorithm, that can be followed to arrive at the gcd of two arbitrary integers is based on a procedure originally developed by Euclid around 300 B.C. It can be stated as follows:

Problem: Find the greatest common divisor of two nonnegative integers u and v.

Step 1: If v equals 0, then we are done and the *gcd* is equal to u.

Step 2: Calculate *temp* $= u \% v, u = v, v = temp$ and go back to Step 1.

Don't concern yourself with the details of how the previous algorithm works— simply take it on faith. We are more concerned here with developing a program to find the greatest common divisor than in performing an analysis of how the algorithm works.

After the solution to the problem of finding the greatest common divisor has been expressed in terms of an algorithm, developing the computer program becomes a much simpler task. An analysis of the steps of the algorithm reveals that step 2 is repetitively executed as long as the value of v is not equal to 0. This realization leads to the natural implementation of this algorithm in Objective-C with the use of a while statement.

The following program finds the gcd of two nonnegative integer values typed in by the user.

Program 5.7

```
// This program finds the greatest common divisor
// of two nonnegative integer values

#import <stdio.h>

int main (int argc, char *argv[])
{
    unsigned int u, v, temp;

    printf ("Please type in two nonnegative integers.\n");
    scanf ("%u%u", &u, &v);
```

Program 5.7 **Continued**

```
while ( v != 0 ) {
    temp = u % v;
    u = v;
    v = temp;
}

printf ("Their greatest common divisor is %u\n", u);
return 0;
}
```

Program 5.7 **Output**

```
Please type in two nonnegative integers.
150 35
Their greatest common divisor is 5
```

Program 5.7 **Output (Rerun)**

```
Please type in two nonnegative integers.
1026 540
Their greatest common divisor is 27
```

After the two integer values have been entered and stored into the variables u and v (using the %u format characters to read in an unsigned integer value), the program enters a while loop to calculate their greatest common divisor. After the while loop is exited, the value of u, which represents the gcd of v and of the original value of u, is displayed at the terminal with an appropriate message.

You will use the algorithm for finding the greatest common divisor again in Chapter 7, "More on Classes," when you return to working with fractions.

For the next program that illustrates the use of the while statement, let's consider the task of reversing the digits of an integer that is entered from the terminal. For example, if the user types in the number 1234, the program should reverse the digits of this number and display the result of 4321.

To write such a program, you first must come up with an algorithm that accomplishes the stated task. Frequently, an analysis of one's own method for solving the problem leads to the development of an algorithm. For the task of reversing the digits of a number, the solution can be simply stated as "successively read the digits of the number from right to left." You can have a computer program successively read the digits of the number by developing a procedure to successively isolate or extract each digit of the number beginning with the rightmost digit. The extracted digit can be subsequently displayed at the terminal as the next digit of the reversed number.

You can extract the rightmost digit from an integer number by taking the remainder of the integer after it is divided by 10. For example, 1234 ÷ 10 gives the value 4, which is the rightmost digit of 1234 and is also the first digit of the reversed number. (Remember that the modulus operator gives the remainder of one integer divided by another.) You can get the next digit of the number by using the same process if you first divide the number by 10, bearing in mind the way integer division works. Thus, 1234 ÷ 10 gives a result of 123, and 123 ÷ 10 gives you 3, which is the next digit of the reversed number.

This procedure can be continued until the last digit has been extracted. In the general case, you know that the last digit of the number has been extracted when the result of the last integer division by 10 is 0.

Program 5.8

```
// Program to reverse the digits of a number

#import <stdio.h>

int main (int argc, char *argv[])
{
  int number, right_digit;

  printf ("Enter your number.\n");
  scanf ("%i", &number);

  while ( number != 0 )  {
        right_digit = number % 10;
        printf ("%i", right_digit);
        number /= 10;
  }

  printf ("\n");
  return 0;
}
```

Program 5.8 **Output**

```
Enter your number.
13579
97531
```

Each digit is displayed as it is extracted by the program. Notice that a newline character is not included inside the `printf` statement contained in the `while` loop. This forces each successive digit to be displayed on the same line. The final `printf` call at the end of the program contains just a newline character, which causes the cursor to advance to the start of the next line.

The do **Statement**

The two looping constructs discussed thus far in this chapter both make a test of the conditions before the loop is executed. Therefore, the body of the loop might never be executed at all if the conditions are not satisfied. When developing programs, you sometimes might want to have the test made at the end of the loop rather than at the beginning. Naturally, the Objective-C language provides a special language construct to handle such a situation, known as the do statement. The syntax of this statement is as follows:

```
do
   program statement
while ( expression );
```

Execution of the do statement proceeds as follows: *program statement* is executed first. Next, the *expression* inside the parentheses is evaluated. If the result of evaluating *expression* is TRUE, the loop continues and *program statement* is again executed. As long as the evaluation of *expression* continues to be TRUE, *program statement* is repeatedly executed. When the evaluation of the expression proves FALSE, the loop is terminated and the next statement in the program is executed in the normal sequential manner.

The do statement is simply a transposition of the while statement, with the looping conditions placed at the end of the loop rather than at the beginning.

Program 5.8 used a while statement to reverse the digits of a number. Go back to that program and try to determine what would happen if the user had typed in the number 0 instead of 13579. The fact of the matter is that the loop of the while statement would never be executed and you would simply end up with a blank line in the display (as a result of the display of the newline character from the second printf statement). If you were to use a do statement instead of a while, you would be assured that the program loop would be executed at least once, thus guaranteeing the display of at least one digit in all cases.

Program 5.9

```
// Program to reverse the digits of a number

#import <stdio.h>

int main (int argc, char *argv[])
{
  int number, right_digit;

  printf ("Enter your number.\n");
  scanf ("%i", &number);

  do {
      right_digit = number % 10;
```

Program 5.9   **Continued**

```
        printf ("%i", right_digit);
        number /= 10;
  }
  while ( number != 0 );

  printf ("\n");

  return 0;
}
```

Program 5.9   **Output**

```
Enter your number.
13579
97531
```

Program 5.9   **Output (Rerun)**

```
Enter your number.
0
0
```

As you can see from the program's output, when 0 is keyed into the program, the program correctly displays the digit 0.

The break Statement

Sometimes when executing a loop, you'll want to leave the loop as soon as a certain condition occurs (for instance, maybe you detect an error condition or reach the end of your data prematurely). The break statement can be used for this purpose. Execution of the break statement causes the program to immediately exit from the loop it is executing, whether it's a for, while, or do loop. Subsequent statements in the loop are skipped and execution of the loop is terminated. Execution continues with whatever statement follows the loop.

If a break is executed from within a set of nested loops, only the innermost loop in which the break is executed is terminated.

The format of the break statement is simply the keyword break followed by a semicolon, like so:

```
break;
```

The `continue` Statement

The `continue` statement is similar to the `break` statement except it doesn't cause the loop to terminate. At the point that the `continue` statement is executed, any statements that appear after the `continue` statement up to the end of the loop are skipped. Execution of the loop otherwise continues as normal.

The `continue` statement is most often used to bypass a group of statements inside a loop based on some condition, but to otherwise continue execution of the loop. The format of the `continue` statement is as follows:

```
continue;
```

Don't use the `break` or `continue` statements until you become very familiar with writing program loops and gracefully exiting from them. These statements are too easy to abuse and can result in programs that are hard to follow.

Now that you are familiar with all the basic looping constructs provided by the Objective-C language, you're ready to learn about another class of language statements that enables you to make decisions during the execution of a program. These decision-making capabilities are described in detail in the next chapter.

Exercises

1. Write a program to generate and display a table of n and n^2, for integer values of n ranging from 1 through 10. Be sure to print the appropriate column headings.

2. A triangular number can also be generated for any integer value of n by this formula:

```
Triangular number = n (n + 1) / 2
```

   For example, the 10th triangular number, 55, can be generated by substituting 10 as the value for n into the previous formula. Write a program that generates a table of triangular numbers using the previous formula. Have the program generate every 5th triangular number between 5 and 50 (that is, 5, 10, 15,…, 50).

3. The factorial of an integer n, written $n!$, is the product of the consecutive integers 1 through n. For example, 5 factorial is calculated as follows:

```
5! = 5 x 4 x 3 x 2 x 1 = 120
```

   Write a program to generate and print a table of the first 10 factorials.

4. A minus sign placed in front of a field width specification causes the field to be displayed left justified. Substitute the following `printf` statement for the corresponding statement in Program 5.2, run the program, and compare the outputs produced by both programs:

```
printf ("%-2i %i\n", n, triangularNumber);
```

5. Program 5.5 allows the user to type in only five different numbers. Modify that program so that the user can type in the number of triangular numbers to be calculated.

6. Rewrite Programs 5.2–5.5, replacing all uses of the `for` statement with equivalent `while` statements. Run each program to verify that both versions are identical.

7. What would happen if you typed a negative number into Program 5.8? Try it and see.

8. Write a program that calculates the sum of the digits of an integer. For example, the sum of the digits of the number 2155 is 2 + 1 + 5 + 5, or 13. The program should accept any arbitrary integer typed in by the user.

6

Making Decisions

A FUNDAMENTAL FEATURE OF ANY PROGRAMMING LANGUAGE lies in its capability to make decisions. Decisions were made when executing the looping statements to determine when to terminate a loop. The Objective-C programming language also provides several other decision-making constructs, which are covered in this chapter:

- The `if` statement
- The `switch` statement
- The `conditional` operator

The `if` Statement

The Objective-C programming language provides a general decision-making capability in the form of a language construct known as the `if` statement. The general format of this statement is

```
if ( expression )
    program statement
```

Imagine if you will that you could translate a statement such as "If it is not raining then I will go swimming" into the Objective-C language. Using the previous format for the `if` statement, this might be "written" in Objective-C as follows:

```
if ( it is not raining )
    I will go swimming
```

The `if` statement is used to stipulate execution of a program statement (or statements if enclosed in braces) based on specified conditions. I will go swimming if it is not raining. Similarly, in the program statement

```
if ( count > MAXIMUM_SONGS )
    [playlist maxExceeded];
```

the maxExceeded message is sent to playlist *only* if the value of count is greater than the value of MAXIMUM_SONGS; otherwise, it is ignored.

An actual program example will help drive the point home. Suppose you want to write a program that accepts an integer typed in from the terminal and then displays the absolute value of that integer. A straightforward way to calculate the absolute value of an integer is to simply negate the number if it is less than zero. The use of the phrase "if it is less than zero" in the previous sentence signals that a decision must be made by the program. This decision can be effected by the use of an if statement as shown in the program that follows.

Program 6.1

```
// Calculate the absolute value of an integer

#import <stdio.h>

int main (int argc, char *argv[])
{
    int number;

    printf ("Type in your number: ");
    scanf ("%i", &number);

    if ( number < 0 )
        number = -number;

    printf ("The absolute value is %i\n", number);

    return 0;
}
```

Program 6.1 **Output**

```
Type in your number: -100
The absolute value is 100
```

Program 6.1 **Output (Rerun)**

```
Type in your number: 2000
The absolute value is 2000
```

The program was run twice to verify that it is functioning properly. Of course, it might be desirable to run the program several more times to get a higher level of confidence so that you know it is indeed working correctly, but at least you know that you have checked both possible outcomes of the decision made by the program.

After a message is displayed to the user and the integer value that is entered is stored into number, the program tests the value of number to see whether it is less than zero. If it is, the following program statement, which negates the value of number, is executed. If the value of number is not less than zero, this program statement is automatically skipped. (If it is already positive, you don't want to negate it.) The absolute value of number is then displayed by the program, and program execution ends.

Let's look at another program that uses the if statement. Let's add one more method to the Fraction class, called convertToNum. This method will provide the value of a fraction expressed as a real number. In other words, it will divide the numerator by the denominator and return the result as a double precision value. So, if you have the fraction 1/2, you want the method to return the value 0.5.

The declaration for such a method might look like this:

```
-(double) convertToNum;
```

And this is how you could write its definition:

```
-(double) convertToNum
{
    return numerator / denominator;
}
```

Well, not quite. There are actually two serious problems with this method as it's defined. Can you spot them? The first has to do with arithmetic conversions. You will recall that numerator and denominator are both integer instance variables. So, what happens when you divide two integers? Correct, it is done as an integer division! So, if you wanted to convert the fraction 1/2, the previous code would give you zero! This is easily corrected by using the type cast operator to convert one or both of the operands to a floating-point value before the division takes place:

```
(double) numerator / denominator
```

Recalling the relatively high precedence of this operator, numerator is first converted to double before the division occurs. Further, you don't need to convert the denominator because the rules of arithmetic conversion take care of that for you.

The second problem with this method is that you should check for division by zero (you should always check for that!). The invoker of this method could inadvertently have forgotten to set the denominator of the fraction or might have set the denominator of the fraction to zero, and you don't want your program to terminate abnormally.

The modified version of the convertToNum method is shown here:

```
-(double) convertToNum
{
    if (denominator != 0)
        return (double) numerator / denominator;
    else
        return 0.0;
}
```

We arbitrarily decided to return 0.0 if the `denominator` of the fraction is zero. Other options are available (such as printing an error message), but we won't go into them here.

Let's put this new method to use. Here's a test program to try it.

Program 6.2

```
#import <stdio.h>
#import <objc/Object.h>

@interface Fraction: Object
{
  int    numerator;
  int    denominator;
}

-(void)   print;
-(void)   setNumerator: (int) n;
-(void)   setDenominator: (int) d;
-(int)    numerator;
-(int)    denominator;
-(double) convertToNum;
@end


@implementation Fraction;
-(void) print
{
  printf (" %i/%i ", numerator, denominator);
}

-(void) setNumerator: (int) n
{
  numerator = n;
}

-(void) setDenominator: (int) d
{
  denominator = d;
}

-(int) numerator
{
  return numerator;
}

-(int) denominator
{
```

Program 6.2   **Continued**

```
  return denominator;
}

-(double) convertToNum
{
  if (denominator != 0)
    return (double) numerator / denominator;
  else
    return 0.0;
}
@end

int main (int argc, char *argv[])
{
    Fraction *aFraction = [[Fraction alloc] init];
    Fraction *bFraction = [[Fraction alloc] init];

    [aFraction setNumerator: 1];  // 1st fraction is 1/4
    [aFraction setDenominator: 4];

    [aFraction print];
    printf (" = ");
    printf ("%g\n", [aFraction convertToNum]);

    [bFraction print];     // never assigned a value
    printf (" = ");
    printf ("%g\n", [bFraction convertToNum]);
    [aFraction free];
    [bFraction free];

    return 0;
}
```

Program 6.2   **Output**

```
1/4 = 0.25
0/0 = 0
```

After setting aFraction to 1/4, the program uses the convertToNum method to convert the fraction to a decimal value. This value is then displayed as 0.25.

In the second case, bFraction's value is not explicitly set, so its numerator and denominator are initialized to zero, which is the default for instance variables. This explains the result from the print method. It also causes the if statement inside the convertToNum method to return the value 0, as verified from the output.

The `if-else` Construct

If someone asks you whether a particular number is even or odd, you will most likely make the determination by examining the last digit of the number. If this digit is either 0, 2, 4, 6, or 8, you will readily state that the number is even. Otherwise, you will claim that the number is odd.

An easier way for a computer to determine whether a particular number is even or odd is effected not by examining the last digit of the number to see whether it is 0, 2, 4, 6, or 8, but by simply determining whether the number is evenly divisible by 2. If it is, the number is even; otherwise, it is odd.

You have already seen how the modulus operator % is used to compute the remainder of one integer divided by another. This makes it the perfect operator to use in determining whether an integer is evenly divisible by 2. If the remainder after division by 2 is 0, it is even; else, it is odd.

Now let's write a program that determines whether an integer value typed in by the user is even or odd and then displays an appropriate message at the terminal.

Program 6.3
```
// Program to determine if a number is even or odd

#import <stdio.h>

int main (int argc, char *argv[])

{
    int number_to_test, remainder;

    printf ("Enter your number to be tested.: ");
    scanf ("%i", &number_to_test);

    remainder = number_to_test % 2;

    if ( remainder == 0 )
        printf ("The number is even.\n");

    if ( remainder != 0 )
        printf ("The number is odd.\n");

    return 0;
}
```

Program 6.3 **Output**
```
Enter your number to be tested: 2455
The number is odd.
```

Program 6.3 **Output (Rerun)**

```
Enter your number to be tested: 1210
The number is even.
```

After the number is typed in, the remainder after division by 2 is calculated. The first
if statement tests the value of this remainder to see whether it is equal to zero. If it is,
the message The number is even is displayed.

The second if statement tests the remainder to see if it's *not* equal to zero and, if
that's the case, displays a message stating that the number is odd.

The fact is that whenever the first if statement succeeds, the second one must fail,
and vice versa. If you recall from our discussions of even/odd numbers at the beginning
of this section, we said that if the number is evenly divisible by 2, it is even; *else* it is odd.

When writing programs, this "else" concept is so frequently required that almost all
modern programming languages provide a special construct to handle this situation. In
Objective-C, this is known as the if-else construct, and the general format is as follows:

```
if ( expression )
   program statement 1
else
   program statement 2
```

The if-else is actually just an extension of the general format of the if statement.
If the result of the evaluation of the expression is TRUE, then *program statement 1*,
which immediately follows, is executed; otherwise, *program statement 2* is executed. In either case, either *program statement 1* or *program statement 2* will be
executed, but not both.

You can incorporate the if-else statement into the previous program, replacing the
two if statements by a single if-else statement. You will see how the use of this new
program construct actually helps somewhat reduce the program's complexity and also
improve its readability.

Program 6.4

```
// Determine if a number is even or odd (Ver. 2)

#import <stdio.h>

int main (int argc, char *argv[])
{
    int number_to_test, remainder;

    printf ("Enter your number to be tested: ");
    scanf ("%i", &number_to_test);

    remainder = number_to_test % 2;
```

Program 6.4   **Continued**

```
if ( remainder == 0 )
    printf ("The number is even.\n");
else
    printf ("The number is odd.\n");
return 0;
}
```

Program 6.4   **Output**

```
Enter your number to be tested: 1234
The number is even.
```

Program 6.4   **Output (Rerun)**

```
Enter your number to be tested: 6551
The number is odd.
```

Don't forget that the double equal sign (==)is the equality test and the single equal sign is the assignment operator. It can lead to a lot of headaches if you forget this and inadvertently use the assignment operator inside the if statement.

Compound Relational Tests

The if statements you have used so far in this chapter set up simple relational tests between two numbers. Program 6.1 compared the value of number against zero, whereas Program 6.2 compared the denominator of the fraction to zero. Sometimes it becomes desirable, if not necessary, to set up more sophisticated tests. Suppose, for example, you wanted to count the number of grades from an exam that were between 70 and 79, inclusive. In such a case, you would want to compare the value of a grade not merely against one limit, but against the two limits 70 and 79 to ensure that it fell within the specified range.

The Objective-C language provides the mechanisms necessary to perform these types of compound relational tests. A *compound relational test* is simply one or more simple relational tests joined by either the logical AND or the logical OR operator. These operators are represented by the character pairs && and || (two vertical bar characters), respectively. As an example, the Objective-C statement

```
if ( grade >= 70 && grade <= 79 )
    ++grades_70_to_79;
```

increments the value of grades_70_to_79 only if the value of grade is greater than or equal to 70 *and* less than or equal to 79. In a like manner, the statement

```
if ( index < 0 || index > 99 )
    printf ("Error - index out of range\n");
```

causes execution of the printf statement if index is less than 0 *or* greater than 99.

The compound operators can be used to form extremely complex expressions in Objective-C. The Objective-C language grants the programmer ultimate flexibility in forming expressions, and this flexibility is a capability that is often abused. Simpler expressions are almost always easier to read and debug.

When forming compound relational expressions, liberally use parentheses to aid readability of the expression and avoid getting into trouble because of a mistaken assumption about the precedence of the operators in the or expression. (The `&&` operator has lower precedence than any arithmetic or relational operator but higher precedence than the `||` operator.) Blank spaces should also be used to aid in the expression's readability. An extra blank space around the `&&` and `||` operators will visually set these operators apart from the expressions that are being joined by these operators.

To illustrate the use of a compound relational test in an actual program example, let's write a program that tests to see whether a year is a leap year. We all know that a year is a leap year if it is evenly divisible by 4. What you might not realize, however, is that a year that is divisible by 100 is not a leap year unless it is also divisible by 400.

Try to think how you would go about setting up a test for such a condition. First, you could compute the remainders of the year after division by 4, 100, and 400 and assign these values to appropriately named variables, such as `rem_4`, `rem_100`, and `rem_400`, respectively. Then you could proceed to test these remainders to determine whether the desired criteria for a leap year were met.

If we rephrase our previous definition of a leap year, we can say that a year is a leap year if it is evenly divisible by 4 and not by 100 or if it is evenly divisible by 400. Stop for a moment to reflect on this last sentence and to verify to yourself that it is equivalent to the previously stated definition. Now that we have reformulated our definition in these terms, it becomes a relatively straightforward task to translate it into a program statement as follows:

```
if ( (rem_4 == 0 && rem_100 != 0) || rem_400 == 0 )
    printf ("It's a leap year.\n");
```

The parentheses around the subexpression

```
rem_4 == 0 && rem_100 != 0
```

are not required because that is how the expression will be evaluated anyway, remembering that or `&&` has higher precedence than `||`.

In fact, in this particular example, the test

```
if ( rem_4 == 0 && ( rem_100 != 0 || rem_400 == 0 ) )
```

would work just as well.

If you add a few statements in front of the test to declare the variables and to enable the user to key in the year from the terminal, you end up with a program that determines whether a year is a leap year, as shown here.

Program 6.5

```c
// This program determines if a year is a leap year

#import <stdio.h>

int main (int argc, char *argv[])
{
    int year, rem_4, rem_100, rem_400;

    printf ("Enter the year to be tested: ");
    scanf ("%i", &year);

    rem_4 = year % 4;
    rem_100 = year % 100;
    rem_400 = year % 400;

    if ( (rem_4 == 0 && rem_100 != 0) || rem_400 == 0 )
        printf ("It's a leap year.\n");
    else
        printf ("Nope, it's not a leap year.\n");
    return 0;
}
```

Program 6.5 **Output**

```
Enter the year to be tested: 1955
Nope, it's not a leap year.
```

Program 6.5 **Output (Rerun)**

```
Enter the year to be tested: 2000
It's a leap year.
```

Program 6.5 **Output (Rerun)**

```
Enter the year to be tested: 1800
Nope, it's not a leap year.
```

The previous examples use a year that is not a leap year because it isn't evenly divisible by 4 (1955), a year that is a leap year because it is evenly divisible by 400 (2000), and a year that isn't a leap year because it is evenly divisible by 100 but not by 400 (1800). To complete the run of test cases, you should also try a year that is evenly divisible by 4 and not by 100. This is left as an exercise for you.

We mentioned that Objective-C gives the programmer a tremendous amount of flexibility in forming expressions. For instance, in the previous program, you did not have to calculate the intermediate results rem_4, rem_100, and rem_400—you could have performed the calculation directly inside the if statement, as follows:

```
if ( ( year % 4 == 0 && year % 100 != 0 ) || year % 400 == 0 )
```

The use of blank spaces to set off the various operators still makes the previous expression readable. If you decided to ignore adding blanks and removed the unnecessary set of parentheses, you could end up with an expression that looked like this:

```
if(year%4==0&&year%100!=0)||year%400==0)
```

This expression is perfectly valid and would (believe it or not) execute identically to the expression shown immediately before it. Obviously, those extra blanks go a long way toward aiding our understanding of complex expressions.

Nested if Statements

In discussions of the general format of the if statement, we indicated that if the result of evaluating the expression inside the parentheses were TRUE, the statement that immediately followed would be executed. It is perfectly valid that this program statement be another if statement, as in the statement

```
if ( [chessGame isOver] == NO )
    if ( [chessGame whoseTurn] == YOU )
        [chessGame yourMove];
```

If the value returned by sending the isOver message to chessGame is NO, the following statement is executed, which is in turn another if statement. This if statement compares the value returned from the whoseTurn method against YOU. If the two values are equal, the yourMove message is sent to the chessGame object. Therefore, the yourMove message is sent only if both the game is not done and it's your turn. In fact, this statement could have been equivalently formulated using compound relationals, like so:

```
if ( [chessGame isOver] == NO && [chessGame whoseTurn] == YOU )
    [chessGame yourMove];
```

A more practical example of nested if statements would be if you added an else clause to the previous example, as shown in the following:

```
if ( [chessGame isOver] == NO )
    if ( [chessGame whoseTurn] == YOU )
        [chessGame yourMove];
    else
        [chessGame myMove];
```

Execution of this statement proceeds as described previously. However, if the game is not over and it's not your move, the else clause is executed. This sends the message myMove to chessGame. If the game is over, the entire if statement that follows, including its associated else clause, is skipped.

Notice how the else clause is associated with the if statement that tests the value returned from the whoseTurn method, and not with the if statement that tests whether the game is over. The general rule is that an else clause is always associated with the last if statement that does not contain an else.

You can go one step further and add an else clause to the outermost if statement in the preceding example. This else clause would be executed if the game is over:

```
if ( [chessGame isOver] == NO )
    if ( [chessGame whoseTurn] == YOU )
        [chessGame yourMove];
    else
        [chessGame myMove];
else
    [chessGame finish];
```

Of course, even if you use indentation to indicate the way you think a statement will be interpreted in the Objective-C language, it might not always coincide with the way the system actually interprets the statement. For instance, removing the first else clause from the previous example

```
if ( [chessGame isOver] == NO )
    if ( [chessGame whoseTurn] == YOU )
        [chessGame yourMove];
else
    [chessGame finish];
```

will *not* result in the statement being interpreted as indicated by its format. Instead, this statement will be interpreted as follows:

```
if ( [chessGame isOver] == NO )
    if ( [chessGame whoseTurn] == YOU )
        [chessGame yourMove];
    else
        [chessGame finish];
```

This is because the else clause is associated with the last un-elsed if. You could use braces to force a different association in those cases in which an innermost if does not contain an else but an outer if does. The braces have the effect of closing off the if statement. Thus,

```
if ( [chessGame isOver] == NO ) {
    if ( [chessGame whoseTurn] == YOU )
        [chessGame yourMove];
}
else
    [chessGame finish];
```

achieves the desired effect.

The else if Construct

You have seen how the else statement comes into play when you have a test against two possible conditions—either the number is even, else it is odd; either the year is a leap year, else it is not. However, programming decisions you have to make are not always so black and white. Consider the task of writing a program that displays −1 if a number typed in by a user is less than zero, 0 if the number typed in is equal to zero, and 1 if the number is greater than zero. (This is actually an implementation of what is commonly called the *sign* function.) Obviously, you must make three tests in this case to determine whether the number that is keyed in is negative, zero, or positive. The simple if-else construct will not work. Of course, in this case, you could always resort to three separate if statements, but this solution will not always work—especially if the tests that are made are not mutually exclusive.

You can handle the situation just described by adding an if statement to your else clause. We mentioned that the statement that follows an else could be any valid Objective-C program statement, so why not another if? Thus, in the general case, you could write the following:

```
if ( expression 1 )
    program statement 1
else
    if ( expression 2 )
            program statement 2
    else
            program statement 3
```

This effectively extends the if statement from a two-valued logic decision to a three-valued logic decision. You can continue to add if statements to the else clauses, in the manner just shown, to effectively extend the decision to an *n*-valued logic decision.

The preceding construct is so frequently used that it is generally referred to as an else if construct and is usually formatted differently from that shown previously, like so:

```
if ( expression 1 )
   program statement 1
else if ( expression 2 )
   program statement 2
else
   program statement 3
```

This latter method of formatting improves the readability of the statement and makes it clearer that a three-way decision is being made.

The next program illustrates the use of the else if construct by implementing the sign function discussed earlier.

Program 6.6

```
// Program to implement the sign function

#import <stdio.h>

int main (int argc, char *argv[])
{
  int number, sign;

  printf ("Please type in a number: ");
  scanf ("%i", &number);

  if ( number < 0 )
     sign = -1;
  else if ( number == 0 )
     sign = 0;
  else        // Must be positive
     sign = 1;

  printf ("Sign = %i\n", sign);
  return 0;
}
```

Program 6.6 **Output**

```
Please type in a number: 1121
Sign = 1
```

Program 6.6 **Output (Rerun)**

```
Please type in a number: -158
Sign = -1
```

Program 6.6 **Output (Rerun)**

```
Please type in a number: 0
Sign = 0
```

If the number that is entered is less than zero, sign is assigned the value -1; if the number is equal to zero, sign is assigned the value 0; otherwise, the number must be greater than zero, so sign is assigned the value 1.

The next program analyzes a character that is typed in from the terminal and classifies it as either an alphabetic character (a–z or A–Z), a digit (0–9), or a special character (anything else). To read a single character from the terminal, the format characters %c are used in the scanf call.

Program 6.7

```
// This program categorizes a single character
//        that is entered at the terminal

#import <stdio.h>

int main (int argc, char *argv[])
{
  char c;

  printf ("Enter a single character:\n");
  scanf ("%c", &c);

  if ( (c >= 'a' && c <= 'z') || (c >= 'A' && c <= 'Z') )
     printf ("It's an alphabetic character.\n");
  else if ( c >= '0' && c <= '9' )
     printf ("It's a digit.\n");
  else
     printf ("It's a special character.\n");
 return 0;
}
```

Program 6.7 **Output**

```
Enter a single character:
&
It's a special character.
```

Program 6.7 **Output (Rerun)**

```
Enter a single character:
8
It's a digit.
```

Program 6.7 **Output (Rerun)**

```
Enter a single character:
B
It's an alphabetic character.
```

The first test that is made after the character is read in determines whether the char variable c is an alphabetic character. This is done by testing whether the character is a lowercase letter or an uppercase letter. The former test is made by the following expression:

```
( c >= 'a' && c <= 'z' )
```

This expression is TRUE if c is within the range of characters 'a' through 'z'; that is, if c is a lowercase letter. The latter test is made by this expression:

```
( c >= 'A' && c <= 'Z' )
```

This expression is TRUE if c is within the range of characters 'A' through 'Z'; that is, if c is an uppercase letter. These tests work on computer systems that store characters inside the machine in a format known as ASCII.[1]

If the variable c is an alphabetic character, the first if test succeeds and the message It's an alphabetic character. is displayed. If the test fails, the else if clause is executed. This clause determines whether the character is a digit. Note that this test compares the character c against the *characters* '0' and '9' and *not* the *integers* 0 and 9. This is because a character was read in from the terminal, and the characters '0' to '9' are not the same as the numbers 0–9. In fact, in ASCII, the character '0' is actually represented internally as the number 48, the character '1' as the number 49, and so on.

If c is a digit character, the phrase It's a digit. is displayed. Otherwise, if c is not alphabetic and is not a digit, the final else clause is executed and displays the phrase It's a special character at the terminal. Execution of the program is then complete.

You should note that even though scanf is used here to read just a single character, the Enter key must still be pressed after the character is typed to send the input to the program. In general, whenever you're reading data from the terminal, the program doesn't see any of the data typed on the line until the Enter key is pressed.

Let's suppose for the next example that you want to write a program that allows the user to type in simple expressions of the following form:

number   operator   number

The program will evaluate the expression and display the results at the terminal. The operators you want to have recognized are the normal operators for addition, subtraction, multiplication, and division. Let's use the Calculator class from Program 4.6 in Chapter 4, "Data Types and Expressions," here. So, each expression will be given to the calculator for computation.

The following program uses a large if statement with many else if clauses to determine which operation is to be performed.

Program 6.8

```
// Program to evaluate simple expressions of the form
//          number operator number

// Implement a Calculator class

#import <objc/Object.h>
#import <stdio.h>
```

---

1. It's better to use routines in the standard library called islower and isupper and avoid the internal representation issue entirely. To do that, include the line #import <ctype.h> in your program. However, we've put this here for illustrative purposes only.

Program 6.8 **Continued**

```objc
@interface Calculator: Object
{
  double accumulator;
}

// accumulator methods
-(void)  setAccumulator: (double) value;
-(void)  clear;
-(double) accumulator;

// arithmetic methods
-(void)  add: (double) value;
-(void)  subtract: (double) value;
-(void)  multiply: (double) value;
-(void)  divide: (double) value;
@end

@implementation Calculator;
-(void) setAccumulator: (double) value
{
    accumulator = value;
}

-(void) clear
{
    accumulator = 0;
}

-(double) accumulator
{
    return accumulator;
}

-(void) add: (double) value
{
    accumulator += value;
}

-(void) subtract: (double) value
{
    accumulator -= value;
}

-(void) multiply: (double) value
{
    accumulator *= value;
}
```

Program 6.8   **Continued**

```objc
-(void) divide: (double) value
{
    accumulator /= value;
}
@end


int main (int argc, char *argv[])
{
  double     value1, value2;
  char       operator;
  Calculator  *deskCalc = [[Calculator alloc] init];

  printf ("Type in your expression.\n");
  scanf ("%lf %c %lf", &value1, &operator, &value2);

  [deskCalc setAccumulator: value1];
  if ( operator == '+' )
    [deskCalc add: value2];
  else if ( operator == '-' )
    [deskCalc subtract: value2];
  else if ( operator == '*' )
    [deskCalc multiply: value2];
  else if ( operator == '/' )
    [deskCalc divide: value2];

  printf ("%.2f\n", [deskCalc accumulator]);
  [deskCalc free];

  return 0;
}
```

Program 6.8   **Output**

```
Type in your expression.
123.5 + 59.3
182.80
```

Program 6.8   **Output (Rerun)**

```
Type in your expression.
198.7 / 26
7.64
```

Program 6.8   **Output (Rerun)**

Type in your expression.
89.3 * 2.5
223.25

The scanf call specifies that three values are to be read into the variables value1, operator, and value2. A double value can be read in with the %lf format characters. This is the format used to read in the value of the variable value1, which is the first operand of the expression.

Next, you read in the operator. Because the operator is a character ('+', '-', '*', or '/') and not a number, you read it into the character variable operator. The %c format characters tell the system to read in the next character from the terminal. The blank spaces inside the format string indicate that an arbitrary number of blank spaces are to be permitted on the input. This enables you to separate the operands from the operator with blank spaces when you type in these values.

After the two values and the operator have been read in, the program stores the first value into the calculator's accumulator. Next, you test the value of operator against the four permissible operators. When a correct match is made, the corresponding message is sent to the calculator to perform the operation. In the last printf, the value of the accumulator is retrieved for display. Execution of the program is then complete.

A few words about program thoroughness are in order at this point. Although the preceding program does accomplish the task that we set out to perform, the program is not really complete because it does not account for mistakes made on the part of the user. For example, what would happen if the user were to type in a ? for the operator by mistake? The program would simply fall through the if statement and no messages would ever appear at the terminal to alert the user that he had incorrectly typed in his expression.

Another case that is overlooked is when the user types in a division operation with zero as the divisor. You know by now that you should never attempt to divide a number by zero in Objective-C. The program should check for this case.

Trying to predict the ways in which a program can fail or produce unwanted results and then taking preventive measures to account for such situations is a necessary part of producing good, reliable programs. Running a sufficient number of test cases against a program can often point a finger to portions of the program that do not account for certain cases. But it goes further than that. It must become a matter of self-discipline while coding a program to always ask, "What would happen if...?" and to insert the necessary program statements to handle the situation properly.

Program 6.8A, a modified version of Program 6.8, accounts for division by zero and the keying in of an unknown operator.

Program 6.8A

```
// Program to evaluate simple expressions of the form
//     value   operator   value

#import <stdio.h>
#import <objc/Object.h>

// Insert interface and implementation sections for
// Calculator class here

int main (int argc, char *argv[])
{
    double    value1, value2;
    char      operator;
    Calculator *deskCalc = [[Calculator alloc] init];

    printf ("Type in your expression.\n");
    scanf ("%lf %c %lf", &value1, &operator, &value2);

    [deskCalc setAccumulator: value1];

    if ( operator == '+' )
        [deskCalc add: value2];
    else if ( operator == '-' )
        [deskCalc subtract: value2];
    else if ( operator == '*' )
        [deskCalc multiply: value2];
    else if ( operator == '/' )
        if ( value2 == 0 )
            printf ("Division by zero.\n");
        else
            [deskCalc divide: value2];
    else
        printf ("Unknown operator.\n");


    printf ("%.2f\n", [deskCalc accumulator]);
    [deskCalc free];

    return 0;
}
```

Program 6.8A   **Output**

```
Type in your expression.
123.5 + 59.3
182.80
```

Program 6.8A   **Output (Rerun)**

```
Type in your expression.
198.7 / 0
Division by zero.
198.7
```

Program 6.8A   **Output (Rerun)**

```
Type in your expression.
125 $ 28
Unknown operator.
125
```

When the operator that is typed in is the slash, for division, another test is made to determine whether value2 is 0. If it is, an appropriate message is displayed at the terminal; otherwise, the division operation is carried out and the results are displayed. Pay careful attention to the nesting of the if statements and the associated else clauses in this case.

The else clause at the end of the program catches any fall throughs. Therefore, any value of operator that does not match any of the four characters tested causes this else clause to be executed, resulting in the display of Unknown operator. at the terminal.

A better way to handle the division by zero problem is to perform the test inside the method that handles division. So, you can modify your divide: method as shown here:

```
-(void) divide: (double) value
{
  if (value != 0.0)
     accumulator /= value;
  else {
     printf ("Division by zero.\n");
     accumulator = 99999999.;
  }
}
```

If value is nonzero, you perform the division; otherwise, you display the message and set the accumulator to 99999999. This is arbitrary; you could have set it to zero or perhaps set a special variable to indicate an error condition. In general, it's better to have the method handle special cases rather than rely on the resourcefulness of the programmer using the method.

The switch Statement

The type of if-else statement chain you encountered in the last program example—
where the value of a variable is successively compared against different values—is so commonly used when developing programs that a special program statement exists in the Objective-C language for performing precisely this function. The name of the statement is the switch statement, and its general format is as follows:

```
switch ( expression )
{
    case value1:
         program statement
         program statement
         ...
         break;
    case value2:
         program statement
         program statement
         ...
         break;
      ...
    case valuen:
         program statement
         program statement
         ...
         break;
    default:
         program statement
         program statement
         ...
         break;
}
```

The expression enclosed within parentheses is successively compared against the values value1, value2, ..., valuen, which must be simple constants or constant expressions. If a case is found whose value is equal to the value of expression, the program statements that follow the case are executed. You will note that when more than one such program statement is included, they do *not* have to be enclosed within braces.

The break statement signals the end of a particular case and causes execution of the switch statement to be terminated. Remember to include the break statement at the end of every case. Forgetting to do so for a particular case causes program execution to continue into the next case whenever that case is executed. Sometimes this is done intentionally; if you elect to do so, be sure to insert comments to alert others of your purpose.

The special optional case called default is executed if the value of expression does not match any of the case values. This is conceptually equivalent to the catchall else used in the previous example. In fact, the general form of the switch statement can be equivalently expressed as an if statement as follows:

```
if ( expression == value1 )
{
     program statement
     program statement
        ...
}
else if ( expression == value2 )
{
     program statement
     program statement
        ...
}
  ...
else if ( expression == valuen )
{
     program statement
     program statement
        ...
}
else
{
     program statement
     program statement
        ...
}
```

Bearing the previous code in mind, you can translate the big if statement from Program 6.8A into an equivalent switch statement. We will call this new program Program 6.9.

Program 6.9

```
// Program to evaluate simple expressions of the form
//        value operator  value

#import <stdio.h>
#import <objc/Object.h>

// Insert interface and implementation sections for
// Calculator class here

int main (int argc, char *argv[])
{
  double  value1, value2;
  char    operator;
  Calculator *deskCalc = [[Calculator alloc] init];
```

Program 6.9   **Continued**

```
printf ("Type in your expression.\n");
scanf ("%lf %c %lf", &value1, &operator, &value2);

[deskCalc setAccumulator: value1];

switch ( operator ) {
  case '+':
     [deskCalc add: value2];
     break;
  case '-':
     [deskCalc subtract: value2];
     break;
  case '*':
     [deskCalc multiply: value2];
     break;
  case '/':
     [deskCalc divide: value2];
     break;
  default:
     printf ("Unknown operator.\n");
     break;
  }
  printf ("%.2f\n", [deskCalc accumulator]);
  [deskCalc free];
  return 0;
}
```

Program 6.9   **Output**

```
Type in your expression.
178.99 - 326.8
-147.81
```

After the expression has been read in, the value of operator is successively compared against the values as specified by each case. When a match is found, the statements contained inside the case are executed. The break statement then sends execution out of the switch statement, where execution of the program is completed. If none of the cases matches the value of operator, the default case, which displays Unknown operator., is executed.

The break statement in the default case is actually unnecessary in the preceding program because no statements follow this case inside the switch. Nevertheless, it is a good programming habit to remember to include the break at the end of every case.

When writing a `switch` statement, you should bear in mind that no two case values can be the same. However, you can associate more than one case value with a particular set of program statements. This is done simply by listing the multiple case values (with the keyword `case` before the value and a colon after the value in each case) before the common statements that are to be executed. As an example, in the `switch` statement

```
switch ( operator )
{
    ...
    case '*':
    case 'x':
        [deskCalc multiply: value2];
        break;
    ...
}
```

the `multiply:` method is executed if `operator` is equal to an asterisk or to the lowercase letter *x*.

Boolean Variables

Just about anyone learning to program soon finds herself with the task of having to write a program to generate a table of prime numbers. To refresh your memory, a positive integer, *p*, is a prime number if it is not evenly divisible by any other integers, other than 1 and itself. The first prime integer is defined to be 2. The next prime is 3 because it is not evenly divisible by any integers other than 1 and 3; and 4 is *not* prime because it *is* evenly divisible by 2.

You could take several approaches to generate a table of prime numbers. If you had the task of generating all prime numbers up to 50, for example, then the most straightforward (and simplest) algorithm to generate such a table would simply test each integer, *p*, for divisibility by all integers from 2 through *p*-1. If any such integer evenly divided *p*, then *p* would not be prime; otherwise, it would be a prime number.

Program 6.10

```
// Program to generate a table of prime numbers

#import <stdio.h>

int main (int argc, char *argv[])
{
    int    p, d, isPrime;
```

Program 6.10 **Continued**

```
for ( p = 2; p <= 50; ++p ) {
    isPrime = 1;

    for ( d = 2; d < p; ++d )
        if ( p % d == 0 )
            isPrime = 0;

    if ( isPrime != 0 )
        printf ("%i ", p);
}

printf ("\n");
return 0;
}
```

Program 6.10 **Output**

```
2  3  5  7  11  13  17  19  23  29  31  37  41  43  47
```

Several points are worth noting about Program 6.10. The outermost `for` statement sets up a loop to cycle through the integers 2–50. The loop variable p represents the value you are currently testing to see whether it is prime. The first statement in the loop assigns the value 1 to the variable `isPrime`. The use of this variable will become apparent shortly.

A second loop is set up to divide p by the integers 2–p-1. Inside the loop, a test is performed to see whether the remainder of p divided by d is 0. If it is, you know that p cannot be prime because an integer other than 1 and itself evenly divides it. To signal that p is no longer a candidate as a prime number, the value of the variable `isPrime` is set equal to 0.

When the innermost loop finishes execution, the value of `isPrime` is tested. If its value is not equal to zero, no integer was found that evenly divided p; therefore, p must be a prime number, and its value is displayed.

You might have noticed that the variable `isPrime` takes on either the value 0 or 1, and no other values. Its value is 1 as long as p still qualifies as a prime number. But as soon as a single even divisor is found, its value is set to 0 to indicate that p no longer satisfies the criteria for being prime. Variables used in such a manner are generally referred to as *Boolean* variables. A flag typically assumes only one of two different values. Furthermore, the value of a flag usually is tested at least once in the program to see whether it is on (TRUE or YES) or off (FALSE or NO) and some particular action is taken based on the results of the test.

In Objective-C, the notion of a flag being TRUE or FALSE is most naturally translated into the values 1 and 0, respectively. So, in Program 6.10, when you set the value of `isPrime` to 1 inside the loop, you are effectively setting it TRUE to indicate that p "is prime." If, during the course of execution of the inner `for` loop, an even divisor is found, the value of `isPrime` is set FALSE to indicate that p no longer "is prime."

It is no coincidence that the value 1 is typically used to represent the TRUE or on state and 0 is used to represent the FALSE or off state. This representation corresponds to the notion of a single bit inside a computer. When the bit is on, its value is 1; when it is off, its value is 0. But in Objective-C, there is an even more convincing argument in favor of these logic values. It has to do with the way the Objective-C language treats the concept of TRUE and FALSE.

When we began our discussions in this chapter, we noted that if the conditions specified inside the if statement were satisfied, the program statement that immediately followed would be executed. But what exactly does *satisfied* mean? In the Objective-C language, *satisfied* means nonzero, and nothing more. Thus, the statement

```
if ( 100 )
    printf ("This will always be printed.\n");
```

results in the execution of the printf statement because the condition in the if statement (in this case simply the value 100) is nonzero and therefore is satisfied.

In each of the programs in this chapter, the notions of "nonzero means satisfied" and "zero means not satisfied" were used. This is because, whenever a relational expression is evaluated in Objective-C, it is given the value 1 if the expression is satisfied and 0 if the expression is not satisfied. So, evaluation of the statement

```
if ( number < 0 )
    number = -number;
```

actually proceeds as follows: The relational expression number < 0 is evaluated. If the condition is satisfied, that is, if number is less than 0, the value of the expression is 1; otherwise, its value is 0.

The if statement tests the result of the expression evaluation. If the result is nonzero, the statement that immediately follows is executed; otherwise, the statement is skipped.

The preceding discussion also applies to the evaluation of conditions inside the for, while, and do statements. Evaluation of compound relational expressions such as in the statement

```
while ( char != 'e' && count != 80 )
```

also proceeds as outlined previously. If both specified conditions are valid, the result is 1; but if either condition is not valid, the result of the evaluation is 0. The results of the evaluation are then checked. If the result is 0, the while loop terminates; otherwise it continues.

Returning to Program 6.10 and the notion of flags, it is perfectly valid in Objective-C, to test whether the value of a flag is TRUE by an expression such as

```
if ( isPrime )
```

which is equivalent to

```
if ( isPrime != 0 )
```

To easily test whether the value of a flag is FALSE, you use the logical negation operator, !. In the expression

```
if ( ! isPrime )
```

the logical negation operator is used to test whether the value of isPrime is FALSE (read this statement as "if not isPrime"). In general, an expression such as

```
! expression
```

negates the logical value of *expression*. So, if *expression* is 0, the logical negation operator produces a 1. And if the result of the evaluation of *expression* is non-zero, the negation operator yields a 0.

The logical negation operator can be used to easily flip the value of a flag, such as in the following expression:

```
my_move = ! my_move;
```

As you might expect, this operator has the same precedence as the unary minus operator, which means that it has higher precedence than all binary arithmetic operators and all relational operators. So, to test whether the value of a variable x is not less than the value of a variable y, such as in

```
! ( x < y )
```

the parentheses are required to ensure proper evaluation of the expression. Of course, you could have equivalently expressed the previous statement as

```
x >= y
```

A couple of built-in features in Objective-C make working with Boolean variables a little easier. One is the special type BOOL, which can be used to declare variables that will contain either a true or false value.[2] The other is the built-in values YES and NO. Using these predefined values in your programs can make them easier to write and read. Here is Program 6.10 rewritten to take advantage of these features.

Program 6.10A

```
// Program to generate a table of prime numbers
// second version using BOOL type and predefined values

#import <stdio.h>
#import <objc/Object.h>

int main (int argc, char *argv[])
{
    int    p, d;
    BOOL   isPrime;
```

---

2. The type BOOL is really added by a mechanism known as the *preprocessor*.

Program 6.10A   **Continued**

```
for ( p = 2; p <= 50; ++p ) {
   isPrime = YES;

   for ( d = 2; d < p; ++d )
      if ( p % d == 0 )
         isPrime = NO;

   if ( isPrime == YES )
      printf ("%i ", p);
   }

printf ("\n");
return 0;
}
```

Program 6.10A   **Output**

```
2 3 5 7 11 13 17 19 23 29 31 37 41 43 47
```

Even though you haven't defined any classes in Program 6.10A, you need to import objc/Object.h because BOOL, YES, and NO are defined there.

The Conditional Operator

Perhaps the most unusual operator in the Objective-C language is one called the conditional operator. Unlike all other operators in Objective-C—which are either unary or binary operators—the conditional operator is a *ternary* operator; that is, it takes three operands. The two symbols used to denote this operator are the question mark (?) and the colon (:). The first operand is placed before the ?, the second between the ? and the :, and the third after the :.

The general format of the conditional expression is

condition ? expression1 : expression2

In this syntax, *condition* is an expression, usually a relational expression, that is evaluated by the Objective-C system first whenever the conditional operator is encountered. If the result of the evaluation of *condition* is TRUE (that is, nonzero), *expression1* is evaluated and the result of the evaluation becomes the result of the operation. If *condition* evaluates FALSE (that is, zero), *expression2* is evaluated and its result becomes the result of the operation.

A conditional expression is most often used to assign one of two values to a variable depending on some condition. For example, suppose you have an integer variable x and another integer variable s. If you wanted to assign -1 to s if x were less than 0, and the value of x^2 to s otherwise, the following statement could be written:

```
s = ( x < 0 ) ? -1 : x * x;
```

The condition x < 0 is first tested when the previous statement is executed. Parentheses are generally placed around the condition expression to aid in the statement's readability. This is usually not required, though, because the precedence of the conditional operator is very low—lower, in fact, than all other operators but the assignment operators and the comma operator.

If the value of x is less than zero, the expression immediately following the ? is evaluated. This expression is simply the constant integer value -1, which is assigned to the variable s if x is less than zero.

If the value of x is not less than zero, the expression immediately following the : is evaluated and assigned to s. So, if x is greater than or equal to zero, the value of x * x, or x^2, is assigned to s.

As another example of the use of the conditional operator, the following statement assigns to the variable max_value the maximum of a and b:

```
max_value = ( a > b ) ? a : b;
```

If the expression that is used after the : (the "else" part) consists of another conditional operator, you can achieve the effects of an "else if" clause. For example, the sign function implemented in Program 6.6 can be written in one program line using two conditional operators, as follows:

```
sign = ( number < 0 ) ? -1 : (( number == 0 ) ? 0 : 1);
```

If number is less than zero, sign is assigned the value -1; else, if number is equal to zero, sign is assigned the value 0; else, it is assigned the value 1. The parentheses around the "else" part of the previous expression are actually unnecessary. This is because the conditional operator associates from right to left, meaning that multiple uses of this operator in a single expression, such as in

```
e1 ? e2 : e3 ? e4 : e5
```

group from right to left and therefore are evaluated as follows:

```
e1 ? e2 : ( e3 ? e4 : e5 )
```

Conditional expressions don't have to be used on the right side of an assignment—they can be used in any situation in which expressions could be used. This means you could display the sign of the variable number without first assigning it to a variable using a printf statement as shown here:

```
printf ("Sign = %i\n", ( number < 0 ) ? -1
                      : ( number == 0 ) ? 0 : 1);
```

The conditional operator is very handy when writing preprocessor macros in Objective-C. This can be seen in detail in Chapter 12, "The Preprocessor."

Exercises

1. Write a program that asks the user to type in two integer values at the terminal. Test these two numbers to determine whether the first is evenly divisible by the second, and then display an appropriate message at the terminal.

2. Program 6.8A displays the value in the accumulator even if an invalid operator is entered or division by zero is attempted. Fix that problem.

3. Modify the `print` method from the `Fraction` class so that whole numbers are displayed as such (so the fraction 5/1 should display as simply 5). Also modify the method to display fractions with a numerator of 0 as simply zero.

4. Write a program that acts as a simple printing calculator. The program should allow the user to type in expressions of the following form:

   ```
   number   operator
   ```

   The following operators should be recognized by the program:

   ```
   +   -   *   /   S   E
   ```

   The S operator tells the program to set the accumulator to the typed-in number, and the E operator tells the program that execution is to end. The arithmetic operations are performed on the contents of the accumulator with the number that was keyed in acting as the second operand. The following is a sample run showing how the program should operate:

   ```
   Begin Calculations
   10 S              Set Accumulator to 10
   = 10.000000       Contents of Accumulator
   2 /               Divide by 2
   = 5.000000        Contents of Accumulator
   55 -              Subtract 55
   -50.000000
   100.25 S          Set Accumulator to 100.25
   = 100.250000
   4 *               Multiply by 4
   = 401.000000
   0 E               End of program
   = 401.000000
   End of Calculations.
   ```

   Make sure that the program detects division by 0 and also checks for unknown operators. Use the `Calculator` class developed in Program 6.8 for performing your calculations.

5. We developed Program 5.9 to reverse the digits of an integer typed in from the terminal. However, this program does not function well if you type in a negative number. Find out what happens in such a case, and then modify the program so that negative numbers are correctly handled. By correctly handled, we mean that if the number −8645 were typed in, for example, the output of the program should be 5468−.

6. Write a program that takes an integer keyed in from the terminal and extracts and displays each digit of the integer in English. So, if the user types in 932, the program should display the following:

```
nine three two
```

(Remember to display zero if the user types in just a 0.) Note: This exercise is a hard one!

7. Program 6.10 has several inefficiencies. One inefficiency results from checking even numbers. Because any even number greater than 2 obviously cannot be prime, the program could simply skip all even numbers as possible primes and as possible divisors. The inner for loop is also inefficient because the value of p is always divided by all values of d from 2 through p–1. This inefficiency could be avoided if you added a test for the value of isPrime in the conditions of the for loop. In this manner, the for loop could be set up to continue as long as no divisor was found and the value of d was less than p. Modify Program 6.10 to incorporate these two changes; then run the program to verify its operation. Note: In a later chapter, you will learn even more efficient ways of generating prime numbers.

7

More on Classes

IN THIS CHAPTER YOU'LL CONTINUE LEARNING HOW to work with classes and write methods. You'll also apply some of the concepts you've learned in the previous chapter, such as program looping, making decisions, and working with expressions. First, we'll talk about splitting your program into multiple files to make working with larger programs easier.

Separate Interface and Implementation Files

It's time to get used to putting your class declarations and definitions in separate files. Typically, a class declaration (that is, the @interface section) is placed in its own file, called `class`.h. The definition (that is, the @implementation section) is normally placed in a file of the same name, using the extension .m instead. So, let's put the declaration of the Fraction class into the file Fraction.h and the definition into Fraction.m. (see Program 7.1).

Program 7.1 **Interface File** `Fraction.h`

```
#import <objc/Object.h>

// The Fraction class

@interface Fraction : Object
{
  int   numerator;
  int   denominator;
}
-(void)     print;
-(void)     setNumerator: (int) n;
-(void)     setDenominator: (int) d;
-(int)      numerator;
-(int)      denominator;
-(double)   convertToNum;

@end
```

The interface file tells the compiler (and other programmers as you'll learn later) what a Fraction looks like—it contains two instance variables called numerator and denominator, which are both integers. It also has six instance methods: print, setNumerator:, setDenominator:, numerator, denominator, and convertToNum. The first three methods don't return a value; the next two return an int; and the last one returns a double. The setNumerator: and setDenominator: methods each take an integer argument.

The details of the implementation for the Fraction class are in the file Fraction.m.

Program 7.1 **Implementation File:** Fraction.m

```
#import "Fraction.h"
#import <stdio.h>

@implementation Fraction;
-(void) print
{
  printf (" %i/%i ", numerator, denominator);
}

-(void) setNumerator: (int) n
{
  numerator = n;
}

-(void) setDenominator: (int) d
{
  denominator = d;
}

-(int) numerator
{
  return numerator;
}

-(int) denominator
{
  return denominator;
}

-(double) convertToNum
{
  if (denominator != 0)
    return (double) numerator / denominator;
  else
    return 1.0;
}
@end
```

Note that the interface file is imported into the implementation file with the following statement:

```
#import "Fraction.h"
```

This is done so that the compiler knows about the class and methods you declared for your `Fraction` class, and it can also ensure consistency between the two files. Recall also that you don't normally (although you can) redeclare the class's instance variables inside the implementation section, so the compiler needs to get that information from the interface section contained in `Fraction.h`.

The other thing you should note is that the file that is imported is enclosed in a set of double quotes and not < and > characters, as was the case with `<obj/Object.h>` and `<stdio.h>`. The double quotes are used for *local* files (files you create yourself), as opposed to system files, and they tell the compiler where to look for the specified file. When you use double quotes, the compiler typically looks inside your current directory first for the specified file and then in a list of other places. The actual places that are searched can be specified to the compiler if necessary.

Here is the test program for our example, which we have typed into the file `main.m`.

Program 7.1   **Main Test Program:** `main.m`

```
#import "Fraction.h"
#import <stdio.h>

int main (int argc, char *argv[])
{
  Fraction   *myFraction = [[Fraction alloc] init];

  // set fraction to 1/3

  [myFraction setNumerator: 1];
  [myFraction setDenominator: 3];

  // display the fraction

  printf ("The value of myFraction is:");
  [myFraction print];
  printf ("\n");
  [myFraction free];

  return 0;
}
```

Note again that the test program, `main.m`, includes the interface file `Fraction.h` and *not* the implementation file `Fraction.m`. This file is specified on the command line for the compiler to process.

Now you have your program split into three separate files. This might seem like a lot of work for a small program example, but the usefulness will become apparent when you start dealing with larger programs and sharing class declarations with other programmers.

To compile this program, give the Objective-C compiler both ".m" filenames on the command line. Using gcc, the command line looks like this:

```
gcc Fraction.m main.m -o fractions -l objc
```

This builds an executable file called fractions. Here's the output after running the program.

Program 7.1   **Output**

```
The value of myFraction is: 1/3
```

Multiple Arguments to Methods

Let's continue to work with the Fraction class and make some additions. You have defined six methods. It would be nice to have a method to set both the numerator and denominator with a single message. You define methods that take multiple arguments simply by listing each successive argument followed by a colon. This becomes part of the method name. For example, the method name addEntryWithName:andEmail: is a method that takes two arguments, presumably a name and an email address. The method addEntryWithName:andEmail:andPhone: is a method that takes three arguments: a name, an email address, and a phone number.

A method to set both the numerator and denominator could be named setNumerator:andDenominator:, and you might use it like this:

```
[myFraction setNumerator: 1 andDenominator: 3];
```

That's not bad. And that was actually the first choice for the method name. But we can come up with a more readable method name. For example, how about setTo:over:? That might not look too appealing at first glance, but compare this message to set myFraction to 1/3 with the previous one:

```
[myFraction setTo: 1 over: 3];
```

I think that reads a little better, but the choice is up to you (some might actually prefer the first name because it explicitly references the instance variable names contained in the class). Again, choosing good method names is important for program readability. Writing out the actual message expression can help you pick a good one.

Let's put this new method to work. First, add the declaration of setTo:over: to the interface file, as shown in Program 7.2.

Program 7.2   **Interface File:** `Fraction.h`

```objc
#import <objc/Object.h>

// Define the Fraction class

@interface Fraction : Object
{
  int numerator;
  int denominator;
}

-(void)    print;
-(void)    setNumerator: (int) n;
-(void)    setDenominator: (int) d;
-(void)    setTo: (int) n over: (int) d;
-(int)     numerator;
-(int)     denominator;
-(double)  convertToNum;
@end
```

Next, add the definition for the new method to the implementation file.

Program 7.2   **Implementation File:** `Fraction.m`

```objc
#import "Fraction.h"
#import <stdio.h>

@implementation Fraction;
-(void) print
{
  printf (" %i/%i ", numerator, denominator);
}

-(void) setNumerator: (int) n
{
  numerator = n;
}

-(void) setDenominator: (int) d
{
  denominator = d;
}

-(int) numerator
{
  return numerator;
}
```

Program 7.2 **Continued**

```
-(int) denominator
{
  return denominator;
}
-(double) convertToNum
{
  if (denominator != 0)
    return (double) numerator / denominator;
  else
    return 1.0;
}

-(void) setTo: (int) n over: (int) d
{
  numerator = n;
  denominator = d;
}
@end
```

The new `setTo:over:` method simply takes its two integer arguments, n and d, and assigns them to the corresponding fields of the fraction, numerator and denominator.

Here's a test program to try your new method.

Program 7.2 **Test File:** `main.m`

```
#import "Fraction.h"
#import <stdio.h>

int main (int argc, char *argv[])
{
  Fraction *aFraction = [[Fraction alloc] init];

  [aFraction setTo: 100 over: 200];
  [aFraction print];

  [aFraction setTo: 1 over: 3];
  [aFraction print];
  [aFraction free];

  return 0;
}
```

Program 7.2   **Output**

```
100/200
1/3
```

Methods Without Argument Names

When creating the name for a method, the argument names are actually optional. For example, you can declare a method like this:

```
-(int) set: (int) n: (int) d;
```

Note that, unlike previous examples, no name is given for the second argument to the method here. This method is named `set::`, and the two colons mean the method takes two arguments, even though they're not all named.

To invoke the `set::` method, you use the colons as argument delimiters, as shown here:

```
[aFraction set: 1 : 3];
```

It's generally not good programming style to omit argument names when writing new methods because it makes the program harder to follow and makes it less intuitive when you're using a method as to what the actual parameters to the method signify.

Operations on Fractions

Let's continue to work with the `Fraction` class. First, you'll write a method that will enable you to add one fraction to another. You'll name the method `add:`, and you have it take a fraction as an argument. Here's the declaration for the new method:

```
-(void) add: (Fraction *) f;
```

Note the declaration for the argument f:

```
(Fraction *) f
```

This says that the argument to the `add:` method is of type class `Fraction`. The asterisk is necessary, so the declaration

```
(Fraction) f
```

is not correct. You will be passing one fraction as an argument to your `add:` method, and you'll have the method add it to the receiver of the message, so the message expression

```
[aFraction add: bFraction];
```

will add the `Fraction` bFraction to the `Fraction` aFraction. Just as a quick math refresher, to add the fractions a/b and c/d, you perform the calculation as follows:

$$\frac{a}{b} + \frac{c}{d} = \frac{ad + bc}{bd}$$

Here is the code for the new method that you will put into the @implementation section:

```
// add a Fraction to the receiver

- (void) add: (Fraction *) f
{
  // To add two fractions:
  // a/b + c/d = ((a*d) + (b*c)) / (b * d)

  numerator = (numerator * [f denominator])
            + (denominator * [f numerator]);
  denominator = denominator * [f denominator];
}
```

Don't forget that you can refer to the Fraction that is the receiver of the message by its fields: numerator and denominator. On the other hand, you can't directly refer to the instance variables of the argument f that way. Instead, you have to obtain them by applying the numerator and denominator methods. Note that this is the first time you have used a method (numerator and denominator) from within another method (add:). Obviously, this is perfectly valid.

Let's assume that you added the previous declarations and definitions for your new add: method to your interface and implementation files. Program 7.3 is a sample test program and output.

Program 7.3   **Test File:** main.m

```
#import "Fraction.h"
3import <stdio.h>

int main (int argc, char *argv[])
{
  Fraction *aFraction = [[Fraction alloc] init];
  Fraction *bFraction = [[Fraction alloc] init];

  // Set two fractions to 1/4 and 1/2 and add them together

  [aFraction setTo: 1 over: 4];
  [bFraction setTo: 1 over: 2];

  // Print the results

  [aFraction print];
  printf (" + ");
  [bFraction print];
  printf (" = ");
```

Program 7.3   **Continued**

```
[aFraction add: bFraction];
[aFraction print];
printf ("\n");
[aFraction free];
[bFraction free];

return 0;
}
```

Program 7.3   **Output**

```
1/4 + 1/2 = 6/8
```

The test program is straightforward enough. Two Fractions, called aFraction and bFraction, are allocated and initialized. Then they are set to the values 1/4 and 1/2, respectively. Next, the Fraction bFraction is added to the Fraction aFraction; the result of the addition is then displayed. Note again that the add: method adds the argument to the object of the message, so the object gets modified. This is verified when you print the value of aFraction at the end of main. You should realize that you had to print the value of aFraction *before* invoking the add: method so that you could get its value displayed before it was changed by the method. Later in this chapter, you'll redefine the add: method so that add: does not affect the value of its argument.

Local Variables

You might have noticed that the result of adding 1/4 to 1/2 was displayed as 6/8, and not as 3/4, which you might have preferred (or even expected!). That's because your addition routine just does the math and no more—it doesn't worry about reducing the result. So, to continue with our exercise of adding new methods to work with fractions, let's make a new reduce method to reduce a fraction to its simplest terms.

Reaching back to your high school math again, you can reduce a fraction by finding the largest number that evenly divides both the numerator and denominator of your fraction and then dividing them by that number. Technically, you want to find the greatest common divisor (gcd) of the numerator and denominator. You already know how to do that from Program 5.7. You might want to refer to that program example just to refresh your memory.

With the algorithm in hand, you can now write your new reduce method:

```
- (void) reduce
{
  int  u = numerator;
  int  v = denominator;
  int  temp;
```

```
  while (v != 0) {
    temp = u % v;
    u = v;
    v = temp;
  }

  numerator /= u;
  denominator /= u;
}
```

Notice something new about this `reduce` method: It declares three integer variables called u, v, and `temp`. These variables are *local* variables, meaning their values exist only during execution of the `reduce` method and that *they can only be accessed from within the method in which they are defined.* In that sense, they are similar to the variables you have been declaring inside your `main` routine; those variables were also local to `main` and could be accessed directly only from within the `main` routine. None of the methods you developed could directly access those variables defined in `main`.

Local variables have no default initial value, so you must set them to some value before using them. The three local variables in the `reduce` method are set to values before they are used, so that's not a problem here. And, unlike your instance variables (which retain their values through method calls), these local variables have no memory. Therefore, after the method returns, the values of these variables disappear. Each time a method is called, each local variable defined in that method is initialized to the value specified (if any) with the variable's declaration.

Method Arguments

The names you use to refer to a method's arguments are also local variables. When the method is executed, whatever arguments are passed to the method are copied into these variables. Because the method is dealing with a copy of the arguments, *it cannot change the original values passed to the method.* This is an important concept. Suppose you had a method `calculate:` defined as follows:

```
-(void) calculate: (double) x
{
  x *= 2;
  ...
}
```

Also suppose you used the following message expression to invoke it:

```
[myData calculate: ptVal];
```

Whatever value contained in the variable `ptVal` would be copied into the local variable x when the `calculate` method was executed. So, changing the value of x inside `calculate:` would have no effect on the value of `ptVal`—only on the copy of its value stored inside x.

Incidentally, in the case of arguments that are objects, you can change the instance variables stored in that object. You'll learn more about that in the next chapter.

The `static` **Keyword**

You can have a local variable retain its value through multiple invocations of a method by placing the keyword `static` in front of the variable's declaration. So, for example

```
static int hitCount = 0;
```

declares the integer `hitCount` to be a static variable. Unlike other normal local variables, a static one does have an initial value of 0, so the initialization shown previously is redundant. Further, they are initialized only once when program execution begins and retain their values through successive method calls.

So the code sequence

```
-(void) showPage
{
    static int pageCount = 0;
    ...
    ++pageCount;
    ...
}
```

might appear inside a `showPage` method that wanted to keep track of the number of times it was invoked (or in this case, perhaps the number of pages that have been printed, for example). The local static variable would be set to 0 only once when the program started and would retain its value through successive invocations of the `showPage` method.

Note the difference between making `pageCount` a local static variable and making it an instance variable. In the former case, `pageCount` could count the number of pages printed by all objects that invoked the `showPage` method. In the latter case, the variable would count the number of pages printed by each individual object because each object would have its own copy of `pageCount`.

Remember that static or local variables can be accessed only from within the method in which they're defined. So, even the static `pageCount` variable can be accessed only from within `showPage`. You can move the declaration of the variable *outside* any method declaration (typically near the beginning of your implementation file) to make it accessible to any methods, like so:

```
#import "Printer.h"
static int pageCount;

@implementation Printer;
    ...
@end
```

The `pageCount` variable can now be accessed by any instance or class method contained in the file. Chapter 10, "More on Variables and Data Types," covers this topic of variable scope in greater detail.

Returning to our fractions, incorporate the code for the `reduce` method into your `Fraction.m` implementation file. Don't forget to declare the `reduce` method in your `Fraction.h` interface file, as well. With that done, you can test your new method in Program 7.4.

Program 7.4   **Test File** `main.m`

```
#import "Fraction.h"
#import <stdio.h>

int main (int argc, char *argv[])
{
  Fraction *aFraction = [[Fraction alloc] init];
  Fraction *bFraction = [[Fraction alloc] init];

  [aFraction setTo: 1 over: 4];    // set 1st fraction to 1/4
  [bFraction setTo: 1 over: 2];    // set 2nd fraction to 1/2

  [aFraction print];
  printf (" + ");
  [bFraction print];
  printf (" = ");

  [aFraction add: bFraction];

  // reduce the result of the addition and print the result

  [aFraction reduce];
  [aFraction print];
  printf ("\n");
  [aFraction free];
  [bFraction free];

  return 0;
}
```

Program 7.4   **Output**

```
1/4 + 1/2 = 3/4
```

That's better!

The `self` **Keyword**

In Program 7.4 we decided to reduce the fraction outside of the `add:` method. We could have done it inside `add:` as well. The decision was completely arbitrary. However, how would we go about identifying the fraction to be reduced to our `reduce` method? We know how to identify instance variables inside a method directly by name, but we don't know how to directly identify the receiver of the message.

The keyword `self` can be used to refer to the object that is the receiver of the current method. If inside your `add:` method you were to write

```
[self reduce];
```

the reduce method would be applied to the `Fraction` that was the receiver of the `add:` method, which is what you want. You will see throughout this book how useful the `self` keyword can be. For now, use it in your `add:` method. Here's what the modified method looks like:

```
- (void) add: (Fraction *) f
{
    // To add two fractions:
    // a/b + c/d = ((a*d) + (b*c)) / (b * d)

    numerator = (numerator * [f denominator]) +
            (denominator * [f numerator]);
    denominator = denominator * [f denominator];

    [self reduce];
}
```

So, after the addition is performed, the fraction is reduced.

Allocating and Returning Objects from Methods

We noted that the `add:` method changes the value of the object that is receiving the message. Let's create a new version of `add:` that will instead make a new fraction to store the result of the addition. In this case, we will need to return the new `Fraction` to the message sender. Here is the definition for the new `add:` method:

```
-(Fraction *) add: (Fraction *) f
{
    // To add two fractions:
    // a/b + c/d = ((a*d) + (b*c)) / (b * d)

    // result will store the result of the addition
    Fraction    *result = [[Fraction alloc] init];
    int         resultNum, resultDenom;

    resultNum = (numerator * [f denominator]) +
            (denominator * [f numerator]);
    resultDenom = denominator * [f denominator];

    [result setTo: resultNum over: resultDenom];
    [result reduce];

    return result;
}
```

The first line of your method definition is

```
-(Fraction *) add: (Fraction *) f;
```

This says that your `add:` method will return a `Fraction` object and that it will take one as its argument as well. The argument will be added to the receiver of the message, which is also a `Fraction`.

The method allocates and initializes a new `Fraction` object called `result` and then defines two local variables called `resultNum` and `resultDenom`. These will be used to store the resulting numerator and denominators from your addition.

After performing the addition as before and assigning the resulting numerators and denominators to your local variables, you then proceed to set `result` with the following message expression:

```
[result setTo: resultNum over: resultDenom];
```

After reducing the result, you return its value to the sender of the message with the `return` statement.

Note that the memory occupied by the `Fraction result` that is allocated inside the `add:` method is returned and does not get released. You can't release it from the `add:` method because the invoker of the method needs it. It is therefore imperative that the user of this method knows that the object being returned is a new instance and must be subsequently released. This can be communicated to the user through suitable documentation that is made available to users of the class.

Program 7.5 tests your new `add:` method.

Program 7.5   **Test File** `main.m`

```
#import "Fraction.h"

int main (int argc, char *argv[])
{
  Fraction *aFraction = [[Fraction alloc] init];
  Fraction *bFraction = [[Fraction alloc] init];

  Fraction *resultFraction;

  [aFraction setTo: 1 over: 4];   // set 1st fraction to 1/4
  [bFraction setTo: 1 over: 2];   // set 2nd fraction to 1/2


  [aFraction print];
  printf (" + ");
  [bFraction print];
  printf (" = ");
```

Program 7.5 **Continued**

```
resultFraction = [aFraction add: bFraction];
[resultFraction print];
printf ("\n");

// This time give the result directly to print
// memory leakage here!

[[aFraction add: bFraction] print];
printf ("\n");


[aFraction free];
[bFraction free];
[resultFraction free];

return 0;
}
```

Program 7.5 **Output**

```
1/4 + 1/2 = 3/4
3/4
```

Some explanation is in order here. First, you define two Fractions—aFraction and bFraction—and set their values to 1/4 and 1/2, respectively. You also define a Fraction called resultFraction (why doesn't it have to be allocated and initialized?). This variable will be used to store the result of your addition operations that follow.

The following lines of code

```
resultFraction = [aFraction add: bFraction];
[resultFraction print];
printf ("\n");
```

first send the add: message to aFraction, passing along the Fraction bFraction as its argument. The resulting Fraction that is returned by the method is stored in resultFraction and then displayed by passing it a print message. Note that you must be careful at the end of the program to release resultFraction, even though you didn't allocate it yourself in main. It was allocated by the add: method, but it's still your responsibility to clean it up. The message expression

```
[[aFraction add: bFraction] print];
```

might look nice, but it actually creates a problem. Because you take the Fraction that add: returns and send it a message to print, you have no way of subsequently releasing the Fraction object that add: created. This is an example of *memory leakage*. If you did this type of nested messaging many times in your program, you would end up accumulating storage for fractions whose memory would not be released. Each time, you would be adding, or *leaking*, just a little bit more memory that you could not directly recover.

One solution to the problem is to have the print method return its receiver, which you could then free. But that seems a little roundabout. A better solution is to divide the nested messages into two separate messages, as was done earlier in the program.

By the way, you could have avoided using the temporary variables resultNum and resultDenom completely in your add: method. Instead, the single message call

```
[result setTo: (numerator * [f denominator]) +
    (denominator * [f numerator])
        over: denominator * [f denominator]];
```

would have done the trick! We're not suggesting you write such concise code. However, you might see it when you examine other programmers' code, so it is useful to learn how to read and understand these powerful expressions.

Let's take one last look at fractions in this chapter. For our example, let's consider calculation of the following series:

$$\sum_{i=1}^{n} 1/2^i$$

The sigma notation is shorthand for a summation. Its use here means to add the values of $1/2^i$, where i varies from 1 to n. That is, add $1/2 + 1/4 + 1/8\ldots$. If you make the value of n large enough, the sum of this series should approach 1. Let's experiment with different values for n to see how close we get.

Program 7.7 prompts for the value of n to be entered and performs the indicated calculation.

Program 7.7   main.m

```
#import "Fraction.h"

int main (int argc, char *argv[])
{
    Fraction *aFraction = [[Fraction alloc] init];
    Fraction *sum = [[Fraction alloc] init], *sum2;
    int i, n, pow2;

    [sum setTo: 0 over: 1]; // set 1st fraction to 0
```

Program 7.7   **Continued**

```
    printf ("Enter your value for n: ");
    scanf ("%i", &n);

    pow2 = 2;
    for (i = 1; i <= n; ++i) {
      [aFraction setTo: 1 over: pow2];
      sum2 = [sum add: aFraction];
      [sum free];   // release previous sum
      sum = sum2;
      pow2 *= 2;
    }

    printf ("After %i iterations, the sum is %g\n", n, [sum convertToNum]);
    [aFraction free];
    [sum free];

    return 0;
}
```

Program 7.7   **Output**

```
Enter your value for n: 5
After 5 iterations, the sum is 0.96875
```

Program 7.7   **Output (Rerun)**

```
Enter your value for n: 10
After 10 iterations, the sum is 0.999023
```

Program 7.7   **Output (Rerun)**

```
Enter your value for n: 15
After 15 iterations, the sum is 0.999969
```

The Fraction sum is set to the value of 0 by setting its numerator to 0 and its denominator to 1 (what would happen if you set both its numerator and denominator to 0?). The program then prompts the user to enter her value for n and reads it using scanf. You then enter a for loop to calculate the sum of the series. First, you initialize the variable pow2 to 2. This variable is used to store the value of 2^i. So, each time through the loop it's value is multiplied by 2.

The for loop starts at 1 and goes through *n*. Each time through the loop, you set aFraction to 1/pow2, or $1/2^i$. This value is then added to the cumulative sum by using the previously defined add: method. The result from add: is assigned to sum2 and not to sum to avoid memory leakage problems. (What would happen if you assigned it directly to sum instead?) The old sum is then freed, and the new sum, sum2, is assigned to sum for the next iteration through the loop. Study the way the fractions are freed in the code so that you feel comfortable with the strategy that is used to avoid memory leakage. And realize that if this were a for loop that was executed hundreds or thousands of times and you weren't judicious about freeing your fractions, you would quickly start to accumulate a lot of wasted memory space.

When the for loop is completed, you display the final result as a decimal value using the convertToNum method. You have just two objects left at that point to release— aFraction and your final Fraction object stored in sum. Program execution is then complete.

The output shows what happens when we ran the program three separate times on a PowerBook G4. You might get slightly different results from your computer. The first time, the sum of the series is calculated and the resulting value of 0.96875 is displayed. The third time we ran the program with a value of 15 for *n*, which gave us a result very close to 1.

Extending Class Definitions and the Interface File

You've now developed a small library of methods for working with fractions. In fact, here is the interface file, listed in its entirety, so you can see all you've accomplished with this class:

```
#import <objc/Object.h>

// Define the Fraction class

@interface Fraction : Object
{
  int   numerator;
  int   denominator;
}

-(void)   print;
-(void)   setNumerator: (int) n;
-(void)   setDenominator: (int) d;
-(void)   setTo: (int) n over: (int) d;
-(int)    numerator;
-(int)    denominator;
-(double) convertToNum;
-(Fraction *) add: (Fraction *) f;
-(void)   reduce;
@end
```

You might not have a need to work with fractions, but these examples have shown how you can continually refine and extend a class by adding new methods. Someone else working with fractions could be handed this interface file and that should be sufficient for him to be able to write his own programs to deal with fractions. If he needed to have a new method added, that could be done either directly by extending the class definition or indirectly by defining his own subclass and adding his own new methods. You'll learn how to do that in the next chapter.

Exercises

1. Add the following methods to the `Fraction` class to round out the arithmetic operations on fractions. Reduce the result within the method in each case:
   ```
   // Subtract argument from receiver
   -(Fraction *) subtract (Fraction *) f;
   // Multiply receiver by argument
   -(Fraction *) multiply (Fraction *) f;
   // Divide receiver by argument
   -(Fraction *) divide (Fraction *) f;
   ```

2. Modify the `print` method from your `Fraction` class so that it takes an optional `BOOL` argument that indicates whether the fraction should be reduced for display. If it is to be reduced, be sure you don't make any permanent changes to the fraction itself.

3. Modify Program 7.7 to also display the resulting sum as a fraction and not just as a real number.

4. Will your `Fraction` class work with negative fractions? For example, can you add −1/4 and −1/2 and get the correct result? After you think you have the answer, write a test program to try it.

5. Modify the `Fraction`'s `print` method to display fractions greater than 1 as mixed numbers. So, the fraction 5/3 should be displayed as 1 2/3.

6. Exercise 7 in Chapter 4, "Data Types and Expressions," defined a new class called `Complex` for working with complex imaginary numbers. Add a new method called `add:` that can be used to add two complex numbers. To add two complex numbers, you simply add the real parts and the imaginary parts, as in:
   ```
   (5.3 + 7i) + (2.7 + 4i) = 10 + 11i
   ```
   Have the `add:` method store and return the result as a new `Complex` number, based on the following method declaration:
   ```
   -(Complex *) add: (Complex * complexNum);
   ```
   Make sure you address any potential memory leakage issues in your test program.

7. Given the `Complex` class developed in exercise 7 of Chapter 4 and the extension made in exercise 6 of this chapter, create separate `Complex.h` and `Complex.m` interface and implementation files. Create a separate test program file to test everything.

Inheritance

I N THIS CHAPTER YOU'LL LEARN ABOUT ONE OF THE KEY PRINCIPLES that makes object-oriented programming so powerful. Through the concept of *inheritance*, you will learn how you can build on existing class definitions and customize them for your own applications.

It All Begins at the Root

You learned about the idea of a parent class in Chapter 3, "Classes, Objects, and Methods." A parent class can itself have a parent. The class that has no parent is at the top of the hierarchy and is known as a *root* class. In Objective-C, you have the ability to define your own root class, but it's something you normally won't want to do. Instead, you'll want to take advantage of existing classes. All the classes we've defined up to this point are descendants of the root class called `Object`, which you specified in your interface file like this:

```
@interface Fraction: Object
...
@end
```

The `Fraction` class is derived from the `Object` class. Because `Object` is at the top of the hierarchy (that is, there are no classes above it), it's called a *root* class, as shown in Figure 8.1. The `Fraction` class is known as a *child* or *subclass*.

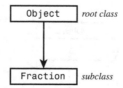

Figure 8.1 Root and subclass.

From a terminology point of view, we can speak of classes, child classes, and parent classes. Analogously, we can talk about classes, subclasses, and superclasses. You should become familiar with both types of terminology.

Whenever a new class (other than a new root class) is defined, certain properties are inherited by the class. For example, all the instance variables and the methods from the parent implicitly become part of the new class definition. That means the subclass can access these methods and instance variables directly, as if they were defined directly within the class definition.

A simple example, albeit contrived, will help illustrate this key concept of inheritance. Here's a declaration for an object called ClassA with one method called initVar:

```
@interface ClassA: Object
{
    int    x;
}

-(void) initVar;
@end
```

The initVar method simply sets the value of ClassA's instance variable to 100:

```
@implementation ClassA;
-(void) initVar
{
    x = 100;
}
@end
```

Now, let's also define a class called ClassB:

```
@interface ClassB: ClassA
-(void) printVar;
@end
```

The first line of the declaration

```
@interface ClassB: ClassA
```

says that instead of ClassB being a subclass of Object, ClassB is a subclass of ClassA. So, although ClassA's parent (or superclass) is Object, ClassB's parent is ClassA. This is shown in Figure 8.2.

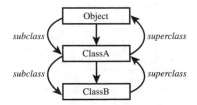

Figure 8.2   Subclasses and superclasses.

As you can see from Figure 8.2, the root class has no superclass and `ClassB`, which is at the bottom of the hierarchy, has no subclass. Therefore, `ClassA` is a subclass of `Object`, and `ClassB` is a subclass of `ClassA` and also of `Object` (technically, it's a sub-subclass, or *grandchild*). Also, `Object` is a superclass of `ClassA`, which is a superclass of `ClassB`. `Object` is also a superclass of `ClassB` because it exists further down its hierarchy.

Here's the full declaration for `ClassB`, which defines one method called `printVar`:

```
@interface ClassB: ClassA
-(void) printVar;
@end

@implementation ClassB;
-(void) printVar
{
    printf ("x = %i\n", x);
}
@end
```

The `printVar` method prints the value of the instance variable x, yet you haven't defined any instance variables in `ClassB`. That's because `ClassB` is a subclass of `ClassA`—it therefore inherits all of `ClassA`'s instance variables (in this case there's just one). This is depicted in Figure 8.3.

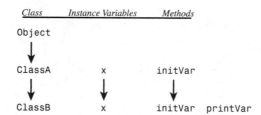

Figure 8.3   Inheriting instance variables and methods.

(Of course, Figure 8.3 doesn't show any of the methods or instance variables that are inherited from the `Object` class, of which there are several.)

Let's see how this works by putting it all together in a complete program example. For the sake of brevity, we'll put all the class declarations and definitions into a single file (see Program 8.1).

Program 8.1

```
// Simple example to illustrate inheritance

#import <objc/Object.h>
#import <stdio.h>
```

Program 8.1 **Continued**

```
// ClassA declaration and definition

@interface ClassA: Object
{
    int  x;
}

-(void) initVar;
@end

@implementation ClassA;
-(void) initVar
{
  x = 100;
}
@end

// Class B declaration and definition

@interface ClassB : ClassA
-(void) printVar;
@end

@implementation ClassB;
-(void) printVar
{
  printf ("x = %i\n", x);
}
@end

int main (int argc, char *argv[])
{
  ClassB  *b = [[ClassB alloc] init];

  [b initVar];      // will use inherited method

  [b printVar];     // reveal value of x;

  [b free];
  return 0;
}
```

Program 8.1 **Output**

```
x = 100
```

You begin by defining b to be a ClassB object. After allocating and initializing b, you send a message to apply the initVar method to it. But looking back at the definition of ClassB, you'll notice that you never defined such a method. The fact is that initVar was defined in ClassA, and because ClassA is the parent of ClassB, ClassB gets to use all of ClassA's methods. So, with respect to ClassB, initVar is an *inherited* method.[1]

After sending the initVar message to b, you invoke the printVar method to display the value of the instance variable x. The output of x = 100 confirms that printVar was capable of accessing this instance variable. That's because, like the initVar method, it was inherited.

Remember that the concept of inheritance works all the way down the chain. So, if you defined a new class called ClassC, whose parent class was ClassB, like so

```
@interface ClassC: ClassB;
...
@end
```

then ClassC would inherit all of ClassB's methods and instance variables, which in turn inherited all of ClassA's methods and instance variables, which in turn inherited all of Object's methods and instance variables.

Be sure you understand that each instance of a class gets it own instance variables, even if they're inherited. A ClassC and a ClassB object would therefore each have their own distinct instance variables.

Finding the Right Method

When you send a message to an object, you might wonder how the correct method is chosen to apply to that object. The rules are actually quite simple. First, the class to which the object belongs is checked to see whether a method is explicitly defined in that class with the specific name. If it is, that's the method that is used. If it's not defined there, the parent class is checked. If the method is defined there, that's what is used. If not, the search continues. Parent classes are checked until one of two things happens: Either you find a class that contains the specified method or you don't find the method after going all the way back to the root class. If the first occurs, you're all set; if the second occurs, you have a problem and a warning message is generated that might look something like this:

```
test1.m: In function 'main':
test1.m:39: warning: 'ClassB' does not respond to 'inity'
```

In this case, you inadvertently sent a message called inity to a variable of type class ClassB. The compiler told you that variables of that type of class do not know how to respond to such a method. Again, this was determined after checking ClassB's methods and its parents' methods back to the root class (which in this case is Object).

In some cases, a message is not generated if the method is not found. It involves using something known as *forwarding*. This idea is briefly discussed in Chapter 9, "Polymorphism, Dynamic Typing, and Dynamic Binding".

---

1. We only briefly mentioned it up to this point, but alloc and init are methods you have used all along that are never defined in your classes. That's because you took advantage of the fact that they were inherited methods.

Extension Through Inheritance— Adding New Methods

Many times the idea of inheritance is used to extend a class. As an example, let's assume you've just been assigned the task of developing some classes to work with 2D graphical objects such as rectangles, circles, and triangles. For now, we'll just worry about rectangles. In fact, let's go back to exercise 7 from Chapter 4, "Data Types and Expressions," and start with the @interface section from that example:

```
@interface Rectangle: Object
{
    int  width;
    int  height;
}

-(void)  setWidth: (int) w;
-(void)  setHeight: (int) h;
-(int)   width;
-(int)   height;
-(int)   area;
-(int)   perimeter;
@end
```

You have methods to set the rectangle's width and height, return those values, and calculate its area and perimeter. Let's also add a method that will allow you to set both the width and the height of the rectangle with the same message call, which is as follows:

```
-(void) setWidth: (int) w andHeight: (int) h;
```

Assume you typed this new class declaration into a file called Rectangle.h. Here's what the implementation file Rectangle.m might look like:

```
#import "Rectangle.h"

@implementation Rectangle;

-(void) setWidth: (int) w
{
    width = w;
}

-(void) setHeight: (int) h
{
    height = h;
}

-(void) setWidth: (int) w andHeight: (int) h
{
```

```
        width = w;
        height = h;
}

-(int) width
{
    return width;
}

-(int) height
{
    return height;
}

-(int) area
{
    return width * height;
}

-(int) perimeter
{
    return (width + height) * 2;
}
@end
```

Each method definition is straightforward enough. Program 8.2 shows a `main` routine to test it.

Program 8.2

```
#import "Rectangle.h"
#import <stdio.h>

int main (int argc, char *argv[])
{
        Rectangle *myRect = [[Rectangle alloc] init];

        [myRect setWidth: 5 andHeight: 8];

        printf ("Rectangle: w = %i, h = %i\n",
                [myRect width], [myRect height]);
        printf ("Area = %i, Perimeter = %i\n",
                [myRect area], [myRect perimeter]);
        [myRect free];

        return 0;
}
```

Program 8.2   **Output**

```
Rectangle: w = 5, h = 8
Area = 40, Perimeter = 26
```

myRect is allocated and initialized; then its width is set to 5 and its height to 8. This is verified by the first printf call. Next, the area and the perimeter of the rectangle are calculated with the appropriate message calls, and the returned values are handed off to printf to be displayed.

After working with rectangles for a while, suppose you now need to work with squares. You could define a new class called Square and define similar methods in it as in your Rectangle class. Alternately, you could recognize the fact that a square is just a special case of a rectangle—one whose width and height just happen to be the same.

Thus, an easy way to handle this is to make a new class called Square and have it be a subclass of Rectangle. That way, you get to use all of Rectangle's methods and variables, in addition to defining your own. For now, the only methods you might want to add would be to set the side of the square to a particular value and retrieve that value. The interface and implementation files for your new Square class are shown in Programs 8.3.

Program 8.3   Square.h **Interface File**

```
#import "Rectangle.h"

@interface Square: Rectangle;

-(void) setSide: (int) s;
-(int) side;
@end
```

Program 8.3   Square.m **Implementation File**

```
#import "Square.h"

@implementation Square: Rectangle;

-(void) setSide: (int) s
{
  [self setWidth: s andHeight: s];
}

-(int) side
{
  return width;
}
@end
```

Notice what you did here. You defined your `Square` class to be a subclass of `Rectangle`, which is declared in the header file `Rectangle.h`. You didn't need to add any instance variables here, but you did add new methods called `setSide:` and `side`.

Even though a square has only one side, and you're internally representing it as two numbers, that's okay. All that is hidden from the user of the `Square` class. You could always redefine your `Square` class later if necessary; any users of the class wouldn't have to be concerned with the internal details because of the notion of data encapsulation discussed earlier.

The `setSide:` method takes advantage of the fact that you already have a method inherited from your `Rectangle` class to set the values of the width and height of a rectangle. So, `setSide:` calls the `setWidth:andHeight:` method from the `Rectangle` class passing the parameter s as the value for both the width and the height. There's really nothing else you have to do. Someone working with a `Square` object can now set the dimensions of the square by using `setSide:` and take advantage of the methods from the `Rectangle` class to calculate the square's area, perimeter, and so on. Program 8.3, "Test Program," shows the test program and output for your new `Square` class.

Program 8.3   **Test Program** `test2.m`

```
#import "Square.h"
#import <stdio.h>

int main (int argc, char *argv[])
{
  Square *mySquare = [[Square alloc] init];

  [mySquare setSide: 5];

  printf ("Square s = %i\n", [mySquare side]);
  printf ("Area = %i, Perimeter = %i\n",
      [mySquare area], [mySquare perimeter]);
  [mySquare free];

  return 0;
}
```

Program 8.3   **Output**

```
Square s = 5
Area - 25, Perimeter = 20
```

To compile your program, remember that you have to tell the compiler that your program consists of three files: `Rectangle.m` and `Square.m`, which define the class methods, and `test2.m`, which contains your test routine. (Remember, you don't specify the .h header files to the compiler because they're imported directly into the programs.) If you're building your program from the command lines, here's what your gcc command line might look like:

```
gcc Square.m Rectangle.m test2.m -o test2 -l objc
```

The way you defined the Square class is a fundamental technique of working with classes in Objective-C: taking what you or someone else has done before and extending it to suit your needs. In addition, a mechanism known as *categories* enables you to add new methods to an existing class definition in a modular fashion—that is, without having to constantly add new definitions to the same interface and implementation files. This is particularly handy when you want to do this to a class for which you don't have access to the source code. You'll learn about categories in Chapter 11, "Categories, Posing, and Protocols."

A Point Class and Memory Allocation

The Rectangle class stores only the rectangle's dimensions. In a real-world graphical application, you might need to keep track of all sorts of additional information, such as the rectangle's fill color, line color, location (origin) inside a window, and so on. You can easily extend your class to do this. For now, let's deal with the idea of the rectangle's origin. Assume that the "*origin*" means the location of the rectangle's lower-left corner within some Cartesian coordinate system (x, y). If you were writing a drawing application, this point might represent the location of the rectangle inside a window, as depicted in Figure 8.4.

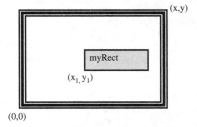

Figure 8.4 A rectangle drawn in a window.

In Figure 8.4 the rectangle's origin is shown at (x_1, y_1).

You could extend your Rectangle class to store the x, y coordinate of the rectangle's origin as two separate values. Or you might realize that, in the development of your graphics application, you'll have to deal with a lot of coordinates and therefore decide to define a class called Point (you might recall this problem from exercise 7 in Chapter 3):

```
#import <objc/Object.h>

@interface Point: Object
{
  int  x;
  int  y;
}
```

```
-(void) setX: (int) xVal;
-(void) setY: (int) yVal;
-(void) setX: (int) xVal andY: (int) yVal;
-(int) x;
-(int) y;
@end
```

`Point` has an x value and a y value, as well as methods that enable you to set them individually (`setX:` and `setY:`), set them collectively (`setX:andY:`), and retrieve their values.

Now let's get back to your `Rectangle` class. You want to be able to store the rectangle's origin, so you're going to add another instance variable called `origin` to the definition of your `Rectangle` class:

```
@interface Rectangle: Object
{
  int  width;
  int  height;
  Point *origin;
}
    . . .
```

It would seem reasonable to add a method to set the rectangle's origin, as well as retrieve it:

```
-(void) setOrigin: (Point *) pt;
-(Point *) origin;
```

The `@class` Directive

Now, you can work with rectangles (and squares as well!) with the ability to set their widths, heights, and origins. First, let's take a complete look at your `Rectangle.h` interface file:

```
#import <objc/Object.h>

@class Point;
@interface Rectangle: Object
{
  int  width;
  int  height;
  Point *origin;
}

-(void)    setWidth: (int) w;
-(void)    setHeight: (int) h;
-(void)    setOrigin: (Point *) pt;
-(Point *) origin;
```

```
-(int)   width;
-(int)   height;
-(int)   area;
-(int)   perimeter;
@end
```

When you start getting a lot of methods for your classes, you should "group" them together in terms of ones that set instance variables (your "setters"), retrieve values (your "getters"), or perform computations, for example. That's what was done previously.

You used a new directive in the Rectangle.h header file:

```
@class Point;
```

You needed this because the compiler needs to know what a Point is when it encounters it as one of the instance variables defined for a Rectangle. It's also used in the argument and return type declarations for your setOrigin: and origin methods, respectively. You do have another choice. You can import the header file instead, like so:

```
#import "Point.h"
```

The use of the @class directive is more efficient because the compiler doesn't need to process the entire Point.h file (even though it is quite small); it just needs to know that Point is the name of a class. If you needed to reference one of the Point classes methods, the @class directive would not suffice because the compiler would need more information. It would need to know how many arguments the method takes, what their types are, and what the method's return type is.

Let's fill in the blanks for your new Point class and Rectangle methods so you can test everything in a program. First, Program 8.4 shows the implementation file for your Point class.

Program 8.4   Point.m Implementation File

```
#import "Point.h"

@implementation Point;

-(void) setX: (int) xVal
{
    x = xVal;
}

-(void) setY: (int) yVal
{
    y = yVal;
}
```

Program 8.4   **Continued**

```
-(void) setX: (int) xVal; andY: (int) yVal
{
    x = xVal;
    y = yVal;
}

-(int) x;
{
    return x;
}

-(int) y;
{
    return y;
}
@end
```

Program 8.4, "Added Methods," shows the new methods for our Rectangle class, followed by the test routine and output.

Program 8.4   Rectangle.m **Added Methods**

```
-(void) setOrigin: (Point *) pt
{
  origin = pt;
}

-(Point *) origin
{
  return origin;
}
```

Program 8.4   **Test Program**

```
#import "Rectangle.h"
#import "Point.h"
#import <stdio.h>
  int main (int argc, char *argv[])
{
  Rectangle *myRect = [[Rectangle alloc] init];
  Point    *myPoint = [[Point alloc] init];

  [myPoint setX: 100 andY: 200];
```

Program 8.4 **Continued**

```
[myRect setWidth: 5 andHeight: 8];
[myRect setOrigin: myPoint];

printf ("Rectangle w = %i, h = %i\n",
    [myRect width], [myRect height]);

printf ("Origin at (%i, %i)\n",
    [[myRect origin] x], [[myRect origin] y]);

printf ("Area = %i, Perimeter = %i\n",
    [myRect area], [myRect perimeter]);
[myRect free];
[myPoint free];

return 0;
}
```

Program 8.4 **Output**

```
Rectangle w = 5, h = 8
Origin at (100, 200)
Area = 40, Perimeter = 26
```

Inside the main routine you allocated and initialized a rectangle identified as myRect and a point called myPoint. Using the setX:andY: method, you set myPoint to (100, 200). After setting the width and the height of the rectangle to 5 and 8, respectively, you invoked the setOrigin method to set the rectangle's origin to the point indicated by myPoint. The values are then retrieved and printed by the three printf calls. The message expression

```
[[myRect origin] x]
```

takes the Point object returned by the origin method and applies the x method to it to get the x-coordinate of the rectangle's origin. In a similar manner, the message expression

```
[[myRect origin] y]
```

retrieves the y-coordinate of the rectangle's origin.

Classes Owning Their Objects

Can you explain the output from Program 8.5?

Program 8.5

```
#import "Rectangle.h"
#import "Point.h"
#import <stdio.h>

int main (int argc, char *argv[])
{
  Rectangle *myRect = [[Rectangle alloc] init];
  Point    *myPoint = [[Point alloc] init];

  [myPoint setX: 100 andY: 200];

  [myRect setWidth: 5 andHeight: 8];
  [myRect setOrigin: myPoint];

  printf ("Origin at (%i, %i)\n",
      [[myRect origin] x], [[myRect origin] y]);
  [myPoint setX: 50 andY: 50];
  printf ("Origin at (%i, %i)\n",
      [[myRect origin] x], [[myRect origin] y]);
  [myRect free];
  [myPoint free];

  return 0;
}
```

Program 8.5 **Output**

```
Origin at (100, 200)
Origin at (50, 50)
```

You changed the Point myPoint from (100, 200) in the program to (50, 50) and apparently it also had the effect of changing the rectangle's origin! But why did that happen? You didn't explicitly reset the rectangle's origin with another setOrigin: method call, so why did the rectangle's origin change? If you go back to the definition of your setOrigin: method, perhaps you'll see why:

```
-(void) setOrigin: (Point *) pt
{
  origin = pt;
}
```

When the setOrigin: method is invoked with the expression

```
[myRect setOrigin: myPoint];
```

the value of myPoint is passed as the argument to the method. This value points to where this Point object is stored in memory, as depicted in Figure 8.5.

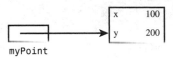

myPoint

Figure 8.5   The Point myPoint in memory.

That value stored inside myPoint, which is a pointer into memory, is copied into the local variable pt as defined inside the method. Now, both pt and myPoint reference the same data stored in memory. This is depicted in Figure 8.6.

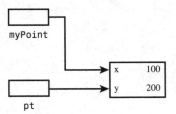

Figure 8.6   Passing the rectangle's origin to the method.

When the origin variable is set to pt inside the method, the pointer stored inside pt is copied into the instance variable origin, as depicted in Figure 8.7.

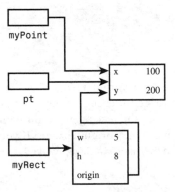

Figure 8.7   Setting the rectangle's origin.

Because myPoint and the origin variable stored in myRect reference the same area in memory (as does the local variable pt), when you subsequently change the value of myPoint to (50, 50), the rectangle's origin is changed as well.

The way to avoid this problem is to modify the setOrigin: method so that it allocates its own point and sets the origin to that point. This is shown here:

```
-(void) setOrigin: (Point *) pt
{
  origin = [[Point alloc] init];

  [origin setX: [pt x] andY: [pt y]];
}
```

The method first allocates and initializes a new Point. The message expression

```
[origin setX: [pt x] andY: [pt y]];
```

sets the newly allocated Point to the x, y coordinate of the argument to the method. Study this message expression until you fully understand how it works.

The change to the setOrigin: method means that each Rectangle instance now owns its origin Point instance. And, even though it is now responsible for allocating the memory for that Point, it should also now become responsible for freeing that memory. In general, when a class contains other objects, at times you will want to have it own some or all of those objects. In the case of a rectangle, it makes sense for it to own its origin because that is a basic attribute of a rectangle.

But how do you free the memory used by your origin? Freeing the rectangle's memory does not also free the memory you allocated for the origin. One way to free the memory is to insert a line such as the following in main:

```
[[myRect origin] free];
```

This frees the Point object returned by the origin method. You must do this before you free the memory for the Rectangle object itself because none of the variables contained in an object are valid after its memory is released. So, the correct code sequence would be as follows:

```
[[myRect origin] free];   // Free the origin's memory
[myRect free];            // Free the rectangle's memory
```

It's a bit of a burden to have to remember to free the origin's memory yourself. After all, you weren't the one who allocated it; the Rectangle class did. In the next section, "Overriding Methods," you learn how to have the Rectangle free the memory.

With your modified method, recompiling and rerunning Program 8.5 produces the following warning messages shown as Program 8.5A.

Program 8.5A   **Compiler Warning Messages**

```
rectangle.m: In function '-[Rectangle setOrigin:]':
rectangle.m:16: warning: 'Point' may not respond to '-x'
rectangle.m:16: warning: cannot find method '-x'; return type 'id' assumed
rectangle.m:16: warning: 'Point' may not respond to '-y'
rectangle.m:16: warning: cannot find method '-y'; return type 'id' assumed
rectangle.m:16: warning: 'Point' may not respond to '-setX:andY:'
rectangle.m:16: warning: cannot find method '-setX:andY:'; return type 'id'
➥assumed
```

Oops! The problem here is that you've used some methods from the `Point` class in your modified method, so now the compiler needs more information about it than is provided by the `@class` directive. In that case, go back and replace that directive with an `import` instead, like so:

```
#import "Point.h"
```

Program 8.5B   **Output**

```
Origin at (100, 200)
Origin at (100, 200)
```

That's better! This time changing the value of `myPoint` to (50, 50) inside `main` had no effect on the rectangle's origin because a copy of the point was created inside the `Rectangle`'s `setOrigin:` method. You should note that, if you try to run the program with the warning messages shown previously, the correct output will still be produced. That's because the compiler issued warning messages and not error messages. In the former case, an executable is still produced, whereas in the latter it is not. When warning messages are produced by the compiler, it makes certain assumptions. Sometimes those assumptions are valid; other times they are not. In any case, it is better to remove as many warning messages as possible because they often indicate poorly written programs or logic errors that you should address.

Overriding Methods

We noted in an earlier section that you can't remove or subtract methods through inheritance. However, you can change the definition of an inherited method by *overriding* it.

Returning to your two classes, `ClassA` and `ClassB`, assume you want to write your own `initVar` method for `ClassB`. You already know that the `initVar` method defined in `ClassA` will be inherited by `ClassB`, but can you make a new method with the same name to replace the inherited method? The answer is yes, and you do so simply by defining a new method with the same name. A method defined with the same name as that of a parent class replaces, or overrides, the inherited definition. Your new method must have the same return type and take the same number and type of arguments as the method you are overriding.

Program 8.6 shows a simple example to illustrate this concept.

Program 8.6

```
// Overriding Methods

#import <objc/Object.h>
#import <stdio.h>

// ClassA declaration and definition

@interface ClassA: Object
{
    int x;
}

-(void) initVar;
@end

@implementation ClassA;
-(void) initVar
{
    x = 100;
}
@end

// ClassB declaration and definition

@interface ClassB: ClassA
-(void) initVar;
-(void) printVar;
@end

@implementation ClassB;
-(void) initVar     // added method
{
    x = 200;
}

-(void) printVar
{
    printf ("x = %i\n", x);
}
@end
```

Program 8.6 **Continued**

```
int main (int argc, char *argv[])
{
   ClassB  *b = [[ClassB alloc] init];

   [b initVar];  // uses overriding method in B

   [b printVar];  // reveal value of x;
   [b free];

   return 0;
}
```

Program 8.6 **Output**

```
x = 200
```

It's clear that the message

```
[b initVar];
```

causes the initVar method defined in ClassB to be used, and not the one defined in ClassA, as was the case with the previous example. This is illustrated in Figure 8.8.

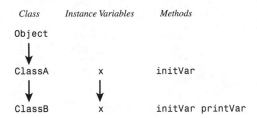

Figure 8.8 Overriding the initVar method.

Which Method Is Selected?

We mentioned how the system searches up the hierarchy for a method to apply to an object. If you have methods in different classes with the same name, the correct method is chosen based on the class of the receiver of the message. Program 8.7 uses the same class definition for ClassA and ClassB from before.

Program 8.7

```
#import <stdio.h>
#import <objc/Object.h>
```

Program 8.7 **Continued**

```
// insert definitions for ClassA and ClassB here

int main (int argc, char *argv[])
{
   ClassA  *a = [[ClassA alloc] init];
   ClassB  *b = [[ClassB alloc] init];

   [a initVar];   // uses ClassA method
   [a printVar];  // reveal value of x;

   [b initVar];   // use overriding ClassB method
   [b printVar];  // reveal value of x;
   [a free];
   [b free];

   return 0;
}
```

Here's what happens when you compile this program using gcc:

gcc main.m -lobjc
```
main.m: In function 'main':
main.m:48: warning: 'ClassA' does not respond to 'printVar'
```

What happened here? We talked about this in an earlier section. Take a look at the declaration for ClassA:

```
// ClassA declaration and definition

@interface ClassA: Object
{
   int  x;
}

-(void) initVar;
@end
```

Notice that no printVar method is declared. That method is declared and defined in ClassB. Therefore, even though ClassB objects and their descendants can use this method through inheritance, ClassA objects cannot because the method is defined further down in the hierarchy.[2]

---

2. There are some ways to coerce the use of this method, but we won't get into that here—besides, it's not good programming practice.

Returning to our example, let's add a printVar method to ClassA so you can display the value of its instance variables:

```
// ClassA declaration and definition

@interface ClassA: Object
{
    int  x;
}

-(void) initVar;
-(void) printVar;
@end

@implementation ClassA;
-(void) initVar
{
    x = 100;
}

-(void) printVar
{
    printf ("x = %i\n", x);
}

@end
```

ClassB's declaration and definition remains unchanged. Now, let's try compiling and running this program again.

Program 8.7 **Output**

```
x = 100
x = 200
```

Now we can talk about the actual example. First, a and b are defined to be ClassA and ClassB objects, respectively. After allocation and initialization, a message is sent to a asking it to apply the initVar method. This method is defined in the definition of ClassA, so it is this method that is selected. The method simply sets the value of the instance variable x to 100 and returns. The printVar method, which you just added to ClassA is invoked next to display the value of x.

Similarly with the ClassB object, b: It is allocated and initialized, then its instance variable x is set to 200, and finally its value displayed.

Be sure you understand how the proper method is chosen for a and b based on which class they belong to. It is a fundamental concept of object-oriented programming in Objective-C.

As an exercise, consider removing the `printVar` method from `ClassB`. Would that work? Why or why not?

Overriding the `free` Method and the Keyword `super`

Now that you know how to override methods, let's return to Program 8.9 to learn a better approach to releasing the memory occupied by the `origin`. The `setOrigin:` method now allocates its own `Point origin` object, and you are responsible for freeing its memory. The approach used in Program 8.6 was to have `main` release that memory with a statement such as follows:

```
[[myRect origin] free];
```

So you don't have to worry about freeing up all the individual members of a class, you can override the inherited `free` method (it's inherited from `Object`) and free the `origin`'s memory there. However, if you decide to override `free`, you also have to be sure to release the memory taken up not only by your own instance variables, but by any inherited ones as well.

To do this, you need to take advantage of the special keyword `super`, which refers to the parent class of the receiver of the message. You can send a message to `super` to execute an overridden method. This is the most common use for this keyword. So, the message expression

```
[super free];
```

when used inside a method invokes the `free` method that is defined in (or inherited by) the parent class. The method is invoked on the receiver of the message—in other words, on `self`.

Therefore, the strategy for overriding the `free` method for your `Rectangle` class is to first release the memory taken up by your `origin` and then invoke the `free` method from the parent class to complete the job. This releases the memory taken up by the `Rectangle` object itself. Here is the new method:

```
-(id) free
{
  if (origin)
    [origin free];
  return [super free];
}
```

The `free` method is defined to return a value of type `id`. You know this by looking inside the header file `objc/Object.h` where it is declared. Inside the `free` method, a test is made to see if `origin` is nonzero before freeing it. It's possible that the origin of the rectangle was never set, in which case it will have its default value of zero. Then we invoke the `free` method from the parent class, which is the same method the `Rectangle` class would have inherited were it not overridden.

It is pointed out that you can also write the `free` method more simply as

```
-(id) free
{
  [origin free];
  return [super free];
}
```

since it's okay to send a message to a nil object.

With your new method, you now have to free only just the rectangles you allocate without having to worry about the `Point` objects they contain. The two `free` messages shown in Program 8.5

```
[myRect free];
[myPoint free];
```

will now suffice to free all the objects you allocated in the program, including the `Point` object that `setOrigin:` creates.

There is still one issue that remains: If you set the origin of a single `Rectangle` object to different values during the execution of your program, you must release the memory taken up by the old origin before you allocate and assign the new one. For example, in the following code sequence

```
[myRect setOrigin: startPoint];
  ...
[myRect setOrigin: endPoint];
  ...
[startPoint free];
[endPoint free];
[myRect free];
```

the copy of the `Point` `startPoint` stored in the `origin` member of `myRect` is never released because it is overwritten by the second origin (`endPoint`) that is stored there. That origin is released properly when the rectangle itself is freed, based on your new `free` method.

You need to ensure that, before you set a new origin in your rectangle, the old one is freed. This can be handled in the `setOrigin:` method as follows:

```
-(void) setOrigin: (Point *) pt
{
  if (origin)
    [origin free];

  origin = [[Point alloc] init];

  [origin setX: [pt x] andY: [pt y]];
}
```

Now you have a clean implementation of your `Rectangle` class that does not leak memory. And that is fundamental to good programming practice in Objective-C (or in any other programming language, for that matter!).

Extension Through Inheritance—Adding New Instance Variables

Not only can you add new methods to effectively extend the definition of a class, but you can also add new instance variables. The effect in both cases is cumulative. You can never subtract methods or instance variables through inheritance; you can only add, or in the case of methods, add or override. Let's return to your simple `ClassA` and `ClassB` classes and make some changes. You'll add a new instance variable y to `ClassB`, like so:

```
@interface ClassB: ClassA
{
   int  y;
}
-(void) printVar;
@end
```

Even though `ClassB` might appear to have only one instance variable called y based on the previous declaration, it actually has two[3]: It inherits the variable x from `ClassA` and adds its own instance variable y.

Let's put this together in a simple example to illustrate this concept (see Program 8.8).

Program 8.8

```
// Extension of instance variables

#import <objc/Object.h>
#import <stdio.h>

// Class A declaration and definition

@interface ClassA: Object
{
   int  x;
}

-(void) initVar;
@end

@implementation ClassA;
-(void) initVar
{
```

3. Of course, it also has instance variables that it inherits from the `Object` class, but we choose to ignore this detail for now.

Program 8.8   **Continued**

```
  x = 100;
}
@end

// ClassB declaration and definition

@interface ClassB: ClassA
{
  int  y;
}
-(void) initVar;
-(void) printVar;
@end

@implementation ClassB;
-(void) initVar
{
  x = 200;
  y = 300;
}

-(void) printVar
{
  printf ("x = %i\n", x);
  printf ("y = %i\n", y);
}
@end

int main (int argc, char *argv[])
{
  ClassB *b = [[ClassB alloc] init];

  [b initVar];  // uses overriding method in ClassB
  [b printVar];  // reveal values of x and y;

  [b free];
  return 0;
}
```

Program 8.8   **Output**

```
x = 200
y = 300
```

The `ClassB` object b is initialized by invoking the `initVar` method defined within `ClassB`. Recall that this method overrides the `initVar` method from `ClassA`. This method also sets the value of x (which was inherited from `ClassA`) to 200 and y (which was defined in `ClassB`) to 300. Next, the `printVar` method is used to display the value of these two instance variables.

There are many more subtleties to the idea of choosing the right method in response to a message, in particular when the receiver can be one of several classes. This is a powerful concept known as *dynamic binding*, and it is the topic of the next chapter.

Abstract Classes

What better way to conclude this chapter than with a bit of terminology? We introduce it here because it's directly related to the notion of inheritance.

Sometimes classes are created just to make it easier for someone to create a subclass. For that reason, these classes are called *abstract* classes or, equivalently, *abstract superclasses*. Methods and instance variables are defined in the class, but no one is expected to actually create an instance from that class. For example, consider the root object `Object`. Can you think of any use for defining an object from that class?

The Foundation framework, covered in Part II, has several of these so-called abstract classes. As an example, the Foundation's `NSNumber` class is an abstract class that was created for working with numbers as objects. Integers and floating-point numbers typically have different storage requirements. So, separate subclasses of `NSNumber` exist for each numeric type. Because these subclasses, unlike their abstract superclasses, actually exist, they are known as *concrete* subclasses. Each concrete subclass falls under the `NSNumber` class umbrella and is collectively referred to as a *cluster*. When you send a message to the `NSNumber` class to create a new integer object, the appropriate subclass is used to allocate the necessary storage for an integer object and to set its value appropriately. These subclasses are actually private. You don't access them directly yourself; they are accessed indirectly through the abstract superclass. The abstract superclass provides a common interface for working with all types of number objects and relieves you of the burden of having to know which type of number you have stored in your number object and how to set and retrieve its value.

Admittedly, this discussion might seem a little "abstract" (sorry!); don't worry, just a basic grasp of the concept is sufficient here.

Exercises

1. Add a new class called `ClassC`, which is a subclass of `ClassB`, to Program 8.1. Make an `initVar` method that sets the value of its instance variable x to 300. Write a test routine that declares `ClassA`, `ClassB`, and `ClassC` objects and invokes their corresponding `initVar` methods.

2. When dealing with higher-resolution devices, you might need to use a coordinate system that enables you to specify points as floating-point values, rather than as simple integers. Modify the `Point` and `Rectangle` classes from this chapter to deal with floating-point numbers. The rectangle's width, height, area, and perimeter should all work with floating-point numbers as well.

3. Modify Program 8.1 to add a new class called `ClassB2` that, like `ClassB`, is a subclass of `ClassA`.

   What can you say about the relationship between `ClassB` and `ClassB2`?

   Identify the hierarchical relationship between the `Object` class, `ClassA`, `ClassB`, and `ClassB2`.

   What is the superclass of `ClassB`?

   What is the superclass of `ClassB2`?

   How many subclasses can a class have, and how many superclasses can it have?

4. Write a `Rectangle` method called `translate:` that takes a vector `Point` (x_v, y_v) as its argument. Have it translate the rectangle's origin by the specified vector.

5. Define a new class called `GraphicObject`, and make it a subclass of `Object`. Define instance variables in your new class as follows:
   ```
   int   fillColor;    // 32-bit color
   BOOL  filled;       // Is the object filled?
   int   lineColor;    // 32-bit line color
   ```
   Write methods to set and retrieve the variables defined previously.

   Make the `Rectangle` class a subclass of `GraphicObject`.

   Define new classes, `Circle` and `Triangle`, that are also subclasses of `GraphicObject`. Write methods to set and retrieve the various parameters for these objects and also to calculate the circle's circumference and area and the triangle's perimeter and area.

6. Write a `Rectangle` method called `intersect:` that takes a rectangle as an argument and returns a rectangle representing the overlapping area between the two rectangles. So, for example, given the two rectangles shown in Figure 8.9, the method should return a rectangle whose origin is at (400, 380), whose width is 50, and whose height is 60.

   If the rectangles do not intersect, return one whose width and height are zero and whose origin is at (0,0).

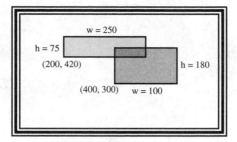

Figure 8.9   Intersecting rectangles.

7. Write a method for the `Rectangle` class called `draw` that draws a rectangle using dashes and vertical bar characters. The following code sequence

```
Rectangle *myRect = [[Rectangle alloc] init];
[myRect setWidth: 10 andHeight: 3];
[myRect draw];
[myRect free];
```

would produce the following output:

9

Polymorphism, Dynamic Typing, and Dynamic Binding

Iₙ THIS CHAPTER YOU'LL LEARN ABOUT THE FEATURES of the Objective-C language that make it such a powerful programming language and that distinguish it from some other object-oriented programming languages such as C++. Three key concepts are described in this chapter: polymorphism, dynamic typing, and dynamic binding. *Polymorphism* enables programs to be developed so that objects from different classes can define methods that share the same name. *Dynamic typing* defers the determination of the class an object belongs to until the program is executing, and *dynamic binding* defers the determination of the actual method to invoke on an object until program execution time.

Polymorphism: Same Name, Different Class

Program 9.1 shows the interface file for a class called `Complex`, which is used to represent complex numbers in a program.

Program 9.1   **Interface File** `Complex.h`

```
// Interface file for Complex class

#import <objc/Object.h>

@interface Complex: Object
{
  double real;
  double imaginary;
}

-(void) print;
-(void) setReal: (double) a;
-(void) setImaginary: (double) b;
```

Program 9.1 **Continued**

```
-(void) setReal: (double) a andImaginary: (double) b;
-(double) real;
-(double) imaginary;
-(Complex *) add: (Complex *) f;
@end
```

We're not going to show the implementation file here; presumably you've already done that in exercise 7 from Chapter 4, "Data Types and Expressions." If you didn't complete that exercise, perhaps now is the time to do so. We added an additional `setReal:andImaginary:` method from that exercise to enable you to set both the real and imaginary parts of your number with a single message.

Program 9.1 **Test Program** `main.m`

```
// Shared Method Names: Polymorphism

#import "Fraction.h"
#import "Complex.h"

int main (int argc, char *argv[])
{
   Fraction *f1 = [[Fraction alloc] init];
   Fraction *f2 = [[Fraction alloc] init];
   Fraction *fracResult;
   Complex *c1 = [[Complex alloc] init];
   Complex *c2 = [[Complex alloc] init];
   Complex *compResult;

   [f1 setTo: 2 over: 5];
   [f2 setTo: 1 over: 4];

   [c1 setReal: 10.0 andImaginary: 2.5];
   [c2 setReal: -5.0 andImaginary: 3.2];

   // add and print 2 complex numbers

   [c1 print]; printf (" + "); [c2 print];
   printf (" = ");
   compResult = [c1 add: c2];
   [compResult print];
   printf ("\n");

   [c1 free];
   [c2 free];
   [compResult free];
```

Program 9.1 **Continued**

```
// add and print 2 fractions

[f1 print]; printf (" + "); [f2 print];
printf (" = ");
fracResult = [f1 add: f2];
[fracResult print];
printf ("\n");

[f1 free];
[f2 free];
[fracResult free];

return 0;
}
```

Program 9.1 **Output**

```
(10 + 2.5i) + (-5 + 3.2i) = (5 + 5.7i)
 2/5 + 1/4 = 13/20
```

Note that both the `Fraction` and `Complex` classes contain `add:` and `print` methods. So, when executing the message expressions

```
compResult = [c1 add: c2];
[compResult print];
```

how does the system know which methods to execute? It's simple: The Objective-C runtime knows that `c1`, the receiver of the first message, is a `Complex` object. Therefore, it selects the `add:` method defined for the `Complex` class.

The Objective-C runtime system also determines that `compResult` is a `Complex` object.[1] So, it selects the `print` method defined in the `Complex` class to display the result of the addition. The same discussion applies to the following message expressions:

```
fracResult = [f1 add: f2];
[fracResult print];
```

The corresponding methods from the `Fraction` class are chosen to evaluate the message expression based on the class of `f1` and `fracResult`.

As mentioned, the ability to share the same method name across different classes is known as polymorphism. It enables you to develop a set of classes that each can respond to the same method name. Each class definition encapsulates the code needed to respond to that particular method, and this makes it independent of the other class definitions. It also enables you to add new classes at a later date that can respond to methods with the same name.

1. As described more completely in Chapter 13, "Underlying C Language Features," the system always carries information about to which class an object belongs. That enables it to make these key decisions at runtime instead of at compile time.

Dynamic Binding and the `id` Type

Chapter 4 briefly touched on the `id` data type and noted that it is a generic object type. That is, it can be used for storing objects that belong to any class. The real power of this data type is exploited when it's used this way to store different types of objects in a variable during the execution of a program. Study Program 9.2 and its associated output.

Program 9.2

```
// Illustrate Dynamic Typing and Binding

#import "Fraction.h"
#import "Complex.h"

int main (int argc, char *argv[])
{
    id      dataValue;
    Fraction *f1 = [[Fraction alloc] init];
    Complex  *c1 = [[Complex alloc] init];

    [f1 setTo: 2 over: 5];
    [c1 setReal: 10.0 andImaginary: 2.5];

    // first dataValue gets a fraction

    dataValue = f1;
    [dataValue print];
    printf ("\n");

    // now dataValue gets a complex number

    dataValue = c1;
    [dataValue print];
    printf ("\n");

    [c1 free];
    [f1 free];

    return 0;
}
```

Program 9.2   **Output**

```
 2/5
10 + 2.5i
```

The variable dataValue is declared as an id object type. Therefore, dataValue can be used to hold any type of object in the program. Make sure to note that there is no asterisk used in the declaration line:

```
id dataValue;
```

The Fraction f1 is set to 2/5, and the Complex number c2 is set to $(10 + 2.5i)$. The assignment

```
dataValue = f1;
```

stores the Fraction f1 into dataValue. Now, what can you do with dataValue? Well, you can invoke any of the methods that you can use on a Fraction object with dataValue, even though the type of dataValue is an id and not a Fraction. But, if dataValue can store any type of object, how does the system know which method to invoke? That is, how does it know when it encounters the message expression

```
[dataValue print];
```

which print method to invoke? You know you have print methods defined for both the Fraction and Complex classes.

As noted previously, the answer lies in the fact that the Objective-C system always keeps track of the class to which an object belongs. It also lies in the concepts of dynamic typing and dynamic binding—that is, making the decision about the class of the object and there-fore which method to invoke dynamically at runtime rather than at compile time.

So, during execution of the program, when the system goes to send the print message to dataValue, it first checks the class of the object stored inside dataValue. In the first case of Program 9.2, this variable contains a Fraction, so it is the print method defined in the Fraction class that is used. This is verified by the output from the program.

In the second case, the same thing happens. First, the Complex number c1 is assigned to dataValue. Next, the message expression

```
[dataValue print];
```

is executed. This time, because dataValue contains an object belonging to the Complex class, the corresponding print method from that class is selected for execution.

This is a simple example, but I think you can extrapolate this concept to more sophisticated applications. When combined with polymorphism, dynamic binding and dynamic typing enable you to easily write code that can send the same message to objects from different classes.

For example, consider a draw method that could be used to paint graphical objects on the screen. You might have different draw methods defined for each of your graphi-cal objects, such as text, circles, rectangles, windows, and so on. If the particular object to be drawn is stored inside an id variable called currentObject, for example, you could paint it on the screen simply by sending it the draw message, like so:

```
[currentObject draw];
```

You could even test it first to ensure that the object stored in currentObject does in fact respond to a draw method. You'll see how to do that later in this chapter.

Compile Time Versus Runtime Checking

Because the type of object stored inside an `id` variable can be indeterminate at compile time, some tests are deferred until runtime—that is, while the program is executing.

Consider the following sequence of code:

```
Fraction *f1 = [[Fraction alloc] init];
[f1 setReal: 10.0 andImaginary: 2.5];
```

Recalling that the `setReal:andImaginary:` method applies to complex numbers and not fractions, the following message will be issued when you compile the program containing these lines:

```
prog3.m: In function 'main':
prog3.m:13: warning: 'Fraction' does not respond to 'setReal:andImaginary:'
```

The Objective-C compiler knows that `f1` is a `Fraction` object because it has been declared that way. It also knows that, when it sees the message expression

```
[f1 setReal: 10.0 andImaginary: 2.5];
```

the `Fraction` class does not have a `setReal:andImaginary:` method (and did not inherit one either), so it issues the warning message shown previously.

Now consider the following code sequence:

```
id dataValue = [[Fraction alloc] init];
  ...
[dataValue setReal: 10.0 andImaginary: 2.5];
```

These lines do not produce a warning message from the compiler because the compiler doesn't know what type of object is stored inside `dataValue` when processing your source file.

It's not until you run the program containing these lines that an error message is reported. The error will look something like this:

```
objc: Fraction: does not recognize selector -setReal:andImaginary:
dynamic3: received signal: Abort trap
When attempting to execute the expression
[dataValue setReal: 10.0 andImaginary: 2.5];
```

The runtime system first checks the type of object stored inside `dataValue`. Because `dataValue` has a `Fraction` stored in it, the runtime system checks to ensure that the method `setReal:andImaginary:` is one of the methods defined for the class `Fraction`. Because it's not, the error message shown previously is issued and the program is terminated.

The `id` Data Type and Static Typing

If an `id` data type can be used to store any object, why don't you just declare all your objects as type `id`? There are several reasons why you don't want to get into the habit of overusing this generic class data type.

First, when you define a variable to be an object from a particular class, you are using what's known as *static* typing. The word *static* refers to the fact the variable is always used to store objects from the particular class. So, the class of the object stored in that type is predeterminate, or *static*. When you use static typing, the compiler ensures, to the best of its ability, that the variable is used consistently throughout the program. The compiler can check to ensure that a method applied to an object is defined or inherited by that class, and it issues a warning message otherwise.[2] Thus, when you declare a `Rectangle` variable called `myRect` in your program, the compiler checks that any methods you invoke on `myRect` are defined in the `Rectangle` class or are inherited from its superclass.

However, if the check is performed for you at runtime anyway, why do you care about static typing? You care because it's better to get your errors out during the compilation phase of your program rather than during the execution phase. If you leave it until runtime, you might not even be the one running the program when the error occurs. If your program is put into production, it might be some poor unsuspecting user who discovers that a method is not recognized by a particular object when she is running the program.

Another reason for using static typing is that it makes your programs more readable. Consider the following declaration:

```
id    f1;
```

versus

```
Fraction *f1;
```

Which do you think is more understandable—that is, which makes it clearer to the reader what the intended use of the variable `f1` is? The combination of static typing and choosing meaningful variable names (which we intentionally did not choose in the previous example) can go a long way toward making your program more self-documenting.

Argument and Return Types with Dynamic Typing

If you use dynamic typing to invoke a method, you need to make note of the following rule: If a method with the same name is implemented in more than one of your classes, each method must agree in the type of each argument and the type of value it returns. That's so that the compiler can generate the correct code for your message expressions.

The compiler performs a consistency check among each class declaration it has seen. If one or more methods conflict either in argument or return types, the compiler issues a warning message. For example, both the `Fraction` and `Complex` classes contain `add:` methods. However, the `Fraction` class takes as its argument and returns a `Fraction` object, whereas the `Complex` class takes and returns a `Complex` object. If `frac1` and

---

2. There are ways to invoke methods that are specified by a variable, in which case the compiler can't check that for you.

myFract are `Fraction` objects, and `comp1` and `myComplex` are `Complex` objects, statements such as

```
result = [myFract add: frac1];
```

and

```
result = [myComplex add: comp1];
```

do not cause any warnings to be issued by the compiler (as you have seen) because in both cases the receiver of the message is statically typed and the compiler can check for consistent use of the method as it is defined in the receiver's class.

However, if `dataValue1` and `dataValue2` are id variables, the statement

```
result = [dataValue1 add: dataValue2];
```

causes the following warning messages from the compiler:

```
ex3.m: In function 'main':
ex3.m:12: warning: multiple declarations for method 'add:'
Fraction.h:18: warning: using '-(Fraction *)add:(Fraction *)f'
Complex.h:18: warning: also found '-(Complex *)add:(Complex *)f'
```

The compiler doesn't know which type of object will be stored in `dataValue1`, but it does know that both the `Fraction` and `Complex` classes define an `add:` method. So, it issues a warning that these two methods have been found and that they are not consistently declared. It then arbitrarily assumes you want the `add:` method from the `Fraction` class. This assumption affects how the compiler generates code to pass arguments to the method and to handle the value returned from the method.

At runtime, the Objective-C runtime system still checks the actual class of the object stored inside `dataValue1` and selects the appropriate method to execute. However, the compiler might have generated the incorrect code to pass arguments to the method or handle its return value. This would likely happen in cases in which one method took an object as its argument and the other took a floating-point value. If the inconsistency between two methods is just a different type of object (for example, the `Fraction`'s `add:` method takes a `Fraction` object as its argument and returns one, whereas the `Complex`'s `add:` method takes and returns a `Complex` object), the correct code is still generated by the compiler because memory addresses are passed for objects anyway. To avoid the warning messages from the compiler, you can declare your arguments and return types to be of type id, like so:

```
-(id) add: (id) value;
```

If you use this when declaring and defining both methods, the compiler no longer complains when the `add:` method is invoked on an id object because the inconsistency no longer exists. You should resort to using these generic definitions only if you will be using dynamic typing on your objects because it makes the methods harder to understand. From the previous declaration, it is not at all clear which type of value the `add:` method takes or returns.

Asking Questions About Classes

As you start working with variables that can contain objects from different classes, you might need to ask questions such as the following:

- Is this object a rectangle?
- Does this object support a print method?
- Is this object a member of the Graphics class or one of its descendants?

The answers to these questions might be used to execute different sequences of code, avoid an error, or check the integrity of your program while it's executing.

Table 9.1 summarizes some of the basic methods supported by the Object class for asking these types of questions. In this table, *class-object* is a class object (typically generated with the class method), and *selector* is a value of type SEL (typically created with the @selector directive).

Table 9.1 **Methods for Working with Dynamic Types**

Method	Question or Action
-(BOOL) isKindOf: *class-object*	Is the object a member of *class-object* or a descendant?
-(BOOL) isMemberOf: *class-object*	Is the object a member of *class-object*?
-(BOOL) respondsTo: *selector*	Can the object respond to the method specified by *selector*?
+(BOOL) instancesRespondTo: *selector*	Can instances of the specified class respond to this particular message?
-(id) perform: *selector*	Apply the method specified by *selector*.

Other methods are available that are not described here and that allow you to ask questions about conformity to a protocol (covered in Chapter 11, "Categories, Posing, and Protocols") and for determining membership in a class given a string representation of the class name.

To generate a class object from a class name or another object, you send it the class message. So, to get a class object from a class named Square, you write the following:

```
[Square class]
```

If mySquare is an instance of Square object, you get its class by writing this:

```
[mySquare class]
```

To see whether the objects stored in the variables obj1 and obj2 are instances from the same class, you could write

```
if ([obj1 class] == [obj2 class])
...
```

To see whether `myFract` is an instance of the `Fraction` class, you would test the result from the expression, like so:

```
[myFract isMemberOf: [Fraction class]]
```

To generate one of the so-called selectors listed in Table 9.1, you apply the `@selector` directive to a method name. For example,

```
@selector (alloc)
```

produces a value of type SEL for the method named `alloc`, which you know is a method inherited from the `Object` class. The expression

```
@selector (setTo:over:)
```

produces a selector for the `setTo:over:` method that you implemented in your `Fraction` class (remember those colon characters in the method names).

To see whether an instance of the `Fraction` class responds to the `setTo:over:` method, you can test the return value from the expression, like so:

```
[Fraction instancesRespondTo: @selector (setTo:over:)]
```

Remember, the test covers inherited methods, not just one that is directly defined in the class definition.

The `perform:` method and its variants (not shown in Table 9.1) allow you to send a message to an object, where the message can be a selector stored inside a variable. For example, consider this code sequence:

```
SEL     action;
id      graphicObject;
  ...
action = @selector (draw);
  ...
[graphicObject perform: action];
```

In this example the method indicated by the SEL variable `action` is sent to whatever graphical object is stored in `graphicObject`. Presumably, the action might vary during program execution—perhaps based on the user's input—even though we've shown the action as `draw`. To first ensure that the object can respond to the action, you might want to use something like this[3]:

```
if ([graphicObject respondsTo: action] == YES)
  [graphicObject perform: action]
else
  // error handling code here
```

---

3. You can also catch an error by overriding the `doesNotRecognize:` method. This method will get invoked whenever an unrecognized message is sent to a class and is passed the unrecognized selector as its argument. You can even forward the message to another message using the `forward::` method.

Program 9.3 asks some questions about the Square and Rectangle classes defined in Chapter 8, "Inheritance." Try to predict the results from this program before looking at the actual output (no peeking now!).

Program 9.3

```
#import "Square.h"
#import <stdio.h>

int main (int argc, char *argv[])
{
  Square *mySquare = [[Square alloc] init];


  // isMemberOf:

  if ( [mySquare isMemberOf: [Square class]] == YES )
    printf ("mySquare is a member of Square class\n");

  if ( [mySquare isMemberOf: [Rectangle class]] == YES )
    printf ("mySquare is a member of Rectangle class\n");

  if ( [mySquare isMemberOf: [Object class]] == YES )
    printf ("mySquare is a member of Object class\n");

  // isKindOf:

  if ( [mySquare isKindOf: [Square class]] == YES )
    printf ("mySquare is a kind of Square\n");

  if ( [mySquare isKindOf: [Rectangle class]] == YES )
    printf ("mySquare is a kind of Rectangle\n");

  if ( [mySquare isKindOf: [Object class]] == YES )
    printf ("mySquare is a kind of Object\n");

  // respondsTo:

  if ( [mySquare respondsTo: @selector (setSide:)] == YES )
    printf ("mySquare responds to setSide: method\n");

  if ( [mySquare respondsTo: @selector (setWidth:andHeight:)] == YES )
    printf ("mySquare responds to setWidth:andHeight: method\n");

  if ( [Square respondsTo: @selector (alloc)] == YES )
    printf ("Square class responds to alloc method\n");
```

Program 9.3 **Continued**

```
// instancesRespondTo:

if ([Rectangle instancesRespondTo: @selector (setSide:)] == YES)
  printf ("Instances of Rectangle respond to setSide: method\n");

if ([Square instancesRespondTo: @selector (setSide:)] == YES)
  printf ("Instances of Square respond to setSide: method\n");
[mySquare free];

return 0;
}
```

Make sure you build this program with the implementation files for the `Square`,
`Rectangle`, and `Point` classes.

Program 9.3 **Output**

```
mySquare is a member of Square class
mySquare is a kind of Square
mySquare is a kind of Rectangle
mySquare is a kind of Object
mySquare responds to setSide: method
mySquare responds to setWidth:andHeight: method
Square class responds to alloc method
Instances of Square respond to setSide: method
```

The output from Program 9.3 should be clear. Remember that `isMemberOf:` tests
for direct membership in a class, whereas `isKindOf:` checks for membership in the
inheritance hierarchy. So, `mySquare` is a member of the `Square` class; but it's also a
"kind of" `Square`, `Rectangle`, and `Object` because it exists in that class hierarchy
(obviously all objects should return `YES` for the `isKindOf:` test on the `Object` class,
unless you've defined a new root object).

The test

```
if ( [Square respondsTo: @selector (alloc)] == YES )
```

tests whether the class `Square` responds to the class method `alloc`, which it does
because it's inherited from the root object `Object`. Realize that you can always use the
class name directly as the receiver in a message expression, and you don't have to write

```
[Square class]
```

in the previous expression (although you could do that if you wanted). That's the only
place you can get away with that. In other places you'll need to apply the `class`
method to obtain the class object.

Message Forwarding

Sometimes you might want to send a message that was sent to your class to another class to handle. This is called *message forwarding*, and it is somewhat analogous to forwarding your phone so that it rings somewhere else: The call is placed to your number and then forwarded to a different one that you specify. The object that is the recipient of the forwarded message is known as the *delegate*. Obviously, if you know which method it is and precisely where you want to send it, you can just write a method of the specified name and invoke the delegate with the corresponding arguments.

However, in the more general case, you might not know precisely which message you're getting and whether the object you want to delegate it to can handle it.

To forward messages, you need to override the `forward::` method from the `Object` class. If you just want to ignore any messages your class doesn't recognize, put the following definition in your class:

```
-(id) forward: (SEL) selector: (marg_list) arglist
{
  return nil;
}
```

Of course, you can also display your own warning messages here or take some other action. Forwarding the message to another class to handle is a bit more complicated and has to be treated differently when working with Foundation's `NSObject` root class (described in Part II). For those reasons, we won't go into any details here on how to do that. For further information, consult the references listed in Appendix E, "Resources."

Exercises

1. What will happen if you insert the message expression
   ```
   [compResult reduce];
   ```
   into Program 9.1 after the addition is performed (but before `compResult` is freed)? Try it and see.

2. Can the `id` variable `dataValue`, as defined in Program 9.2, be assigned a `Rectangle` object as you defined it in Chapter 8, "Inheritance"? That is, is the statement
   ```
   dataValue = [[Rectangle alloc] init];
   ```
   valid? Why or why not?

3. Add a `print` method to your `Point` class defined in Chapter 8. Have it display the point in the format (x, y). Then modify Program 9.2 to incorporate a `Point` object. Have the modified program create a `Point` object, set its value, assign it to the `id` variable `dataValue`, and then display its value.

4. Based on the discussions about argument and return types in this chapter, modify both add: methods in the Fraction and Complex classes to take and return id objects. Then write a program that incorporates the following code sequence:

```
result = [dataValue1 add: dataValue2];
[result print];
```

where result, dataValue1, and dataValue2 are id objects. Make sure you set dataValue1 and dataValue2 appropriately in your program and free all objects before your program terminates.

5. Given the Fraction and Complex class definitions you have been using in this text and the following definitions

```
Fraction *fraction = [[Fraction alloc] init];
Complex *complex = [[Complex alloc] init];
id     number = [[Complex alloc] init];
```

determine the return value from the following message expressions. Then type them into a program to verify the results.

```
[fraction isMemberOf: [Complex class]];
[complex isMemberOf: [Object class]];
[complex isKindOf: [Object class]];
[fraction isKindOf: [Fraction class]];
[fraction respondsTo: @selector (print)];
[complex respondsTo: @selector (print)];
[Fraction instancesRespondTo: @selector (print)];
[number respondsTo: @selector (print)];
[number isKindOf: [Complex class]];
[number respondsTo: @selector (free)];
[[number class] respondsTo: @selector (alloc)];
```

10

More on Variables and Data Types

Iɴ ᴛʜɪs ᴄʜᴀᴘᴛᴇʀ, ᴡᴇ'ʟʟ ɢᴏ ɪɴᴛᴏ ᴍᴏʀᴇ ᴅᴇᴛᴀɪʟ about variable scope, initialization methods for objects, and data types.

The initialization of an object needs some special attention, which we'll give it here.

We talked briefly about the scope of instance variables and also static and local variables in Chapter 7, "More on Classes." We'll talk more about static variables here and introduce the concept of global and external ones as well. In addition, certain directives can be given to the Objective-C compiler to more precisely control the scope of your instance variables. These are covered in this chapter as well.

An *enumerated* data type enables you to define the name for a data type that will only be used to store a specified list of values. The Objective-C language's `typedef` statement lets you assign your own name to a built-in or derived data type. Finally, in this chapter, we'll describe in more detail the precise steps the Objective-C compiler follows when converting data types in the evaluation of expressions.

Initializing Classes

You've seen the pattern before: You allocate a new instance of an object and then initialize it, using a familiar sequence, like so:

```
Fraction *myFract = [[Fraction alloc] init];
```

After these two methods are invoked, you typically assign some values to the new object, like this:

```
[myFract setTo: 1 over: 3];
```

The process of initializing an object followed by setting it to some initial values is often combined into a single method. For example, you could define an `initWith::` method that initializes a fraction and sets its numerator and denominator to the two (unnamed) supplied arguments.

A class that contains many methods and instance variables in it commonly has several initialization methods as well. For example, the Foundation framework's NSArray class contains the following six initialization methods:

```
initWithArray:
initWithArray:copyItems:
initWithContentsOfFile:
initWithContentsOfURL:
initWithObjects:
initWithObjects:count:
```

An array might be allocated and then initialized with a sequence like this:

```
myArray = [[NSArray alloc] initWithArray: myOtherArray];
```

It's common practice for all the initializers in a class to begin with init.... As you can see, the NSArray's initializers follow that convention. You should adhere to the following two strategies when writing initializers.

If your class contains more than one initializer, one of them should be your *designated* initializer and all the other initialization methods should use it. Typically, that is your most complex initialization method (usually the one that takes the most arguments). By creating a designated initializer, your main initialization code will be centralized in a single method. Anyone subclassing your class can then override your designated initializer to ensure that new instances are properly initialized.

Ensure that any inherited instance variables get properly initialized. The easiest way to do that is to first invoke the parent's designated initialization method, which is most often init. After that, you can initialize your own instance variables.

Based on that discussion, your initialization method initWith:: for your Fraction class might look like this:

```
-(Fraction *) initWith: (int) n: (int) d
{
  self = [super init];

  if (self)
    [self setTo: n over: d];
  return self;
}
```

This method invokes the parent initializer first, which is Object's init method (you'll recall that that is Fraction's parent). You need to assign the result back to self because an initializer has the right to change or move the object in memory.

Following super's initialization (and its success as indicated by the return of a nonzero value) you use the setTo:over: method to set the numerator and denominator of your Fraction. As with other initialization methods, you are expected to return it yourself, which is what you do here.

Program 10.1 tests your new initWith:: initialization method.

Program 10.1

```
#import "Fraction.h"

int main (int argc, char *argv[])
{
  Fraction *a, *b;

  a = [[Fraction alloc] initWith: 1: 3];
  b = [[Fraction alloc] initWith: 3: 7];

  [a print]; printf ("\n");
  [b print]; printf ("\n");
  [a free];
  [b free];

  return 0;
}
```

Program 10.1 **Output**

```
1/3
3/7
```

Initializing Classes: The `initialize` Method

When your program begins execution, it sends the `initialize` call method to all your classes. If you have a class and associated subclasses, the parent class gets the message first. This message is sent only once to each class, and it is guaranteed to be sent before any other messages are sent to the class. The purpose is for you to perform any class initialization at that point. For example, you might want to initialize some static variables associated with that class at that time.

Scope Revisited

You can influence the scope of the variables in your program in several ways. This can be done with instance variables as well as with normal variables defined either outside or inside functions. In the discussion that follows, we use the term *module* to refer to any number of method or function definitions contained within a single source file.

Directives for Controlling Instance Variable Scope

You know by now that instance variables have scope that is limited to the instance methods defined for the class. So, any instance method can access its instance variables directly by name, without having to do anything special.

And you also know that instance variables are inherited by a subclass. Inherited instance variables can also be accessed directly by name from within any method defined in that subclass. Once again, this is without having to do anything special.

You can put three directives in front of your instance variables when they are declared in the interface section to more precisely control their scope; these are

- @protected—The instance variables that follow can be directly accessed by methods defined in the class and by any subclasses. This is the default case.

- @private—The instance variables that follow can be directly accessed by methods defined in the class but not by any subclasses.

- @public—The instance variables that follow can be directly accessed by methods defined in the class and by any other classes or modules.

If you wanted to define a class called Printer that kept two instance variables called pageCount and tonerLevel private and accessible only by methods in the Printer class, you might use an interface section that looked like this:

```
@interface Printer: Object
{
@private
  int  pageCount;
  int  tonerLevel;
@protected
  // other instance variables
}
  ...
@end
```

Anyone subclassing Printer would be incapable of accessing these two instance variables because they were made private.

These special directives act like "switches"; all variables that appear after one of these directives (until the right curly brace that marks the end of the variable declarations) has the specified scope unless another directive is used. In the previous example, the @protected directive ensures that instance variables that follow up to the } will be accessible by subclasses as well as by the Printer class methods.

The @public directive makes instance variables accessible by other methods or functions through the use of the pointer operator (->), which is covered in Chapter 13, "Underlying C Language Features." Making an instance variable public is not considered good programming practice because it defeats the concept of data encapsulation (that is, a class hiding its instance variables).

External Variables: extern **and** static

If you write the statement

```
int gMoveNumber - 0;
```

at the beginning of your program—outside any method, class definition, or function—its value can be referenced from anywhere in that module. In such a case, we say that gMoveNumber is defined as a *global* variable. By convention, a lowercase *g* is commonly used as the first letter of a global variable to indicate its scope to the program's reader.

Actually, this very same definition of the variable gMoveNumber also makes its value accessible from other files. Specifically, the preceding statement defines the variable gMoveNumber not just as a global variable, but in fact as an *external* global variable.

An *external* variable is one whose value can be accessed and changed by any other methods or functions. Inside the module that wants to access the external variable, the variable is declared in the normal fashion and the keyword extern is placed before the declaration. This signals to the system that a globally defined variable from another file is to be accessed. The following is an example of how to declare the variable gMoveNumber as an external variable:

```
extern int gMoveNumber;
```

The value of gMoveNumber can now be accessed and modified by the module in which the preceding declaration appeared. Other modules can also access the value of gMoveNumber by using a similar extern declaration in the file.

Here is an important rule you must follow when working with external variables: The variable must be defined in some place among your source files. This is done by declaring the variable outside any method or function, *not* preceded by the keyword extern, like so:

```
int gMoveNumber;
```

Here, an initial value can be optionally assigned to the variable, as was shown previously.

The second way to define an external variable is to declare the variable outside any function, placing the keyword extern in front of the declaration, and explicitly assigning an initial value to it, like this:

```
extern int gMoveNumber = 0;
```

This, however, is not the preferred way to do things, and the compiler will give you a warning to the effect that you've declared the variable extern and assigned it a value at the same time. That's because using the word extern makes it a declaration for the variable and not a definition. Remember, a declaration doesn't cause storage for a variable to be allocated, but a definition does. So, the previous example violates this rule by forcing a declaration to be treated as a definition (by assigning it an initial value).

When dealing with external variables, a variable can be declared as `extern` in many places but can be defined only once.

Let's take a look at a small program example to illustrate the use of external variables. Suppose we have defined a class called `Foo` and we type the following code into a file called `main.m`:

```
#import "Foo.h"
int gGlobalVar = 5;

int main (int argc, char *argc[])
{
    Foo *myFoo = [[Foo alloc] init];
    printf ("%i ", gGlobalVar);

    [myFoo setgGlobalVar: 100];

    printf ("%i\n", gGlobalVar);
    [myFoo free];
    return 0;
}
```

The definition of the global variable `gGlobalVar` in the previous program makes its value accessible by any method (or function) that uses an appropriate `extern` declaration. Suppose your `Foo` method `setgGlobalVar:` looks like this:

```
-(void) setgGlobalVar: (int) val
{
    extern int gGlobalVar;
    gGlobalVar = val;
}
```

This program would produce the following output at the terminal:

```
100
```

This would verify that the method `setgGlobalVar:` is capable of accessing and changing the value of the external variable `gGlobalVar`.

If many methods needed to access the value of `gGlobalVar`, making the `extern` declaration just once at the front of the file would be easier. However, if only one method or a small number of methods needed to access this variable, there would be something to be said for making separate `extern` declarations in each such method; it would make the program more organized and would isolate the use of the particular variable to those functions that actually used it. Note that if the variable is defined inside the file containing the code that accesses the variable, the individual `extern` declarations are not required.

Static Versus Extern Variables

The example just shown goes against the notion of data encapsulation and good object-oriented programming techniques. However, you might need to work with variables whose values are shared across different method invocations. Even though it might not make sense to make gGlobalVar an instance variable in the Foo class, a better approach than that shown might be to "hide" it within the Foo class by restricting its access to setter and getter methods defined for that class.

You now know that any variable defined outside a method is not only a global variable, but an external one as well. Many situations arise in which you want to define a variable to be global but not external. In other words, you want to define a global variable to be local to a particular module (file). It would make sense to want to define a variable this way if no methods other than those contained inside a particular class definition needed access to the particular variable. This can be accomplished by defining the variable to be *static* inside the file that contains the implementation for the particular class.

The statement

```
static int gGlobalVar = 0;
```

if made outside any method (or function), makes the value of gGlobalVar accessible from any subsequent point in the file in which the definition appears but not from methods or functions contained in other files.

You'll recall that class methods do not have access to instance variables (you might want to think about why that's the case again). However, you might want a class method to be capable of setting and accessing variables. A simple example would be a class allocator method that wanted to keep track of the number of objects it had allocated. The way to accomplish this task would be to set up a static variable inside the implementation file for the class. The allocation method could then access this variable directly because it would not be an instance variable. The users of the class do not need to know about this variable. Because it's defined as a static variable in the implementation file, its scope would be restricted to that file. So, users wouldn't have direct access to it and the concept of data encapsulation would not be violated. A method can be written to retrieve the value of this variable if access is needed from outside the class.

Program 10.2 extends the Fraction class definition with the addition of two new methods. The allocF class method allocates a new Fraction and keeps track of how many Fractions it has allocated, whereas the count method returns that count. Note that this latter method is also a class method. It could have been implemented as an instance method as well, but it makes more sense to ask the class how many instances it has allocated rather than sending the message to a particular instance of the class.

Here are the declarations for the two new class methods to be added to the Fraction.h header file:

```
+(Fraction *) allocF;
+(int)      count;
```

You might have noticed that the inherited `alloc` method wasn't overridden here; that's risky business. Instead, you defined your own allocator method. Your method will take advantage of the inherited `alloc` method. Here's the code to be placed into your `Fraction.m` implementation file:

```
static int gCounter;

@implementation Fraction;

+(Fraction *) allocF
{
    extern int gCounter;
    ++gCounter;

    return [Fraction alloc];
}

+(int) count
{
    extern int gCounter;

    return gCounter;
}
// other methods from Fraction class go here
   ...
@end
```

The static declaration of counter makes it accessible to any method defined in the implementation section yet does not make it accessible from outside the file. The `allocF` method simply increments the gCounter variable and then uses the `alloc` method to create a new `Fraction`, returning the result. The `count` method simply returns the value of the counter, thus isolating its direct access from the user.

Recall that the `extern` declarations are not required in the two methods because the gCounter variable is defined within the file. It simply helps the reader of the method understand that a variable defined outside the method is being accessed. The *g* prefix for the variable name also serves the same purpose for the reader; for that reason, most programmers typically do not include the `extern` declarations.

Program 10.2 tests the new methods.

Program 10.2

```
#import "Fraction.h"

int main (int argc, char *argv[])
{
  Fraction *a, *b, *c;
```

Program 10.2   **Continued**

```
printf ("Fractions allocated: %i\n", [Fraction count]);

a = [Fraction allocF];
b = [[Fraction allocF] init];
c = [Fraction allocF];

printf ("Fractions allocated: %i\n", [Fraction count]);
[a free];
[b free];
[c free];

return 0;
}
```

Program 10.2   **Output**

```
Fractions allocated: 0
Fractions allocated: 3
```

When the program begins execution, the value of counter is automatically set to 0 (you'll recall that you could override the inherited class initialize method if you wanted to perform any special initialization of the class as a whole, such as set the value of other static variables to some nonzero values). After allocating three Fractions using the allocF method, the count method retrieves the counter variable, which is correctly set to 3. You could also add a setter method to the class if you wanted to reset the counter or set it to a particular value. You don't need that for this application, though.

Storage Class Specifiers

You've already encountered storage class specifiers you can place in front of variable names, such as extern and static. Here are some more.

auto

This keyword is used to declare an automatic local variable, as opposed to a static one. It is the default for a variable declared inside a function or method, and you'll never see anyone using it. Here's an example:

```
auto int index;
```

This declares index to be an automatic local variable, meaning it will automatically be allocated when the block (which can be a curly-braced sequence of statements, a method, or a function) is entered and automatically deallocated when the block is exited. Because this is the default inside a block, the statement

```
int index;
```

is equivalent to

```
auto int index;
```

Unlike static variables, which have default initial values of 0, automatic variables have no default initial values; their values are undefined unless you explicitly assign them values.

register

If a local variable is used heavily, you can request that the value of that variable be stored in one of the machine's registers whenever the method or function is executed. This is done by prefixing the declaration of the variable with the keyword `register`, like so:

```
register int  index;
```

Both local variables and parameters can be declared as `register` variables. The types of variables that can be assigned to registers vary among machines. The basic data types can usually be assigned to registers, as well as objects.

Even if you declare a variable as a register variable, it is still not guaranteed that it will in fact be assigned to a register. In fact, the compiler is free to ignore the presence of this keyword. This keyword was more important years ago when compilers needed hints in producing optimized code. As such, it is not used much any more.

Additionally, a `restrict` modifier is available that you can use with pointer variables to help optimization (such as the `register` modifier). Consult Appendix B, "Objective-C Language Summary," for more information.

const

The compiler enables you to associate the `const` attribute to variables whose values will not be changed by the program. That is, this tells the compiler that the specified variables have a *const*ant value throughout the program's execution. If you try to assign a value to a `const` variable after initializing it, or try to increment or decrement it, the compiler issues a warning message. As an example of the `const` attribute, the line

```
const double pi = 3.141592654;
```

declares the `const` variables `pi`. This tells the compiler that this variable will not be modified by the program. Of course, because the value of a `const` variable cannot be subsequently modified, you must initialize it when it is defined.

Defining a variable as a `const` variable aids in the self-documentation process and tells the reader of the program that the variable's value will not be changed by the program.

volatile

This is sort of the inverse to `const`. It tells the compiler explicitly that the specified variable *will* change its value. It's included in the language to prevent the compiler from optimizing away seemingly redundant assignments to a variable or repeated examination of a variable without its value seemingly changing. A good example to consider is an I/O port and involves an understanding of pointers (see Chapter 13).

Let's say you have the address of an output port stored in a variable in your program called outPort. If you wanted to write two characters to the port—let's say an *O* followed by an *N*—you might write the following code:

```
*outPort = 'O';
*outPort = 'N';
```

This first line says to store the character O at the memory address specified by outPort. The second says to then store the character N at the same location. A smart compiler might notice two successive assignments to the same location and, because outPort isn't being modified in between, simply remove the first assignment from the program. To prevent this from happening, you declare outPort to be a volatile variable, like so:

```
volatile char *outPort;
```

Enumerated Data Types

The Objective-C language enables you to specify a range of values that can be assigned to a variable. An enumerated data type definition is initiated by the keyword enum. Immediately following this keyword is the name of the enumerated data type, followed by a list of identifiers (enclosed in a set of curly braces) that define the permissible values that can be assigned to the type. For example, the statement

```
enum flag { false, true };
```

defines a data type flag. In theory, this data type can be assigned the values true and false inside the program, and no other values. Unfortunately, the Objective-C compiler does not generate warning messages if this rule is violated.

To declare a variable to be of type enum flag, you again use the keyword enum, followed by the enumerated type name, followed by the variable list. So the statement

```
enum flag endOfData, matchFound;
```

defines the two variables endOfData and matchFound to be of type flag. The only values (in theory, that is) that can be assigned to these variables are the names true and false. So, statements such as

```
endOfData = true;
```

and

```
if ( matchFound == false )
   ...
```

are valid.

If you want to have a specific integer value associated with an enumeration identifier, the integer can be assigned to the identifier when the data type is defined. Enumeration

identifiers that subsequently appear in the list are assigned sequential integer values
beginning with the specified integer value plus one.

In the definition

```
enum direction { up, down, left = 10, right };
```

an enumerated data type, `direction`, is defined with the values up, down, left, and
right. The compiler assigns the value 0 to up because it appears first in the list, assigns
1 to down because it appears next, assigns 10 to left because it is explicitly assigned
this value, and assigns 11 to right because it is the incremented value of the preceding
enum in the list.

Enumeration identifiers can share the same value. For example, in

```
enum boolean { no = 0, false = 0, yes = 1, true = 1 };
```

assigning either the value no or false to an enum boolean variable assigns it the
value 0; assigning either yes or true assigns it the value 1.

As another example of an enumerated data type definition, the following defines the
type enum month, with permissible values that can be assigned to a variable of this type
being the names of the months of the year:

```
enum month { january = 1, february, march, april, may, june, july,
        august, september, october, november, december };
```

The Objective-C compiler actually treats enumeration identifiers as integer constants.
If your program contains these two lines

```
enum month thisMonth;
    ...
thisMonth = february;
```

the value 2 would be assigned to thisMonth (and not the name february).

Program 10.3 shows a simple program using enumerated data types. The program
reads a month number and then enters a switch statement to see which month was
entered. Recall that enumeration values are treated as integer constants by the compiler,
so they're valid case values. The variable days is assigned the number of days in the
specified month, and its value is displayed after the switch is exited. A special test is
included to see whether the month is February.

Program 10.3

```
// print the number of days in a month
int main (int argc, char *argv[])
{
  enum month { january = 1, february, march, april, may, june,
              july, august, september, october, november,
              december };
  enum month amonth;
  int     days;
```

Program 10.3   **Continued**

```
printf ("Enter month number: ");
scanf ("%i", &amonth);

switch (amonth) {
  case january:
  case march:
  case may:
  case july:
  case august:
  case october:
  case december:
            days = 31;
            break;
  case april:
  case june:
  case september:
  case november:
            days = 30;
            break;
  case february:
            days = 28;
            break;
  default:
            printf ("bad month number\n");
            days = 0;
            break;
}

if ( days != 0 )
  printf ("Number of days is %i\n", days);

if ( amonth == february )
  printf ("...or 29 if it's a leap year\n");
return 0;
}
```

Program 10.3   **Output**

```
Enter month number: 5
Number of days is 31
```

Program 10.3   **Output (Rerun)**

```
Enter month number: 2
Number of days is 28
...or 29 if it's a leap year
```

You can explicitly assign an integer value to an enumerated data type variable; this should be done using the type cast operator. Therefore, if `monthValue` were an integer variable that had the value 6, for example, the expression

```
lastMonth = (enum month) (monthValue - 1);
```

would be permissible. If you don't use the type cast operator, the compiler (unfortunately) won't complain about it.

When using programs with enumerated data types, try not to rely on the fact that the enumerated values are treated as integers. Instead, try to treat them as distinct data types. The enumerated data type gives you a way to associate a symbolic name with an integer number. If you subsequently need to change the value of that number, you must change it only in the place where the enumeration is defined. If you make assumptions based on the actual value of the enumerated data type, you defeat this benefit of using an enumeration.

Some variations are permitted when defining an enumerated data type: The name of the data type can be omitted, and variables can be declared to be of the particular enumerated data type when the type is defined. As an example showing both of these options, the statement

```
enum { east, west, south, north } direction;
```

defines an (unnamed) enumerated data type with values `east`, `west`, `south`, or `north` and declares a variable (`direction`) to be of that type.

Defining an enumerated data type within a block limits the scope of that definition to the block. On the other hand, defining an enumerated data type at the beginning of the program, outside any block, makes the definition global to the file.

When defining an enumerated data type, you must make certain that the enumeration identifiers are unique with respect to other variable names and enumeration identifiers defined within the same scope.

The `typedef` Statement

Objective-C provides a capability that enables the programmer to assign an alternative name to a data type. This is done with a statement known as `typedef`. The statement

```
typedef int Counter;
```

defines the name `Counter` to be equivalent to the Objective-C data type `int`. Variables can subsequently be declared to be of type `Counter`, as in the following statement:

```
Counter  j, n;
```

The Objective-C compiler actually treats the declaration of the variables `j` and `n`, shown previously, as normal integer variables. The main advantage of the use of the `typedef` in this case is in the added readability it lends to the definition of the variables. It is clear from the definition of `j` and `n` what the intended purpose of these variables is in the program. Declaring them to be of type `int` in the traditional fashion would not have made the intended use of these variables at all clear.

The following `typedef` defines a type named `NumberObject` to be a `Number` object:

```
typedef Number *NumberObject;
```

Variables subsequently declared to be of type `NumberObject`, as in

```
NumberObject myValue1, myValue2, myResult;
```

are treated as if they were declared in the normal way in your program, like so:

```
Number *myValue1, *myValue2, *myResult;
```

To define a new type name with `typedef`, follow this procedure:

1. Write the statement as if a variable of the desired type were being declared.
2. Where the name of the declared variable would normally appear, substitute the new type name.
3. In front of everything, place the keyword `typedef`.

As an example of this procedure, to define a type called `Direction` to be an enumerated data type that consists of the directions east, west, north, and south, write out the enumerated type definition and substitute the name `Direction` where the variable name would normally appear. Before everything, place the keyword `typedef`:

```
typedef enum { east, west, south, north } Direction;
```

With this `typedef` in place, you can subsequently declare variables to be of type `Direction`, as in the following:

```
Direction step1, step2;
```

The Foundation framework, which is covered in Part II, "The Foundation Framework," has the following `typedef` definition for `NSComparisonResult` in one of its header files:

```
typedef enum _NSComparisonResult {
    NSOrderedAscending = -1, NSOrderedSame, NSOrderedDescending
} NSComparisonResult;
```

Some of the methods in the Foundation framework that perform comparisons return a value of this type. For example, Foundation's string comparison method, called `compare:`, returns a value of type `NSComparisonResult` after comparing two strings that are `NSString` objects. The method is declared like this:

```
-(NSComparisonResult) compare: (NSString *) string;
```

To test whether two `NSString` objects called `userName` and `savedName` are equal, you might include a line like this in your program:

```
if ( [userName compare: savedName] == NSOrderedSame)
   // The names match
   ...
```

This actually tests whether the result from the `compare:` method is zero.

Data Type Conversions

Chapter 4, "Data Types and Expressions," briefly addressed the fact that sometimes conversions are implicitly made by the system when expressions are evaluated. The case you examined was with the data types `float` and `int`. You saw how an operation that involves a `float` and an `int` was carried out as a floating-point operation, the integer data item being automatically converted to floating point.

You have also seen how the type cast operator can be used to explicitly dictate a conversion. So, given that `total` and `n` are both integer variables

```
average = (float) total / n;
```

the value of the variable `total` is converted to type `float` before the operation is performed, thereby guaranteeing that the division will be carried out as a floating-point operation.

The Objective-C compiler adheres to very strict rules when it comes to evaluating expressions that consist of different data types.

The following summarizes the order in which conversions take place in the evaluation of two operands in an expression:

1. If either operand is of type `long double`, the other is converted to `long double`, and that is the type of the result.

2. If either operand is of type `double`, the other is converted to `double`, and that is the type of the result.

3. If either operand is of type `float`, the other is converted to `float`, and that is the type of the result.

4. If either operand is of type `_Bool`, `char`, `short int`, `bit field`,[1] or of an enumerated data type, it is converted to `int`.

5. If either operand is of type `long long int`, the other is converted to `long long int`, and that is the type of the result.

6. If either operand is of type `long int`, the other is converted to `long int`, and that is the type of the result.

7. If this step is reached, both operands are of type `int`, and that is the type of the result.

This is actually a simplified version of the steps involved in converting operands in an expression. The rules get more complicated when `unsigned` operands are involved. For the complete set of rules, see Appendix B, "Objective-C Language Summary."

Realize from this series of steps that, whenever you reach a step that says "that is the type of the result," you're done with the conversion process.

---

1. Bit fields are briefly discussed in Chapter 13.

As an example of how to follow these steps, let's see how the following expression would be evaluated, where f is defined to be a float, i an int, l a long int, and s a short int variable:

```
f * i + l / s
```

Consider first the multiplication of f by i, which is the multiplication of a float by an int. From step 3, you know that, because f is of type float, the other operand (i) will also be converted to type float and that will be the type of the result of the multiplication.

Next, the division of l by s occurs, which is the division of a long int by a short int. Step 4 tells you that the short int will be promoted to an int. Continuing, step 6 shows that, because one of the operands (l) is a long int, the other operand will be converted to a long int, which will also be the type of the result. This division will therefore produce a value of type long int, with any fractional part resulting from the division truncated.

Finally, step 3 indicates that, if one of the operands in an expression is of type float (as is the result of multiplying f * i), the other operand will be converted to type float, which will be the type of the result. Therefore, *after* the division of l by s has been performed, the result of the operation will be converted to type float and then added into the product of f and i. The final result of the preceding expression will therefore be a value of type float.

Remember, the type cast operator can always be used to explicitly force conversions and thereby control the way in which a particular expression is evaluated.

Thus, if you didn't want the result of dividing l by s to be truncated in the preceding expression evaluation, you could have type cast one of the operands to type float, thereby forcing the evaluation to be performed as a floating-point division, like so:

```
f * i + (float) l / s
```

In this expression, l would be converted to float before the division operation was performed because the type cast operator has higher precedence than the division operator. Because one of the operands of the division would then be of type float, the other (s) would be automatically converted to type float, and that would be the type of the result.

Sign Extension

Whenever a signed int or signed short int is converted into an integer of a larger size, the sign is extended to the left when the conversion is performed. This ensures that a short int having a value of -5, for example, will also have the value -5 when converted to a long int. Whenever an unsigned integer is converted to an integer of a larger size, no sign extension occurs, as you would expect.

On some machines (such as a Mac G4/G5 and Pentium processors) characters are treated as signed quantities. This means that when a character is converted to an integer, sign extension occurs. As long as characters are used from the standard ASCII character set, this never poses a problem. However, if a character value is used that is not part of the standard character set, its sign can be extended when converted to an integer. For example, on a Mac, the character constant `'\377'` is converted to the value –1 because its value is negative when treated as a signed 8-bit quantity.

Recall that the Objective-C language permits character variables to be declared unsigned, thus avoiding this potential problem. That is, an `unsigned char` variable never has its sign extended when converted to an integer; its value always is greater than or equal to zero. For the typical 8-bit character, a signed character variable therefore has the range of values from –128 to +127, inclusive. An unsigned character variable can range in value from 0 to 255, inclusive.

If you want to force sign extension on your character variables, you can declare such variables to be of type `signed char`. This ensures that sign extension occurs when the character value is converted to an integer, even on machines that don't do so by default.

In Chapter 15, "Numbers, Strings, and Collections," you'll learn about dealing with multibyte Unicode characters. This is the preferred way to deal with strings that can contain characters from character sets containing millions of characters.

Exercises

1. Using the `Rectangle` class from Chapter 8, "Inheritance," add an initializer method according to the following declaration:
   ```
   -(Rectangle *) initWithWidth: (int) w: andHeight: (int) h;
   ```

2. Given that you label the method developed in exercise 1 the designated initializer for the `Rectangle` class, and based on the `Square` and `Rectangle` class definitions from Chapter 8, add an initializer method to the `Square` class according to the following declaration:
   ```
   -(Square *) initWithSide: (int) side;
   ```

3. Add a counter to the `Fraction` class's `add:` method to count the number of times it is invoked. How can you retrieve the value of the counter?

4. Using `typedef` and enumerated data types, define a type called `Day` with the possible values `Sunday`, `Monday`, `Tuesday`, `Wednesday`, `Thursday`, `Friday`, and `Saturday`.

5. Using `typedef`, define a type called `FractionObj` that enables you to write the statements such as the following:
   ```
   FractionObj f1 = [[Fraction alloc] init],
               f2 = [[Fraction alloc] init];
   ```

6. Based on the following definitions
```
float     f = 1.00;
short int i = 100;
long int  l = 500L;
double    d = 15.00;
```

and the seven steps outlined in this chapter for the conversion of operands in expressions, determine the type and value of the following expressions:
```
f + i
l / d
i / l + f
l * i
f / 2
i / (d + f)
l / (i * 2.0)
l + i / (double) l
```

7. Write a program to ascertain whether sign extension is performed on signed char variables on your machine.

11

Categories, Posing, and Protocols

In this chapter you'll learn about how to add methods to a class in a modular fashion through the use of categories, how one class can substitute for another one, and how to create a standardized list of methods for others to implement.

Categories

Sometimes you might be working with a class definition and want to add some new methods to it. For example, you might decide for your Fraction class that, in addition to the add: method for adding two fractions, you'd like to have methods to subtract, multiply, and divide two fractions.

As another example, say you are working on a large programming project and as part of that project a new class is being defined containing many different methods. You have been assigned the task of writing methods for the class that work with the file system, for example. Other project members have been assigned methods responsible for creating and initializing instances of the class, performing operations on objects in the class, and drawing representations of objects from the class on the screen.

As a final example, suppose you've learned how to use a class from the library (for example, the Foundation framework's array class called NSArray) and realize that there are one or more methods that you wish the class had implemented. Of course, you could write a new subclass of the NSArray class and implement the new methods, but perhaps an easier way exists.

A practical solution for all these situations is one word: *categories*. A category provides an easy way for you to modularize the definition of a class into groups or categories of related methods. It also gives you an easy way to extend an existing class definition without even having access to the original source code for the class and without having to create a subclass. It is a powerful yet easy concept for you to learn.

Let's get back to the first case and show how to add a new category to the Fraction class to handle the four basic math operations. We'll first show you the original Fraction interface section:

```
#import <objc/Object.h>
#import <stdio.h>


// Define the Fraction class

@interface Fraction . Object
{
  int  numerator;
  int  denominator;
}
// setters
-(void)  setNumerator: (int) n;
-(void)  setDenominator:  (int) d;
-(void)  setTo: (int) n over: (int) d;

// getters
-(int)  numerator;
-(int)  denominator;

// utility
-(Fraction *) add: (Fraction *) f;
-(void)   reduce;
-(double) convertToNum;
-(void)   print;
@end
```

Next, let's remove the add: method from this interface section and add it to a new category, along with the other three math operations you want to implement. Here's what the interface section would look like for your new MathOps category:

```
#import "Fraction.h"
@interface Fraction (MathOps)
-(Fraction *) add: (Fraction *) f;
-(Fraction *) mul: (Fraction *) f;
-(Fraction *) sub: (Fraction *) f;
-(Fraction *) div: (Fraction *) f;
@end
```

Realize that, even though this is an interface section definition, it is an extension to an existing one. Therefore, you must include the original interface section so that the compiler knows about the Fraction class (unless you incorporate the new category directly into the original Fraction.h header file, which is an option).

After the #import, you see the following line:

```
@interface Fraction (MathOps)
```

This tells the compiler you are defining a new category for the Fraction class and that it's name is MathOps. The category name is enclosed in a pair of parentheses after the class name. Notice that you don't list the Fraction's parent class here; the compiler already knows it from Fraction.h. Also, you don't tell it about the instance variables, as you've done in all the previous interface sections you've defined. In fact, if you try to list the parent class or the instance variables, you'll get a syntax error from the compiler.

This interface section tells the compiler you are adding an extension to the class called Fraction under the category named MathOps. The MathOps category contains four instance methods: add:, mul:, sub:, and div:. Each method takes a fraction as its argument and returns one as well.

You can put the definitions for all your methods into a single implementation section. That is, you could define all the methods from the interface section in Fraction.h plus all the methods from the MathOps category in one implementations section. Alternatively, you could define your category's methods in a separate implementation section. In such a case, the implementation section for these methods must also identify the category to which the methods belong. As with the interface section, you do this by enclosing the category name inside parentheses after the class name, like so:

```
@implementation Fraction (MathOps)
  // code for category methods
   ...
@end
```

In Program 11.1, the interface and implementation sections for the new MathOps category are grouped together, along with a test routine, into a single file.

Program 11.1 **MathOps Category and Test Program**

```
#import "Fraction.h"
@interface Fraction (MathOps)
-(Fraction *) add: (Fraction *) f;
-(Fraction *) mul: (Fraction *) f;
-(Fraction *) sub: (Fraction *) f;
-(Fraction *) div: (Fraction *) f;
@end

@implementation Fraction (MathOps);
-(Fraction *) add: (Fraction *) f
{
  // To add two fractions:
  // a/b + c/d = ((a*d) + (b*c)) / (b * d)

  Fraction *result = [[Fraction alloc] init];
  int     resultNum, resultDenom;
```

Program 11.1 **Continued**

```
resultNum = (numerator * [f denominator]) +
   (denominator * [f numerator]);
resultDenom = denominator * [f denominator];

[result setTo: resultNum over: resultDenom];
[result reduce];

return result;
}

-(Fraction *) sub: (Fraction *) f
{
  // To sub two fractions:
  // a/b - c/d = ((a*d) - (b*c)) / (b * d)

  Fraction *result = [[Fraction alloc] init];
  int      resultNum, resultDenom;

  resultNum = (numerator * [f denominator]) -
        (denominator * [f numerator]);
  resultDenom = denominator * [f denominator];

  [result setTo: resultNum over: resultDenom];
  [result reduce];

  return result;
}

-(Fraction *) mul: (Fraction *) f
{
  Fraction  *result = [[Fraction alloc] init];

  [result setTo: numerator * [f numerator]
            over: denominator * [f denominator]];
  [result reduce];

  return result;
}

-(Fraction *) div: (Fraction *) f
{
  Fraction  *result = [[Fraction alloc] init];
```

Program 11.1 **Continued**

```
  [result setTo: numerator * [f denominator]
             over: denominator * [f numerator]];
  [result reduce];

  return result;
}
@end
int main (int argc, char *argv[])
{
  Fraction *a = [[Fraction alloc] init];
  Fraction *b = [[Fraction alloc] init];
  Fraction *result;

  [a setTo: 1 over: 3];
  [b setTo: 2 over: 5];

  [a print]; printf (" + "); [b print]; printf (" = ");
  result = [a add: b];
  [result print];
  printf ("\n");
  [result free];

  [a print]; printf (" - "); [b print]; printf (" = ");
  result = [a sub: b];
  [result print];
  printf ("\n");
  [result free];

  [a print]; printf (" * "); [b print]; printf (" = ");
  result = [a mul: b];
  [result print];
  printf ("\n");
  [result free];

  [a print]; printf (" / "); [b print]; printf (" = ");
  result = [a div: b];
  [result print];
  printf ("\n");
  [result free];
  [a free];
  [b free];

  return 0;
}
```

Program 11.1 **Output**

```
1/3 + 2/5 = 11/15
1/3 - 2/5 = -1/15
1/3 * 2/5 = 2/15
1/3 / 2/5 = 5/6
```

Realize once again that it is certainly legal in Objective-C to write a statement such as this:

```
[[a div: b] print];
```

This line directly prints the result of dividing `Fraction` a by b and thereby avoids the intermediate assignment to the variable `result`, as was done in Program 11.1. However, you need to perform this intermediate assignment so you can capture the resulting `Fraction` and subsequently release its memory. Otherwise, your program will leak memory every time you perform an arithmetic operation on a fraction.

Program 11.1 puts the interface and implementation sections for the new category into the same file with the test program. As mentioned previously, the interface section for this category could either go in the original `Fraction.h` header file so that all methods would be declared in one place or in its own header file.

If you put your category into a master class definition file, all users of the class will have access to the methods in the category. If you don't have the ability to modify the original header file directly (consider adding a category to an existing class from a library, as shown in Part II, "The Foundation Framework"), you have no choice but to keep it separate.

Some Notes About Categories

Some points are worth mentioning about categories. First, although a category has access to the instance variables of the original class, it can't add any of its own. If you need to do that, consider subclassing.

Also, a category can override another method in the class, but this is typically considered poor programming practice. For one thing, after you override a method, you can no longer access the original method. Therefore, you must be careful to duplicate all the functionality of the overridden method in your replacement. If you do need to override a method, subclassing might be the right choice. If you override a method in a subclass, you can still reference the parent's method by sending a message to `super`. So, you don't have to understand all the intricacies of the method you are overriding; you can simply invoke the parent's method and add your own functionality to the subclass's method.

You can have as many categories as you like, following the rules we've outlined here. If a method is defined in more than one category, the language does not specify which one will be used.

Unlike a normal interface section, you don't need to implement all the methods in a category. That's useful for incremental program development because you can declare all the methods in the category and implement them over time.

Remember that extending a class by adding new methods with a category affects not just that class, but all its subclasses as well. This can be potentially dangerous if you add new methods to the root object Object, for example, because everyone will inherit those new methods, whether that was your intention.

The new methods you add to an existing class through a category can serve your purposes just fine, but they might be inconsistent with the original design or intentions of the class. Turning a Square into a Circle (admittedly an exaggeration), for example, by adding a new category and some methods muddies the definition of the class and is not good programming practice.

Also, object/category named pairs must be unique. Only one NSString (Private) category can exist in a given Objective-C namespace. This can be tricky because the Objective-C namespace is shared between the program code and all the libraries, frameworks, and plug-ins. This is especially important for Objective-C programmers writing screensavers, preference panes, and other plug-ins because their code will be injected into application or framework code they do not control.

Posing

You can "fake out" the Objective-C system by pretending to be a class that you're not. This act of deception is known as *posing*, and it is supported by the poseAs: method.[1]

For this substitution to occur, you have to be a subclass of the class you want to masquerade as. You also need to send the poseAs: message to the class before you've allocated any instances of the class or sent it any messages. The subclass also can't add any new instance variables, which makes sense when you consider it will be filling in for the parent when it poses for it.

Program 11.2 shows how a class called FractionB can be used to pose as the Fraction class. We did this to override the print method from the Fraction class, but without having to change all references of the class named Fraction to FractionB. This is one of the qualities that makes posing so appealing.

Program 11.2
```
#import "Fraction.h"

@interface FractionB: Fraction
-(void) print;
@end
```

1. Note that when using NSObject as your root object, this method is poseAsClass:.

Program 11.2 **Continued**

```
@implementation FractionB;
-(void) print
{
  printf (" (%i/%i) ", numerator, denominator);
}
@end


int main (int argc, char *argv[])
{
  Fraction *a;
  Fraction *b;
  Fraction *result;

  [FractionB poseAs: [Fraction class]];

  a = [[Fraction alloc] init];
  b = [[Fraction alloc] init];

  [a setTo: 1 over: 3];
  [b setTo: 2 over: 5];

  [a print]; printf (" + "); [b print]; printf (" = ");
  result = [a add: b];
  [result print];
  printf ("\n");
  [a free];
  [b free];
  [result free];

  return 0;
}
```

Program 11.2 **Output**

```
(1/3) + (2/5) = (11/15)
```

FractionB is defined as a subclass of Fraction. It contains one method called print, which is defined to override the parent's method. Of course, posing is not just used for overriding methods; new methods can be added as well. The new print method puts parentheses around each fraction it displays, just for the heck of it!

Before you send any messages to the Fraction class, you must invoke the poseAs: method on it with the following message expression:

```
[FractionB poseAs: [Fraction class]];
```

The argument to `poseAs:` is a class object, which you've seen how to obtain using the `class` method.

After sending the `poseAs:` message to the `FractionB` class, all messages sent to the `Fraction` class instead go to the `FractionB` class. Naturally, because `FractionB` is a subclass of `Fraction`, it gets all its methods, except those it overrides.

Now when you allocate and initialize a `Fraction` with

```
a = [[Fraction alloc] init];
```

the inherited methods in the `FractionB` class are invoked. And when you print the result of the addition with

```
[result print];
```

the overridden `print` method is invoked. The nice thing here is that you can define one class to replace another and simply plug it in by issuing the `poseAs:` message. This eliminates the need to go through the program and change all the class uses to the name of the new subclass.

Categories and posing share much in common. One subtle difference, though, is that if you override a method with a category, you can't access the overridden method. When posing, however, you can access the overridden method by sending a message to `super`. So, the `print` method from `FractionB` could have still invoked the `print` method from `Fraction` if it wanted to, as follows:

```
[super print];
```

Posing also comes in handy when you need to fix a bug in a method for which you don't have access to the source code. You can define a subclass, override the method, and then pose as the parent class.

Protocols

A *protocol* is a list of methods that is shared among classes. The methods listed in the protocol do not have corresponding implementations; they're meant to be implemented by someone else (like you!). A protocol provides a way to define a set of methods with a specified name that are somehow related. The methods are typically documented so you know how they are to perform and so you can implement them in your own class definitions if desired.

If you decide to implement all of the methods for a particular protocol, you are said to *conform to* or *adopt* that protocol.

Defining a protocol is easy: You simply use the `@protocol` directive followed by the name of the protocol, which is up to you. After that, you declare methods just as you have done with your interface section. All the method declarations, up to the `@end` directive, become part of the protocol.

If you choose to work with the Foundation framework, you'll find that several protocols are defined. One of them is called `NSCopying`, and it declares a method you need to implement if your class is to support copying of objects through the `copy` (or `copyWithZone:`) method. (The topic of copying objects is covered in detail in Chapter 18, "Copying Objects.")

Here's how the `NSCopying` protocol is defined in the standard Foundation header file `NSObject.h`:

```
@protocol NSCopying

- (id)copyWithZone: (NSZone *)zone;

@end
```

If you adopt the `NSCopying` protocol in your class, you must implement a method called `copyWithZone:`. You tell the compiler you are adopting a protocol by listing the protocol name inside a pair of angular brackets (`<...>`) on the `@interface` line. The protocol name comes after the name of the class and its parent class, as in the following:

```
@interface AddressBook: NSObject <NSCopying>
```

This says that `AddressBook` is an object whose parent is `NSObject` and which conforms to the `NSCopying` protocol.[2] Because the system already knows about the method(s) previously defined for the protocol (in this example it knows from the header file `NSObject.h`), you don't declare the methods in the interface section. However, you need to define them in your implementation section.

So, in this example, in the implementation section for `AddressBook`, the compiler expects to see the `copyWithZone:` method defined.

If your class adopts more than one protocol, just list them inside the angular brackets, separated by commas, like so:

```
@interface AddressBook: NSObject <NSCopying, NSCoding>
```

This tells the compiler that the `AddressBook` class adopts the `NSCopying` and `NSCoding` protocols. Again, the compiler will expect to see all the methods listed for those protocols implemented in the `AddressBook` implementation section.

If you define your own protocol, you don't have to actually implement it yourself. However, you're alerting other programmers that if they want to adopt the protocol that they in fact do have to implement the methods. Those methods can be inherited from a superclass. Thus, if one class conforms to the `NSCopying` protocol, its subclasses do as well (although that doesn't mean the methods are correctly implemented for that subclass).

A protocol can be used to define methods you want other people who subclass your class to implement. Perhaps a `Drawing` protocol could be defined for your

---

2. As you'll learn in Part II, the root object for the Foundation framework is not `Object` but `NSObject`.

`GraphicObject` class, and in it you could define `paint`, `erase`, and `outline` methods, as in the following:

```
@protocol Drawing
-(void) paint;
-(void) erase;
-(void) outline;
@end
```

As the creator of `GraphicObject` class, you don't necessarily want to implement these painting methods. However, you want to specify the methods that someone who subclasses the `GraphicObject` class needs to implement to conform to a standard for drawing objects he's trying to create.

So, if you create a subclass of `GraphicObject` called `Rectangle` and advertise (that is, *document*) that your `Rectangle` class conforms to the `Drawing` protocol, users of the class will know that they can send `paint`, `erase`, and `outline` messages to instances from that class.[3] Notice that the protocol doesn't reference any classes; it's *classless*. Any class can conform to the `Drawing` protocol, not just subclasses of `GraphicObject`.

You can check to see whether an object conforms to a protocol by using the `conformsTo:` method. For example, if you had an object called `currentObject` and wanted to see whether it conformed to the `Drawing` protocol so you could send it drawing messages, you could write this:

```
id currentObject;
  ...
if ([currentObject conformsTo: @protocol (Drawing)] == YES)
{
  // Send currentObject paint, erase and/or outline msgs
  ...
}
```

The special `@protocol` directive as used here takes a protocol name and produces a `Protocol` object, which is what the `conformsTo:` method expects as its argument.

You can enlist the aid of the compiler to check for conformance with your variables by including the protocol name inside angular brackets after the type name, like so:

```
id <Drawing> currentObject;
```

This tells the compiler that `currentObject` will contain objects that conform to the `Drawing` protocol. If you assign a statically typed object to `currentObject` that does not conform to the `Drawing` protocol (say you have a `Square` class that does not conform), the compiler issues a warning message that looks like this:

```
prot1.m:61: warning: class 'Square' does not implement the 'Drawing' protocol
```

---

3. Well that's the theory, anyway. The compiler lets you say you conform to a protocol and issues warning messages only if you don't implement the methods.

This is a compiler check here, so assigning an id variable to currentObject would not generate this message because the compiler has no way of knowing whether the object stored inside an id variable conforms to the Drawing protocol.

You can list more than one protocol if the variable will hold an object conforming to more than one protocol, as in this line:

```
id <NSCopying, NSCoding> myDocument;
```

When you define a protocol, you can extend the definition of an existing one. So, the protocol declaration

```
@protocol Drawing3D <Drawing>
```

says that the Drawing3D protocol also adopts the Drawing protocol. Thus, whichever class adopts the Drawing3D protocol must implement the methods listed for that protocol as well as the methods from the Drawing protocol.

Finally, a category can adopt a protocol too, like so:

```
@interface Fraction (Stuff) <NSCopying, NSCoding>
```

Here Fraction has a category Stuff (okay, not the best choice of names!) that adopts the NSCopying and NSCoding protocols.

As with class names, protocol names must be unique.

Informal Protocols

You might come across the notion of an *informal* protocol in your readings. This is really a category that lists a group of methods but does not implement them. Everyone (or just about everyone) inherits from the same root object, so informal categories are often defined for the root class. Sometimes informal protocols are also referred to as *abstract* protocols.

If you look at the header file objc/Object.h, you might find some lines that look like this:

```
/* Abstract Protocol for Archiving */

@interface Object (Archiving)

- startArchiving: (void *)stream;
- finishUnarchiving;

@end
```

This defines a category called Archiving for the Object class. This informal protocol lists a group of methods (here, two are listed) that can be implemented as part of this protocol. An informal protocol is really no more than a grouping of methods under a name. This can help somewhat from the point of documentation and modularization of methods.

The class that declares the informal protocol doesn't implement the methods in the class itself, and a subclass that chooses to implement the methods needs to redeclare them in its interface section as well as implement one or more of them. Unlike formal protocols, the compiler gives no help with informal protocols; there's no concept of conformance or testing by the compiler.

If an object adopts a formal protocol, the object must conform to all the messages in the protocol. This can be enforced at runtime as well as compile time. If an object adopts an informal protocol, the object might not need to adopt all the methods in the protocol, depending on the protocol. Conformance to an informal protocol can be enforced at runtime (via respondsToSelector:) but not at compile time.

Composite Objects

You've learned several ways to extend the definition of a class through techniques such as subclassing, categories, and posing. Another technique involves defining a class that consists of one or more objects from other classes. An object from this new class is known as a *composite* object because it is composed of other objects.

As an example, consider the Square class you defined in Chapter 8. You defined this as a subclass of a Rectangle because you recognized that a square was just a rectangle with equal sides. When you define a subclass, it inherits all the instance variables and methods of the parent class. In some cases, this is undesirable—for example, some of the methods defined in the parent class might not be appropriate for use by the subclass. The Rectangle's setWidth:andHeight: method is inherited by the Square class but really does not apply to a square (even though it will in fact work properly). Further, when you create a subclass, you must ensure that all the inherited methods work properly because users of the class will have access to them.

As an alternative to subclassing, you can define a new class that contains as one of its instance variables an object from the class you want to extend. Then you only have to define those methods in the new class that are appropriate for that class. Getting back to the Square example, here's an alternative way to define a Square:

```
@interface Square: Object
{
    Rectangle *rect;
}
-(int) setSide: (int) s;
-(int) side;
-(int) area;
-(int) perimeter;
@end
```

The Square class is defined here with four methods. Unlike the subclass version, which gives you direct access to the Rectangle's methods (setWidth:, setHeight:, setWidth:andHeight:, width, and height), those methods are not in this definition for a `Square`. That makes sense here because those methods really don't fit in when you deal with squares.

If you define your `Square` this way, it becomes responsible for allocating the memory for the rectangle it contains. For example, without overriding methods, the statement

```
Square *mySquare = [[Square alloc] init];
```

allocates a new `Square` object but does not allocate a `Rectangle` object stored in its instance variable, `rect`.

A solution is to override `init` or add a new method such as `initWithSide:` to do the allocation. That method can allocate the `Rectangle rect` and set its side appropriately. You'll also need to override the `free` method (which you saw how to do with the `Rectangle` class in Chapter 8) to release the memory used by the `Rectangle rect` when the `Square` itself is freed.

When defining your methods in your `Square` class, you can still take advantage of the `Rectangle`'s methods. For example, here's how you could implement the `area` method:

```
-(int) area
{
   return [rect area];
}
```

Implementation of the remaining methods is left as an exercise for you (see exercise 5 that follows).

Exercises

1. Extend the `MathOps` category from Program 11.1 to also include an `invert` method, which returns a `Fraction` that is an inversion of the receiver.

2. Add a category to the `Fraction` class called `Comparison`. In this category add two methods according to these declarations:
   ```
   -(BOOL) isEqualTo: (Fraction *) f;
   -(int) compare: (Fraction *) f;
   ```
   The first method should return YES if the two fractions are identical and return NO otherwise. Be careful about comparing fractions (for example, comparing 3/4 to 6/8 should return YES).

   The second method should return −1 if the receiver compares less than the fraction represented by the argument, return 0 if the two are equal, and return 1 if the receiver is greater than the argument.

3. The functions `sin ()`, `cos ()`, and `tan ()` are part of the Standard Library (like `printf ()` and `scanf ()` are). These functions are declared in the header file `<math.h>`, which you should import into your program with the following line:

   ```
   #import <math.h>
   ```

   These functions can be used to calculate the sine, cosine, or tangent, respectively, of their `double` argument, which is expressed in radians. The result is also returned as a double precision floating-point value. So

   ```
   result = sin (d);
   ```

   can be used to calculate the sine of `d`, with the angle `d` expressed in radians. Add a category called `Trig` to the `Calculator` class defined in Chapter 6, "Making Decisions." Add methods to this category to calculate the sine, cosine, and tangent based on these declarations:

   ```
   -(double) sin;
   -(double) cos;
   -(double) tan;
   ```

4. Assume the developer of the `Trig` category from exercise 3 goofed and was supposed to write the methods to take arguments as angles expressed in degrees and not radians. Given that an angle can be converted from degrees to radians by multiplying it by $\pi/180$,[4] override the three methods developed in exercise 3 and use `poseAs:` to correct this mistake with the `Calculator` class.

5. Given the discussion on composite objects from this chapter and the following interface section:

   ```
   @interface Square: Object
   {
      Rectangle *rect;
   }
   -(Square*) initWithSide: (int) s;
   -(void) setSide: (int) s;
   -(int) side;
   -(int) area;
   -(int) perimeter;
   -(id)  free;  // Override to release the Rectangle object
   @end
   ```

   write the implementation section for a `Square` and a test program to check its methods.

---

4. For the value of π, you can use the value 3.141592654 or take advantage of the special defined value `M_PI` from the `math.h` header file.

12

The Preprocessor

THE PREPROCESSOR PROVIDES THE TOOLS that enable you to develop programs that are easier to develop, read, modify, and port to different systems. You can also use the preprocessor to literally customize the Objective-C language to suit a particular programming application or your own programming style.

The preprocessor is a part of the Objective-C compilation process that recognizes special statements that can be interspersed throughout a program. As its name implies, the preprocessor actually processes these statements before analysis of the Objective-C program itself takes place. Preprocessor statements are identified by the presence of a pound sign (#), which must be the first nonspace character on the line. As you will see, preprocessor statements have a syntax that is slightly different from that of normal Objective-C statements. We will begin by examining the #define statement.

The #define Statement

One of the primary uses of the #define statement is to assign symbolic names to program constants. The preprocessor statement

```
#define   TRUE   1
```

defines the name TRUE and makes it equivalent to the value 1. The name TRUE can subsequently be used anywhere in the program where the constant 1 could be used. Whenever this name appears, its defined value of 1 is automatically substituted into the program by the preprocessor. For example, you might have the following Objective-C statement that uses the defined name TRUE:

```
gameOver = TRUE;
```

This statement assigns the value of TRUE to gameOver. You don't need to concern yourself with the actual value you defined for TRUE, but because you do know that you defined it to be 1, the preceding statement would have the effect of assigning 1 to gameOver. The preprocessor statement

```
#define   FALSE   0
```

defines the name FALSE and makes its subsequent use in the program equivalent to specifying the value 0. Therefore, the statement

```
gameOver = FALSE;
```

assigns the value of FALSE to gameOver, and the statement

```
if ( gameOver == FALSE )
 ...
```

compares the value of gameOver against the defined value of FALSE.

A defined name is *not* a variable. Therefore, you cannot assign a value to it, unless the result of substituting the defined value is in fact a variable. Whenever a defined name is used in a program, whatever appears to the right of the defined name in the #define statement is automatically substituted into the program by the preprocessor. It's analogous to doing a search and replace with a text editor; in this case, the preprocessor replaces all occurrences of the defined name with its associated text.

You will notice that the #define statement has a special syntax: No equal sign is used to assign the value 1 to TRUE. Furthermore, a semicolon does *not* appear at the end of the statement. Soon you will understand why this special syntax exists.

#define statements are often placed toward the beginning of the program, after #import or #include statements. This is not required; they can appear anywhere in the program. However, a name must be defined before it is referenced by the program. Defined names do not behave like variables: There is no such thing as a local define. After a name has been defined, it can subsequently be used *anywhere* in the program. Most programmers place their defines inside header files so they can be used by more than one source file.

As another example of the use of a defined name, suppose you wanted to write two methods to find the area and circumference of a Circle object. Because both of these methods need to use the constant π, which is not a particularly easy constant to remember, it might make sense to define the value of this constant once at the start of the program and then use this value where necessary in each method.

So, you could include the following in your program:

```
#define PI     3.141592654
```

Then, you could use it in your two Circle methods (this assumes the Circle class has an instance variable called radius), like so:

```
-(double) area
{
    return PI * radius * radius;
}

-(double) circumference
{
    return 2.0 * PI * radius;
}
```

Assignment of a constant to a symbolic name frees you from having to remember the particular constant value every time you want to use it in a program. Furthermore, if you ever needed to change the value of the constant (if perhaps you found out that you were using the wrong value, for example), you would have to change the value in only one place in the program: in the #define statement. Without this approach, you would have to search throughout the program and explicitly change the value of the constant whenever it was used.

You might have realized that all the defines shown so far (TRUE, FALSE, and PI) have been written in capital letters. The reason this is done is to visually distinguish a defined value from a variable. Some programmers adopt the convention that all defined names be capitalized, so that determining when a name represents a variable or an object, a class name, or a defined name is easy. Another common convention is to prefix the define with the letter *k*. In that case, the following characters of the name are not capitalized. kMaximumValues and kSignificantDigits are examples of two defined names that adhered to this convention.

Using a defined name for a constant value helps make programs more readily extendable. For example, when you learn how to work with arrays, instead of hard-coding in the size of the array you want to allocate, you can define a value such as follows:

```
#define MAXIMUM_DATA_VALUES  1000
```

Then you can base all references on the array's size (such as allocation of the array in memory) and valid indices into this array on this defined value.

Also, if the program were written to use MAXIMUM_DATA_VALUES in all cases where the size of the array was used, the preceding definition could be the only statement in the program that would have to be changed if you later needed to change the array size.

More Advanced Types of Definitions

A definition for a name can include more than a simple constant value. It can include an expression and, as you will see shortly, just about anything else!

The following defines the name TWO_PI as the product of 2.0 and 3.141592654:

```
#define TWO_PI  2.0 * 3.141592654
```

You can subsequently use this defined name anywhere in a program where the expression 2.0 * 3.141592654 would be valid. So, you could have replaced the return statement of the circumference method from the previous example with the following statement:

```
return TWO_PI * radius;
```

Whenever a defined name is encountered in an Objective-C program, everything that appears to the right of the defined name in the #define statement is literally substituted for the name at that point in the program. Thus, when the preprocessor encounters the name TWO_PI in the return statement shown previously, it substitutes for this name whatever appeared in the #define statement for this name. Therefore, 2.0 * 3.141592654 is literally substituted by the preprocessor whenever the defined name TWO_PI occurs in the program.

The fact that the preprocessor performs a literal text substitution whenever the defined name occurs explains why you don't usually want to end your #define statement with a semicolon. If you did, the semicolon would also be substituted into the program wherever the defined name appeared. If you had defined PI as

```
#define PI    3.141592654;
```

and then written

```
return 2.0 * PI * r;
```

the preprocessor would replace the occurrence of the defined name PI by `3.141592654;`. The compiler would therefore see this statement as

```
return 2.0 * 3.141592654; * r;
```

after the preprocessor had made its substitution, which would result in a syntax error. Remember not to put a semicolon at the end of your define statements unless you're really sure you want one there.

A preprocessor definition does not have to be a valid Objective-C expression in its own right, as long as the resulting expression is valid wherever it is used. For instance, you could set up these definitions:

```
#define AND    &&
#define OR     ||
```

Then, you could write expressions such as

```
if ( x > 0 AND x < 10 )
    ...
```

and

```
if ( y == 0 OR y == value )
    ...
```

You could even include a define for the equality test:

```
#define EQUALS  ==
```

Then, you could write the following statement:

```
if ( y EQUALS 0 OR y EQUALS value )
    ...
```

This removes the very real possibility of mistakenly using a single equal sign for the equality test.

Although these examples illustrate the power of the #define, you should note that it is commonly considered bad programming practice to redefine the syntax of the underlying language in such a manner. Plus, it makes it harder for someone else to understand your code.

To make things even more interesting, a defined value can itself reference another defined value. So, the two defines

```
#define PI      3.141592654
#define TWO_PI  2.0 * PI
```

are perfectly valid. The name TWO_PI is defined in terms of the previously defined name PI, thus obviating the need to spell out the value 3.141592654 again.

Reversing the order of the defines, as in

```
#define TWO_PI  2.0 * PI
#define PI      3.141592654
```

is also valid. The rule is that you can reference other defined values in your definitions provided everything is defined at the time the defined name is used in the program.

Good use of defines often reduces the need for comments within the program. Consider the following statement:

```
if ( year % 4 == 0 && year % 100 != 0 || year % 400 == 0 )
  ...
```

This expression tests whether the variable year is a leap year. Now, consider the following define and the subsequent if statement:

```
#define IS_LEAP_YEAR  year % 4 == 0 && year % 100 != 0 \
                || year % 400 == 0
  ...
if ( IS_LEAP_YEAR )
  ...
```

Normally, the preprocessor assumes that a definition is contained on a single line of the program. If a second line is needed, the last character on the line must be a backslash character. This character signals a continuation to the preprocessor and is otherwise ignored. The same holds true for more than one continuation line; each line to be continued must be ended with a backslash character.

The preceding if statement is far easier to understand than the one shown directly before it. No comment is needed because the statement is self-explanatory. Of course, the definition restricts you to testing the variable year to see whether it's a leap year. If would be nice if you could write a definition to see whether any year were a leap year and not just the variable year. Actually, you can write a definition to take one or more arguments, which leads us to our next point of discussion.

IS_LEAP_YEAR can be defined to take an argument called y as follows:

```
#define IS_LEAP_YEAR(y)  y % 4 == 0 && y % 100 != 0 \
                || y % 400 == 0
```

Unlike a method definition, you do not define the type of the argument y here because you are merely performing a literal text substitution and not calling a function.

Note that when defining a name with arguments, no spaces are permitted between the defined name and the left parenthesis of the argument list.

With the previous definition, you can write a statement such as follows:

```
if ( IS_LEAP_YEAR (year) )
  ...
```

This tests whether the value of year is a leap year. Or, you could write

```
if ( IS_LEAP_YEAR (nextYear) )
  ...
```

to test whether the value of nextYear is a leap year. In the preceding statement, the definition for IS_LEAP_YEAR is directly substituted inside the if statement, with the argument nextYear replacing y wherever it appears in the definition. So, the if statement would actually be seen by the compiler as follows:

```
if ( nextYear % 4 == 0 && nextYear % 100 != 0 || nextYear % 400 == 0 )
  ...
```

Definitions are frequently called *macros*. This terminology is more often applied to definitions that take one or more arguments.

Here's a macro called SQUARE that simply squares its argument:

```
#define SQUARE(x) x * x
```

Although the macro definition for SQUARE is straightforward, there is an interesting pitfall that you must be careful to avoid when defining macros. As we have described, the statement

```
y = SQUARE (v);
```

assigns the value of v^2 to y. What do you think would happen in the case of the statement

```
y = SQUARE (v + 1);
```

This statement does *not* assign the value of $(v + 1)^2$ to y as you would expect. Because the preprocessor performs a literal text substitution of the argument into the macro definition, the preceding expression is actually evaluated as follows:

```
y = v + 1 * v + 1;
```

This obviously does not produce the expected results. To handle this situation properly, parentheses are needed in the definition of the SQUARE macro:

```
#define SQUARE(x)  ( (x) * (x) )
```

Even though the previous definition might look strange, remember that it is the entire expression as given to the SQUARE macro that is literally substituted wherever x appears in the definition. With your new macro definition for SQUARE, the statement

```
y = SQUARE (v + 1);
```

is then correctly evaluated as

```
y = ( (v + 1) * (v + 1) );
```

The following macro lets you to easily create new fractions from your Fraction class "on-the-fly":

```
#define MakeFract(x,y) ([[Fraction alloc] initWith: x over: y]])
```

Then you can write expressions such as

```
myFract = MakeFract (1, 3);  // Make the fraction 1/3
```

or even

```
sum = [MakeFract (n1, d1) add: MakeFract (n2, d2)];
```

to add the fractions n1/d1 and n2/d2 together.

The conditional expression operator can be particularly handy when defining macros. The following defines a macro called MAX that gives the maximum of two values:

```
#define MAX(a,b)  ( ((a) > (b)) ? (a) : (b) )
```

This macro enables you to subsequently write statements such as this:

```
limit = MAX (x + y, minValue);
```

This assigns to limit the maximum of x + y and minValue. Parentheses are placed around the entire MAX definition to ensure that an expression such as

```
MAX (x, y) * 100
```

is evaluated properly; and parentheses are individually placed around each argument to ensure that expressions such as the following are correctly evaluated:

```
MAX (x & y, z)
```

The & operator is the bitwise AND operator, and it has lower precedence than the > operator used in the macro. Without the parentheses in the macro definition, the > operator would be evaluated before the bitwise AND, producing the incorrect result.

The following macro tests whether a character is a lowercase letter:

```
#define IS_LOWER_CASE(x) ( ((x) >= 'a') && ((x) <= 'z') )
```

It thereby permits expressions such as

```
if ( IS_LOWER_CASE (c) )
    ...
```

to be written. You can even use this macro in another macro definition to convert a character from lowercase to uppercase, leaving any nonlowercase character unchanged:

```
#define TO_UPPER(x) ( IS_LOWER_CASE (x) ? (x) - 'a' + 'A' : (x) )
```

Again, you are dealing with a standard ASCII character set here. When you learn about Foundation string objects in Part II, you'll see how to perform case conversion that will work for international (Unicode) character sets as well.

The # Operator

If you place a # in front of a parameter in a macro definition, the preprocessor creates a constant C-style string out of the macro argument when the macro is invoked. For example, the definition

```
#define str(x)   # x
```

causes the subsequent invocation

```
str (testing)
```

to be expanded into

```
"testing"
```

by the preprocessor. The `printf` call

```
printf (str (Programming in Objective-C is fun.\n));
```

is therefore equivalent to

```
printf ("Programming in Objective-C is fun.\n");
```

The preprocessor literally inserts double quotation marks around the actual macro argument. Any double quotation marks or backslashes in the argument are preserved by the preprocessor. So

```
str ("hello")
```

produces

```
"\"hello\""
```

A more practical example of the use of the # operator might be in the following macro definition:

```
#define printint(var)  printf (# var " = %i\n", var)
```

This macro is used to display the value of an integer variable. If `count` is an integer variable with a value of `100`, the statement

```
printint (count);
```

is expanded into

```
printf ("count" " = %i\n", count);
```

The compiler concatenates two adjacent literal strings together to make a single string out of them. Therefore, after concatenation is performed on the two adjacent strings, the statement becomes the following:

```
printf ("count = %i\n", count);
```

The ## Operator

This operator is used in macro definitions to join two tokens together. It is preceded (or followed) by the name of a parameter to the macro. The preprocessor takes the actual argument to the macro that is supplied when the macro is invoked and creates a single token out of that argument and whatever token follows (or precedes) the ##.

Suppose, for example, you have a list of variables x1 through x100. You can write a macro called printx that simply takes as its argument an integer value 1–100 and displays the corresponding x variable as shown here:

```
#define printx(n)   printf ("%i\n", x ## n)
```

The portion of the define that reads

```
x ## n
```

says to take the tokens that occur before and after the ## (the letter x and the argument n, respectively) and make a single token out of them. So the call

```
printx (20);
```

is expanded into the following:

```
printf ("%i\n", x20);
```

The printx macro can even use the previously defined printint macro to get the variable name as well as its value displayed:

```
#define printx(n)   printint(x ## n)
```

The invocation

```
printx (10);
```

first expands into

```
printint (x10);
```

and then into

```
printf ("x10" " = %i\n", x10);
```

and finally into the following:

```
printf ("x10 = %i\n", x10);
```

The #import and #include Statements

After you have programmed in Objective-C for a while, you will find yourself developing your own set of macros, which you will want to use in each of your programs. But instead of having to type these macros into each new program you write, the preprocessor enables you to collect all your definitions into a separate file and then include them in your program, using the #import statement. These files—similar to the ones you've previously encountered but haven't written yourself—normally end with the characters .h and are referred to as *header* or *include* files.

The #include statement can also be used to include the contents of a file into your program. The difference is that using #import guarantees that the file is included only once in your program and not multiple times, which frequently causes compiler errors. This can happen inadvertently—for example, when you include a class definition header file in your program. That header file likely includes its own header files, some of which can overlap with previously included files When #include is used instead of #import, the file is included at that point in the program, whether it has been previously included or not.[1] You can work around this when using #include, and we'll talk about that later in this chapter.

Suppose you were writing a series of programs for performing various metric conversions. You might want to set up some defines for the various constants you would need for performing your conversions:

```
#define INCHES_PER_CENTIMETER   0.394
#define CENTIMETERS_PER_INCH   (1 / INCHES_PER_CENTIMETER)

#define QUARTS_PER_LITER        1.057
#define LITERS_PER_QUART       (1 / QUARTS_PER_LITER)

#define OUNCES_PER_GRAM         0.035
#define GRAMS_PER_OUNCE        (1 / OUNCES_PER_GRAM)
    . . .
```

Suppose you entered the previous definitions into a separate file on the system called metric.h. Any program that subsequently needed to use any of the definitions contained in the metric.h file could then do so by simply issuing the preprocessor directive:

```
#import "metric.h"
```

This statement must appear before any of the defines contained in metric.h are referenced and is typically placed at the beginning of the source file. The preprocessor looks for the specified file on the system and effectively copies the contents of the file into the program at the precise point at which the #import statement appears. So, any statements inside the file are treated just as if they had been directly typed into the program at that point.

The double quotation marks around the header filename instruct the preprocessor to look for the specified file in one or more file directories (typically, first in the same directory that contains the source file, but the actual places the preprocessor searches are

---

1. GNU advocates do not encourage use of the #import and claim its support might be phased out. Apple uses the #import directive extensively and will likely continue supporting it into the future. Because #import enables a programmer to more easily avoid accidental multiple inclusion of a file and thus reduce the chance of errors, we've chosen to adopt that method in this text for the inclusion of files.

system dependent). If the file isn't located, the preprocessor automatically searches other special directories as described in the following.

Enclosing the filename within the characters < and > instead, as in

```
#import <stdio.h>
```

causes the preprocessor to look for the include file in the special "system" header file directory or directories. Once again, these directories are system dependent. On Unix (including Mac OS X) systems, the system include file directory is /usr/include. So, on those systems the standard header file objc/Object.h is found in /usr/include/objc/Object.h.

To see how include files are used in an actual program example, type the six defines given previously into a file called metric.h. Then type and run Program 12.1 in the normal manner.

Program 12.1

```
/* Illustrate the use of the #import statement
   Note: This program assumes that definitions are
   set up in a file called metric.h        */

#import "metric.h"

main ()
{
   float liters, gallons;

   printf ("*** Liters to Gallons ***\n\n");
   printf ("Enter the number of liters: ");
   scanf ("%f", &liters);

   gallons = liters * QUARTS_PER_LITER / 4.0;
   printf ("%g liters = %g gallons\n", liters, gallons);
}
```

Program 12.1   **Output**

```
*** Liters to Gallons ***

Enter the number of liters: 55.75
55.75 liters = 14.7319 gallons.
```

Program 12.1 is a rather simple one because it shows only a single defined value (QUARTS_PER_LITER) being referenced from the include file metric.h. Nevertheless, the point is well made: After the definitions have been entered into metric.h, they can be used in any program that uses an appropriate #import statement.

One of the nicest things about the import file capability is that it enables you to centralize your definitions, thus ensuring that all programs reference the same value. Furthermore, errors discovered in one of the values contained in the include file need be corrected in only that one spot, thus eliminating the need to correct each and every program that uses the value. Any program that referenced the incorrect value would simply have to be recompiled and would not have to be edited.

Besides `stdio.h` and `objc/Object.h`, two other useful system include files are `limits.h` and `float.h`. The first file, `limits.h`, contains system-dependent values that specify the sizes of various character and integer data types.[2] For instance, the maximum size of an `int` is defined by the name `INT_MAX` inside this file. The maximum size of an `unsigned long int` is defined by `ULONG_MAX`, and so on.

The `float.h` header file gives information about floating-point data types. For example, `FLT_MAX` specifies the maximum floating-point number, and `FLT_DIG` specifies the number of decimal digits of precision for a `float` type.

Other system include files contain declarations for various functions stored inside the system library. For example, the include file `string.h` contains declarations for the library routines that perform character string operations such as copying, comparing, and concatenating. If you're working with the Foundation string classes exclusively (discussed in Chapter 15, "Numbers, Strings, and Collections"), you probably won't need to use any of these routines in your programs.

Conditional Compilation

The Objective-C preprocessor offers a feature known as *conditional compilation*. Conditional compilation is often used to create one program that can be compiled to run on different computer systems. It is also often used to switch on or off various statements in the program, such as debugging statements that print the values of variables or trace the flow of program execution.

The `#ifdef`, `#endif`, `#else`, and `#ifndef` Statements

Unfortunately, a program sometimes must rely on system-dependent parameters—on a filename, for example—that can be specified differently on different systems or on a particular feature of the operating system.

If you had a large program that had many such dependencies on the particular hardware and/or software of the computer system (and this should be minimized as much as possible), you might end up with many defines whose values would have to be changed when the program was moved to another computer system.

You can help reduce the problem of having to change these defines when the program is moved and can incorporate into the program the values of these defines for each

---

2. With gcc implementations, these values are not specified directly in `limits.h` but in a header file that is included by `limits.h`.

different machine by using the conditional compilation capabilities of the preprocessor. As a simple example, the statements

```
#ifdef UNIX
#  define DATADIR  "/uxn1/data"
#else
#  define DATADIR  "\usr\data"
#endif
```

have the effect of defining `DATADIR` to `"/uxn1/data"` if the symbol `UNIX` has been previously defined and to `"\usr\data"` otherwise. As you can see here, you are allowed to put one or more spaces after the # that begins a preprocessor statement.

The `#ifdef`, `#else`, and `#endif` statements behave as you would expect. If the symbol specified on the `#ifdef` line has been already defined—through a `#define` statement or through the command line when the program is compiled—lines that follow up to a `#else`, `#elif`, or `#endif` are processed by the compiler; otherwise, they are ignored.

To define the symbol `UNIX` to the preprocessor, the statement

```
#define UNIX  1
```

or even just

```
#define UNIX
```

will suffice. As you can see, no text at all has to appear after the defined name to satisfy the `#ifdef` test. The compiler also permits you to define a name to the preprocessor when the program is compiled by using a special option to the compiler command. The command line

```
gcc -D UNIX program.m -lobjc
```

defines the name `UNIX` to the preprocessor, causing all `#ifdef UNIX` statements inside `program.m` to evaluate as `TRUE` (note that the `-D UNIX` must be typed before the program name on the command line). This technique enables names to be defined without having to edit the source program.

A value can also be assigned to the defined name on the command line. For example

```
gcc -D GNUDIR=/c/gnustep program.m
```

invokes the compiler on the file `program.m`, defining the name `GNUDIR` to be the text `/c/gnustep`.

The `#ifndef` statement follows along the same lines as the `#ifdef`. This statement is used in a similar way, except it causes the subsequent lines to be processed if the indicated symbol is *not* defined. This statement is often used to avoid multiple inclusion of a file in a program, and it is the method recommended by GNU developers as the way around use of the `#import` statement.

For example, inside a header file you want to include just once in a program, you typically define a unique identifier that can be tested later. Consider this sequence of statements:

```
#ifndef _OBJC_OBJECT_H_
#define _OBJC_OBJECT_H_
...
#endif /* _OBJC_OBJECT_H */
```

Suppose you typed this into a file called `obj.h`.

If you included this file in your program with an `#include` statement, such as

```
#include "obj.h"
```

The `#ifndef` would test whether `OBJC_OBJECT_H` were defined. Because it wouldn't be, the lines between the `#ifndef` and the matching `#endif` would be included in the program. Notice that the very next line defines `_OBJC_OBJECT_H`. If an attempt were made to again include the file in the program, `_OBJC_OBJECT_H` would be defined, so the statements that followed would not be included in the program, thus avoiding multiple inclusion of the header file in the program.

The lines shown previously are actually from the standard header file `<objc/Object.h>`. So, if you did use `#include` instead of `#import` in your program, you could do so without worrying about duplicate inclusion of the file.

As already mentioned, conditional compilation is useful when debugging programs. You might have many `printf` calls embedded in your program that are used to display intermediate results and trace the flow of execution. These statements can be turned on by conditionally compiling them into the program if a particular name, say `DEBUG`, is defined. For example, a sequence of statements such as the following could be used to display the value of some variables only if the program had been compiled with the name `DEBUG` defined:

```
#ifdef DEBUG
  printf ("User name = %s, id = %i\n", userName, userId);
#endif
```

You might have many such debugging statements throughout the program. Whenever the program is being debugged, it can be compiled with the `-D DEBUG` command-line option to·have all the debugging statements compiled. When the program is working correctly, it can be recompiled without the `-D` option. This also has the added benefit of reducing the size of the program because all your debugging statements are not compiled in.

The `#if` and `#elif` Preprocessor Statements

The `#if` preprocessor statement offers a more general way of controlling conditional compilation. The `#if` statement can be used to test whether a constant expression evaluates to nonzero. If the result of the expression is nonzero, subsequent lines up to a `#else`, `#elif`, or `#endif` are processed; otherwise, they are skipped. As an example of how this can be used, assume you define the name `OS`, which is set to `1` if the operating system is Macintosh OS, to `2` if the operating system is Windows, to `3` if the operating system is Unix, and so on. You could write a sequence of statements to conditionally compile statements based on the value of OS as follows:

```
#if  OS == 1 /* Mac OS */
 ...
#elif OS == 2 /* Windows */
 ...
#elif OS == 3 /* Unix */
 ...
#else
 ...
#endif
```

With most compilers, you can assign a value to the name OS on the command line using the -D option discussed earlier. The command line

```
gcc -D OS=2 program.m -lobjc
```

compiles program.m with the name OS defined as 2. This causes the program to be compiled to run under Windows.

The special operator

```
defined (name)
```

can also be used in #if statements. The set of preprocessor statements

```
#if defined (DEBUG)
 ...
#endif
```

and

```
#ifdef DEBUG
 ...
#endif
```

do the same thing. The statements

```
#if defined (WINDOWS) || defined (WINDOWSNT)
# define BOOT_DRIVE "C:/"
#else
# define BOOT_DRIVE "D:/"
#endif
```

define BOOT_DRIVE as "C:/" if either WINDOWS or WINDOWSNT is defined and define it as "D:/" otherwise.

Another common use of #if is in code sequences that look like this:

```
#if defined (DEBUG) && DEBUG
 ...
#endif
```

This causes the statements after the #if and up to the #endif to be processed only if DEBUG is defined and has a nonzero value.

The #undef Statement

On some occasions, you might need to cause a defined name to become undefined. This is done with the #undef statement. To remove the definition of a particular name, you write the following:

```
#undef name
```

Thus, the statement

```
#undef LINUX
```

removes the definition of LINUX. Subsequent #ifdef LINUX or #if defined (LINUX) statements evaluate to FALSE.

This concludes our discussion on the preprocessor. Some other preprocessor statements that weren't described here are described in Appendix B, "Objective-C Language Summary."

Exercises

1. Locate the system header files stdio.h, limits.h, and float.h on your machine (on Unix systems, look inside the /usr/include directory). Examine the files to see what's in them. If these files include other header files, be sure to track them down as well to examine their contents.

2. Define a macro called MIN that gives the minimum of two values. Then write a program to test the macro definition.

3. Define a macro called MAX3 that gives the maximum of three values. Write a program to test the definition.

4. Write a macro called IS_UPPER_CASE that gives a nonzero value if a character is an uppercase letter.

5. Write a macro called IS_ALPHABETIC that gives a nonzero value if a character is an alphabetic character. Have the macro use the IS_LOWER_CASE macro defined in the chapter text and the IS_UPPER_CASE macro defined in exercise 4.

6. Write a macro called IS_DIGIT that gives a nonzero value if a character is a digit '0' through '9'. Use this macro in the definition of another macro called IS_SPECIAL, which gives a nonzero result if a character is a special character— that is, not alphabetic and not a digit. Be sure to use the IS_ALPHABETIC macro developed in exercise 5.

7. Write a macro called ABSOLUTE_VALUE that computes the absolute value of its argument. Make sure that an expression such as

```
ABSOLUTE_VALUE (x + delta)
```

is properly evaluated by the macro.

8. Consider the definition of the printint macro from this chapter:

```
#define printx(n)  printf ("%i\n", x ## n)
```

Could the following be used to display the values of the 100 variables x1–x100? Why or why not?

```
for ( i = 1; i <= 100; ++i )
   printx (i);
```

13

Underlying C Language Features

THIS CHAPTER DESCRIBES FEATURES OF THE Objective-C language that you don't necessarily need to know to write Objective-C programs. In fact, most of these come from the underlying C programming language. Features such as functions, structures, pointers, unions, and arrays are best learned on a need-to-know basis. Because C is a procedural language, some of these features go against the grain of object-oriented programming. They can also interfere with some of the strategies implemented by the Foundation framework, such as the memory allocation methodology or working with character strings containing multibyte characters.[1]

On the other hand, some applications can require you to use a lower-level approach, perhaps for the sake of optimization. If you're working with large arrays of data for example, you might want to use Objective-C's built-in array data structures rather than Foundation's array objects (which are described in Chapter 15, "Numbers, Strings, and Collections"). Functions can also come in handy if used properly to group repetitive operations together and modularize a program.

It is recommended that you just skim through this chapter to get an overview of the material and come back after you've finished reading Part II, "The Foundation Framework." Or you can skip it all together and go on to Part II, which covers the Foundation framework. If you end up supporting someone else's code or start digging through some of the Foundation framework header files, you will encounter some of the constructs covered in this chapter. Several of the Foundation data types, such as `NSRange`, `NSPoint`, and `NSRect`, require a rudimentary understanding of structures, which are described here. In such cases, you can return to this chapter and read the appropriate section to gain an understanding of the concepts.

---

1. There are ways to work with multibyte characters at the Objective-C level, but Foundation provides a much more elegant solution with its `NSString` class.

Arrays

The Objective-C language provides a capability that enables the user to define a set of ordered data items known as an *array*. This section describes how arrays can be defined and manipulated. In later sections, we'll include further discussions on arrays to illustrate how they work together with functions, structures, character strings, and pointers.

Suppose you had a set of grades that you wanted to read into the computer, and suppose that you wanted to perform some operations on these grades, such as rank them in ascending order, compute their average, or find their median. If you think about the process of ranking a set of grades, you will quickly realize that you cannot perform such an operation until each and every grade has been entered.

In Objective-C, you can define a variable called `grades`, which represents not a single value of a grade but an entire set of grades. Each element of the set can then be referenced by means of a number called an *index* number, or *subscript*. Whereas in mathematics a subscripted variable, x_i, refers to the *i*th element *x* in a set, in Objective-C the equivalent notation is this:

```
x[i]
```

So, the expression

```
grades[5]
```

(read as "grades sub 5") refers to element number 5 in the array called `grades`. In Objective-C, array elements begin with the number 0, so

```
grades[0]
```

actually refers to the first element of the array.

An individual array element can be used anywhere that a normal variable can be. For example, you can assign an array value to another variable with a statement such as follows:

```
g = grades[50];
```

This statement takes the value contained in `grades[50]` and assigns it to `g`. More generally, if `i` is declared to be an integer variable, the statement

```
g = grades[i];
```

takes the value contained in element number `i` of the `grades` array and assigns it to `g`.

A value can be stored into an element of an array simply by specifying the array element on the left side of an equal sign. In the statement

```
grades[100] = 95;
```

the value 95 is stored into element number 100 of the `grades` array.

You can easily sequence through the elements in the array by varying the value of a variable that is used as a subscript into the array. Therefore, the `for` loop

```
for ( i = 0; i < 100; ++i )
  sum += grades[i];
```

sequences through the first 100 elements of the array `grades` (elements 0–99) and adds the value of each grade into `sum`. When the `for` loop is finished, the variable `sum` contains the total of the first 100 values of the `grades` array (assuming `sum` was set to 0 before the loop was entered).

Just as with other types of variables, arrays must also be declared before they are used. The declaration of an array involves declaring the type of element that will be contained in the array, such as `int`, `float`, or an object, as well as the maximum number of elements that will be stored inside the array.

The definition

```
Fraction *fracts [100];
```

defines `fracts` to be an array containing 100 fractions. Valid references to this array can be made by using subscripts 0–99.

The expression

```
fracts[2] = [fracts[0] add: fracts[1]];
```

invokes the `Fraction`'s `add:` method to add the first two fractions from the `fracts` array and stores the result in the third location of the array.

Program 13.1 generates a table of the first 15 Fibonacci numbers. Try to predict its output. What relationship exists between each number in the table?

Program 13.1

```
// Program to generate the first 15 Fibonacci numbers
#import <stdio.h>

int main (int argc, char *argv[])
{
  int Fibonacci[15], i;

  Fibonacci[0] = 0;  /* by definition */
  Fibonacci[1] = 1;  /*   ditto   */

  for ( i = 2; i < 15; ++i )
     Fibonacci[i] = Fibonacci[i-2] + Fibonacci[i-1];

  for ( i = 0; i < 15; ++i )
     printf ("%i\n", Fibonacci[i]);

  return 0;
}
```

Program 13.1   **Output**

```
0
1
1
2
3
5
8
13
21
34
55
89
144
233
377
```

The first two Fibonacci numbers, which we will call F_0 and F_1, are defined to be 0 and 1, respectively. Thereafter, each successive Fibonacci number F_i is defined to be the sum of the two preceding Fibonacci numbers F_{i-2} and F_{i-1}. So, F_2 is calculated by adding the values of F_0 and F_1. In the preceding program, this corresponds directly to calculating Fibonacci[2] by adding the values Fibonacci[0] and Fibonacci[1]. This calculation is performed inside the for loop, which calculates the values of F_2–F_{14} (or, equivalently, Fibonacci[2] through Fibonacci[14]).

Initializing Array Elements

Just as you can assign initial values to variables when they are declared, you can also assign initial values to the elements of an array. This is done by simply listing the initial values of the array, starting from the first element. Values in the list are separated by commas and the entire list is enclosed in a pair of braces.

The statement

```
int integers[5] = { 0, 1, 2, 3, 4 };
```

sets the value of integers[0] to 0, integers[1] to 1, integers[2] to 2, and so on.

Arrays of characters are initialized in a similar manner; thus the statement

```
char letters[5] = { 'a', 'b', 'c', 'd', 'e' };
```

defines the character array letters and initializes the five elements to the characters 'a', 'b', 'c', 'd', and 'e', respectively.

You don't have to completely initialize an entire array. If fewer initial values are specified, only an equal number of elements are initialized and the remaining values in the array are set to zero. Thus, the declaration

```
float sample_data[500] = { 100.0, 300.0, 500.5 };
```

initializes the first three values of `sample_data` to `100.0`, `300.0`, and `500.5` and sets the remaining 497 elements to 0.

By enclosing an element number in a pair of brackets, specific array elements can be initialized in any order. For example

```
int x = 1233;
int a[] = { [9] = x + 1, [2] = 3, [1] = 2, [0] = 1 };
```

defines a 10-element array called a (based on the highest index into the array) and initializes the last element to the value of x + 1 (`1234`). In addition, it initializes the first three elements to 1, 2, and 3, respectively.

Character Arrays

The purpose of Program 13.2 is to simply illustrate how a character array can be used. However, there is one point worthy of discussion. Can you spot it?

Program 13.2

```
#import <stdio.h>

int main (int argc, char *argv[])
{
  char word[] - { 'H', 'e', 'l', 'l', 'o', '!' };
  int  i;

  for ( i = 0; i < 6; ++i )
        printf ("%c", word[i]);

  printf ("\n");
  return 0;
}
```

Program 13.2   Output

```
Hello!
```

The most notable point in the preceding program is the declaration of the character array word. There is no mention of the number of elements in the array. The Objective-C language enables you to define an array without specifying the number of elements. If this is done, the size of the array is determined automatically based on the number of initialization elements. Because Program 13.2 has six initial values listed for the array word, the Objective-C language implicitly dimensions the array to six elements.

This approach works fine as long as you initialize every element in the array at the point that the array is defined. If this is not to be the case, you must explicitly dimension the array.

If you put a terminating null character (`'\0'`) at the end of a character array, you create what is often-called a *character string*. If you substituted the initialization of word in Program 13.2 with this line

```
char word[] = { 'H', 'e', 'l', 'l', 'o', '!', '\0' };
```

you could have subsequently displayed the string with a single `printf` call, like this:

```
printf ("%s\n", word);
```

This works because the `%s` format characters tell `printf` to keep displaying characters until a terminating null character is reached. That's the character you put at the end of your word array.

Multidimensional Arrays

The types of arrays you've seen thus far are all linear arrays—that is, they all deal with a single dimension. The language enables arrays of any dimension to be defined. This section takes a look at two-dimensional arrays.

One of the most natural applications for a two-dimensional array arises in the case of a matrix. Consider the 4×5 matrix shown here:

10	5	−3	17	82
9	0	0	8	−7
32	20	1	0	14
0	0	8	7	6

In mathematics, it is common to refer to an element of a matrix by using a double subscript. If the preceding matrix was called M, the notation $M_{i,j}$ would refer to the element in the ith row, jth column, where i ranges from 1 through 4 and j ranges from 1 through 5. The notation $M_{3,2}$ would refer to the value 20, which is found in the third row, second column of the matrix. In a similar fashion, $M_{4,5}$ would refer to the element contained in the fourth row, fifth column (the value 6).

In Objective-C, an analogous notation is used when referring to elements of a two-dimensional array. However, because Objective-C likes to start numbering things at 0, the first row of the matrix is actually row 0 and the first column of the matrix is column 0. The preceding matrix would then have row and column designations as shown in the following diagram:

Row (i)   Column (j)

	0	1	2	3	4
0	10	5	−3	17	82
1	9	0	0	8	−7
2	32	20	1	0	14
3	0	0	8	7	6

Whereas in mathematics the notation $M_{i,j}$ is used, in Objective-C the equivalent notation is as follows:

```
M[i][j]
```

Remember, the first index number refers to the row number, whereas the second index number references the column. The statement

```
sum = M[0][2] + M[2][4];
```

therefore adds the value contained in row 0, column 2 (which is -3) to the value contained in row 2, column 4 (which is 14) and assigns the result of 11 to the variable sum.

Two-dimensional arrays are declared the same way that one-dimensional arrays are; thus

```
int M[4][5];
```

declares the array M to be a two-dimensional array consisting of 4 rows and 5 columns, for a total of 20 elements. Each position in the array is defined to contain an integer value.

Two-dimensional arrays can be initialized in a manner analogous to their one-dimensional counterparts. When listing elements for initialization, the values are listed by row. Brace pairs are used to separate the list of initializers for one row from the next. Thus, to define and initialize the array M to the elements listed in the preceding table, a statement such as the following could be used:

```
int M[4][5] = {
            { 10, 5, -3, 17, 82 },
            { 9, 0, 0, 8, -7 },
            { 32, 20, 1, 0, 14 },
            { 0, 0, 8, 7, 6 }
    };
```

Pay particular attention to the syntax of the previous statement. Note that commas are required after each brace that closes off a row, except in the case of the last row. The use of the inner pairs of braces is actually optional. If it's not supplied, initialization proceeds by row. Therefore, the previous statement could also have been written as follows:

```
int M[4][5] = { 10, 5, -3, 17, 82, 9, 0, 0, 8, -7, 32,
            20, 1, 0, 14, 0, 0, 8, 7, 6 };
```

As with one-dimensional arrays, the entire array need not be initialized. A statement such as

```
int M[4][5] = {
            { 10, 5, -3 },
            { 9, 0, 0 },
            { 32, 20, 1 },
            { 0, 0, 8 }
    };
```

initializes only the first three elements of each row of the matrix to the indicated values. The remaining values are set to 0. Note that, in this case, the inner pairs of braces are required to force the correct initialization. Without them, the first two rows and the first two elements of the third row would have been initialized instead. (Verify for yourself that this would be the case.)

Functions

The printf routine is an example of a function that you have used in every program so far. Indeed, each and every program also has used a function called main. Let's go back to the very first program you wrote (Program 2.1), which displayed the phrase Programming is fun. at the terminal:

```
#import <stdio.h>
int main (int argc, char *argv[])
{
    printf ("Programming is fun.\n");
    return 0;
}
```

Here is a function called printMessage that produces the same output:

```
void printMessage (void)
{
    printf ("Programming is fun.\n");
}
```

The only difference between printMessage and the function main from Program 2.1 is in the first line. The first line of a function definition tells the compiler four things about the function:

- Who can call it
- The type of value it returns
- Its name
- The number and type of arguments it takes

The first line of the printMessage function definition tells the compiler that printMessage is the name of the function and that it returns no value (the first use of the keyword void). Unlike methods, you don't put the function's return type inside a set of parentheses. In fact, you'll get a compiler error message if you do!

After telling the compiler that printMessage doesn't return a value, the second use of the keyword void says that it takes no arguments.

You will recall that main is a specially recognized name in the Objective-C system that always indicates where the program is to begin execution. There always must be a main. So, you can add a main function to the preceding code to end up with a complete program, as shown in Program 13.3.

Program 13.3

```
#import <stdio.h>
void printMessage (void)
{
        printf ("Programming is fun.\n");
}


int main (int argc, char *argv[])
{
        printMessage ();
        return 0;
}
```

Program 13.3 **Output**

```
Programming is fun.
```

Program 13.3 consists of two functions: `printMessage` and `main`. As mentioned earlier, the idea of calling a function is not new. Because `printMessage` takes no arguments, you call it simply by listing its name followed by a pair of open and close parentheses.

Arguments and Local Variables

In Chapter 5, "Program Looping," you developed programs for calculating triangular numbers. Here you'll define a function to generate a triangular number and call it, appropriately enough, `calculateTriangularNumber`. As an argument to the function, you'll specify which triangular number to calculate. The function will then calculate the desired number and display the results at the terminal. Program 13.4 shows the function to accomplish the task and a `main` routine to try it.

Program 13.4

```
#import <stdio.h>
// Function to calculate the nth triangular number

void calculateTriangularNumber (int n)
{
   int i, triangularNumber = 0;

   for ( i = 1; i <= n; ++i )
       triangularNumber += i;

   printf ("Triangular number %i is %i\n", n, triangularNumber);
}
```

Program 13.4 **Continued**

```
int main (int argc, char *argv[])
{
    calculateTriangularNumber (10);
    calculateTriangularNumber (20);
    calculateTriangularNumber (50);
    return 0;
}
```

Program 13.4 **Output**

```
Triangular number 10 is 55
Triangular number 20 is 210
Triangular number 50 is 1275
```

The first line of the `calculateTriangularNumber` function is

```
void calculateTriangularNumber (int n)
```

and it tells the compiler that `calculateTriangularNumber` is a function that returns no value (the keyword `void`) and that it takes a single argument, called n, which is an `int`. Note again that you can't put the argument type inside parentheses, as you are accustomed to doing when you write methods.

The beginning of the function's definition is indicated by the opening curly brace. Because you want to calculate the *n*th triangular number, you have to set up a variable to store the value of the triangular number as it is being calculated. You also need a variable to act as your loop index. The variables `TriangularNumber` and i are defined for these purposes and are declared to be of type `int`. These variables are defined and initialized in the same manner that you defined and initialized your variables inside the `main` routine in previous programs.

Local variables in functions behave the same way they do in methods: If an initial value is given to a variable inside a function, that initial value is assigned to the variable each time the function is called.

Variables defined inside a function (as in methods) are known as *automatic local* variables because they are automatically "created" each time the function is called and because their values are local to the function.

Static local variables are declared with the keyword `static`, retain their values through function calls, and have default initial values of 0.

The value of a local variable can be accessed only by the function in which the variable is defined. Its value cannot be accessed from outside the function.

Returning to our program example, after the local variables have been defined, the function calculates the triangular number and displays the results at the terminal. The closed brace then defines the end of the function.

Inside the main routine, the value 10 is passed as the argument in the first call to calculateTriangularNumber. Execution is then transferred directly to the function where the value 10 becomes the value of the formal parameter n inside the function. The function then calculates the value of the 10th triangular number and displays the result.

The next time that calculateTriangularNumber is called, the argument 20 is passed. In a similar process, as described earlier, this value becomes the value of n inside the function. The function then calculates the value of the 20th triangular number and displays the answer at the terminal.

Returning Function Results

As with methods, a function can return a value. The type of value returned with the return statement must be consistent with the return type declared for the function. A function declaration that starts like this

```
float kmh_to_mph (float km_speed)
```

begins the definition of a function kmh_to_mph, which takes one float argument called km_speed and returns a floating-point value. Similarly

```
int gcd (int u, int v)
```

defines a function called gcd with integer arguments u and v and returns an integer value.

Let's rewrite the greatest common divisor algorithm used in Program 5.7 in function form. The two arguments to the function are the two numbers whose greatest common divisor (gcd) you want to calculate (see Program 13.5).

Program 13.5

```
#import <stdio.h>
// This function finds the greatest common divisor of two
//  nonnegative integer values and returns the result

int gcd (int u, int v)
{
    int temp;

    while ( v != 0 )
    {
        temp = u % v;
        u = v;
        v = temp;
    }
```

Program 13.5   **Continued**

```
    return u;
}

main ()
{
    int result;

    result = gcd (150, 35);
    printf ("The gcd of 150 and 35 is %i\n", result);

    result = gcd (1026, 405);
    printf ("The gcd of 1026 and 405 is %i\n", result);

    printf ("The gcd of 83 and 240 is %i\n", gcd (83, 240));
    return 0;
}
```

Program 13.5   **Output**

```
The gcd of 150 and 35 is 5
The gcd of 1026 and 405 is 27
The gcd of 83 and 240 is 1
```

The function gcd is defined to take two integer arguments. The function refers to these arguments through their formal parameter names: u and v. After declaring the variable temp to be of type int, the program displays the values of the arguments u and v, together with an appropriate message at the terminal. The function then calculates and returns the greatest common divisor of the two integers.

The statement

```
result = gcd (150, 35);
```

says to call the function gcd with the arguments 150 and 35 and to store the value that is returned by this function into the variable result.

If the return type declaration for a function is omitted, the compiler assumes the function will return an integer—if it returns a value at all. Many programmers take advantage of this fact and omit the return type declaration for functions that return integers. This, however, is a bad programming habit that should be avoided.

The default return type for functions differs from that for methods. You'll recall that, if no return type is specified for a method, the compiler assumes it returns a value of type id. Once again, you should always declare the return type for a method and not rely on this fact.

Declaring Return Types and Argument Types

We mentioned earlier that the Objective-C compiler assumes that a function returns a value of type `int` as the default case. More specifically, whenever a call is made to a function, the compiler assumes that the function returns a value of type `int` unless either of the following has occurred:

- The function has been defined in the program before the function call is encountered.

- The value returned by the function has been declared before the function call is encountered. Declaring the return and argument types for a function is known as a *prototype* declaration.

Not only is the function declaration used to declare the function's return type, but it is also used to tell the compiler how many arguments the function takes and what their types are. This is analogous to declaring methods inside the `@interface` section when defining a new class.

To declare `absoluteValue` as a function that returns a value of type `float` and that takes a single argument, also of type `float`, you could use the following prototype declaration:

```
float absoluteValue (float);
```

As you can see, you just have to specify the argument type inside the parentheses, and not its name. You can optionally specify a "dummy" name after the type if you like:

```
float absoluteValue (float x);
```

This name doesn't have to be the same as the one used in the function definition—the compiler ignores it anyway.

A foolproof way to write a prototype declaration is to simply use your text editor to make a copy of the first line from the actual definition of the function. Remember to place a semicolon at the end.

If the function takes a variable number of arguments (such as is the case with `printf` and `scanf`), the compiler must be informed. The declaration

```
int printf (char *format, ...);
```

tells the compiler that `printf` takes a character pointer as its first argument (more on that later) and is followed by any number of additional arguments (the use of the `...`). `printf` and `scanf` are declared in the special file `stdio.h`, which is why you have been placing the following line at the start of each of your programs:

```
#import <stdio.h>
```

Without this line, the compiler can assume `printf` takes a fixed number of arguments, which can result in incorrect code being generated.

The compiler automatically converts your numeric arguments to the appropriate types when a function is called only if you have placed the function's definition or have declared the function and its argument types before the call.

Here are some reminders and suggestions about functions:

- By default, the compiler assumes that a function returns an `int`.
- When defining a function that returns an `int`, define it as such.
- When defining a function that doesn't return a value, define it as `void`.
- The compiler converts your arguments to agree with the ones the function expects only if you have previously defined or declared the function.

To be safe, declare all functions in your program, even if they are defined before they are called. (You might decide later to move them someplace else in your file or even to another file.) A good strategy is to put your function declarations inside a header file and then just import that file into your modules.

Functions are *external* by default. That is, the default scope for a function is that it can be called by any functions or methods contained in any files that are linked together with the function. You can limit the scope of a function by making it static. You do this by placing the keyword `static` in front of the function declaration, as shown here:

```
static int gcd (int u, int v)
{
   ...
}
```

A static function can be called only by other functions or methods that appear in the same file that contains the function's definition.

Functions, Methods, and Arrays

To pass a single array element to a function or method, the array element is specified as an argument in the normal fashion. So, if you had a `squareRoot` function to calculate square roots and wanted to take the square root of `averages[i]` and assign the result to a variable called `sq_root_result`, a statement such as this one would work:

```
sq_root_result = squareRoot (averages[i]);
```

Passing an entire array to a function or method is an entirely new ball game. To pass an array, you only need to list the name of the array, without any subscripts, inside the call to the function or method invocation. As an example, if you assume that `grade_scores` has been declared as an array containing 100 elements, the expression

```
minimum (grade_scores)
```

in effect passes the entire 100 elements contained in the array `grade_scores` to the function called `minimum`. Naturally, on the other side of the coin, the `minimum` function must be expecting an entire array to be passed as an argument and must make the appropriate formal parameter declaration.

Here is a function that finds the minimum integer value in an array containing a specified number of elements:

```
// Function to find the minimum in an array

int minimum (int values[], int numElements)
{
    int minValue, i;

    minValue = values[0];

    for ( i = 1; i < numElements; ++i )
        if ( values[i] < minValue )
            minValue = values[i];

    return (minValue);
}
```

The function `minimum` is defined to take two arguments: first, the array whose minimum you want to find and, second, the number of elements in the array. The open and close brackets that immediately follow `values` in the function header serve to inform the Objective-C compiler that `values` is an array of integers. The compiler doesn't care how large it is.

The formal parameter `numElements` serves as the upper limit inside the `for` statement. Thus, the `for` statement sequences through the array from `values[1]` through the last element of the array, which is `values[numElements - 1]`.

If a function or method changes the value of an array element, that change is made to the original array that was passed to the function or method. This change remains in effect even after the function or method has completed execution.

The reason an array behaves differently from a simple variable or an array element—whose value cannot be changed by a function or method—is worthy of a bit of explanation. We stated that, when a function or method is called, the values passed as arguments are copied into the corresponding formal parameters. This statement is still valid. However, when dealing with arrays, the entire contents of the array are not copied into the formal parameter array. Instead, a pointer is passed indicating where in the computer's memory the array is located. So, any changes made to the formal parameter array are actually made to the original array and not to a copy of the array. Therefore, when the function or method returns, these changes still remain in effect.

Multidimensional Arrays

A multidimensional array element can be passed to a function or method just as any ordinary variable or single-dimensional array element can. The statement

```
result = squareRoot (matrix[i][j]);
```

calls the `squareRoot` function, passing the value contained in `matrix[i][j]` as the argument.

An entire multidimensional array can be passed as an argument the same way in which a single-dimensional array can: You simply list the name of the array. For example, if the matrix `measuredValues` is declared to be a two-dimensional array of integers, the Objective-C statement

```
scalarMultiply (measuredValues, constant);
```

could be used to invoke a function that multiplies each element in the matrix by the value of `constant`. This implies, of course, that the function itself can change the values contained inside the `measuredvalues` array. The discussion pertaining to this topic for single-dimensional arrays also applies here: An assignment made to any element of the formal parameter array inside the function makes a permanent change to the array that was passed to the function.

When declaring a single-dimensional array as a formal parameter, it was stated that the actual dimension of the array was not needed. It suffices to simply use a pair of empty brackets to inform the Objective-C compiler that the parameter is in fact an array. This does not totally apply in the case of multidimensional arrays. For a two-dimensional array, the number of rows in the array can be omitted but the declaration must contain the number of columns in the array. The declarations

```
int arrayValues[100][50]
```

and

```
int arrayValues[][50]
```

are both valid declarations for a formal parameter array called `arrayValues` containing 100 rows by 50 columns; but the declarations

```
int arrayValues[100][]
```

and

```
int arrayValues[][]
```

are not because the number of columns in the array must be specified.

Structures

The Objective-C language provides another tool for grouping elements together besides arrays. *Structures* can also be used, and they form the basis for the discussions in this section.

Suppose you wanted to store a date—say, 7/18/03—inside a program, perhaps to be used for the heading of some program output or even for computational purposes. A natural method for storing the date would be to simply assign the month to an integer variable called `month`, the day to an integer variable `day`, and the year to an integer variable `year`. So the statements

```
int month = 7, day = 18, year = 2003;
```

would work just fine. This is a totally acceptable approach. But what if your program also needed to store several dates? It would be much better if you could somehow group these sets of three variables together.

You can define a structure called `date` in the Objective-C language that consists of three components that represent the month, day, and year. The syntax for such a definition is rather straightforward, as shown by the following:

```
struct date
{
  int month;
  int day;
  int year;
};
```

The `date` structure just defined contains three integer members called `month`, `day`, and `year`. The definition of `date` in a sense defines a new type in the language in that variables can subsequently be declared to be of type `struct date`, as in the following definition:

```
struct date today;
```

You can also define a variable called `purchaseDate` to be of the same type by a separate definition, such as follows:

```
struct date purchaseDate;
```

Or, you can simply include the two definitions on the same line, as in this line:

```
struct date today, purchaseDate;
```

Unlike variables of type `int`, `float`, or `char`, a special syntax is needed when dealing with structure variables. A member of a structure is accessed by specifying the variable name, followed by a period (called the *dot operator*), and then the member name. For example, to set the value of `day` in the variable `today` to 21, you write

```
today.day = 21;
```

Note that no spaces are permitted between the variable name, period, and member name. To set `year` in `today` to 2003, the expression

```
today.year = 2003;
```

can be used. Finally, to test the value of `month` to see whether it is equal to 12, a statement such as

```
if ( today.month == 12 )
  next_month = 1;
```

will work.

Program 13.6 incorporates the preceding discussions into an actual program.

Program 13.6

```
#import <stdio.h>
int main (int argc, char *argv[])
{
    struct date
    {
        int month;
        int day;
        int year;
    };

    struct date today;

    today.month = 9;
    today.day = 25;
    today.year = 2004;

    printf ("Today's date is %i/%i/%.2i.\n", today.month,
            today.day, today.year % 100);

    return 0;
}
```

Program 13.6 **Output**

```
Today's date is 9/25/04.
```

The first statement inside main defines the structure called date to consist of three integer members called month, day, and year. In the second statement, the variable today is declared to be of type struct date. So, the first statement simply defines what a date structure looks like to the Objective-C compiler and causes no storage to be reserved inside the computer. The second statement declares a variable to be of type struct date and therefore does cause memory to be reserved for storing the three integer members of the structure variable today.

After the assignments have been made, the values contained inside the structure are displayed by an appropriate printf call. The remainder of today.year divided by 100 is calculated prior to being passed to the printf function so that just 04 is displayed for the year. The %.2i format characters in the printf call specify a minimum of two characters to be displayed, thus forcing the display of the leading zero for the year.

When it comes to the evaluation of expressions, structure members follow the same rules as do ordinary variables in the Objective-C language. Division of an integer structure member by another integer is therefore performed as an integer division, as shown here:

```
century = today.year / 100 + 1;
```

Suppose you wanted to write a simple program that accepted today's date as input and displayed tomorrow's date to the user? Now, at first glance, this seems a perfectly simple task to perform. You can ask the user to enter today's date and then calculate tomorrow's date by a series of statements, like so:

```
tomorrow.month = today.month;
tomorrow.day   = today.day + 1;
tomorrow.year = today.year;
```

Of course, the previous statements would work fine for the majority of dates, but the following two cases would not be properly handled:

- If today's date fell at the end of a month
- If today's date fell at the end of a year (that is, if today's date were December 31)

One way to easily determine whether today's date falls at the end of a month is to set up an array of integers that corresponds to the number of days in each month. A lookup inside the array for a particular month then gives the number of days in that month (see Program 13.7).

Program 13.7

```
// Program to determine tomorrow's date

#import <stdio.h>
#import <objc/Object.h>

struct date
{
    int month;
    int day;
    int year;
};

// Function to calculate tomorrow's date

struct date dateUpdate (struct date today)
{
    struct date tomorrow;
    int numberOfDays (struct date d);

    if ( today.day != numberOfDays (today) )
    {
      tomorrow.day = today.day + 1;
      tomorrow.month = today.month;
      tomorrow.year = today.year;
    }
    else if ( today.month == 12 )    // end of year
    {
```

Program 13.7   **Continued**

```c
    tomorrow.day = 1;
    tomorrow.month = 1;
    tomorrow.year = today.year + 1;
  }
  else
  {                      // end of month
    tomorrow.day = 1;
    tomorrow.month = today.month + 1;
    tomorrow.year = today.year;
  }

  return (tomorrow);
}

// Function to find the number of days in a month

int numberOfDays (struct date d)
{
   int answer;
   BOOL isLeapYear (struct date d);
   int daysPerMonth[12] =
     { 31, 28, 31, 30, 31, 30, 31, 31, 30, 31, 30, 31 };

   if ( isLeapYear (d) == YES && d.month == 2 )
     answer = 29;
   else
     answer = daysPerMonth[d.month - 1];

   return (answer);
}

// Function to determine if it's a leap year

BOOL isLeapYear (struct date d)
{
 if ( (d.year % 4 == 0 && d.year % 100 != 0) ||
       d.year % 400 == 0 )
    return YES;
 else
    return NO;
}

int main (int argc, char *argv[])
{
   struct date dateUpdate (struct date today);
   struct date thisDay, nextDay;
```

Program 13.7   **Continued**

```
    printf ("Enter today's date (mm dd yyyy): ");
    scanf ("%i%i%i", &thisDay.month, &thisDay.day,
                &thisDay.year);

    nextDay = dateUpdate (thisDay);

    printf ("Tomorrow's date is %i/%i/%.2i.\n",nextDay.month,
                nextDay.day, nextDay.year % 100);
    return 0;
}
```

Program 13.7   **Output**

```
Enter today's date (mm dd yyyy): 2 28 2004
Tomorrow's date is 2/29/04.
```

Program 13.7   **Output (Rerun)**

```
Enter today's date (mm dd yyyy): 10 2 2005
Tomorrow's date is 10/3/05.
```

Program 13.7   **Output (Rerun)**

```
Enter today's date (mm dd yyyy): 12 31 2005
Tomorrow's date is 1/1/06.
```

Even though you're not working with any classes in this program, the file Object.h was imported nevertheless because you wanted to use the BOOL type and the defines YES and NO. They're defined in that file.

You'll notice that the definition of the date structure appears first and outside of any function. This is because structure definitions behave very much like variables: If a structure is defined within a particular function, only that function knows of its existence. This is a *local* structure definition. If you define the structure outside any function, that definition is *global*. A global structure definition enables any variables that are subsequently defined in the program (either inside or outside a function) to be declared to be of that structure type. Structure definitions that are shared among more than one file are typically centralized in a header file and then imported into the files that want to use the structure.

Inside the main routine, the declaration

```
struct date dateUpdate (struct date today);
```

tells the compiler that the `dateUpdate` function takes a `date` structure as its argument and returns one as well. You don't need the declaration here because the compiler has already seen the actual function definition earlier in the file. However, it's still good programming practice. For example, consider if you subsequently separated the function definition and `main` into separate source files. In that case, the declaration would be necessary.

As with ordinary variables—and unlike arrays—any changes made by the function to the values contained in a structure argument have no effect on the original structure. They affect only the copy of the structure that is created when the function is called.

After a date has been entered and stored inside the `date` structure variable `thisDay`, the `dateUpdate` function is called like this:

```
nextDay = dateUpdate (thisDay);
```

This statement calls `dateUpdate`, passing it the value of the `date` structure `thisDay`.

Inside the `dateUpdate function`, the prototype declaration

```
int numberOfDays (struct date d);
```

informs the Objective-C compiler that the `numberOfDays` function returns an integer value and takes a single argument of type `struct date`.

The statement

```
if ( today.day != numberOfDays (today) )
```

specifies that the structure `today` is to be passed as an argument to the `numberOfDays` function. Inside that function, the appropriate declaration must be made to inform the system that a structure is expected as an argument, like so:

```
int numberOfDays (struct date d)
```

The `numberOfDays` function begins by determining whether it is a leap year and whether the month is February. The former determination is made by calling another function called `isLeapYear`.

The `isLeapYear` function is straightforward enough; it simply tests the year contained in the `date` structure given as its argument and returns `YES` if it is a leap year and `NO` if it is not.

Make sure that you understand the hierarchy of function calls in the Program 13.7: The `main` function calls `dateUpdate`, which in turn calls `numberOfDays`, which itself calls the function `isLeapYear`.

Initializing Structures

Initializing structures is similar to initializing arrays—the elements are simply listed inside a pair of braces, with each element separated by a comma.

To initialize the `date` structure variable `today` to July 2, 2004, the statement

```
struct date today = { 7, 2, 2004 };
```

can be used.

As with the initialization of an array, fewer values can be listed than are contained in the structure. So, the statement

```
struct date today = { 7 };
```

sets `today.month` to 7 but gives no initial value to `today.day` or `today.year`. In such a case, their default initial values are undefined.

Specific members can be designated for initialization in any order with the notation

```
.member = value
```

in the initialization list, as in

```
struct date today = { .month = 7, .day = 2, .year = 2004 };
```

and

```
struct date today = { .year = 2004 };
```

The last statement just sets the year in the structure to 2004. As you know, the other two members are undefined.

Arrays of Structures

Working with arrays of structures is pretty straightforward. The definition

```
struct date birthdays[15];
```

defines the array `birthdays` to contain 15 elements of type `struct date`. Referencing a particular structure element inside the array is quite natural. To set the second birthday inside the `birthdays` array to February 22, 1996, the sequence of statements

```
birthdays[1].month = 2;
birthdays[1].day  = 22;
birthdays[1].year = 1996;
```

will work just fine. The statement

```
n = numberOfDays (birthdays[0]);
```

sends the first date in the array to the `numberOfDays` function to find out how many days are contained in the month specified by that date.

Structures Within Structures

Objective-C provides an enormous amount of flexibility in defining structures. For instance, you can define a structure that itself contains other structures as one or more of its members, or you can define structures that contain arrays.

You have seen how to logically group the month, day, and year into a structure called `date`. Suppose you had an analogous structure called `time` that you used to group the hour, minutes, and seconds representing a time. In some applications, you might need to logically group both a date and a time together. For example, you might need to set up a list of events that are to occur at a particular date and time.

The previous discussion implies that you want to have a convenient means for associating both the date and the time together. You can do this in Objective-C by defining a new structure (called, perhaps, `date_and_time`), which contains as its members two elements: the date and the time. It is shown here:

```
struct date_and_time
{
    struct date  sdate;
    struct time  stime;
};
```

The first member of this structure is of type `struct date` and is called `sdate`, and the second member of the `date_and_time` structure is of type `struct time` and is called `stime`. This definition of a `date_and_time` structure requires that a `date` structure and a `time` structure have been previously defined to the compiler.

Variables can now be defined to be of type `struct date_and_time`, like so:

```
struct date_and_time event;
```

To reference the `date` structure of the variable `event`, the syntax is the same:

```
event.sdate
```

You could therefore call your `dateUpdate` function with this date as the argument and assign the result back to the same place by a statement, like so:

```
event.sdate = dateUpdate (event.sdate);
```

You can do the same type of thing with the `time` structure contained within your `date_and_time` structure:

```
event.stime = time_update (event.stime);
```

To reference a particular member inside one of these structures, a period followed by the member name is added onto the end:

```
event.sdate.month = 10;
```

This statement sets the `month` of the `date` structure contained within `event` to October, and the statement

```
++event.stime.seconds;
```

adds one to the `seconds` contained within the `time` structure.

The event variable can be initialized in the expected manner:

```
struct date_and_time event =
    { { 12, 17, 1989 }, { 3, 30, 0 } };
```

This sets the date in the variable `event` to December 17, 1989, and sets the time to 3:30:00.

Naturally, you can set up an array of date_and_time structures, as is done with the following declaration:

```
struct date_and_time events[100];
```

The array events is declared to contain 100 elements of type struct date_and_time. The 4th date_and_time contained within the array is referenced in the usual way as events[3], and the 25th date in the array can be sent to your dateUpdate function as follows:

```
events[24].sdate = dateUpdate (events[24].sdate);
```

To set the first time in the array to noon, the following series of statements can be used:

```
events[0].stime.hour    = 12;
events[0].stime.minutes = 0;
events[0].stime.seconds = 0;
```

Additional Details About Structures

There is some flexibility in defining a structure that we should mention here. First, it is valid to declare a variable to be of a particular structure type at the same time that the structure is defined. This is done simply by including the variable name(s) before the terminating semicolon of the structure definition. For example, the statement

```
struct date
{
    int month;
    int day;
    int year;
} todaysDate, purchaseDate;
```

defines the structure date and also declares the variables todaysDate and purchaseDate to be of this type. You can also assign initial values to the variables in the normal fashion. Thus

```
struct date
{
    int month;
    int day;
    int year;
} todaysDate = { 9, 25, 2004 };
```

defines the structure date and the variable todaysDate with initial values as indicated.

If all the variables of a particular structure type are defined when the structure is defined, the structure name can be omitted. So the statement

```
struct
{
    int month;
    int day;
    int year;
} dates[100];
```

defines an array called dates to consist of 100 elements. Each element is a structure containing three integer members: month, day, and year. Because you did not supply a name to the structure, the only way to subsequently declare variables of the same type would be by explicitly defining the structure again.

Bit Fields

Two methods in Objective-C can be used to pack information together. One way is to simply represent the data inside an integer and then access the desired bits of the integer using the bit operators described in Chapter 4, "Data Types and Expressions."

Another way is to define a structure of packed information using an Objective-C construct known as a *bit field*. This method uses a special syntax in the structure definition that enables you to define a field of bits and assign a name to that field.

To define bit field assignments, you can define a structure called packedStruct, for example, as follows:

```
struct packedStruct
{
    unsigned int f1:1;
    unsigned int f2:1;
    unsigned int f3:1;
    unsigned int type:4;
    unsigned int index:9;
};
```

The structure packedStruct is defined to contain five members. The first member, called f1, is an unsigned int. The :1 that immediately follows the member name specifies that this member is to be stored in 1 bit. The flags f2 and f3 are similarly defined as being a single bit in length. The member type is defined to occupy 4 bits, whereas the member index is defined as being 9 bits long.

The compiler automatically packs the preceding bit field definitions together. The nice thing about this approach is that the fields of a variable defined to be of type packedStruct can now be referenced in the same convenient way that normal structure members are referenced. So, if you were to declare a variable called packedData as follows:

```
struct packedStruct packedData;
```

you could easily set the `type` field of `packedData` to 7 with this simple statement:

```
packedData.type = 7;
```

You could also set this field to the value of n with this similar statement:

```
packedData.type = n;
```

In this last case, you needn't worry about whether the value of n is too large to fit into the `type` field; only the low-order 4 bits of n are assigned to `packedData.type`.

Extraction of the value from a bit field is also automatically handled, so the statement

```
n = packedData.type;
```

extracts the `type` field from `packedData` (automatically shifting it into the low-order bits as required) and assigns it to n.

Bit fields can be used in normal expressions and are automatically converted to integers. The statement

```
i = packedData.index / 5 + 1;
```

is therefore perfectly valid, as is the following:

```
if ( packedData.f2 )
    ...
```

This tests whether flag `f2` is on or off. One thing worth noting about bit fields is that there is no guarantee whether the fields are internally assigned from left to right or from right to left. So, if bit fields are assigned from right to left, `f1` would be in the low-order bit position, `f2` in the bit position immediately to the left of `f1`, and so on. This should not present a problem unless you are dealing with data that was created by a different program or by a different machine.

You can also include normal data types within a structure that contains bit fields. So, if you wanted to define a structure that contains an `int`, a `char`, and two 1-bit flags, the following definition would be valid:

```
struct table_entry
{
  int      count;
  char     c;
  unsigned int f1:1;
  unsigned int f2:1;
};
```

Bit fields are packed into *units* as they appear in the structure definition, where the size of a *unit* is defined by the implementation and is most likely a word. The Objective-C compiler does not rearrange the bit field definitions to try to optimize storage space.

A bit field that has no name can be specified to cause bits inside a word to be skipped, meaning the definition

```
struct x_entry
{
  unsigned int type:4;
  unsigned int :3;
  unsigned int count:9;
};
```

defines a structure, x_entry, that contains a 4-bit field called type and a 9-bit field called count. The unnamed field specifies that 3 bits separate the type from the count field.

A final point concerning the specification of fields concerns the special case of an unnamed field of length 0. This can be used to force alignment of the next field in the structure at the start of a unit boundary.

Don't Forget About Object-Oriented Programming!

Now you know how to define a structure to store a date. And you've written various routines to manipulate that date structure. But what about object-oriented programming? Shouldn't you have made a class called Date instead and then developed methods to work with a Date object? Wouldn't that be a better approach? Well, the answer is yes. Hopefully, that's what entered your mind when we led the discussion in this section about storing dates in your program.

Certainly, if you had to work with a lot of dates in your programs, defining a class and methods to work with dates would be a better approach. In fact, the Foundation framework has a couple of classes called NSDate and NSCalendarDate defined for such purposes. It's left as an exercise for you to implement a Date class to deal with dates as objects instead of as structures.

Pointers

Pointers enable you to effectively represent complex data structures, change values passed as arguments to functions and methods, and more concisely and efficiently deal with arrays. At the end of this chapter, we'll also clue you in about how important they are to the implementation of objects in the Objective-C language.

We introduced the concept of a pointer in Chapter 8, "Inheritance," when we talked about the Point and Rectangle classes and how you can have multiple references to the same object.

To understand the way in which pointers operate, you first must understand the concept of *indirection*. We are used to this concept in our everyday life. For example, suppose I needed to buy a new toner cartridge for my printer. In the company that I work for, all purchases are handled by the purchasing department. So, I would call Jim in purchasing and ask him to order the new cartridge for me. Jim, in turn, would call the local supply store to order the cartridge. The approach that I would take in obtaining my new cartridge would actually be an indirect one because I would not be ordering the cartridge directly from the supply store myself.

This same notion of indirection applies to the way pointers work in Objective-C. A pointer provides an indirect means of accessing the value of a particular data item. And just as there are reasons it makes sense to go through the purchasing department to order new cartridges (I don't have to know which particular store the cartridges are being ordered from, for example), so are there good reasons why, at times, it makes sense to use pointers in Objective-C.

But enough talk; it's time to see how pointers actually work. Suppose you've defined a variable called count as follows:

```
int count = 10;
```

You can define another variable, called intPtr, that will enable you to indirectly access the value of count by the following declaration:

```
int *intPtr;
```

The asterisk defines to the Objective-C system that the variable intPtr is of type pointer to int. This means that intPtr will be used in the program to indirectly access the value of one or more integer variables.

You have seen how the & operator was used in the scanf calls of previous programs. This unary operator, known as the *address* operator, is used to make a pointer to a variable in Objective-C. So, if x is a variable of a particular type, the expression &x is a pointer to that variable. The expression &x can be assigned to any pointer variable, if desired, that has been declared to be a pointer to the same type as x.

Therefore, with the definitions of count and intPtr as given, you can write a statement such as

```
intPtr = &count;
```

to set up the indirect reference between intPtr and count. The address operator has the effect of assigning to the variable intPtr not the value of count, but a pointer to the variable count. The link that has been made between intPtr and count is conceptualized in Figure 13.1. The directed line illustrates the idea that intPtr does not directly contain the value of count but a pointer to the variable count.

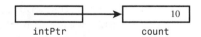

Figure 13.1   Pointer to an integer.

To reference the contents of count through the pointer variable intPtr, you use the indirection operator, which is the asterisk (*). If x were defined to be of type int, the statement

```
x = *intPtr;
```

would assign the value that is indirectly referenced through `intPtr` to the variable x. Because `intPtr` was previously set pointing to `count`, this statement would have the effect of assigning the value contained in the variable `count`—which is `10`—to the variable x.

The previous statements have been incorporated into Program 13.8, which illustrates the two fundamental pointer operators: the address operator (&) and the indirection operator (*).

Program 13.8

```
// Program to illustrate pointers

#import <stdio.h>

int main (int argc, char *argv[])
{
    int  count = 10, x;
    int  *intPtr;

    intPtr = &count;
    x = *intPtr;

    printf ("count = %i, x = %i\n", count, x);

    return 0;
}
```

Program 13.8 **Output**

```
count = 10, x = 10
```

The variables `count` and x are declared to be integer variables in the normal fashion. On the next line, the variable `intPtr` is declared to be of type "pointer to `int`." Note that the two lines of declarations could have been combined into the single line, like so:

```
int count = 10, x, *intPtr;
```

Next, the address operator is applied to the variable `count`, which has the effect of creating a pointer to this variable, which is then assigned by the program to the variable `intPtr`.

Execution of the next statement in the program

```
x = *intPtr;
```

proceeds as follows: The indirection operator tells the Objective-C system to treat the variable `intPtr` as containing a pointer to another data item. This pointer is then used to access the desired data item, whose type is specified by the declaration of the pointer variable. Because you told the compiler that intPtr points to integers when you declared the variable, the compiler knows that the value referenced by the expression *intPtr is an integer. Also, because you set intPtr to point to the integer variable count in the previous program statement, the value of count is indirectly accessed by this expression.

Program 13.9 illustrates some interesting properties of pointer variables. Here, a pointer to a character is used.

Program 13.9

```
#import <stdio.h>

int main (int argc, char *argv[])
{
    char c = 'Q';
    char *charPtr = &c;

    printf ("%c %c\n", c, *charPtr);

    c = '/';
    printf ("%c %c\n", c, *charPtr);

    *charPtr = '(';
    printf ("%c %c\n", c, *charPtr);

    return 0;
}
```

Program 13.9 **Output**

```
Q Q
/ /
( (
```

The character variable c is defined and initialized to the character 'Q'. In the next line of the program, the variable charPtr is defined to be of type "pointer to char," meaning that whatever value is stored inside this variable should be treated as an indirect reference (pointer) to a character. You will notice that you can assign an initial value to this variable in the normal fashion. The value you assign to charPtr in the program is a pointer to the variable c, which is obtained by applying the address operator to the variable c. (Note that this initialization would have generated a compiler error had c been defined after this statement because a variable must always be declared before its value can be referenced in an expression.)

The declaration of the variable `charPtr` and the assignment of its initial value could have been equivalently expressed in two separate statements as follows:

```
char *charPtr;
charPtr = &c;
```

(and not by the statements

```
char *charPtr;
*charPtr = &c;
```

as might be implied from the single line declaration).

Always remember that the value of a pointer in Objective-C is meaningless until it is set pointing to something.

The first `printf` call simply displays the contents of the variable `c` and the contents of the variable referenced by `charPtr`. Because you set `charPtr` to point to the variable `c`, the value displayed is the contents of `c`, as verified by the first line of the program's output.

In the next line of the program, the character `'/'` is assigned to the character variable `c`. Because `charPtr` still points to the variable `c`, displaying the value of `*charPtr` in the subsequent `printf` call correctly displays this new value of `c` at the terminal. This is an important concept. Unless the value of `charPtr` is changed, the expression `*charPtr` will always access the value of `c`. Thus, as the value of `c` changes, so does the value of `*charPtr`.

The previous discussion can help you understand how the program statement that appears next in the program works. We mentioned that unless `charPtr` were changed, the expression `*charPtr` would always reference the value of `c`. Therefore, in the expression

```
*charPtr = '(';
```

the left parenthesis character is being assigned to `c`. More formally, the character `'('` is assigned to the variable that is pointed to by `charPtr`. You know that this variable is `c` because you placed a pointer to `c` in `charPtr` at the beginning of the program.

The previous concepts are the key to your understanding of the operation of pointers. Please review them at this point if they still seem a bit unclear.

Pointers and Structures

You have seen how a pointer can be defined to point to a basic data type such as an `int` or a `char`. But pointers can also be defined to point to structures. Earlier in this chapter, you defined your `date` structure as follows:

```
struct date
{
    int month;
    int day;
    int year;
};
```

Just as you defined variables to be of type struct date, as in

```
struct date  todaysDate;
```

so can you define a variable to be a pointer to a struct date variable:

```
struct date *datePtr;
```

The variable datePtr, as just defined, can then be used in the expected fashion. For example, you can set it to point to todaysDate with the following assignment statement:

```
datePtr = &todaysDate;
```

After such an assignment has been made, you can then indirectly access any of the members of the date structure pointed to by datePtr in the following way:

```
(*datePtr).day = 21;
```

This statement will have the effect of setting the day of the date structure pointed to by datePtr to 21. The parentheses are required because the structure member operator . has higher precedence than the indirection operator *.

To test the value of month stored in the date structure pointed to by datePtr, a statement such as

```
if ( (*datePtr).month == 12 )
    ...
```

can be used.

Pointers to structures are so often used that a special operator exists in the language. The structure pointer operator ->, which is the dash followed by the greater than sign, permits expressions that would otherwise be written as

```
(*x).y
```

to be more clearly expressed as

```
x->y
```

So, the previous if statement can be conveniently written as follows:

```
if ( datePtr->month == 12 )
    ...
```

Program 13.6, which was the first program that illustrated structures, was rewritten using the concept of structure pointers. This program is presented here as Program 13.10.

Program 13.10

```
// Program to illustrate structure pointers
#import <stdio.h>

int main (int argc, char *argv[])
{
    struct date
    {
```

Program 13.10   **Continued**

```
    int month;
    int day;
    int year;
};

struct date today, *datePtr;

datePtr = &today;
datePtr->month = 9;
datePtr->day = 25;
datePtr->year = 2004;

printf ("Today's date is %i/%i/%.2i.\n",
        datePtr->month, datePtr->day, datePtr->year % 100);
return 0;
}
```

Program 13.10   **Output**

```
Today's date is 9/25/04.
```

Pointers, Methods, and Functions

You can pass a pointer as an argument to a method or function in the normal fashion, and you can have a function or method return a pointer as its result. When you think about it, that's what your `alloc` and `init` methods have been doing all along—returning pointers. That's covered in more detail at the end of this chapter.

Now consider Program 13.11.

Program 13.11

```
// Pointers as arguments to functions
#import <stdio.h>

void exchange (int *pint1, int *pint2)
{
   int temp;

   temp = *pint1;
   *pint1 = *pint2;
   *pint2 = temp;
}
```

Program 13.11   **Continued**

```
int main (int argc, char *argv[])
{
   void exchange (int *pint1, int *pint2);
   int   i1 = -5, i2 = 66, *p1 = &i1, *p2 = &i2;

   printf ("i1 = %i, i2 = %i\n", i1, i2);

   exchange (p1, p2);
   printf ("i1 = %i, i2 = %i\n", i1, i2);

   exchange (&i1, &i2);
   printf ("i1 = %i, i2 = %i\n", i1, i2);

   return 0;
}
```

Program 13.11   **Output**

```
i1 = -5, i2 = 66
i1 = 66, i2 = -5
i1 = -5, i2 = 66
```

The purpose of the exchange function is to interchange the two integer values pointed to by its two arguments. The local integer variable temp is used to hold one of the integer values while the exchange is made. Its value is set equal to the integer that is pointed to by pint1. The integer pointed to by pint2 is then copied into the integer pointed to by pint1, and the value of temp is then stored into the integer pointed to by pint2, thus making the exchange complete.

The main routine defines integers i1 and i2 with values of –5 and 66, respectively. Two integer pointers, p1 and p2, are then defined and set to point to i1 and i2, respectively. The program next displays the values of i1 and i2 and calls the exchange function, passing the two pointers (p1 and p2) as arguments. The exchange function exchanges the value contained in the integer pointed to by p1 with the value contained in the integer pointed to by p2. Because p1 points to i1, and p2 to i2, the values of i1 and i2 are exchanged by the function. The output from the second printf call verifies that the exchange worked properly.

The second call to exchange is a bit more interesting. This time, the arguments passed to the function are pointers to i1 and i2 that are manufactured right on the spot by applying the address operator to these two variables. Because the expression &i1 produces a pointer to the integer variable i1, this is in line with the type of argument your function expects for the first argument (a pointer to an integer). The same applies for the second argument as well. And as you can see from the program's output, the exchange function did its job and switched the values of i1 and i2 back to their original values.

Study Program 13.11 in detail. It illustrates with a small example the key concepts to be understood when dealing with pointers in Objective-C.

Pointers and Arrays

If you have an array of 100 integers called values, you can define a pointer called valuesPtr, which can be used to access the integers contained in this array with the following statement:

```
int *valuesPtr;
```

When you define a pointer that will be used to point to the elements of an array, you don't designate the pointer as type "pointer to array"; rather you designate the pointer as pointing to the type of element contained in the array.

If you had an array of Fraction objects called fracts, you could similarly define a pointer to be used to point to elements in fracts with the following statement:

```
Fraction *fractsPtr;
```

Note that this is the same declaration used to define a Fraction object.

To set valuesPtr to point to the first element in the values array, you simply write

```
valuesPtr = values;
```

The address operator is not used in this case because the Objective-C compiler treats the occurrence of an array name without a subscript as a pointer to the first element of the array. Therefore, simply specifying values without a subscript has the effect of producing a pointer to the first element of values.

An equivalent way of producing a pointer to the start of values is to apply the address operator to the first element of the array. Thus the statement

```
valuesPtr = &values[0];
```

can be used to serve the same purpose of placing a pointer to the first element of values in the pointer variable valuesPtr.

To display the Fraction object in the array fracts that is pointed to by fractsPtr, you could write this statement:

```
[fractsPtr print];
```

The real power of using pointers to arrays comes into play when you want to sequence through the elements of an array. If valuesPtr is defined as mentioned previously and is set pointing to the first element of values, the expression

```
*valuesPtr
```

can be used to access the first integer of the `values` array—that is, `values[0]`. To reference `values[3]` through the `valuesPtr` variable, you can add three to `valuesPtr` and then apply the indirection operator:

```
*(valuesPtr + 3)
```

In general, the expression

```
*(valuesPtr + i)
```

can be used to access the value contained in `values[i]`.

So, to set `values[10]` to 27, you could obviously write the following expression:

```
values[10] = 27;
```

Or, using `valuesPtr`, you could write this:

```
*(valuesPtr + 10) = 27;
```

To set `valuesPtr` to point to the second element of the `values` array, you can apply the address operator to `values[1]` and assign the result to `valuesPtr`:

```
valuesPtr = &values[1];
```

If `valuesPtr` points to `values[0]`, you can set it to point to `values[1]` by simply adding one to the value of `valuesPtr`:

```
valuesPtr += 1;
```

This is a perfectly valid expression in Objective-C and can be used for pointers to any data type.

So, in general, if a is an array of elements of type x, px is of type "pointer to x," and i and n are integer constants of variables, the statement

```
px = a;
```

sets px to point to the first element of a, and the expression

```
*(px + i)
```

subsequently references the value contained in `a[i]`. Furthermore, the statement

```
px += n;
```

sets px to point n elements further in the array, no matter what type of element is contained in the array.

Suppose `fractsPtr` points to a fraction stored inside an array of fractions. Further suppose you want to add it to the fraction contained in the next element of the array and assign the result to the `Fraction` object `result`. You could do this by writing the following:

```
result = [fractsPtr add: fractsPtr + 1];
```

The increment and decrement operators (++ and --) are particularly handy when dealing with pointers. Applying the increment operator to a pointer has the same effect as adding one to the pointer, whereas applying the decrement operator has the same effect as subtracting one from the pointer. So, if textPtr were defined as a char pointer and were set pointing to the beginning of an array of chars called text, the statement

```
++textPtr;
```

would set textPtr pointing to the next character in text, which is text[1]. In a similar fashion, the statement

```
--textPtr;
```

would set textPtr pointing to the previous character in text, assuming of course that textPtr was not pointing to the beginning of text prior to the execution of this statement.

Comparing two pointer variables in Objective-C is perfectly valid. This is particularly useful when comparing two pointers into the same array. For example, you could test the pointer valuesPtr to see whether it points past the end of an array containing 100 elements by comparing it to a pointer to the last element in the array. So, the expression

```
valuesPtr > &values[99]
```

would be TRUE (nonzero) if valuesPtr was pointing past the last element in the values array, and it would be FALSE (zero) otherwise. From our earlier discussions, you can replace the previous expression with its equivalent:

```
valuesPtr > values + 99
```

This is possible because values used without a subscript is a pointer to the beginning of the values array. (Remember that it's the same as writing &values[0].)

Program 13.12 illustrates pointers to arrays. The arraySum function calculates the sum of the elements contained in an array of integers.

Program 13.12

```
#import <stdio.h>
// Function to sum the elements of an integer array

int arraySum (int array[], int n)
{
    int sum = 0, *ptr;
    int *arrayEnd = array + n;

    for ( ptr = array; ptr < arrayEnd; ++ptr )
        sum += *ptr;

    return (sum);
}
```

Program 13.12   **Continued**

```
int main (int argc, char *argv[])
{
    int arraySum (int array[], int n);
    int values[10] = { 3, 7, -9, 3, 6, -1, 7, 9, 1, -5 };

    printf ("The sum is %i\n", arraySum (values, 10));
    return 0;
}
```

Program 13.12   **Output**

```
The sum is 21
```

Inside the arraySum function, the integer pointer arrayEnd is defined and set pointing immediately after the last element of array. A for loop is then set up to sequence through the elements of array; then the value of ptr is set to point to the beginning of array when the loop is entered. Each time through the loop, the element of array pointed to by ptr is added into sum. The value of ptr is then incremented by the for loop to set it pointing to the next element in array. When ptr points past the end of array, the for loop is exited and the value of sum is returned to the caller.

Is It an Array, or Is It a Pointer?

To pass an array to a function, you simply specify the name of the array, as you did previously with the call to the arraySum function. But we also mentioned in this section that to produce a pointer to an array, you need only specify the name of the array. This implies that in the call to the arraySum function, what was passed to the function was actually a pointer to the array values. This is precisely the case and explains why you are able to change the elements of an array from within a function.

But if it is indeed the case that a pointer to the array is passed to the function, then why isn't the formal parameter inside the function declared to be a pointer? In other words, in the declaration of array in the arraySum function, why isn't the declaration

```
int *array;
```

used? Shouldn't all references to an array from within a function be made using pointer variables?

To answer these questions, we must first reiterate what we have said before about pointers and arrays. We mentioned that, if valuesPtr points to the same type of element as contained in an array called values, the expression *(valuesPtr + i) is in all ways equivalent to the expression values[i], assuming that valuesPtr has been set to point to the beginning of values. What follows from this is that you can also use the expression *(values + i) to reference the ith element of the array values, and, in general, if x is an array of any type, the expression x[i] can always be equivalently expressed in Objective-C as *(x + i).

As you can see, pointers and arrays are intimately related in Objective-C, which is why you can declare array to be of type "array of ints" inside the arraySum function or to be of type "pointer to int." Either declaration works just fine in the preceding program—try it and see.

If you will be using index numbers to reference the elements of an array, declare the corresponding formal parameter to be an array. This more correctly reflects the usage of the array by the function. Similarly, if you will be using the argument as a pointer to the array, declare it to be of type pointer.

Pointers to Character Strings

One of the most common applications of using a pointer to an array is as a pointer to a character string. The reasons are ones of notational convenience and efficiency. To show how easily pointers to character strings can be used, let's write a function called copyString to copy one string into another. If you were writing this function using your normal array indexing methods, the function might be coded as follows:

```
void copyString (char to[], char from[])
{
    int i;

    for ( i = 0; from[i] != '\0'; ++i )
        to[i] = from[i];

    to[i] = '\0';
}
```

The for loop is exited before the null character is copied into the to array, thus explaining the need for the last statement in the function.

If you write copyString using pointers, you no longer need the index variable i. A pointer version is shown in Program 13.13.

Program 13.13

```
#import <stdio.h>
void copyString (char *to, char *from)
{
    for ( ; *from != '\0'; ++from, ++to )
        *to = *from;

    *to = '\0';
}

int main (int argc, char *argv[])
{
    void copyString (char *to, char *from);
    char string1[] = "A string to be copied.";
    char string2[50];
```

Program 13.13   **Continued**

```
copyString (string2, string1);
printf ("%s\n", string2);

copyString (string2, "So is this.");
printf ("%s\n", string2);
return 0;
}
```

Program 13.13   **Output**

```
A string to be copied.
So is this.
```

The copyString function defines the two formal parameters, to and from, as character pointers and not as character arrays as was done in the previous version of copyString. This reflects how these two variables will be used by the function.

A for loop is then entered (with no initial conditions) to copy the string pointed to by from into the string pointed to by to. Each time through the loop, the from and to pointers are each incremented by one. This sets the from pointer pointing to the next character that is to be copied from the source string and sets the to pointer pointing to the location in the destination string where the next character is to be stored.

When the from pointer points to the null character, the for loop is exited. The function then places the null character at the end of the destination string.

In the main routine, the copyString function is called twice—the first time to copy the contents of string1 into string2 and the second time to copy the contents of the constant character string "So is this." into string2.

Constant Character Strings and Pointers

The fact that the call

```
copyString (string2, "So is this.");
```

works in the previous program implies that when a constant character string is passed as an argument to a function, what is actually passed is a pointer to that character string. Not only is this true in this case, but it can also be generalized by saying that whenever a constant character string is used in Objective-C, a pointer to that character string is produced.[2]

---

2. The following point might sound a bit confusing now, but in Chapter 15, "Numbers, Strings, and Collections," we'll clear this up: The constant character strings we mention here are called C-style strings. These are *not* objects. In Objective-C, a constant character string *object* can be created by putting an @ sign in front of the string, as in @"This is okay." You can't substitute one for the other. Again, Chapter 15 clears up this point for you.

So, if `textPtr` is declared to be a character pointer, as in

```
char *textPtr;
```

then the statement

```
textPtr = "A character string.";
```

assigns to `textPtr` a pointer to the constant character string `"A character string."` Be careful to make the distinction here between character pointers and character arrays because the type of assignment shown previously is not valid with a character array. For example, if `text` were defined instead to be an array of `char`s, with a statement such as

```
char text[80];
```

you could not write a statement such as this:

```
text = "This is not valid.";
```

The only time Objective-C lets you get away with performing this type of assignment to a character array is when initializing it, like so:

```
char text[80] = "This is okay.";
```

Initializing the `text` array in this manner does not have the effect of storing a pointer to the character string `"This is okay."` inside `text`, but rather the actual characters themselves followed by a terminating null character, inside corresponding elements of the `text` array.

If `text` were a character pointer, initializing `text` with the statement

```
char *text = "This is okay.";
```

would assign to it a pointer to the character string `"This is okay."`

The Increment and Decrement Operators Revisited

Up to this point, whenever you used the increment or decrement operator it was the only operator that appeared in the expression. When you write the expression ++x, you know that this adds one to the value of the variable x. And as you have just seen, if x is a pointer to an array, this sets x to point to the next element of the array.

The increment and decrement operators can be used in expressions in which other operators also appear. In such cases, it becomes important to know more precisely how these operators work.

Whenever you used the increment and decrement operators, you always placed them before the variables that were being incremented or decremented. So, to increment a variable i, you simply wrote the following:

```
++i;
```

Actually, it is also valid to place the increment operator after the variable, like so:

```
i++;
```

Both expressions are valid and both achieve the same result—namely, incrementing the value of i. In the first case, where the ++ is placed before its operand, the increment operation is more precisely identified as a *pre-increment*. In the second case, where the ++ is placed after its operand, the operation is identified as a *post-increment*.

The same discussion applies to the decrement operator. So, the statement

```
--i;
```

technically performs a pre-decrement of i, whereas the statement

```
i--;
```

performs a post-decrement of i. Both have the same net result of subtracting one from the value of i.

When the increment and decrement operators are used in more complex expressions, the distinction between the pre- and post- nature of these operators is realized.

Suppose you have two integers called i and j. If you set the value of i to 0 and then write the statement

```
j = ++i;
```

the value assigned to j is 1—not 0 as you might expect. In the case of the pre-increment operator, the variable is incremented before its value is used in an expression. Therefore, in the previous expression, the value of i is first incremented from 0 to 1 and then its value is assigned to j, as if the following two statements had been written instead:

```
++i;
j = i;
```

If you use the post-increment operator in the statement

```
j = i++;
```

i is incremented after its value has been assigned to j. So, if i were 0 before the previous statement were executed, 0 would be assigned to j and then i would be incremented by 1, as if the statements

```
j = i;
++i;
```

were used instead.

As another example, if i is equal to 1, the statement

```
x = a[--i];
```

has the effect of assigning the value of a[0] to x because the variable i is decremented before its value is used to index into a. The statement

```
x = a[i--];
```

used instead assigns the value of a[1] to x because i would be decremented after its value had been used to index into a.

As a third example of the distinction between the pre- and post- increment and decrement operators, the function call

```
printf ("%i\n", ++i);
```

increments i and then sends its value to the `printf` function, whereas the call

```
printf ("%i\n", i++);
```

increments i after its value has been sent to the function. So, if i were equal to 100, the first `printf` call would display 101 at the terminal, whereas the second `printf` call would display 100. In either case, the value of i would be equal to 101 after the statement had been executed.

As a final example on this topic before we present a program, if `textPtr` is a character pointer, the expression

```
*(++textPtr)
```

first increments `textPtr` and then fetches the character it points to, whereas the expression

```
*(textPtr++)
```

fetches the character pointed to by `textPtr` before its value is incremented. In either case, the parentheses are not required because the * and ++ operators have equal precedence but associate from right to left.

Let's go back to the `copyString` function from Program 13.13 and rewrite it to incorporate the increment operations directly into the assignment statement.

Because the `to` and `from` pointers are incremented each time after the assignment statement inside the `for` loop is executed, they should be incorporated into the assignment statement as post-increment operations. The revised `for` loop of Program 13.13 then becomes

```
for ( ; *from != '\0'; )
    *to++ = *from++;
```

Execution of the assignment statement inside the loop would proceed as follows. The character pointed to by `from` would be retrieved, and then `from` would be incremented to point to the next character in the source string. The referenced character would be stored inside the location pointed to by `to`; then `to` would be incremented to point to the next location in the destination string.

The previous `for` statement hardly seems worthwhile because it has no initial expression and no looping expression. In fact, the logic would be better served when expressed in the form of a `while` loop. This has been done in Program 13.14. This program presents the new version of the `copyString` function. The `while` loop uses the fact that the null character is equal to the value 0, as is commonly done by experienced Objective-C programmers.

Program 13.14

```
// Function to copy one string to another
//          pointer version 2
#import <stdio.h>

void copyString (char *to, char *from)
{
    while ( *from )
        *to++ = *from++;
    *to = '\0';
}


int main (int argc, char *argv[])
{
    void copyString (char *to, char *from);
    char string1[] = "A string to be copied.";
    char string2[50];

    copyString (string2, string1);
    printf ("%s\n", string2);

    copyString (string2, "So is this.");
    printf ("%s\n", string2);
    return 0;
}
```

Program 13.14   **Output**

```
A string to be copied.
So is this.
```

Operations on Pointers

As you have seen in this chapter, you can add or subtract integer values from pointers. Furthermore, you can compare two pointers to see whether they are equal or whether one pointer is less than or greater than another pointer. The only other operation permitted on pointers is the subtraction of two pointers of the same type. The result of subtracting two pointers in Objective-C is the number of elements contained between the two pointers. Thus, if a points to an array of elements of any type and b points to another element somewhere further along in the same array, the expression b - a represents the number of elements between these two pointers. For example, if p points to some element in an array x, the statement

```
n = p - x;
```

assigns to the variable n (assumed here to be an integer variable) the index number of the element inside x that p points to. Therefore, if p had been set pointing to the 100th element in x by a statement such as

```
p = &x[99];
```

the value of n after the previous subtraction was performed would be 99.

Pointers to Functions

Of a slightly more advanced nature, but presented here for the sake of completeness, is the notion of a pointer to a function. When working with pointers to functions, the Objective-C compiler needs to know not only that the pointer variable points to a function, but also the type of value returned by that function as well as the number and types of its arguments. To declare a variable, fnPtr, to be of type "pointer to function that returns an int and that takes no arguments," the declaration

```
int (*fnPtr) (void);
```

can be written. The parentheses around *fnPtr are required; otherwise, the Objective-C compiler would treat the preceding statement as the declaration of a function called fnPtr that returns a pointer to an int (because the function call operator () has higher precedence than the pointer indirection operator *).

To set your function pointer pointing to a specific function, you simply assign the name of the function to it. Therefore, if lookup were a function that returned an int and that took no arguments, the statement

```
fnPtr = lookup;
```

would store a pointer to this function inside the function pointer variable fnPtr. Writing a function name without a subsequent set of parentheses is treated in an analogous way to writing an array name without a subscript. The Objective-C compiler automatically produces a pointer to the specified function. An ampersand is permitted in front of the function name, but it's not required.

If the lookup function has not been previously defined in the program, you must declare the function before the previous assignment can be made. A statement such as

```
int lookup (void);
```

would be needed before a pointer to this function could be assigned to the variable fnPtr.

You can call the function indirectly referenced through a pointer variable by applying the function call operator to the pointer, listing any arguments to the function inside the parentheses. For example

```
entry = fnPtr ();
```

calls the function pointed to by fnPtr, storing the returned value inside the variable entry.

One common application for pointers to functions is passing them as arguments to other functions. The Standard Library uses this in the function qsort, which performs a *quick sort* on an array of data elements. This function takes as one of its arguments a pointer to a function that is called whenever qsort needs to compare two elements in the array being sorted. In this manner, qsort can be used to sort arrays of any type because the actual comparison of any two elements in the array is made by a user-supplied function, and not by the qsort function itself.

In the Foundation framework some methods take a function pointer as an argument. For example, the method sortUsingFunction:context: is defined in the NSMutableArray class and calls the specified function whenever two elements in an array to be sorted need to be compared.

Another common application for function pointers is to create *dispatch* tables. You can't store functions themselves inside the elements of an array. However, you can store function pointers inside an array. Given this, you can create tables that contain pointers to functions to be called. For example, you might create a table for processing different commands that will be entered by a user. Each entry in the table could contain both the command name and a pointer to a function to call to process that particular command. Now, whenever the user entered a command, you could look up the command inside the table and invoke the corresponding function to handle it.

Pointers and Memory Addresses

Before we end this discussion of pointers in Objective-C, we should point out the details of how they are actually implemented. A computer's memory can be conceptualized as a sequential collection of storage cells. Each cell of the computer's memory has a number, called an *address*, associated with it. Typically, the first address of a computer's memory is numbered 0. On most computer systems, a *cell* is one byte.

The computer uses memory for storing the instructions of your computer program and for storing the values of the variables associated with a program. So, if you declare a variable called count to be of type int, the system would assign location(s) in memory to hold the value of count while the program is executing. This location might be at address $1000FF_{16}$, for example, inside the computer's memory.

Luckily, you don't need to concern yourself with the particular memory addresses assigned to variables—they are automatically handled by the system. However, the knowledge that associated with each variable is a unique memory address will help you to understand the way pointers operate.

Whenever you apply the address operator to a variable in Objective-C, the value generated is the actual address of that variable inside the computer's memory. (Obviously, this is where the address operator gets its name.) So, the statement

```
intPtr = &count;
```

assigns to intPtr the address in the computer's memory that has been assigned to the variable count. Thus, if count were located at address $1000FF_{16}$, this statement would assign the value 0x1000FF to intPtr.

Applying the indirection operator to a pointer variable, as in the expression

```
*intPtr
```

has the effect of treating the value contained in the pointer variable as a memory address. The value stored at that memory address is then fetched and interpreted in accordance with the type declared for the pointer variable. So, if `intPtr` were of type pointer to `int`, the value stored in the memory address given by `*intPtr` would be interpreted as an integer by the system.

Unions

One of the more unusual constructs in the Objective-C programming language is the *union*. This construct is used mainly in more advanced programming applications where you need to store different types of data into the same storage area. For example, if you wanted to define a single variable called x that could be used to store a single character, a floating-point number, or an integer, you would first define a union, called (perhaps) `mixed`, as follows:

```
union mixed
{
  char  c;
  float f;
  int   i;
};
```

The declaration for a union is identical to that of a structure, except the keyword `union` is used where the keyword `struct` is otherwise specified. The real difference between structures and unions has to do with the way memory is allocated. Declaring a variable to be of type `union mixed`, as in

```
union mixed x;
```

does not define x to contain three distinct members called c, f, and i; rather it defines x to contain a single member that is called either c, f, or i. In this way, the variable x can be used to store either a `char`, a `float`, or an `int`, but not all three (or not even two of the three). You can store a character into the variable x with the following statement:

```
x.c = 'K';
```

To store a floating-point value into x, the notation `x.f` is used:

```
x.f = 786.3869;
```

Finally, to store the result of dividing an integer count by 2 into x, the statement

```
x.i = count / 2;
```

could be used.

Because the `float`, `char`, and `int` members of x coexist in the same place in memory, only one value can be stored into x at a time. Furthermore, it is your responsibility to ensure that the value retrieved from a union is consistent with the way it was last stored in the union.

When defining a union, the name of the union is not required and variables can be declared at the same time that the union is defined. Pointers to unions can also be declared, and their syntax and rules for performing operations are the same as for structures. Finally, a union variable can be initialized like so:

```
union mixed x = { '#' };
```

This sets the first member of x, which is c, to the character #. A particular member can also be initialized by name, like this

```
union mixed x = {.f=123.4;};
```

An automatic union variable can also be initialized to another union variable of the same type.

The use of a union enables you to define arrays that can be used to store elements of different data types. For example, the statement

```
struct
{
    char *name;
    int  type;
    union
    {
        int   i;
        float f;
        char  c;
    } data;
} table [kTableEntries];
```

sets up an array called `table`, consisting of `kTableEntries` elements. Each element of the array contains a structure consisting of a character pointer called `name`, an integer member called `type`, and a union member called `data`. Each `data` member of the array can contain an `int`, a `float`, or a `char`. The integer member `type` might be used to keep track of the type of value stored in the member `data`. For example, you could assign it the value `INTEGER` (defined appropriately, we assume) if it contained an `int`, `FLOATING` if it contained a `float`, and `CHARACTER` if it contained a `char`. This information would enable you to know how to reference the particular `data` member of a particular array element.

To store the character `'#'` into `table[5]`, and subsequently set the `type` field to indicate that a character is stored in that location, the following two statements could be used:

```
table[5].data.c = '#';
table[5].type = CHARACTER;
```

When sequencing through the elements of table, you could determine the type of data value stored in each element by setting up an appropriate series of test statements. For example, the following loop would display each name and its associated value from table at the terminal:

```
enum symbolType { INTEGER, FLOATING, CHARACTER };
   ...

for ( j = 0; j < kTableEntries; ++j )
{
  printf ("%s ", table[j].name);

  switch ( table[j].type )
  {
     case INTEGER:
          printf ("%i\n", table[j].data.i);
          break;
     case FLOATING:
          printf ("%g\n", table[j].data.f);
          break;
     case CHARACTER:
          printf ("%c\n", table[j].data.c);
          break;
     default:
          printf ("Unknown type (%i), element %i\n",
                    table[j].type, j );
          break;
  }
}
```

The type of application illustrated previously might be practical for storage of a symbol table, which might contain the name of each symbol, its type, and its value (and perhaps other information about the symbol as well).

They're Not Objects!

Now you know how to define arrays, structures, character strings, and unions and how to manipulate them in your program. Just remember one fundamental thing: *They're not objects.* That means you can't send messages to them. It also means they can't be used to take maximal advantage of nice things such as the memory allocation strategy provided by the Foundation framework. That's one of the reasons I encouraged you to skip this chapter and return to it later. In general, I'd rather you learned how to use the Foundation's classes that define things like arrays and strings as objects than the ones built in to the language. You should resort to using the types defined in this chapter only if you really need to. And hopefully you won't!

Miscellaneous Language Features

Some language features didn't fit well into any of the other chapters, so they've been included here.

Compound Literals

A *compound literal* is a type name enclosed in parentheses followed by an initialization list. It creates an unnamed value of the specified type, which has scope limited to the block in which it is created or global scope if defined outside of any block. In the latter case, the initializers must all be constant expressions.

Here's an example:

```
(struct date) {.month = 7, .day = 2, .year = 2004}
```

This is an expression that produces a structure of type `struct date` with the specified initial values. This can be assigned to another `struct date` structure, like so:

```
theDate = (struct date) {.month = 7, .day = 2, .year = 2004};
```

Or, it can be passed to a function or method expecting an argument of `struct date`, like so:

```
setStartDate ((struct date) {.month = 7, .day = 2, .year = 2004});
```

Types other than structures can be defined as well—for example, if `intPtr` is of type `int *`, the statement

```
intPtr = (int [100]) {[0] = 1, [50] = 50, [99] = 99 };
```

(which can appear anywhere in the program) sets `intptr` pointing to an array of 100 integers, whose 3 elements are initialized as specified.

If the size of the array is not specified, it is determined by the initializer list.

The `goto` Statement

Execution of a `goto` statement causes a direct branch to be made to a specified point in the program. To identify where in the program the branch is to be made, a label is needed. A *label* is a name formed with the same rules as variable names and must be immediately followed by a colon. The label is placed directly before the statement to which the branch is to be made and must appear in the same function or method as the `goto`.

For example, the statement

```
goto out_of_data;
```

causes the program to branch immediately to the statement that is preceded by the label `out_of_data;`. This label can be located anywhere in the function or method, before or after the `goto`, and might be used as shown here:

```
out_of_data: printf ("Unexpected end of data.\n");
    ...
```

Programmers who are lazy frequently abuse the goto statement to branch to other portions of their code. The goto statement interrupts the normal sequential flow of a program. As a result, programs are harder to follow. Using many gotos in a program can make it impossible to decipher. For this reason, goto statements are not considered part of good programming style.

The null Statement

Objective-C permits a solitary semicolon to be placed wherever a normal program statement can appear. The effect of such a statement, known as the *null* statement, is that nothing is done. This might seem quite useless, but it is often used by programmers in while, for, and do statements. For example, the purpose of the following statement is to store all the characters read in from *standard input* (your terminal by default) into the character array pointed to by text until a newline character is encountered. It uses the library routine getchar, which reads and returns a single character at a time from standard input:

```
while ( (*text++ = getchar ()) != '\n' )
    ;
```

All the operations are performed inside the looping conditions part of the while statement. The null statement is needed because the compiler takes the statement that follows the looping expression as the body of the loop. Without the null statement, whatever statement that follows in the program would be treated as the body of the program loop by the compiler.

The Comma Operator

At the bottom of the precedence totem pole, so to speak, is the comma operator. In Chapter 5,"Program Looping," we pointed out that inside a for statement you could include more than one expression in any of the fields by separating each expression with a comma. For example, the for statement that begins

```
for ( i = 0, j = 100; i != 10; ++i, j -= 10 )
    ...
```

initializes the value of i to 0 and j to 100 before the loop begins, and it increments the value of i and subtracts 10 from the value of j each time after the body of the loop is executed.

Because all operators in Objective-C produce a value, the value of the comma operator is that of the rightmost expression.

The sizeof Operator

Although you should never make any assumptions about the size of a data type in your program, sometimes you will need to know this information. This might be needed when performing dynamic memory allocation using library routines such as malloc or when writing or archiving data to a file. Objective-C provides an operator called `sizeof` that you can use to determine the size of a data type or object. The `sizeof` operator returns the size of the specified item in bytes. The argument to the `sizeof` operator can be a variable, an array name, the name of a basic data type, an object, the name of a derived data type, or an expression. For example, writing

```
sizeof (int)
```

gives the number of bytes needed to store an integer. On a Mac with a G5 processor, this produces a result of 4 (or 32 bits). If x is declared as an array of 100 ints, the expression

```
sizeof (x)
```

would give the amount of storage required to store the 100 integers of x.

Given that `myFract` is a `Fraction` object that contains two int instance variables (`numerator` and `denominator`), the expression

```
sizeof (myFract)
```

produces the value 4 on any system that represents pointers using 4 bytes. In fact, this is the value that `sizeof` yields for any object because here you are asking for the size of the pointer to the object's data. To get the size of the actual data structure to store an instance of a `Fraction` object, you would instead write the following:

```
sizeof (*myFract)
```

On my PowerBook G4 OS X system, this gives me a value of 12. That's 4 bytes each for the `numerator` and `denominator` plus another 4 bytes for the inherited `isa` member mentioned in the section "How Things Work" at the end of this chapter.

The expression

```
sizeof (struct data_entry)
```

has as its value the amount of storage required to store one `data_entry` structure. If data is defined as an array of `struct data_entry` elements, the expression

```
sizeof (data) / sizeof (struct data_entry)
```

gives the number of elements contained in `data` (`data` must be a previously defined array and not a formal parameter or externally referenced array). The expression

```
sizeof (data) / sizeof (data[0])
```

also produces the same result.

Use the `sizeof` operator wherever possible to avoid having to calculate and hard-code sizes into your programs.

Command–Line Arguments

Many times a program is developed that requires the user to enter a small amount of information at the terminal. This information might consist of a number indicating the triangular number you want to have calculated or a word you want to have looked up in a dictionary.

Rather than having the program request this type of information from the user, you can supply the information to the program at the time the program is executed. This capability is provided by what is known as *command-line arguments*.

We have pointed out that the only distinguishing quality of the function main is that its name is special; it specifies where program execution is to begin. In fact, the function main is actually called upon at the start of program execution by the runtime system, just as you would call a function from within your own program. When main completes execution, control is returned to the runtime system, which then knows that your program has completed execution.

When main is called by the runtime system, two arguments are passed to the function. The first argument, which is called argc by convention (for *arg*ument *c*ount), is an integer value that specifies the number of arguments typed on the command line. The second argument to main is an array of character pointers, which is called argv by convention (for *arg*ument *v*ector). In addition, argc + 1 character pointers are contained in this array. The first entry in this array is either a pointer to the name of the program that is executing or a pointer to a null string if the program name is not available on your system. Subsequent entries in the array point to the values specified in the same line as the command that initiated execution of the program. The last pointer in the argv array, argv[argc], is defined to be null.

To access the command-line arguments, the main function must be appropriately declared as taking two arguments. The conventional declaration we have used in all the programs in this book will suffice:

```
int main (int argc, char *argv[])
{
    ...
}
```

Remember, the declaration of argv defines an array that contains elements of type "pointer to char." As a practical use of command-line arguments, suppose you had developed a program that looks up a word inside a dictionary and prints its meaning. You can use command-line arguments so that the word whose meaning you want to find can be specified at the same time that the program is executed, as in the following command:

```
lookup aerie
```

This eliminates the need for the program to prompt the user to enter a word because it is typed on the command line.

If the previous command were executed, the system would automatically pass to the main function a pointer to the character string "aerie" in argv[1]. As you will recall, argv[0] would contain a pointer to the name of the program, which in this case would be "lookup".

The `main` routine might appear as shown:

```
#include <stdio.h>

int main (int argc, char *argv[])
{
    struct entry dictionary[100] =
      { { "aardvark", "a burrowing African mammal"    },
        { "abyss",   "a bottomless pit"            },
        { "acumen",  "mentally sharp; keen"         },
        { "addle",   "to become confused"           },
        { "aerie",   "a high nest"               },
        { "affix",   "to append; attach"            },
        { "agar",    "a jelly made from seaweed"     },
        { "ahoy",    "a nautical call of greeting"    },
        { "aigrette", "an ornamental cluster of feathers" },
        { "ajar",    "partially opened"            } };

    int  entries = 10;
    int  entryNumber;
    int  lookup (struct entry dictionary [], char search[],
                 int entries);

    if ( argc != 2 )
    {
        printf ("No word typed on the command line.\n");
        return (1);
    }

    entryNumber = lookup (dictionary, argv[1], entries);

    if ( entryNumber != -1 )
        printf ("%s\n", dictionary[entryNumber].definition);
    else
        printf ("Sorry, %s is not in my dictionary.\n", argv[1]);

    return (0);
}
```

The `main` routine tests to ensure that a word was typed after the program name when the program was executed. If it wasn't, or if more than one word was typed, the value of `argc` is not equal to 2. In that case, the program writes an error message to standard error and terminates, returning an exit status of 1.

If `argc` is equal to 2, the `lookup` function is called to find the word pointed to by `argv[1]` in the dictionary. If the word is found, its definition is displayed.

It should be remembered that command-line arguments are always stored as character strings. So, execution of the program `power` with the command-line arguments 2 and 16, as in

```
power 2 16
```

stores a pointer to the character string `"2"` inside `argv[1]` and a pointer to the string `"16"` inside `argv[2]`. If the arguments are to be interpreted as numbers by the program (as we suspect is the case in the `power` program), they must be converted by the program itself. Several routines are available in the program library for doing such conversions, such as `sscanf`, `atof`, `atoi`, `strtod`, and `strtol`. In Part II, "The Foundation Framework," you'll learn how to use a class called `NSProcessInfo` to access the command-line arguments as string objects instead of as C strings.

How Things Work

We would be remiss if we finished this chapter without first trying to tie a couple of things together. Because the Objective-C language has the C language lying underneath, it's worthwhile mentioning some of the connections between the former and the latter. These are implementation details you can ignore or can use to perhaps give you a better understanding of how things work, in the same way learning that pointers are actually memory addresses can help give you a better understanding about pointers. We won't get too detailed here; we'll just state four facts about the relationship between Objective-C and C.

Fact #1: Instance variables are stored in structures. When you define a new class and its instance variables, those instance variables are actually stored inside a structure. That's how you can manipulate objects; they're really structures whose members are your instance variables. So, the inherited instance variables plus the ones you added in your class all comprise a single structure. When you `alloc` a new object, enough space is reserved to hold one of these structures.

One of the inherited members (it comes from the root object) of the structure is a protected member called `isa` that identifies the class to which the object belongs. Because it's part of the structure (and therefore part of the object), it is carried around with the object. In that way the runtime system can always identify the class of an object (even if you assign it to a generic `id` object variable) by just looking at its `isa` member.

You can gain direct access to the members of an object's structure by making them `@public` (see the discussion in Chapter 10, "More on Variables and Data Types"). If you did that with the `numerator` and `denominator` members of your `Fraction` class, for example, you could write expressions such as

```
myFract->numerator
```

in your program to directly access the `numerator` member of the `Fraction` object `myFract`. But we strongly advise against your doing that! As we mentioned in Chapter 10, it goes against the grain of data encapsulation.

Fact #2: An object variable is really a pointer. When you define an object variable like a `Fraction`, as in

```
Fraction *myFract;
```

you're really defining a pointer variable called `myFract`. This variable is defined to point to something of type `Fraction`, which is the name of your class. When you allocate a new instance of a `Fraction`, with

```
myFract = [Fraction alloc];
```

you're allocating space to store a new `Fraction` object in memory (that is, space for a structure) and then taking the pointer to that structure that is returned and storing it inside the pointer variable `myFract`.

When you assign one object variable to another, as in

```
myFract2 = myFract1;
```

you're simply copying pointers. Both variables end up pointing to the same structure stored somewhere in memory. Making a change to one of the members referenced (that is, pointed to) by `myFract2` therefore changes the same instance variable (that is, structure member) referenced by `myFract1`.

Fact #3: Methods are functions and message expressions are function calls. Methods are really functions. When you invoke a method, you are calling a function associated with the class of the receiver. The arguments passed to the function are the receiver (`self`) and the method's arguments. So, all the rules about passing arguments to functions, return values, and automatic and static variables are the same whether you're talking about a function or a method. The Objective-C compiler creates a unique name for each function using a combination of the class name and the method name.

Fact #4: The `id` type is a generic pointer type. Because objects are referenced through pointers, which in turn are just memory addresses, you can freely assign them back and forth between `id` variables. A method that returns an `id` type consequently just returns a pointer to some object in memory. You can then take that value and assign it to any object variable you like. Because the object always carries around its `isa` member wherever it goes, its class can always be identified, even if you store it in a generic object variable of type `id`.

Exercises

1. Write a function that calculates the average of an array of 10 floating-point values and returns the result.

2. The reduce method from your Fraction class finds the greatest common divisor of the numerator and denominator to reduce the fraction. Modify that method so that it uses the gcd function from Program 13.5 instead. Where do you think you should place the function definition? Are there any benefits to making the function static? Which approach do you think is better—using a gcd function or incorporating the code directly into the method as you did previously? Why?

3. Prime numbers can be generated by an algorithm known as the *Sieve of Erastosthenes*. The algorithm for this procedure is presented here. Write a program that implements this algorithm. Have the program find all prime numbers up to n = 150. What can you say about this algorithm as compared to the ones used in the text for calculating prime numbers?

   Step 1: Define an array of integers P. Set all elements P_i to 0, $2 <= i <= $ n.

   Step 2: Set i to 2.

   Step 3: If $i > n$, the algorithm terminates.

   Step 4: If P_i is 0, i is prime.

   Step 5: For all positive integer values of j, such that $i \times j < \neq n$, set P_{ixj} to 1.

   Step 6: Add 1 to i and go to step 3.

4. Write a function to add all the Fractions passed to it in an array and to return the result as a Fraction.

5. Write a typedef definition for a struct date called Date that will allow you to make declarations like

   ```
   Date todaysDate;
   ```

   in your program.

6. As noted in the text, defining a Date class instead of a date structure would be more consistent with the notion of object-oriented programming. Define such a class with appropriate setter and getter methods. Also, add a method called dateUpdate to return the day after its argument.

   Do you see any advantages of defining a Date as a class instead of as a structure? Do you see any disadvantages?

7. Given the following definitions:

```
char *message = "Programming in Objective-C is fun\n";
char message2[] = "You said it\n";
char *format = "x = %i\n";
int  x = 100;
```

determine whether each printf call from the following sets is valid and produces the same output as other calls from the set.

```
/*** set 1 ***/
printf ("Programming in Objective-C is fun\n");
printf ("%s", "Programming in Objective-C is fun\n");
printf ("%s", message);
printf (message);
/*** set 2 ***/
printf ("You said it\n");
printf ("%s", message2);
printf (message2);
printf ("%s", &message2[0]);
/*** set 3 ***/
printf ("said it\n");
printf (message2 + 4);
printf ("%s", message2 + 4);
printf ("%s", &message2[4]);
/*** set 4 ***/
printf ("x = %i\n", x);
printf (format, x);
```

8. Write a program that prints all its command-line arguments, one per line at the terminal. Notice the effect of enclosing arguments containing space characters inside quotation marks.

II

The Foundation Framework

14

Introduction to the
Foundation Framework

A *FRAMEWORK* IS A COLLECTION OF classes, methods, functions, and documentation logically grouped together to make developing programs easier. On the Mac under OS X, about 50 frameworks exist for developing applications, working with the Mac's Address Book structure, burning CDs, developing QuickTime applications, using audio devices, and so on.

The framework that provides the base or foundation for all your program development is called the Foundation framework. This framework is the subject of this second part of this book. It allows you to work with basic objects, such as numbers and strings, and with collections of objects, such as arrays, dictionaries, and sets. Other capabilities provide for working with dates and times, automated memory management, working with the underlying file system, storing (or *archiving*) objects, and working with geometric data structures such as points and rectangles.

The Application Kit framework contains an extensive collection of classes and methods to develop interactive graphical applications. These give the capability to easily work with text, menus, toolbars, tables, documents, the pasteboard, and windows. On Mac OS X the term *Cocoa* collectively refers to the Foundation framework and the Application Kit framework. After you have finished the material in this book, you will be well suited to learning how to develop Cocoa applications. Many resources for this subject are listed in Appendix E, "Resources."

The Foundation framework can be found on the Mac as noted. It also exists as part of the free GNUStep distribution, which means you can use it on any Unix system that has GNUStep installed or under Windows as part of the CygWin or MinGW system. Linux users can install LinuxSTEP as their development environment. As with the programs developed in the first part of this book, all the programs using the Foundation framework run under all these environments. Consult Appendix E for links to Web sites where you can download these development environments.

Foundation Programs on the Mac

This section tells how to access the large volumes of documentation and how to compile Foundation programs on Mac OS X.

Foundation Documentation

For reference purposes, you should know that the Foundation header files are stored in the directory /System/Library/Frameworks/Foundation.framework/Headers. Take a look at that directory and familiarize yourself with its contents. You should also take advantage of the Foundation framework documentation stored on your system. This documentation exists both in the form of a single Acrobat .pdf file (at /Developer/ Documentation/Cocoa/Reference/Foundation/ObjC_classic/Foundation. pdf) and as HTML files for viewing by a browser (at /Developer/Documentation/ Cocoa/CocoaTopics.html or /Developer/Documentation/Cocoa/Cocoa.html under panther). Contained in this documentation is a description of all the Foundation classes and all the implemented methods and functions.

If you're using the HTML files, open the CocoaTopics.html file in your browser and click Foundation under the heading Objective-C Framework Reference (see Figure 14.1). Under the topic heading Programming Topics further down on the page you will also find a wide assortment of documents covering specific programming issues, such as Memory Management, Strings, and File Management. The reference documentation is also available online from Apple's Web site at the following URL: http://developer. apple.com/documentation/Cocoa/Reference/Foundation/ObjC_classic/ index.html. The online documentation might be more current than that stored on your hard disk, so you should take that into consideration.

If you're using Project Builder (or X code), one of the nice things is that you have easy access to all the documentation stored on your disk, which includes the header files, method descriptions, and related programming topics, through the sideways Classes tab. For example, Figure 14.2 shows the Programming Topics documentation for the NSObject class in the rightmost window. You get this by clicking the book icon next to NSObject in the upper-left window. Clicking NSObject itself gives you the actual interface section for the class. The lower-left window gives you access to the instance methods for a particular class, in this case for NSObject.

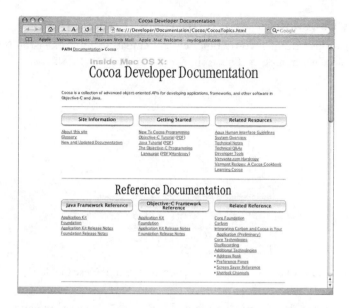

Figure 14.1 Online Foundation documentation.

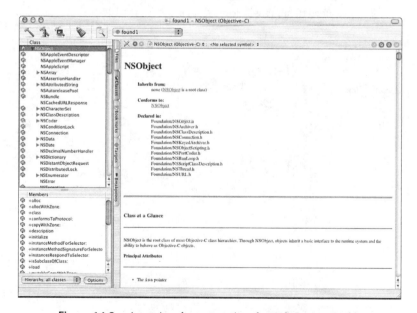

Figure 14.2 Accessing documentation through Project Builder.

Compiling Foundation Programs Using Project Builder

If you're using Project Builder, you should select Foundation Tool under the New Project window when it appears. This is shown in Figure 14.3.

Figure 14.3   Selecting Foundation Tool from Project Builder.

In the menu screen that follows, you should specify the project name and its location in the normal way. After that, the new project is created. If you examine the template file that is created for you (main.m), it will look similar to Figure 14.4.

Figure 14.4   The initial main.m file that is created in Project Builder.

There are some new things in the main.m file, which we will talk about in Chapter 15, "Numbers, Strings, and Collections." You can delete the NSLog function call from the template file; the rest can remain.

You can then enter the lines for your program into the editor window and can subsequently build and run your application as you did with all the previous program examples.

Compiling Foundation Programs Using Terminal

You can easily compile programs using gcc to work with the Foundation framework. All you have to do is add the -framework foundation option on the gcc command line. This can then be followed by the list of Objective-C files to be compiled. So, the command line

```
$ gcc -framework Foundation main.m
```

compiles the program main.m and automatically links it with the appropriate libraries. Note that you do not use the -l objc option any longer.

Assuming your program was divided into three files called addressbook.m, addresscard.m, and main.m, the command line

```
$ gcc -framework Foundation addressbook.m addresscard.m main.m -o addrbk
```

would compile the three specified Objective-C files and name the executable output file addrbk.

Foundation Programs Under GNUStep

If you've installed MinGW or CygWin on your Windows system, you should note that GNUStep is not part of the standard MinGW distribution, so you'll have to get it yourself from www.gnustep.org and follow the directions for installation.

After GNUStep is installed, you can compile your programs using gcc. You can use two approaches here. One is to create your own gcc command line, and the other is to use the make utility and create a GNUmakefile. In either case, you need to ensure that the GNUStep environment variables are set up properly on your system. This is done by executing the GNUStep.sh file when you start your shell. Check with your system administrator if you were not the one who installed GNUStep on your system to ensure that your GNUStep environment is properly set up.

If you use the gcc command line approach, your command line might vary based on how GNUStep was installed on your system. In the general case, it might look something like this:

```
$ gcc -fconstant-string-class=NSConstantString -I header-dirs \
   -L lib-dirs source-files -lobjc -lgnustep-base
```

(The \ at the end of the line is for continuing the command line over the following line.)

The directory -I *header-dir* option specifies the directory containing the header files needed by your program. You will need more than one of these. Similarly, the -L *lib-dir* option specifies the location of the GNUStep library files, which you will also need more than one of. On my Windows XP system with GNUStep installed in the directory C:\gnustep (which can also be referenced through the variable $GNUSTEP_ROOT), I would use the following command line to compile the program main.m:

```
$ gcc -fconstant-string-class=NSConstantString \
 -I /c/gnustep/system/library/headers \
 -I /c/gnustep/system/library/headers/gnustep \
 -I /c/gnustep/system/library/headers/ix86/mingw32 \
 -L /c/gnustep/system/library/libraries/ix86/mingw32 \
 -L /c/gnustep/system/library/libraries/ix86/mingw32/gnu-gnu-gnu \
 main.m -lobjc -lgnustep-base
```

Obviously, you won't want to type this in each time. So, you should create a simple shell script that enables you to specify the name of the file(s) to compile, like this:

```
$ fgcc main.m
```

You can also use a special program called make to build your programs more easily. To use make, you must make sure you have the GNU make utility installed. Then, you'll need to create a makefile under the name GNUmakefile.

Assuming you are compiling a program called main.m and want the executable named test1.exe (under Windows), your GNUmakefile would look like this:

```
$ cat GNUmakefile
include $(GNUSTEP_MAKEFILES)/common.make

TOOL_NAME = test1
test1_OBJC_FILES = main.m

include $(GNUSTEP_MAKEFILES)/tool.make
$
```

Here, test1 should be replaced in two spots by the name of your program. If your program contains more than one source file, they all should be listed on the OBJC_FILES line, as in the following:

```
TOOL_NAME = addrbook
addrbk_OBJC_FILES = addressbook.m addresscard.m main.m
```

To compile your test1 program (assuming that the source file and the makefile are in the current directory), you can issue the make command:

```
$ make
Making all for tool test1...
 Compiling file main.m ...
main.m:1:2: warning: #import is obsolete, use an #ifndef wrapper in the header
file
 Linking tool test1 ...
$
```

The executable for the program is not placed in your current directory. Instead it is buried in a directory called shared_obj, which is created for you if it doesn't already exist. In our example, you can locate your executable as follows:

```
$ cd shared_obj/ix86/mingw32/gnu-gnu-gnu
$ test1
Programming is fun.
$
```

You can also have all your programs installed into the same directory by setting and exporting the variable GNUSTEP_INSTALLATION_DIR. This variable can also be set inside the makefile and should be a path to a directory to which you can write. After your program compiles and links successfully, typing in

```
$ make install
```

places your executable into that directory. More precisely, the executable is placed into the directory $GNUSTEP_INSTALLATION_DIR/ Tools/ix86/mingw32/ gnu-gnu-gnu (or something slightly different, depending on your machine and development environment). This directory path can then be added to your PATH so you can execute your installed programs from anywhere.

Before leaving this section, we should talk a little about documentation. Appendix E lists resources for locating the online GNUStep Foundation framework documentation. You can also look at Apple's online documentation. You will find that, for the most part, its Foundation documentation (as far as class and method descriptions are concerned) corresponds closely to your GNUStep implementation.

The Root Object: NSObject

Before leaving this chapter, we should mention that you will be using a new root object in your Foundation programs. In all the programs up to this point, you used the root object Object. The Foundation framework uses a different root object called NSObject. If you're not including <Foundation/Foundation.h> (it's put there automatically by Project Builder), include the line

```
#import <Foundation/NSObject.h>
```

at the beginning of each of your Foundation programs. Any new class you define when working with the Foundation framework should also have NSObject as its root class, unless, of course it's a subclass of some other object.

You should also note that, as far as memory allocation strategy is concerned, the free method is no longer used to release an object's memory. Instead, you will use NSObject's release method. Foundation also uses a new memory allocation strategy that involves what is known as the *autorelease pool*. You'll learn more about that in the upcoming chapters.

Exercises

1. Locate the header file NSObject.h and examine its contents.

2. Look up the documentation for the Foundation's NSArray class; then find the documentation for the objectAtIndex: method. If you're using a Mac OS X system, locate the documentation on your disk and also online. If you're using Project Builder, locate the documentation on your disk through the application. Don't worry if you don't fully understand the description of the class or the method (we'll cover that in the next chapter). This exercise is just to get you familiar with how to use the documentation.

3. Modify the Fraction class defined in Part I, "The Objective-C Language," to run under the Foundation framework. Be sure you change the root object in that class to NSObject. Compile and run a test program.

15

Numbers, Strings, and Collections

THIS CHAPTER DESCRIBES HOW TO WORK with some of the basic objects provided in the Foundation framework. These include numbers; strings; and collections, which refers to the capability to work with groups of objects in the form of arrays, dictionaries, and sets.

The Foundation framework contains a plethora of classes, methods, and functions for you to use. Approximately 100 header files are available on the Mac, and 70 are available as part of GNUStep that you can import into your program. As a convenience, you can simply use the following import:

```
#import <Foundation/Foundation.h>
```

Then you don't have to worry about whether you are importing the correct header file. This header file is automatically imported into your program by Project Builder when you create a Foundation Tool, as described previously in Chapter 14, "Introduction to the Foundation Framework."

Because the `Foundation.h` file imports virtually all the other Foundation header files, using this statement can add a significant amount of time to your compiles. You can, however, avoid this extra time by using *precompiled* headers. These are files that have been preprocessed by the compiler. By default, all Project Builder projects benefit from pre-compiled headers. In this chapter, you'll use the specific header files for each object you use. This will help you become familiar with what's contained in each header file.

Number Objects

All the numeric data types we've dealt with up to now, such as integers, floats, and longs, are basic data types in the Objective-C language; that is, they are not objects. For example, you can't send messages to them. Sometimes, though, you need to work with these values as objects. For example, the Foundation object `NSArray` enables you to set up an array in which you can store values. These values have to be objects, so you can't directly store any of your basic data types in these arrays. Instead, to store any of the basic numeric data types (including the `char` data type), you can use the `NSNumber` class to create objects from these data types. This is shown in Program 15.1.

Program 15.1

```
// Working with Numbers

#import <Foundation/NSObject.h>
#import <Foundation/NSAutoreleasePool.h>
#import <Foundation/NSValue.h>

#import <Foundation/NSString.h>

int main (int argc, char *argv[])
{
    NSAutoreleasePool *pool = [[NSAutoreleasePool alloc] init];
    NSNumber           *myNumber, *floatNumber, *intNumber;
    int                i;

    // integer value

    intNumber = [NSNumber numberWithInt: 100];
    printf ("%i\n", [intNumber intValue]);

    // long value

    myNumber = [NSNumber numberWithLong: 0xabcdef];
    printf ("%lx\n", [myNumber longValue]);

    // char value

    myNumber = [NSNumber numberWithChar: 'X'];
    printf ("%c\n", [myNumber charValue]);


    // float value

    floatNumber = [NSNumber numberWithFloat: 100.00];
    printf ("%g\n", [floatNumber floatValue]);

    // double

    myNumber = [NSNumber numberWithDouble: 12345e+15];
    printf ("%Lg\n", [myNumber doubleValue]);

    // Wrong access here

    printf ("%i\n", [myNumber intValue]);

    // Test two Numbers for equality
```

Program 15.1 **Continued**

```
if ([intNumber isEqualToNumber: floatNumber] == YES)
    printf ("Numbers are equal\n");
else
    printf ("Numbers are not equal\n");


// Test if one Number is <, ==, or > second Number

if ([intNumber compare: myNumber] == NSOrderedAscending)
    printf ("First number is less than second\n");

[pool release];
return 0;
}
```

Program 15.1 **Output**

```
100
abcdef
X
100
1.2345e+19
2147483647
Numbers are equal
First number is less than second
```

The interface file `<Foundation/NSValue.h>` is needed to work with objects from the NSNumber class.

A Quick Look at the Autorelease Pool

The line in Program 15.1 that reads

```
NSAutoreleasePool *pool = [[NSAutoreleasePool alloc] init];
```

reserves space in memory for an autorelease pool that you assign to pool. Put this line at the beginning of main in all your Foundation programs—if you're using Project Builder (and following the steps outlined in Chapter 14), it has already been put there for you. If not, you'll also need to include the header file `<Foundation/NSAutoreleasePool.h>` in your program.

At the end of main, before you exit your program, you should release the allocated memory pool with a line such as follows:

```
[pool release];
```

Again, Project Builder automatically inserts this line into your program for you.

In a nutshell, the autorelease pool provides for the automatic release of memory used by objects that are added to this pool. An object is added to the pool when it is sent an `autorelease` message. When the pool is released, so are all the objects that were added to it. Therefore, all such objects are destroyed unless they have been specified to exist beyond the scope of the autorelease pool (as indicated by their *reference counts*).

In general, you don't need to worry about releasing an object returned by a Foundation method. Sometimes the object is owned by the method that returns it. Other times, the object is newly created and added to the autorelease pool by the method. As described in detail in Part I, "The Objective-C Language," you do still need to release any objects (including Foundation objects) that you explicitly create using the `alloc` method when you're done using them.[1]

Reference counts and the autorelease pool are described in full detail in Chapter 17, "Memory Management."

Let's return to Program 15.1. The `NSNumber` class contains many methods that allow you to create `NSNumber` objects with initial values. For example, the line

```
intNumber = [NSNumber numberWithInt: 100];
```

creates an object from an integer whose value is `100`.

The value retrieved from an `NSNumber` object must be consistent with the type of value that was stored in it. So, in the `printf` statement that follows in the program, the message expression

```
[intNumber intValue]
```

retrieves the integer value stored inside `intNumber` and displays it using the correct `printf` formatting characters.

For each basic value, a class method allocates an `NSNumber` object and sets it to a specified value. These methods begin with `numberWith` followed by the type, as in `numberWithLong:`, `numberWithFloat:`, and so on. In addition, instance methods can be used to set a previously allocated `NSNumber` object to a specified value. These all begin with `initWith`—as in `initWithLong:` and `initWithFloat:`.

Table 15.1 lists the class and instance methods for setting values for `NSNumber` objects and the corresponding instance methods for retrieving their values.

Table 15.1   NSNumber **Creation and Retrieval Methods**

Creation and Initialization Class Method	Initialization Instance Method	Retrieval Instance Method
numberWithChar:	initWithChar:	charValue
numberWithUnsignedChar:	initWithUnsignedChar:	unsignedCharValue
numberWithShort:	initWithShort:	shortValue
numberWithUnsignedShort:	initWithUnsignedShort:	unsignedShortValue

1. You also need to release objects created by a copy method, as you'll learn in Chapter 17, "Memory Management."

Table 15.1 **Continued**

Creation and Initialization Class Method	Initialization Instance Method	Retrieval Instance Method
numberWithInt:	initWithInt:	intValue
numberWithUnsignedInt:	initWithUnsignedInt:	unsignedIntValue
numberWithLong:	initWithLong:	longValue
numberWithUnsignedLong:	initWithUnsignedLong:	unsignedLongValue
numberWithLongLong:	initWithLongLong:	longlongValue
numberWithUnsignedLongLong:	initWithUnsignedLongLong:	unsignedLongLongValue
numberWithFloat:	initWithFloat:	floatValue
numberWithDouble:	initWithDouble:	doubleValue
numberWithBool:	initWithBool:	boolValue

Returning to Program 15.1, the program next uses the class methods to create `long`, `char`, `float`, and `double` NSNumber objects. Notice what happens after you create a `double` object with the line

```
myNumber = [NSNumber numberWithDouble: 12345e+15];
```

and then try to (incorrectly) retrieve and display its value with the following line:

```
printf ("%i\n", [myNumber intValue]);
```

You get this output:

```
2147483647
```

Also, you get no error message from the system. In general, it's up to you to ensure that, if you store a value in an NSNumber object, you retrieve it in a consistent manner.

Inside the `if` statement, the message expression

```
[intNumber isEqualToNumber: floatNumber]
```

uses the `isEqualToNumber:` method to numerically compare two NSNumber objects. The Boolean value returned is tested by the program to see whether the two values are equal.

The `compare:` method can be used to test whether one numeric value is numerically less than, equal to, or greater than another. The message expression

```
[intNumber compare: myNumber]
```

returns the value NSOrderedAscending if the numeric value stored in `intNumber` is less than the numeric value contained in `myNumber`, returns the value NSOrderedSame if the two numbers are equal, and returns the value NSOrderedDescending if the first number is greater than the second. The values returned are defined in the header file NSObject.h for you.

You should note that you can't reinitialize the value of a previously created NSNumber object. For example, you can't set the value of an integer stored in the NSNumber object myNumber with a statement such as follows:

```
[myNumber initWithInt: 1000];
```

This statement generates an error when the program is executed. All number objects must be newly created, meaning you must invoke either one of the methods listed in the first column of Table 15.1 on the NSNumber class or one of the methods listed in column two with the result from the alloc method, like so:

```
myNumber = [[NSNumber alloc] initWithInt: 1000];
```

Of course, based on previous discussions, if you create myNumber this way, you are responsible for subsequently releasing it when you're done using it with a statement such as follows:

```
[myNumber release];
```

You'll encounter NSNumber objects again in programs throughout the remainder of this chapter.

String Objects

You've encountered character strings in your programs before. Whenever you enclosed a sequence of character strings inside a pair of double quotes, as in

```
"Programming is fun"
```

you created a character string in Objective-C. Each time you used printf you also specified the format of the output with a character string. These character strings are often referred to as *C-strings* or *C-style strings* because they are a basic data type from the underlying C language.

Like the basic data types in Objective-C, C-strings are not objects. The Foundation framework supports a class called NSString for working with character string objects. Whereas C-strings are composed of char characters, NSString objects are composed of unichar characters. A unichar character is a multibyte character according to the Unicode standard. This enables you to work with character sets that can contain literally millions of characters. Luckily, you don't have to worry about the internal representation of the characters in your strings because it's all handled for you automatically by the NSString class.[2] By using the methods from this class, you can more easily develop applications that can be *localized*—that is, made to work in different languages all over the world.

---

2. Currently, unichar characters occupy 16 bits, but the Unicode standard provides for characters larger than that size. So, in the future, unichar characters might be larger than 16 bits. The bottom line is to never make any assumption about the size of a Unicode character.

To create a constant character string object in Objective-C, you put the @ character in front of the string. So, the expression

```
@"Programming is fun"
```

creates a constant character string object. In particular, it is a constant character string belonging to the class NSConstantString.[3] Make sure you understand the distinction between writing a character string with and without the @ character in front of it.

NSConstantString is a subclass of the string object class NSString. To use string objects in your program, include the following line:

```
#import <Foundation/NSString.h>
```

The NSLog Function

A function in the Foundation library called NSLog is similar to printf. The first argument to NSLog is the format string; however, in this case it expects a string object. Program 15.2 illustrates the use of NSLog to duplicate in functionality what you did in your first program.

Program 15.2

```
#import <Foundation/NSObject.h>
#import <Foundation/NSString.h>
#import <Foundation/NSAutoreleasePool.h>

int main (int argc, char *argv[])
{
  NSAutoreleasePool *pool = [[NSAutoreleasePool alloc] init];

  NSLog (@"Programming is fun\n");

  [pool release];
  return 0;
}
```

Program 15.2 **Output**

```
2003-07-10 13:31:53.664 a.out[3621] Programming is fun
```

Note that the output from NSLog includes the date and time as well as the name of the program that generated the log message.

3. If you're using GNUStep, the default data type for a constant character string might be NXConstantString. If that's the case, you'll run into problems when working with the NSString class. You might need to use the gcc command-line option -fconstant-string-class=NSConstantString to change the default for the constant string class.

Program 15.3, which follows, shows how to define an NSString object and assign an initial constant character string to it. You can use NSLog to display a string object using the format characters %@. In the case of printf, it doesn't know about string objects, so an NSString object has to be converted back to a C-string, where it can be displayed with the %s format characters.[4] You should realize that C strings do not store Unicode characters, so you might lose data when you convert an NSString object to a C string.

Program 15.3

```
#import <Foundation/NSObject.h>
#import <Foundation/NSString.h>
#import <Foundation/NSAutoreleasePool.h>

int main (int argc, char *argv[])
{
  NSAutoreleasePool *pool = [[NSAutoreleasePool alloc] init];
  NSString *str = @"Programming is fun";

  NSLog (@"%@\n", str);
  printf ("%s\n", [str cString]);
  [pool release];
  return 0;
}
```

Program 15.3 **Output**

```
2003-07-10 13:32:53.894 a.out[3629] Programming is fun
Programming is fun
```

In the line

```
NSString *str = @"Programming is fun";
```

the constant string object Programming is fun is assigned to the NSString variable str. Its value is then displayed using NSLog and printf. In the latter case, as mentioned, it must first be converted to a C string using the cString method from the NSString class.

The NSLog format characters %@ can be used not just to display NSString objects, but to display any object as well. For example, given the following:

```
NSNumber *intNumber = [NSNumber numberWithInt: 100];
```

the NSLog call

```
NSLog (@"%@\n", intNumber);
```

4. The printf function comes from the underlying C language, which doesn't know anything about objects.

produces the following output:

```
2003-07-27 21:02:49.054 nslogn[1921] 100
```

The %@ format characters can even be used to display the entire contents of arrays, dictionaries, and sets. In fact, they can be used to display your own class objects as well, provided you override the description method inherited by your class. If you don't override the method, NSLog simply displays the name of the class and the address of your object in memory (that's the default implementation for the description method that is inherited from the NSObject class).

Mutable Versus Immutable Objects

When you create a string object by writing an expression such as

```
@"Programming is fun"
```

you create an object whose contents cannot be changed. This is referred to as an *immutable* object. The NSString class deals with immutable strings. Frequently, you'll want to deal with strings and change characters within the string. For example, you might want to delete some characters from a string or perform a search-and-replace operation on a string. These types of strings are handled through the NSMutableString class.

Program 15.4 shows basic ways to work with immutable character strings in your programs.

Program 15.4

```
// Basic String Operations

#import <Foundation/NSObject.h>
#import <Foundation/NSString.h>
#import <Foundation/NSAutoreleasePool.h>

int main (int argc, char *argv[])
{
  NSAutoreleasePool *pool = [[NSAutoreleasePool alloc] init];
  NSString *str1 = @"This is string A";
  NSString *str2 = @"This is string B";
  NSString *res;
  NSComparisonResult compareResult;

  // Count the number of characters

  printf ("Length of str1: %i\n", [str1 length]);

  // Copy one string to another
```

Program 15.4 **Continued**

```
res = [NSString stringWithString: str1];
printf ("Copy: %s\n", [res cString]);

// Copy one string to the end of another

str2 = [str1 stringByAppendingString: str2];
printf ("Concatentation: %s\n", [str2 cString]);

// Test if 2 strings are equal

if ([str1 isEqualToString: res] == YES)
     printf ("str1 == res\n");
else
     printf ("str1 != res\n");

// Test if one string is <, == or > than another

compareResult = [str1 compare: str2];

if (compareResult == NSOrderedAscending)
     printf ("str1 < str2\n");
else if (compareResult == NSOrderedSame)
     printf ("str1 == str2\n");
else // must be NSOrderedDescending
     printf ("str1 > str2\n");

// Convert a string to uppercase

res = [str1 uppercaseString];
printf ("Uppercase conversion: %s\n", [res cString]);

// Convert a string to lowercase

res = [str1 lowercaseString];
printf ("Lowercase conversion: %s\n", [res cString]);

printf ("Original string: %s\n", [str1 cString]);

[pool release];
return 0;
}
```

Program 15.4 **Output**

```
Length of str1: 16
Copy: This is string A
Concatentation: This is string AThis is string B
str1 == res
str1 < str2
Uppercase conversion: THIS IS STRING A
Lowercase conversion: this is string a
Original string: This is string A
```

Program 15.4 first declares three immutable NSString objects: str1, str2, and res. The first two are initialized to constant character string objects. The declaration

```
NSComparisonResult compareResult;
```

declares compareResult to hold the result of the string comparison that will be performed later in the program.

The length method can be used to count the number of characters in a string. The output verifies that the string

```
@"This is string A"
```

contains 16 characters. The statement

```
res = [NSString stringWithString: str1];
```

shows how to create a new character string with the contents of another. The resulting NSString object is assigned to res and is then displayed to verify the results. An actual copy of the string contents is made here, not just another reference to the same string in memory. That means that str1 and res refer to two different string objects, which is different from simply performing a simple assignment, as follows:

```
res = str1;
```

This simply creates another reference to the same object in memory.

The stringByAppendingString: method can be used to join two character strings. So, the expression

```
[str1 stringByAppendingString: str2]
```

creates a new string object that consists of the characters str1 followed by str2, returning the result. The original string objects, str1 and str2, are not affected by this operation (they can't be because they're both immutable string objects).

The isEqualToString: method is used next to test to see whether two character strings are equal—that is, contain the same characters. The compare: method can be used instead if you need to determine the ordering of two character strings—for example, if you wanted to sort an array of them. Similar to the compare: method you used earlier for comparing two NSNumber objects, the result of the comparison is NSOrderedAscending if the first string is lexically less than the second string, NSOrderedSame if the two strings are equal, and NSOrderedDescending if the first string is lexically greater than the second. If you don't want to perform a case-sensitive comparison, use the caseInsensitiveCompare: method instead of compare: to compare two strings. In such a case, the two string objects @"Gregory" and @"gregory" would compare as equal with caseInsensitiveCompare:.

The uppercaseString and lowercaseString are the last two NSString methods used in Program 15.4 to convert strings to uppercase and lowercase, respectively. Once again, the conversion does not affect the original strings, as verified by the last line of output.

Program 15.5 illustrates additional methods for dealing with strings. These methods enable you to extract substrings from a string as well as search one string for the occurrence of another.

Some methods require that you identify a substring by specifying a range. A *range* consists of a starting index number plus a character count. Index numbers begin with zero, so the first three characters in a string would be specified by the pair of numbers {0, 3}. The special data type NSRange is used by some methods from the NSString class (and other Foundation classes as well) to create a range specification. It is defined in <Foundation/NSRange.h> (which is included for you from inside <Foundation/NSString.h>) and is actually a typedef definition for a structure that has two members, called location and length.[5] This data type is used in Program 15.5.

Program 15.5

```
// Basic String Operations - Continued

#import <Foundation/NSObject.h>
#import <Foundation/NSString.h>
#import <Foundation/NSAutoreleasePool.h>

int main (int argc, char *argv[])
{
  NSAutoreleasePool *pool = [[NSAutoreleasePool alloc] init];
  NSString *str1 = @"This is string A";
  NSString *str2 = @"This is string B";
  NSString *res;
  NSRange   subRange;

  // Extract first 4 chars from string

  res = [str1 substringToIndex: 3];
  printf ("First 3 chars of str1: %s\n", [res cString]);

  // Extract chars to end of string starting at index 5
```

---

5. You can read about structures in Chapter 13, "Underlying C Language Features." However, you can probably gain enough information to work with them from the discussion that follows in the text.

Program 15.5   **Continued**

```
res = [str1 substringFromIndex: 5];
printf ("Chars from index 5 of str1: %s\n", [res cString]);

// Extract chars from index 8 through 13 (6 chars)

res = [[str1 substringFromIndex: 8] substringToIndex: 6];
printf ("Chars from index 8 through 13: %s\n", [res cString]);

// An easier way to do the same thing

res = [str1 substringWithRange: NSMakeRange (8, 6)];
printf ("Chars from index 8 through 13: %s\n", [res cString]);

// Locate one string inside another

subRange = [str1 rangeOfString: @"string A"];
printf ("String is at index %i, length is %i\n",
            subRange.location, subRange.length);

subRange = [str1 rangeOfString: @"string B"];

if (subRange.location == NSNotFound)
      printf ("String not found\n");
else
      printf ("String is at index %i, length is %i\n",
            subRange.location, subRange.length);

[pool release];
return 0;
}
```

Program 15.5   **Output**

```
First 3 chars of str1: Thi
Chars from index 5 of str1: is string A
Chars from index 8 through 13: string
Chars from index 8 through 13: string
String is at index 8, length is 8
String not found
```

The substringToIndex: method creates a substring from the leading characters in a string up to but not including the specified index number. Because indexing begins at zero, the argument of 3 extracts characters 0, 1, and 2 from the string and returns the resulting string object. For any of the string methods that take an index number as one of their arguments, you'll get a `Range or index out of bounds` error message if you provide an invalid index number in the string.

The `substringFromIndex:` method returns a substring from the receiver beginning with the character at the specified index and up through the end of the string.

The expression

```
res = [[str1 substringFromIndex: 8] substringToIndex: 6];
```

shows how the two methods can be combined to extract a substring of characters from inside a string. The `substringFromIndex:` method is first used to extract characters from index number 8 through the end of the string; then `substringToIndex:` is applied to the result to get the first six characters. The net result is a substring representing the range of characters {8, 6} from the original string.

The `substringWithRange:` method does in one step what we just did in two: It takes a range and returns a character in the specified range. The special function

```
NSMakeRange (8, 6)
```

creates a range from its argument and returns the result. This is given as the argument to the `substringWithRange:` method.

To locate one string inside another, you can use the `rangeOfString:` method. If the specified string is found inside the receiver, the returned range specifies precisely where in the string it was found. If, however, the string is not found, the range that is returned has its `location` member set to `NSNotFound`.

So, the statement

```
subRange = [str1 rangeOfString: @"string A"];
```

assigns the `NSRange` structure returned by the method to the `NSRange` variable `subRange`. Be sure to note that `subRange` is not an object variable, but a *structure* variable (the declaration for `subRange` in the program also does not contain an asterisk). Its members can be retrieved by using the structure member operator dot (.). So, the expression `subRange.location` gives the value of the `location` member of the structure and `subRange.length` gives the `length` member. These values are passed to the `printf` function to be displayed.

Mutable Strings

The `NSMutableString` class can be used to create string objects whose characters can be changed. Because this class is a subclass of `NSString`, all `NSString`'s methods can be used as well.

When we speak of mutable versus immutable string objects, we talk about changing the actual characters within the string. Either a mutable or an immutable string object can always be set to a completely different string object during execution of the program. For example, consider the following:

```
str1 = @"This is a string";
    ...
str1 = [str1 stringFromIndex: 5];
```

In this case, str1 is first set to a constant character string object. Later in the program, it is set to a substring. In such a case, str1 can be declared as either a mutable or an immutable string object. Be sure you understand this point.

Program 15.6 shows some ways to work with mutable strings in your programs.

Program 15.6

```
// Basic String Operations - Mutable Strings

#import <Foundation/NSObject.h>
#import <Foundation/NSString.h>
#import <Foundation/NSAutoreleasePool.h>

int main (int argc, char *argv[])
{
  NSAutoreleasePool   *pool = [[NSAutoreleasePool alloc] init];
  NSString            *str1 = @"This is string A";
  NSString            *search, *replace;
  NSMutableString     *mstr;
  NSRange             substr;

  // Create mutable string from immutable

  mstr = [NSMutableString stringWithString: str1];
  printf ("%s\n", [mstr cString]);

  // Insert characters starting at a specific index

  [mstr insertString: @" mutable" atIndex: 7];
  printf ("%s\n", [mstr cString]);

  // Effective concatentation if insert at end

  [mstr insertString: @" and string B" atIndex: [mstr length]];
  printf ("%s\n", [mstr cString]);

  // Or can use appendString directly

  [mstr appendString: @" and string C"];
  printf ("%s\n", [mstr cString]);
```

Program 15.6   **Continued**

```
// Delete substring based on range

[mstr deleteCharactersInRange: NSMakeRange (16, 13)];
printf ("%s\n", [mstr cString]);

// Find range first and then use it for deletion

substr = [mstr rangeOfString: @"string B and "];

if (substr.location != NSNotFound) {
    [mstr deleteCharactersInRange: substr];
    printf ("%s\n", [mstr cString]);
}

// Set the mutable string directly

[mstr setString: @"This is string A"];
printf ("%s\n", [mstr cString]);

// Now let's replace a range of chars with another

[mstr replaceCharactersInRange: NSMakeRange(8, 8)
    withString: @"a mutable string"];
printf ("%s\n", [mstr cString]);

// Search and replace

search = @"This is";
replace = @"An example of";

substr = [mstr rangeOfString: search];

if (substr.location != NSNotFound) {
    [mstr replaceCharactersInRange: substr
        withString: replace];
    printf ("%s\n", [mstr cString]);
}

// Search and replace all occurrences

search = @"a";
replace = @"X";

substr = [mstr rangeOfString: search];
```

Program 15.6   **Continued**

```
    while (substr.location != NSNotFound) {
        [mstr replaceCharactersInRange: substr
            withString: replace];
        substr = [mstr rangeOfString: search];
    }

    printf ("%s\n", [mstr cString]);

    [pool release];
    return 0;
}
```

Program 15.6   **Output**

```
This is string A
This is mutable string A
This is mutable string A and string B
This is mutable string A and string B and string C
This is mutable string B and string C
This is mutable string C
This is string A
This is a mutable string
An example of a mutable string
An exXmple of X mutXble string
```

The declaration

```
NSMutableString *mstr;
```

declares `mstr` to be a variable that will hold a character string object whose contents might change during execution of the program. The line

```
    mstr = [NSMutableString stringWithString: str1];
```

sets `mstr` to the string object whose contents are a copy of the characters in `str1`, or `"This is string A"`. When the `stringWithString:` method is sent to the NSMutableString class, a mutable string object is returned. When it's sent to the NSString class, as you did in Program 15.5, you get an immutable string object instead.

The `insertString:atIndex:` method inserts the specified character string into the receiver beginning at the specified index number. In this case, you insert the string `@" mutable"` into the string beginning at index number 7, or in front of the eighth character in the string. Unlike the immutable string object methods, no value is returned here because the receiver is modified—you can do that because it's a mutable string object.

The second `insertString:atIndex:` invocation uses the `length` method to insert one character string at the end of another. The `appendString:` method makes this task a little simpler.

By using the `deleteCharactersInRange:` method, you can remove a specified number of characters from a string. The range {16, 13}, when applied to the string

```
This is mutable string A and string B and string C
```

deletes the 13 characters `"string A and "` beginning with index number 16 (or the 17th character in the string). This is depicted in Figure 15.1.

```
This is mutable string A and string B and string C
```

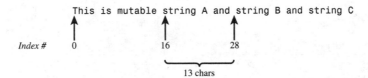

Figure 15.1   Indexing into a string.

The `rangeOfString:` method is used in the lines that follow in Program 15.6 to show how a string can first be located and then deleted. After first verifying that the string @`"string B and"` does in fact exist in `mstr`, the `deleteCharactersInRange:` method is then used to delete the characters using the range returned from the `rangeOfString:` method as its argument.

The `setString:` method can be used to set the contents of a mutable string object directly. After using this method to set `mstr` to the string @`"This is string A"`, the `replaceCharactersInRange:` method replaces some of the characters in the string with another string. The size of the strings do not have to be the same; you can replace one string with another of equal or unequal sizes. So, in the statement

```
[mstr replaceCharactersInRange: NSMakeRange(8, 8)
                 withString: @"a mutable string"];
```

the 8 characters `"string A"` are replaced with the 16 characters `"a mutable string"`.

The remaining lines in the program example show how to perform a search and replace. First, you locate the string @"This is" inside the string mstr, which contains @"This is a mutable string". If the search is successful (which it is), you replace the matched string with the replacement string, which in this case is @"An example of".

The program next sets up a loop to illustrate how to implement a search-and-replace-all operation. The search string is set to @"a" and the replacement string is set to @"X". You want to replace all occurrences of the letter *a* with the letter *X*. The `while` loop continues executing as long as you continue to find the search string inside mstr. The output verifies that all *a*s were in fact replaced by *X*s.

If the replacement string also contains the search string (for example, consider replacing the string "a" with the string "aX"), you would end up with an infinite loop.

Second, if the replacement string is empty (that is, contains no characters), you will effectively delete all occurrences of the search string. An empty constant character string object is specified by an adjacent pair of quotation marks, with no intervening spaces, like so:

```
replace = @"";
```

Of course, if you just wanted to delete an occurrence of a string, you could use the `deleteCharactersInRange:` method instead, as you've already seen.

Finally, the `NSString` class also contains a method called `replaceOccurrencesOfString:withString:options:range:` that can be used to do a search-and-replace-all on a string. In fact, the `while` loop from Program 15.6 could have been replaced with this single statement:

```
[mstr replaceOccurrencesOfString: search
                withString: replace
                   options: nil
                     range: NSMakeRange (0, [mstr length])];
```

This would achieve the same result and avert the potential of setting up an infinite loop because the method prevents such a thing from happening.

Where Are All Those Objects Going?

Programs 15.5 and 15.6 deal with many string objects that are created and returned by various `NSString` and `NSMutableString` methods. As discussed at the beginning of this chapter, you are not responsible for releasing the memory used by these objects; the objects' creators are. Presumably, all these objects have been added to the autorelease pool by their creators and will be freed when the pool is released. However, you should be aware that if you are developing a program that creates a lot of temporary objects, the memory used by these objects can accumulate. In such cases, you might need to adopt different strategies that allow for memory to be released during your program's execution, and not just at the end. This concept is described in Chapter 17. For now, just realize that these objects do take up memory that can expand as your program executes.

The `NSString` class contains more than 100 methods that can be used to work with immutable string objects. Table 15.2 summarizes some of the more commonly used ones, and Table 15.3 lists some of the additional methods provided by the `NSMutableString` class. Some other `NSString` methods (such as working with pathnames and reading the contents of a file into a string) will be introduced to you throughout the remainder of this book.

In Tables 15.2 and 15.3, *cstring* refers to a C-style character string, *url* is an `NSURL` object, *path* is an `NSString` object specifying the path to a file, *nsstring* is an `NSString` object, *i* is an integer representing a valid character number in a string, *size* and *opts* are unsigned integers, and *range* is an `NSRange` object indicating a valid range of characters within a string.

Table 15.2 **Common** NSString **Methods**

Method	Description
+(id) stringWithCString: *cstring*	Creates an NSString object from *cstring*
+(id) stringWithContentsOfFile: *path*	Creates a new string and sets it to the contents of file specified by *path*
+(id) stringWithContentsOfURL: *url*	Creates a new string and sets it to the contents of *url*
+(id) string	Creates a new empty string
+(id) stringWithString: *nsstring*	Creates a new string, setting it to *nsstring*
-(id) initWithCString: *nsstring*	Sets a newly allocated string to *cstring*
-(id) initWithString: *nsstring*	Sets a newly allocated string to *nsstring*
-(id) initWithContentsOfFile: *path*	Sets a string to the contents of a file specified by *path*
-(id) initWithContentsOfURL: (NSURL *) *url*	Sets a string to the contents of *url*
-(unsigned int) length	Returns the number of characters in the string
-(unichar) characterAtIndex: *i*	Returns the Unicode character at index *i*
- (NSString *) substringFromIndex: *i*	Returns a substring from the character at *i* to the end
- (NSString *) substringWithRange: *range*	Returns a substring based on a specified range
-(NSString *) substringToIndex: *i*	Returns a substring from the start of the string up to the character at index *i*
-(NSComparator *) caseInsensitiveCompare: *nsstring*	Compares two strings, ignoring case
-(NSComparator *) compare: *nsstring*	Compares two strings
-(BOOL) hasPrefix: *nsstring*	Tests whether a string begins with *nsstring*
-(BOOL) hasSuffix: *nsstring*	Tests whether a string ends with *nsstring*
-(BOOL) isEqualToString: *nsstring*	Tests whether two strings are equal
- (NSString *) capitalizedString	Returns a string with the first letter of every word capitalized (and the remaining letters in each word converted to lowercase)
-(NSString *) lowercaseString	Returns a string converted to lowercase
-(NSString *) uppercaseString	Returns a string converted to uppercase
-(const char *) cString	Returns a string converted to a C-style string
-(const char *) UTF8String	Returns a string converted to a UTF-8 string
-(double) doubleValue	Returns a string converted to a double
-(float) floatValue	Returns a string converted to a floating value
-(int) intValue	Returns a string converted to an integer

The following either create or modify `NSMutableString` objects.

Table 15.3 **Common** `NSMutableString` **Methods**

Method	Description
`+(id) stringWithCapacity: size`	Creates a string initially containing `size` characters.
`-(id) initWithCapacity: size`	Initializes a string with an initial capacity of `size` characters.
`-(void) setString: nsstring`	Sets a string to `nsstring`.
`-(void) appendString: nsstring`	Appends `nsstring` to the end of the receiver.
`-(void) deleteCharactersInRange: range`	Deletes characters in a specified `range`.
`-(void) insertString: nstring atIndex: i`	Inserts `nsstring` into the receiver starting at index `i`.
`-(void) replaceCharactersInRange: range withString: nsstring`	Replaces characters in a specified `range` with `nsstring`.
`-(void) replaceOccurrencesOf String: nsstring withString: nsstring2 options: opts range: range`	Replaces all occurrences of `nsstring` with `nsstring2` within a specified `range` and according to options `opt`. Options can include a bitwise-ORed combination of `NSBackwardsSearch` (the search starts from the end of range), `NSAnchoredSearch` (`nsstring` must match from the beginning of the range only), `NSLiteralSearch` (performs a byte-by-byte comparison), and `NSCaseInsensitiveSearch`.

`NSString` objects are used extensively throughout the remainder of this text. If you need to parse strings into tokens, you can take a look at Foundation's `NSScanner` class.

Array Objects

A Foundation array is an ordered collection of objects. Most often, elements in an array are of one particular type, but that's not required. Just as there are mutable and immutable strings, so too are there mutable and immutable arrays. *Immutable* arrays are handled by the `NSArray` class, whereas *mutable* ones are handled by `NSMutableArray`. The latter is a subclass of the former, which means it inherits its methods. To work with array objects in your programs, include the following line:

```
#import <Foundation/NSArray.h>
```

Program 15.7 sets up an array to store the names of the months of the year and then prints them.

Program 15.7

```
#import <Foundation/NSObject.h>
#import <Foundation/NSArray.h>
#import <Foundation/NSString.h>
#import <Foundation/NSAutoreleasePool.h>

int main (int argc, char *argv[])
{

  NSAutoreleasePool  *pool = [[NSAutoreleasePool alloc] init];

  // Create an array to contain the month names

  NSArray *monthNames = [NSArray arrayWithObjects:
    @"January", @"February", @"March", @"April",
    @"May", @"June", @"July", @"August", @"September",
    @"October", @"November", @"December", nil ];

  int   i;

  // Now list all the elements in the array

  printf ("Month  Name\n=====  ====\n");

  for (i = 0; i < 12; ++i)
       printf (" %2i   %s\n", i + 1,
              [[monthNames objectAtIndex: i] cString]);

  [pool release];
  return 0;
}
```

Program 15.7 **Output**

Month	Name
=====	====
1	January
2	February
3	March
4	April
5	May
6	June
7	July
8	August
9	September

Program 15.7   **Continued**

10	October
11	November
12	December

The class method `arrayWithObjects:` can be used to create an array with a list of objects as its elements. In such a case, the objects are listed in order and are separated by commas. This is a special syntax used by methods that can take a variable number of arguments. To mark the end of the list, `nil` must be specified as the last value in the list—it isn't actually stored inside the array.

In Program 15.7 `monthNames` is set to the 12 string values specified by the arguments to `arrayWithObjects:`.

Elements are identified in an array by their index numbers. Similar to `NSString` objects, indexing begins with zero. So, an array containing 12 elements would have valid index numbers 0–11. To retrieve an element of an array using its index number, you use the `objectAtIndex:` method.

The program simply executes a `for` loop to extract each element from the array using the `objectAtIndex:` method. Each retrieved element is converted to a C string and then displayed with `printf`.

Program 15.8 generates a table of prime numbers. Because you are going to be adding prime numbers to your array as they are generated, a mutable array is required. The `NSMutableArray` primes is allocated using the `arrayWithCapacity:` method. The argument of 20 that you give specifies the initial capacity of the array; a mutable array's capacity automatically is increased as necessary while the program is running.

Even though prime numbers are integers, you can't directly store `int` values inside your array. Your array can hold only objects. So, you need to store `NSNumber` integer objects inside your `primes` array.

Program 15.8

```
// Generate a table of prime numbers
#import <Foundation/NSObject.h>
#import <Foundation/NSArray.h>
#import <Foundation/NSString.h>
#import <Foundation/NSAutoreleasePool.h>
#import <Foundation/NSValue.h>

#define kMaxPrime   50

int main (int argc, char *argv[])
{
  int    i, p, n, prevPrime;
  BOOL   isPrime;
  NSAutoreleasePool  *pool = [[NSAutoreleasePool alloc] init];
```

Program 15.8 **Continued**

```
// Create an array to store the prime numbers

NSMutableArray *primes =
     [NSMutableArray arrayWithCapacity: 20];

// Store the first two primes (2 and 3) into the array

[primes addObject: [NSNumber numberWithInt: 2]];
[primes addObject: [NSNumber numberWithInt: 3]];

// Calculate the remaining primes

for (p = 5; p <= kMaxPrime; p += 2) {
// we're testing to see if p is prime

     isPrime = YES;

     i = 1;

     do {
       prevPrime = [[primes objectAtIndex: i] intValue];

       if (p % prevPrime == 0)
          isPrime = NO;

       ++i;
     } while ( isPrime == YES && p / prevPrime >= prevPrime);

     if (isPrime)
          [primes addObject: [NSNumber numberWithInt: p]];
}


// Display the results
n = [primes count];

for (i = 0; i < n; ++i)
     printf ("%i ", [[primes objectAtIndex: i] intValue]);

printf ("\n");

[pool release];
return 0;
}
```

Program 15.8   **Output**

```
2  3  5  7  11  13  17  19  23  29  31  37  41  43  47
```

You define kMaxPrime to the maximum prime number you want the program to calculate, which in this case is 50.

After allocating your primes array, you set the first two elements of the array using these statements:

```
[primes addObject: [NSNumber numberWithInt: 2]];
[primes addObject: [NSNumber numberWithInt: 3]];
```

The addObject: method adds an object to the end of an array. Here you add the NSNumber objects created from the integer values 2 and 3, respectively.

The program then enters a for loop to find prime numbers starting with 5, going up to kMaxPrime and skipping the even numbers in between (p += 2).

For each possible prime candidate p, you want to see whether it is evenly divisible by the previously discovered primes. If it is, it's not prime. As an added optimization, you test the candidate for even division only by earlier primes up to its square root. That's because, if a number is not prime, it must be divisible by a prime number that is less than or equal to its square root (ahh, back to high school math again!). So, the expression

```
p / prevPrime >= prevPrime
```

remains true only as long as prevPrime is less than the square root of p.

If the do-while loop exits with the flag isPrime still equal to YES, you have found another prime number. In that case, the candidate p is added to the primes array and execution continues.

Just a comment about program efficiency here. The Foundation classes for working with arrays provide many conveniences. However, in the case of manipulating large arrays of numbers with complex algorithms, learning how to perform such a task using the lower-level array constructs provided by the language might be more efficient, both in terms of memory usage and execution speed. Refer to the section titled "Arrays" in Chapter 13 for more information.

Making an Address Book

Let's take a look at an example that starts to combine a lot of what you've learned to this point by creating an address book.[6] Your address book will contain address cards. For the sake of simplicity, your address cards will contain only a person's name and email address. It is straightforward to extend this concept to other information, such as address and phone number, but that's left as an exercise for you at the end of this chapter.

---

6. Mac OS X provides an entire Address Book framework, which offers extremely powerful capabilities for working with address books.

Creating an Address Card

You're going to start by defining a new class called AddressCard. You'll want the ability to create a new address card, set its name and email fields, retrieve those fields, and print the card. In a graphics environment, you could use some nice routines such as those provided by the Application Kit framework to draw your card onscreen. But here you're going to stick to a simple terminal interface to display your address cards.

Program 15.9 shows the interface file for your new AddressCard class.

Program 15.9 **Interface File** AddressCard.h

```
#import <Foundation/NSObject.h>
#import <Foundation/NSString.h>

@interface AddressCard: NSObject
{
  NSString  *name;
  NSString  *email;
}


-(void) setName: (NSString *) theName;
-(void) setEmail: (NSString *) theEmail;

-(NSString *) name;
-(NSString *) email;

-(void) print;

@end
```

This is straightforward, as is the implementation file in Program 15.9.

Program 15.9 **Implementation File** AddressCard.m

```
#import "AddressCard.h"

@implementation AddressCard;

-(void) setName: (NSString *) theName
{
   name = [[NSString alloc] initWithString: theName];
}

-(void) setEmail: (NSString *) theEmail
{
   email = [[NSString alloc] initWithString: theEmail];
}
```

Program 15.9 **Continued**

```
-(NSString *) name
{
  return name;
}


-(NSString *) email
{
  return email;
}

-(void) print
{
    printf ("====================================\n");
    printf ("|                                  |\n");
    printf ("|  %-31s |\n", [name cString]);
    printf ("|  %-31s |\n", [email cString]);
    printf ("|                                  |\n");
    printf ("|                                  |\n");
    printf ("|                                  |\n");
    printf ("|        O                O        |\n");
    printf ("====================================\n");

}
@end
```

You could have the setName: and setEmail: methods store the objects directly in their respective instance variables with method definitions like these:

```
-(void) setName: (NSString *) theName
{
  name = theName;
}

-(void) setEmail: (NSString *) theEmail
{
  email = theEmail;
}
```

But the AddressCard object would not own its member objects. We talked about the motivation for an object to take ownership with respect to the Rectangle class owning its origin object in Chapter 8, "Inheritance."

Defining the two methods this way:

```
-(void) setName: (NSString *) theName
{
  name = [NSString stringWithString: theName];
}

-(void) setEmail: (NSString *) theEmail
{
  email = [NSString stringWithString: theEmail];
}
```

would also be the incorrect approach because the `AddressCard` methods would still not own their name and email objects—`NSString` would own them.

Returning to Program 15.9, the print method tries to present a nice display of an address card to the user in a format resembling a Rolodex card (remember those?). The `%-31s` characters to `printf` indicate to print a C-string within a field width of 31 characters, left-justified. That ensures the right edges of your address card line up in the output.

With your AddressCard class in hand, you can write a test program to create an address card, set its values, and display it (see Program 15.9).

Program 15.9 **Test Program**

```
#import "AddressCard.h"
#import <Foundation/NSAutoreleasePool.h>

int main (int argc, char *argv[])
{
  NSAutoreleasePool *pool = [[NSAutoreleasePool alloc] init];
  NSString    *aName = @"Julia Kochan";
  NSString    *aEmail = @"jewls337@axlc.com";
  AddressCard  *card1 = [[AddressCard alloc] init];

  [card1 setName: aName];
  [card1 setEmail: aEmail];

  [card1 print];

  [card1 release];
  [pool release];
  return 0;
}
```

Program 15.9 **Output**

```
========================================
|                                      |
| Julia Kochan                         |
| jewls337@axlc.com                    |
|                                      |
|                                      |
|                                      |
|        O                 O           |
========================================
```

Releasing Objects: `release` and `dealloc`

The line

```
[card1 release];
```

is used in Program 15.9 to release the memory used by your address card. You should realize from previous discussions that releasing an `AddressCard` object this way does not also release the memory you allocated for its `name` and `email` members. To make the `AddressCard` leak-free, you need to override a method called `dealloc` to release these members whenever the memory for an `AddressCard` object is released.

Whereas in Part I you saw how to override the `free` method to release the space used by objects contained in an object being freed, with `NSObject` you override `dealloc` instead. The `dealloc` method is called whenever the memory used by an object is to be returned to the system, or *deallocated*. It differs from the `release` method in a subtle but important way: The `release` method does not necessarily deallocate the memory used by an object, whereas `dealloc` does. In fact, when `release` is ready to free an object's memory, it does so with `dealloc`. This will become clear in Chapter 17 when we talk about retaining `objects`. Here is the `dealloc` method for your `AddressCard` class:

```
-(void) dealloc
{
   [name release];
   [email release];
   [super dealloc];
}
```

The `dealloc` method must release its own instance variables before using `super` to destroy the object itself. That's because an object is no longer valid after it has been deallocated.

To make your `AddressCard` leak-free, you must also modify your `setName:` and `setEmail:` methods to release the memory used by the objects stored in their respective instance variables. If someone changes the name on a card, you need to release the memory taken up by the old name before replacing it with the new one. Similarly for the email address, you need to release the memory used by the old email address before replacing it with the new one.

Here are the new `setName:` and `setEmail:` methods that will ensure we have a class that handles memory management properly:

```
-(void) setName: (NSString *) theName
{
  [name release];
  name = [[NSString alloc] initWithString: theName];
}


-(void) setEmail: (NSString *) theEmail
{
  [email release];
  email = [[NSString alloc] initWithString: theEmail];
}
```

You can send a message to a nil object; therefore, the message expressions

```
[name release];
```

and

```
[email release];
```

are okay even if `name` or `email` have not been previously set.

Let's add another method to your `AddressCard` class. You might want to set both the name and email fields of your card with one call. To do so, add a new method, `setName:andEmail:`.[7] Here's what the new method looks like:

```
-(void) setName: (NSString *) theName andEmail: (NSString *) theEmail
{
  [self setName: theName];
  [self setEmail: theEmail];
}
```

By relying on the `setName:` and `setEmail:` methods to set the appropriate instance variables (instead of setting them directly inside the method yourself), you add a level of abstraction and therefore make the program slightly more independent of its internal data structures.

Program 15.10 tests your new method.

---

7. You also might want an `initWithName:andEmail:` initialization method, but we won't show that here.

Program 15.10   **Test Program**

```
#import<Foundations/NSAutoreleasePool.h>
#import "AddressCard.h"

int main (int argc, char *argv[])
{
  NSAutoreleasePool *pool = [[NSAutoreleasePool alloc] init];

  NSString  *aName = @"Julia Kochan";
  NSString  *aEmail = @"jewls337@axlc.com";
  NSString  *bName = @"Tony Iannino";
  NSString  *bEmail = @"tony.iannino@techfitness.com";

  AddressCard   *card1 = [[AddressCard alloc] init];
  AddressCard   *card2 = [[AddressCard alloc] init];

  [card1 setName: aName andEmail: aEmail];
  [card2 setName: bName andEmail: bEmail];

  [card1 print];
  [card2 print];
  [card1 release];
  [card2 release];
  [pool release];
  return 0;
}
```

Program 15.10   **Output**

```
====================================
|                                  |
| Julia Kochan                     |
| jewls337@axlc.com                |
|                                  |
|                                  |
|                                  |
|      O           O               |
====================================
====================================
|                                  |
| Tony Iannino                     |
| tony.iannino@techfitness.com     |
|                                  |
|                                  |
|                                  |
|      O           O               |
====================================
```

Your `AddressCard` class seems to be working okay. What if you wanted to work with a lot of `AddressCards`? It would make sense to collect them together, which is exactly what you'll do by defining a new class called `AddressBook`. The `AddressBook` class will store the name of an address book and a collection of `AddressCards`, which you'll store in an array object. To start with, you'll want the ability to create a new address book, add new address cards to it, find out how many entries are in it, and list its contents. Later, you'll want to be able to search the address book, remove entries, possibly edit existing entries, sort it, or even make a copy of its contents.

Let's get started with a simple `interface` file (see Program 15.11).

Program 15.11 `Addressbook.h` Interface File

```
#import <Foundation/NSArray.h>
#import "AddressCard.h"

@interface AddressBook: NSObject
{
  NSString        *bookName;
  NSMutableArray  *book;
}

-(AddressBook *) initWithName: (NSString *) name;
-(void) addCard: (AddressCard *) theCard;
-(int) entries;
-(void) list;
-(void) dealloc;

@end
```

The `initWithName:` method sets up the initial array to hold the address cards and store the name of the book, whereas the `addCard:` method adds an `AddressCard` to the book. The `entries` method reports the number of address cards in your book, and the `list` method gives a concise listing of its entire contents. The implementation file for your `AddressBook` class is shown in Program 15.11.

Program 15.11 `Addressbook.m` Implementation File

```
#import "AddressBook.h"

@implementation AddressBook;

// set up the AddressBook's name and an empty book

-(id) initWithName: (NSString *) name
{
  self = [super init];
```

Program 15.11   **Continued**

```
  if (self) {
    bookName = [[NSString alloc] initWithString: name];
    book = [[NSMutableArray alloc] init];
  }

  return self;
}

-(void) addCard: (AddressCard *) theCard
{
  [book addObject: theCard];
}

-(int) entries
{
  return [book count];
}

-(void) list
{
  int     i, elements;
  AddressCard *theCard;

  printf ("\n======== Contents of: %s =========\n",
          [bookName cString]);
  elements = [book count];

  for ( i = 0; i < elements; ++i ) {
      theCard = [book objectAtIndex: i];
      printf ("%-20s  %-32s\n", [[theCard name] cString],
                  [[theCard email] cString]);
  }

  printf("=======================================\
          ============\n\n");
}

-(void) dealloc
{
  [bookName release];
  [book release];
  [super dealloc];
}
@end
```

The `initWithName:` method first calls the `init` method for the superclass to perform its initialization. Next, it creates a string object (using `alloc` so it owns it) and sets it to the name of the address book passed in as name. This is followed by the allocation and initialization of an empty mutable array that is stored in the instance variable `book`.

You defined `initWithName:` to return an `id` object, instead of an `AddressBook` one. If `AddressBook` is subclassed, the argument to `initWithName:` isn't an `AddressBook` object; its type is that of the subclass. For that reason, you define the return type as a generic object type.

Notice also that in `initWithName:`, you take ownership of the `bookName` and `book` instance variables by using `alloc`. For example, if you created the array for `book` using `NSMutableArray`'s array method, as in

```
book = [NSMutableArray array];
```

you would still not be the owner of the `book` array; `NSMutableArray` would own it. Thus, you wouldn't be able to release its memory when you freed up the memory for an `AddressBook` object.

The `addCard:` method takes the `AddessCard` object given as its argument and adds it to the address book.

The `count` method gives the number of elements in an array. This is used by the `entries` method to return the number of address cards stored in the address book.

Finally, the `list` method goes through each entry in the address book and displays the name and email fields at the terminal.

Following is a test program for your new `AddressBook` class.

Program 15.11 **Test Program**

```
#import "AddressBook.h"
#import <Foundation/NSAutoreleasePool.h>

int main (int argc, char *argv[])
{
  NSAutoreleasePool *pool = [[NSAutoreleasePool alloc] init];

  NSString   *aName = @"Julia Kochan";
  NSString   *aEmail = @"jewls337@axlc.com";
  NSString   *bName = @"Tony Iannino";
  NSString   *bEmail = @"tony.iannino@techfitness.com";
  NSString   *cName = @"Stephen Kochan";
  NSString   *cEmail = @"steve@kochan-wood.com";
  NSString   *dName = @"Jamie Baker";
  NSString   *dEmail = @"jbaker@kochan-wood.com";

  AddressCard *card1 = [[AddressCard alloc] init];
  AddressCard *card2 = [[AddressCard alloc] init];
  AddressCard *card3 = [[AddressCard alloc] init];
  AddressCard *card4 = [[AddressCard alloc] init];
```

Program 15.11   **Continued**

```
AddressBook  *myBook = [AddressBook alloc];

// First set up four address cards

[card1 setName: aName andEmail: aEmail];
[card2 setName: bName andEmail: bEmail];
[card3 setName: cName andEmail: cEmail];
[card4 setName: dName andEmail: dEmail];

// Now initialize the address book

myBook = [myBook initWithName: @"Linda's Address Book"];

printf ("Entries in address book after creation: %i\n",
         [myBook entries]);

// Add some cards to the address book

[myBook addCard: card1];
[myBook addCard: card2];
[myBook addCard: card3];
[myBook addCard: card4];

printf ("Entries in address book after adding cards: %i\n\n",
         [myBook entries]);

// List all the entries in the book now

[myBook list];

[card1 release];
[card2 release];
[card3 release];
[card4 release];
[myBook release];
[pool release];
return 0;
}
```

Program 15.11   **Output**

```
Entries in address book after creation: 0
Entries in address book after adding cards: 4
```

Program 15.11   **Continued**

```
======== Contents of: Linda's Address Book =========
Julia Kochan       jewls337@axlc.com
Tony Iannino       tony.iannino@techfitness.com
Stephen Kochan     steve@kochan-wood.com
Jamie Baker        jbaker@kochan-wood.com
===================================================
```

The program sets up four address cards and then creates a new address book called "Linda's Address Book." The four cards are then added to the address book using the addCard: method, and the list method is used to list the contents of the address book and verify its contents.

Looking Up Someone in the Address Book

When you have a large address book, you won't want to list its complete contents each time you want to look up someone. It therefore makes sense to add a method to do that for you. Let's call the method lookup: and have it take as its argument the name to locate. The method will search the address book for a match (ignoring case) and return the matching entry if found. If the name does not appear in the phone book, you'll have it return nil.

Here's the new lookup: method:

```
// lookup address card by name -- assumes an exact match

-(AddressCard *) lookup: (NSString *) theName
{
    AddressCard *nextCard;

    int    i, elements;
    elements = [book count];

    for ( i = 0; i < elements; ++i) {
        nextCard = [book objectAtIndex: i];

        if ( [[nextCard name] caseInsensitiveCompare: theName]
                == NSOrderedSame )
                    return nextCard;
    }

    return nil;
}
```

If you put the declaration for this method in your interface file and the definition in the implementation file, you can write a test program to try your new method. Program 15.12 shows such a program, followed immediately by its output.

Program 15.12 **Test Program**

```
#import "AddressBook.h"
#import <Foundation/NSAutoreleasePool.h>

int main (int argc, char *argv[])
{

   NSAutoreleasePool *pool = [[NSAutoreleasePool alloc] init];

   NSString   *aName = @"Julia Kochan";
   NSString   *aEmail = @"jewls337@axlc.com";
   NSString   *bName = @"Tony Iannino";
   NSString   *bEmail = @"tony.iannino@techfitness.com";
   NSString   *cName = @"Stephen Kochan";
   NSString   *cEmail = @"steve@kochan-wood.com";
   NSString   *dName = @"Jamie Baker";
   NSString   *dEmail = @"jbaker@kochan-wood.com";
   AddressCard   *card1 = [[AddressCard alloc] init];
   AddressCard   *card2 = [[AddressCard alloc] init];
   AddressCard   *card3 = [[AddressCard alloc] init];
   AddressCard   *card4 = [[AddressCard alloc] init];

   AddressBook  *myBook = [AddressBook alloc];
   AddressCard  *myCard;

   // First set up four address cards

   [card1 setName: aName andEmail: aEmail];
   [card2 setName: bName andEmail: bEmail];
   [card3 setName: cName andEmail: cEmail];
   [card4 setName: dName andEmail: dEmail];

   myBook = [myBook initWithName: @"Linda's Address Book"];

   // Add some cards to the address book

   [myBook addCard: card1];
   [myBook addCard: card2];
   [myBook addCard: card3];
   [myBook addCard: card4];

   // Look up a person by name

   printf ("Lookup: Stephen Kochan\n");
   myCard = [myBook lookup: @"stephen kochan"];
```

Program 15.12 **Continued**

```
if (myCard != nil)
     [myCard print];
else
     printf ("Not found!\n");

// Try another lookup

printf ("\nLookup: Wes Rosenberg\n");
myCard = [myBook lookup: @"Wes Rosenberg"];

if (myCard != nil)
     [myCard print];
else
     printf ("Not found!\n");

[card1 release];
[card2 release];
[card3 release];
[card4 release];
[myBook release];

[pool release];
return 0;
}
```

Program 15.12 **Output**

```
Lookup: Stephen Kochan
=====================================
|                                   |
| Stephen Kochan                    |
| steve@kochan-wood.com             |
|                                   |
|                                   |
|                                   |
|      O            O               |
=====================================

Lookup: Wes Rosenberg
Not found!
```

When Stephen Kochan was located in the address book (taking advantage of the fact that a case-insensitive match was made) by the lookup: method, the resulting address card that was returned was given to the AddressCard's print method for display. In the case of the second lookup, the name Wes Rosenberg was not found, thus explaining the resulting message.

This lookup message is very primitive because it needs to find an exact match of the entire name. A better method would perform partial matches and be able to handle multiple matches as well. For example, the message expression

```
[myBook lookup: @"steve"]
```

could match entries for "Steve Kochan", "Fred Stevens", and "steven levy". Because multiple matches would exist, a good approach might be to create an array containing all the matches and return the array to the method caller (see exercise 2 at the end of this chapter), like so:

```
matches = [myBook lookup: @"steve"];
```

Removing Someone from the Address Book

No address book manager that enables you to add an entry would be complete without the capability to also remove one. You can make a `removeCard:` method to remove a particular `AddressCard` from the address book. Another possibility would be to create a `remove:` method that removes someone based on her name (see exercise 6 at the end of this chapter).

Because you've made a couple of changes to your interface file, Program 15.13 shows it again with the new `removeCard:` method. It's followed by your new `removeCard:` method.

Program 15.13   `Addressbook.h` **Interface File**

```
#import <Foundation/NSArray.h>
#import "AddressCard.h"

@interface AddressBook: NSObject
{
  NSString        *bookName;
  NSMutableArray  *book;
}

-(AddressBook *) initWithName: (NSString *) name;

-(void) addCard: (AddressCard *) theCard;
-(void) removeCard: (AddressCard *) theCard;

-(AddressCard *) lookup: (NSString *) theName;
-(int) entries;
-(void) list;

@end
```

Here's the new `removeCard` method:

```
-(void) removeCard: (AddressCard *) theCard
{
  [book removeObjectIdenticalTo: theCard];
}
```

For purposes of what's considered an *identical* object, we are using the idea of the same location in memory. So, two address cards that contain the same information, but which are located in different places in memory (which might happen if you made a copy of an `AddressCard`, for example), would *not* be considered identical by the `removeObjectIdenticalTo:` method.

Incidentally, the `removeObjectIdenticalTo:` method removes all objects identical to its argument. However, that's only an issue if you have multiple occurrences of the same object in your arrays.

You can get more sophisticated with your approach to equal objects by using the `removeObject:` method and then writing your own `isEqual:` method for testing whether two objects are equal. If you use `removeObject:`, the system automatically invokes the `isEqual:` method for each element in the array, giving it the two elements to compare. In this case, because your address book contains `AddressCard` objects as its elements, you would have to add an `isEqual:` method to that class (you would be overriding the method that the class inherits from `NSObject`). The method could then decide for itself how to determine equality. It would make sense to compare the two corresponding names and emails, and if they were both equal, you could return YES from the method. Otherwise, you could return NO. Your method might look like this:

```
-(BOOL) isEqual (AddressCard *) theCard
{
  if ([name isEqualToString: [theCard name]] == YES &&
        [email isEqualToString: [theCard email]] == YES)
    return YES;
  else
    return NO;
}
```

You should note that other `NSArray` methods, such as `containsObject:` and `indexOfObject:`, also rely on this `isEqual:` strategy for determining whether two objects are considered equal.

Program 15.14 tests the new `removeCard:` method.

Program 15.14

```
#import "AddressBook.h"
#import <Foundation/NSAutoreleasePool.h>

int main (int argc, char *argv[])
{
  NSAutoreleasePool *pool = [[NSAutoreleasePool alloc] init];
```

Program 15.14 **Continued**

```
NSString  *aName = @"Julia Kochan";
NSString  *aEmail = @"jewls337@axlc.com";
NSString  *bName = @"Tony Iannino";
NSString  *bEmail = @"tony.iannino@techfitness.com";
NSString  *cName = @"Stephen Kochan";
NSString  *cEmail = @"steve@kochan-wood.com";
NSString  *dName = @"Jamie Baker";
NSString  *dEmail = @"jbaker@kochan-wood.com";

AddressCard *card1 = [[AddressCard alloc] init];
AddressCard *card2 = [[AddressCard alloc] init];
AddressCard *card3 = [[AddressCard alloc] init];
AddressCard *card4 = [[AddressCard alloc] init];

AddressBook  *myBook = [AddressBook alloc];
AddressCard  *myCard

// First set up four address cards

[card1 setName: aName andEmail: aEmail];
[card2 setName: bName andEmail: bEmail];
[card3 setName: cName andEmail: cEmail];
[card4 setName: dName andEmail: dEmail];

myBook = [myBook initWithName: @"Linda's Address Book"];

// Add some cards to the address book

[myBook addCard: card1];
[myBook addCard: card2];
[myBook addCard: card3];
[myBook addCard: card4];

// Look up a person by name

printf ("Lookup: Stephen Kochan\n");
myCard = [myBook lookup: @"Stephen Kochan"];

if (myCard != nil)
      [myCard print];
else
      printf ("Not found!\n");

// Now remove the entry from the phone book
```

Program 15.14 **Continued**

```
[myBook removeCard: myCard];
[myBook list];    // verify it's gone

[card1 release];
[card2 release];
[card3 release];
[card4 release];
[myBook release];
[pool release];

return 0;
}
```

Program 15.14 **Output**

```
Lookup: Stephen Kochan
======================================
|                                    |
| Stephen Kochan                     |
| steve@kochan-wood.com              |
|                                    |
|                                    |
|                                    |
|      O            O                |
======================================

======== Contents of: Linda's Address Book =========
Julia Kochan       jewls337@axlc.com
Tony Iannino       tony.iannino@techfitness.com
Jamie Baker        jbaker@kochan-wood.com
====================================================
```

After looking up Stephen Kochan in the address book and verifying he's there, you pass the resulting `AddressCard` to your new `removeCard:` method to be removed. The resulting listing of the address book verifies the removal.

Sorting Arrays

If you end up with a lot of entries in your address book, alphabetizing it might be convenient. You can easily do this by adding a `sort` method to your `AddressBook` class and by taking advantage of an `NSMutableArray` method called `sortUsingSelector:`. This method takes as its argument a selector that is used by the `sortUsingSelector:` method to compare two elements. Arrays can contain any type of objects in them, so the only way to implement a generic sorting method is to have

8. There's also a method called `sortUsingFunction:context:` that lets you use a function instead of a method for performing the comparison.

you decide whether elements in the array are in order. To do this, you have to add a method that will be used to compare two elements in the array.[8] The result returned from that method is to be of type NSComparisonResult, and it should return NSOrderedAscending if you want the sorting method to place the first element before the second in the array, return NSOrderedSame if the two elements are considered equal, and return NSOrderedDescending if the first element should come after the second element in the sorted array.

First, here's the new sort method from your AddressBook class:

```
-(void) sort
{
    [book sortUsingSelector: @selector(compareNames:)];
}
```

As you learned in Chapter 9, "Polymorphism, Dynamic Typing, and Dynamic Binding," the expression

```
@selector (compareNames:)
```

creates a selector, which is of type SEL, from a specified method name; this is the method used by sortUsingSelector: to compare two elements in the array. When it needs to make such a comparison, it invokes the specified method, sending the message to the first element in the array (the receiver) to be compared against its argument. The returned value should be of type NSComparisonResult, as previously described.

Because the elements of your address book are AddressCard objects, the comparison method must be added to the AddressCard class. So, you have to go back to your AddressCard class and add a compareNames: method to it. This is shown here:

```
// Compare the two names from the specified address cards
-(NSComparisonResult) compareNames: (id) element
{
    return [name compare: [element name]];
}
```

Because you are doing a string comparison of the two names from the address book, you can use the NSString compare: method to do the work for you.

If you add the sort method to the AddressBook class and the compareNames: method to the AddressCard class, you can write a test program to test it (see Program 15.15).

Program 15.15   **Test Program**

```
#import "AddressBook.h"
#import <Foundation/NSAutoreleasePool.h>

int main (int argc, char *argv[])
{

  NSAutoreleasePool *pool = [[NSAutoreleasePool alloc] init];
```

Program 15.15 **Continued**

```
NSString  *aName = @"Julia Kochan";
NSString  *aEmail = @"jewls337@axlc.com";
NSString  *bName = @"Tony Iannino";
NSString  *bEmail = @"tony.iannino@techfitness.com";
NSString  *cName = @"Stephen Kochan";
NSString  *cEmail = @"steve@kochan-wood.com";
NSString  *dName = @"Jamie Baker";
NSString  *dEmail = @"jbaker@kochan-wood.com";

AddressCard  *card1 = [[AddressCard alloc] init];
AddressCard  *card2 = [[AddressCard alloc] init];
AddressCard  *card3 = [[AddressCard alloc] init];
AddressCard  *card4 = [[AddressCard alloc] init];

AddressBook   *myBook = [AddressBook alloc];

// First set up four address cards

[card1 setName: aName andEmail: aEmail];
[card2 setName: bName andEmail: bEmail];
[card3 setName: cName andEmail: cEmail];
[card4 setName: dName andEmail: dEmail];

myBook = [myBook initWithName: @"Linda's Address Book"];

// Add some cards to the address book

[myBook addCard: card1];
[myBook addCard: card2];
[myBook addCard: card3];
[myBook addCard: card4];

// List the unsorted book

[myBook list];

// Sort it and list it again

[myBook sort];
[myBook list];

[card1 release];
[card2 release];
[card3 release];
[card4 release];
```

Program 15.15   **Continued**

```
[myBook release];
[pool release];
return 0;
}
```

Program 15.15   **Output**

```
======== Contents of: Linda's Address Book =========
Julia Kochan        jewls337@axlc.com
Tony Iannino        tony.iannino@techfitness.com
Stephen Kochan      steve@kochan-wood.com
Jamie Baker         jbaker@kochan-wood.com
====================================================


======== Contents of: Linda's Address Book =========
Jamie Baker         jbaker@kochan-wood.com
Julia Kochan        jewls337@axlc.com
Stephen Kochan      steve@kochan-wood.com
Tony Iannino        tony.iannino@techfitness.com
====================================================
```

You should note that the sort is an ascending one. However, you can easily perform a descending sort by modifying the compareNames: method in the AddressCard class to reverse the sense of the values that are returned.

More than 60 methods are available for working with array objects. Tables 15.4 and 15.5 list some commonly used methods for working with immutable and mutable arrays, respectively. Because NSMutableArray is a subclass of NSArray, the former inherits the methods of the latter.

In Tables 15.4 and 15.5, *obj*, *obj1*, and *obj2* are any objects; *i* is an integer representing a valid index number into the array; *selector* is a selector object of type SEL; and *size* is an unsigned integer.

Table 15.4   **Common NSArray Methods**

Method	Description
+(id) arrayWithObjects: *obj1*, *obj2*, … nil	Creates a new array with *obj1*, *obj2*, … as its elements
-(BOOL) containsObject: *obj*	Determines whether the array contains *obj* (uses the isEqual: method)
-(unsigned int) *count*	The number of elements in the array
-(unsigned int) indexOfObject: *obj*	The index number of the first element that contains *obj* (uses the isEqual: method)

Table 15.4 **Continued**

-(id) objectAtIndex: *i*	The object stored in element *i*
-(NSEnumerator *) objectEnumerator	Returns an object enumerator that can be used with nextObject to retrieve successive elements from the array
-(void) makeObjectsPerformSelector: (SEL) *selector*	Sends the message indicated by *selector* to every element of the array
-(NSArray *) sortedArrayUsingSelector: (SEL) *selector*	Sorts the array according to the comparison method specified by *selector*
-(BOOL) writeToFile: *path* atomically: (BOOL) *flag*	Writes the array to the specified file, creating a temporary file first if *flag* is YES

Table 15.5 **Common** NSMutableArray **Methods**

Method	Description
+(id) array	Creates an empty array
+(id) arrayWithCapacity: *size*	Creates an array with a specified initial *size*
-(id) initWithCapacity: *size*	Initializes a newly allocated array with a specified initial *size*
-(void) addObject: *obj*	Adds *obj* to the end of the array
-(void) insertObject: *obj* atIndex: *i*	Inserts *obj* into element *i* of the array
-(void) replaceObjectAtIndex: *i* withObject: *obj*	Replaces element *i* of the array with *obj*
-(void) removeObject: *obj*	Removes all occurrences of *obj* from the array
-(void) removeObjectAtIndex: *i*	Removes element *i* from the array, moving down elements *i*+1 through the end of the array
-(void) sortUsingSelector: (SEL) *selector*	Sorts the array based on the comparison method indicated by *selector*

Dictionary Objects

A *dictionary* is a collection of data consisting of key-object pairs. Just as you would look up the definition of a word in a dictionary, you obtain the value (object) from an Objective-C dictionary by its key. The keys in a dictionary must be unique, and they can be of any object type, although they are typically strings. The value associated with the key can also be of any object type, but it cannot be nil.

Dictionaries can be mutable or immutable; mutable ones can have entries dynamically added and removed. Dictionaries can be searched based on a particular key, and their contents can be enumerated. Program 15.16 sets up a mutable dictionary to be used as a glossary of Objective-C terms and fills in the first three entries.

To use dictionaries in your programs, include the following line:

```
#import <Foundation/NSDictionary.h>
```

Program 15.16
```
#import <Foundation/NSObject.h>
#import <Foundation/NSString.h>
#import <Foundation/NSDictionary.h>
#import <Foundation/NSAutoreleasePool.h>

int main (int argc, char *argv[])
{
  NSAutoreleasePool  *pool = [[NSAutoreleasePool alloc] init];

  NSMutableDictionary *glossary = [NSMutableDictionary dictionary];
  // Store three entries in the glossary

  [glossary setObject:
      @"A class defined so other classes can inherit from it"
       forKey: @"abstract class" ];
  [glossary setObject:
      @"To implement all the methods defined in a protocol"
       forKey: @"adopt"];
  [glossary setObject:
      @"Storing an object for later use"
       forKey: @"archiving"];

  // Retrieve and display them

  printf ("abstract class: %s\n\n",
    [[glossary objectForKey: @"abstract class"] cString]);
  printf ("adopt: %s\n\n",
    [[glossary objectForKey: @"adopt"] cString]);
  printf ("archiving: %s\n\n",
    [[glossary objectForKey: @"archiving"] cString]);

  [pool release];
  return 0;
}
```

Program 15.16 **Output**

```
abstract class: A class defined so other classes can inherit from it

adopt: To implement all the methods defined in a protocol

archiving: Storing an object for later use
```

The expression

```
[NSMutableDictionary dictionary]
```

creates an empty mutable dictionary. Key-value pairs can subsequently be added to the dictionary using the `setObject:forKey:` method. After the dictionary has been constructed, you can retrieve the value for a given key using the `objectForKey:` method. Program 15.17 shows how the three entries in the glossary were retrieved and displayed. In a more practical application, the user would type in the word he wanted to define and the program would search the glossary for its definition.

Enumerating a Dictionary

Program 15.17 illustrates how a dictionary can be defined with initial key-value pairs using the `dictionaryWithObjectsAndKeys:` method. An immutable dictionary is created, and the program also shows how the `keyEnumerator` method can be used to retrieve each element from a dictionary one key at a time. This process is known as *enumeration*. Unlike array objects, dictionary objects are not ordered. So, the first key-object pair placed in a dictionary might not be the first key extracted when the dictionary is enumerated.

Program 15.17

```
#import <Foundation/NSObject.h>
#import <Foundation/NSString.h>
#import <Foundation/NSDictionary.h>
#import <Foundation/NSEnumerator.h>
#import <Foundation/NSAutoreleasePool.h>

int main (int argc, char *argv[])
{
  NSAutoreleasePool  *pool = [[NSAutoreleasePool alloc] init];
  NSEnumerator *keyEnum;
  NSString     *key;

  NSDictionary *glossary =
   [NSDictionary dictionaryWithObjectsAndKeys:
     @"A class defined so other classes can inherit from it",
     @"abstract class",
```

Program 15.17   **Continued**

```
    @"To implement all the methods defined in a protocol",
    @"adopt",
    @"Storing an object for later use",
    @"archiving",
        nil
    ];

    // Print all key-value pairs from the dictionary

    keyEnum = [glossary keyEnumerator];

    while ( (key = [keyEnum nextObject]) != nil ) {
      printf ("%s: %s\n\n", [key cString],
          [[glossary objectForKey: key] cString]);
    }

    [pool release];
    return 0;
}
```

Program 15.17   **Output**

```
abstract class: A class defined so other classes can inherit from it

adopt: To implement all the methods defined in a protocol

archiving: Storing an object for later use     -
```

The argument to `dictionaryWithObjectsAndKeys:` is a list of object–key pairs (yes, in that order!), each separated by a comma. The list must be terminated with the special `nil` object.

After the program creates the dictionary, it sets up a loop to enumerate its contents. To use the special enumeration features provided by the Foundation framework, you need to add this line to your program:

```
#import <Foundation/NSEnumerator.h>
```

The loop you set up can be used for a dictionary of any size. The statement

```
keyEnum = [glossary keyEnumerator];
```

uses the `keyEnumerator` method to create a list of all the keys in `glossary`. The returned value is an `NSEnumerator` object, which is stored in the variable `keyEnum`. This object is used inside the loop as the receiver of the `nextObject` message. This method retrieves the next key from the dictionary (keys are not stored in any particular order, as noted) and returns it. When no more keys are left in the dictionary, it returns `nil`. The value associated with each enumerated key is obtained using the `objectForKey:` method and is then displayed.

Enumerations can be performed on arrays and sets (discussed in the next section) as well. The `objectEnumerator` method is used first on the dictionary, array, or set, followed by repeated calls to the `nextObject` method to retrieve successive elements. After the last element from the dictionary, array, or set is retrieved, `nil` is returned. In the case of an array, the elements are retrieved in order, whereas in the case of dictionaries and sets, the order is not defined.

If you wanted to display the contents of a dictionary in alphabetical order, you could first retrieve all the keys from the dictionary, sort them, and then retrieve all the values for those sorted keys in order. The method `keysSortedByValueUsingSelector:` does half of the work for you, returning the sorted keys in an array based on your sorting criteria.

As an example of array enumeration, you could replace the loop that prints all the generated prime numbers from Program 15.8

```
// Display the results
n = [primes count];
for (i = 0; i < n; ++i)
  printf ("%i ", [[primes objectAtIndex: i] intValue]);

printf ("\n");
```

with the following functionally equivalent code:

```
#import <Foundation/NSEnumerator.h>
    ...
NSEnumerator *pElems;
NSNumber    *pNum;
    ...
// Display the results

pElems = [primes objectEnumerator];

while ( (pNum = [pElems nextObject]) != nil)
  printf ("%i ", [pNum intValue]);

printf ("\n");
```

We have just shown some basic operations with dictionaries here. Tables 15.6 and 15.7 summarize some of the more commonly used methods for working with immutable and mutable dictionaries, respectively. Because `NSMutableDictionary` is a subset of `NSDictionary`, it inherits its methods.

In Tables 15.6 and 15.7, *key*, *key1*, *key2*, *obj*, *obj1*, and *obj2* are any objects and *size* is an unsigned integer.

Table 15.6 **Common** NSDictionary **Methods**

Method	Description
+(id) dictionaryWithObjectsAndKeys: *obj1, key1,obj2, key2, ..., nil*	Creates a dictionary with key-object pairs {*key1, obj1*},{*key2, obj2*},...
-(id) initWithObjectsAndKeys: *obj1, key1, obj2,key2,..., nil*	Initializes a newly allocated dictionary with key-object pairs {*key1, obj1*}, {*key2, obj2*},...
-(unsigned int) count	Returns the number of entries in the dictionary
-(NSEnumerator *) keyEnumerator	Returns an NSEnumerator object for all the keys in the dictionary
-(NSArray *) keysSortedByValueUsingSelector: (SEL) *selector*	Returns an array of keys in the dictionary sorted according to the comparison method specified by *selector*
-(NSEnuerator *) objectEnumerator	Returns an NSEnumerator object for all the values in the dictionary
-(id) objectForKey: *key*	Returns the object for the specified *key*

Table 15.7 **Common** NSMutableDictionary **Methods**

Method	Description
+(id) dictionaryWithCapacity: *size*	Creates a mutable dictionary with an initial specified *size*
-(id) initWithCapacity: *size*	Initializes a newly allocated dictionary to be of an initial specified *size*
-(void) removeAllObjects	Removes all entries from the dictionary
-(void) removeObjectForKey: *key*	Removes the entry for the specified *key* from the dictionary
-(void) setObject: *obj* forKey: *key*	Adds *obj* to the dictionary for the key *key* and replaces the value if *key* already exists

Set Objects

A *set* is a collection of unique objects, and it can be mutable or immutable. Operations
include searching, adding, and removing members (mutable sets); comparing two sets;
and finding the intersection and union of two sets.

To work with sets in your program, include the following line:

```
#import <Foundation/NSSet.h>
```

Program 15.18 shows some basic operations on sets. Say you wanted to display the contents of your sets several times during execution of the program. You therefore have decided to create a new method called print. You add the print method to the NSSet class by creating a new category called Printing. NSMutableSet is a subclass of NSSet, so mutable sets can use the new print method as well.

Program 15.18

```
#import <Foundation/NSObject.h>
#import <Foundation/NSSet.h>
#import <Foundation/NSValue.h>
#import <Foundation/NSEnumerator.h>
#import <Foundation/NSAutoreleasePool.h>
#import <Foundation/NSString.h>

// Create an integer object
#define INTOBJ(v) [NSNumber numberWithInt: v]

// Add a print method to NSSet with the Printing category
@interface NSSet (Printing);
-(void) print;
@end

@implementation NSSet (Printing);
-(void) print {
    NSEnumerator *setEnum;
    NSNumber    *element;

    setEnum = [self objectEnumerator];

    printf (" {");

    while ((element = [setEnum nextObject]) != nil)
        printf (" %i ", [element intValue]);

    printf ("}\n");
}
@end


int main (int argc, char *argv[])
{
    NSAutoreleasePool  *pool = [[NSAutoreleasePool alloc] init];
```

Program 15.18   **Continued**

```
NSMutableSet *set1 = [NSMutableSet setWithObjects:
      INTOBJ(1), INTOBJ(3), INTOBJ(5), INTOBJ(10), nil];
NSSet *set2 = [NSSet setWithObjects:
      INTOBJ(-5), INTOBJ(100), INTOBJ(3), INTOBJ(5), nil];
NSSet *set3 = [NSSet setWithObjects:
      INTOBJ(12), INTOBJ(200), INTOBJ(3), nil];

printf ("set1: "); [set1 print];
printf ("set2: "); [set2 print];

// Equality test
if ([set1 isEqualToSet: set2] == NO)
      printf ("set1 equals set2\n");
else
      printf ("set1 is not equal to set2\n");

// Membership test

if ([set1 containsObject: INTOBJ(10)] == YES)
      printf ("set1 contains 10\n");
else
      printf ("set1 does not contain 10\n");

if ([set2 containsObject: INTOBJ(10)] == YES)
      printf ("set2 contains 10\n");
else
      printf ("set2 does not contain 10\n");

// add and remove objects from mutable set set1

[set1 addObject: INTOBJ(4)];
[set1 removeObject: INTOBJ(10)];
printf ("set1 after adding 4 and removing 10: "); [set1 print];

// get intersection of two sets

[set1 intersectSet: set2];
printf ("set1 intersect set2: "); [set1 print];

// union of two sets

[set1 unionSet:set3];
printf ("set1 union set3: "); [set1 print];

[pool release];
return 0;
}
```

Program 15.18   **Output**

```
set1: { 1 10 3 5 }
set2: { 3 100 -5 5 }
set1 is not equal to set2
set1 contains 10
set2 does not contain 10
set1 after adding 4 and removing 10: { 1 3 4 5 }
set1 intersect set2: { 3 5 }
set1 union set3: { 200 3 12 5 }
```

The `print` method uses the enumeration technique previously described to retrieve each element from the set. You also defined a macro called `INTOBJ` to create an integer object from an integer value. This enabled you to make your program more concise and saved some unnecessary typing. Of course, your `print` method is not that general because it works only with sets that have integer members in them. But it's a good reminder here about how to add methods to a class through a category.[9]

The `setWithObjects:` creates a new set from a `nil`-terminated list of objects. After creating three sets, the program displays the first two using your new `print` method. The `isEqualToSet:` method is then used to test whether `set1` is equal to `set2`—it isn't.

The `containsObject:` method is used to first see whether the integer `10` is in `set1` and then whether it is in `set2`. The Boolean values returned by the method verifies that it is in fact in the first set and not in the second.

The program next uses the `addObject:` and `removeObject:` methods to add and remove `4` and `10` from `set1`, respectively. Displaying the contents of the set verifies that the operations were successful.

The `intersect:` and `union:` methods can be used to calculate the intersection and union of two sets. In both cases, the result of the operation replaces the receiver of the message.

The Foundation framework also provides a class called `NSCountedSet`. These sets can represent more than one occurrence of the same object; however, instead of the object appearing multiple times in the set, a count of the number of times is maintained. So, the first time an object is added to the set, its count is 1. Subsequently, adding the object to the set increments the count, whereas removing the object from the set decrements the count. If it reaches zero, the actual object itself is removed from the set. The `countForObject:` is used to retrieve the count for a specified object in a set.

One application for a counted set might be a word counter application. Each time a word is found in some text, it can be added to the counted set. When the scan of the text is complete, each word can be retrieved from the set along with its count, which indicates the number of times the word appeared in the text.

---

9. A more general method could implement an `NSLog` approach and invoke each object's `description` method for displaying each member of the set. That would allow sets containing any types of objects to be displayed in a readable format.

We have just shown some basic operations with sets here. Tables 15.8 and 15.9 summarize commonly used methods for working with immutable and mutable sets, respectively. Because `NSMutableSet` is a subclass of `NSSet`, it inherits its methods.

In Tables 15.8 and 15.9, *obj*, *obj1*, and *obj2* are any objects; *nsset* is an `NSSet` or `NSMutableSet` object; and *size* is an unsigned integer.

Table 15.8   **Common `NSSet` Methods**

Method	Description
`+(id) setWithObjects:` *obj1, obj2, ..., nil*	Creates a new set from the list of objects
`-(id) initWithObjects:` *obj1, obj2, ..., nil*	Initializes a newly allocated set with a list of objects
`-(unsigned int) count`	Returns the number of members in the set
`-(BOOL) containsObject:` *obj*	Determines whether the set contains *obj*
`-(BOOL) member:` *obj*	Determines whether the set contains *obj* (using the `isEqual:` method)
`-(NSEnumerator *) objectEnumerator`	Returns an `NSEnumerator` object for all the objects in the set
`-(BOOL) isSubsetOfSet:` *nsset*	Determines whether every member of the receiver is present in *nsset*
`-(BOOL) intersectsSet:` *nsset*	Determines whether at least one member of the receiver appears in *nsset*
`-(BOOL) isEqualToSet:` *nsset*	Determines whether the two sets are equal

Table 15.9   **Common `NSMutableSet` Methods**

Method	Description
`-(id) setWithCapacity:` *size*	Creates a new set with an initial capacity to store *size* members
`-(id) initWithCapacity:` *size*	Sets the initial capacity of a newly allocated set to *size* members
`-(void) addObject:` *obj*	Adds *obj* to the set
`-(void) removeObject:` *obj*	Removes *obj* from the set
`-(void) removeAllObjects`	Removes all members of the receiver
`-(void) unionSet:` *nsset*	Adds each member of *nsset* to the receiver
`-(void) minusSet:` *nsset*	Removes all members of *nsset* from the receiver
`-(void) intersectSet:` *nsset*	Removes all members from the receiver that are not also in *nsset*

Exercises

1. Look up the NSCalendarDate class in your documentation. Then add a new category to NSCalendarDate called ElapsedDays. In that new category, add a method based on the following method declaration:

   -(unsigned long) numberOfElapsedDays: (NSCalendarDate *) theDate;

   Have the new method return the number of elapsed days between the receiver and the argument to the method. Write a test program to test your new method. (Hint: Look at the years:months:days:hours:minutes:seconds: sinceDate: method.)

2. Modify the lookup: method developed in this chapter for the AddressBook class so that partial matches of a name can be made. The message expression

   [myBook lookup: @"steve"]

   should match an entry that contains the string steve anywhere within the name.

3. Modify the lookup: method developed in this chapter for the AddressBook class to search the address book for all matches. Have the method return an array of all such matching address cards or nil if no match is made.

4. Add new fields of your choice to the AddressCard class. Some suggestions are separating the name field into first and last name fields and adding address (perhaps with separate state, city, ZIP, and country fields) and phone number fields. Write appropriate setter and getter methods, and ensure that the fields are displayed properly by the print and list methods.

5. After completing exercise 3, modify the lookup: method from exercise 2 to perform a search on all the fields of an address card. Can you think of a way to design your AddressCard and AddressBook classes so that the latter does not have to know all the fields stored in the former?

6. Add the method removeName: to the AddressBook class to remove someone from the address book given this declaration for the method:

   -(BOOL) removeName: (NSString *) theName;

   Use the lookup: method developed in exercise 2. If the name is not found, or multiple entries exist, have the method return NO. If the person is successfully removed, have it return YES.

7. Using the Fraction class defined in Part I, "The Objective-C Language," set up an array of fractions with some arbitrary values. Then write some code that finds the sum of all the fractions stored in the array. Make sure you modify the Fraction class as appropriate to run under Foundation.

8. Using the `Fraction` class defined in Part I, set up a mutable array of fractions with arbitrary values. Then sort the array using the `sortUsingSelector:` method from the `NSMutableArray` class. Add a `Comparison` category to the `Fraction` class and implement your comparison method in that category. Make sure you modify the `Fraction` class as appropriate to run under Foundation.

9. Define three new classes, called `Song`, `PlayList`, and `MusicCollection`. A `Song` object will contain information about a particular song, such as its title, artist, album, and playing time. A `PlayList` object will contain the name of the playlist and a collection of songs, and a `MusicCollection` object will contain a collection of playlists, including a special master playlist called `library` that contains every song in the collection. Define these three classes and write methods to do the following:

   - Create a `Song` object and set its information.
   - Create a `Playlist` object and add and remove songs to and from a playlist. A new song should be added to the master playlist if it's not already there. Make sure that, if a song is removed from the master playlist, it is removed from all playlists in the music collection as well.
   - Create a `MusicCollection` object and add and remove playlists to and from the collection.
   - Search and display the information about any song, playlist, or the entire music collection.

   Make sure all your classes do not leak memory!

10. Write a program that takes an array of integer objects and produces a frequency chart that lists each integer and how many times it occurs in the array. Use an `NSCountedSet` object for constructing your frequency counts.

16

Working with Files

THE FOUNDATION FRAMEWORK ENABLES YOU TO GET ACCESS to the file system to perform basic operations on files and directories. This is provided by `NSFileManager`, whose methods include the capability to

- Create a new file
- Read from an existing file
- Write data to a file
- Rename a file
- Remove (delete) a file
- Test for the existence of a file
- Determine the size of a file as well as other attributes
- Make a copy of a file
- Test two files to see whether their contents are equal

Many of these operations can also be performed on directories. For example, you can create a directory, read its contents, or delete it. Another feature is the ability to *link* files. That is, the ability to have the same file exist under two different names, perhaps even in different directories.

To open a file and perform multiple read and write operations on the file, you use the methods provided by `NSFileHandle`. The methods in this class enable you to

- Open a file for reading, writing, or updating (reading and writing)
- Seek to a specified position within a file
- Read or write a specified number of bytes from and to a file

The methods provided by `NSFileHandle` can also be applied to devices or sockets. However, we will focus only on dealing with ordinary files in this chapter.

If you want to write programs that will run on different machines (or even under different operating system versions on the same machine), you should try to make your programs as independent of the underlying structure of the file system as possible. This implies that you should not make any assumptions about the existence of particular directories (for example, /tmp) or the location of particular files. Luckily, the Foundation framework provides routines that enable you to more easily write portable programs.

Managing Files and Directories: NSFileManager

A file or directory is uniquely identified to NSFileManager using a *pathname* to the file. A pathname is an NSString object that can either be a relative or full pathname. A *relative* pathname is one that is relative to the current directory. So, the filename copy1.m would mean the file copy1.m in the current directory. Slash characters separate a list of directories in a path. The filename ch16/copy1.m is also a relative pathname, identifying the file copy1.m stored in the directory ch16, which is contained in the current directory.

Full pathnames, also known as *absolute* pathnames, begin with a leading /. Slash is actually a directory, called the *root* directory. On my Mac, the full pathname to my home directory is /Users/stevekochan. This pathname specifies three directories: / (the root directory), Users, and stevekochan.[1]

The special tilde character (~) is used as an abbreviation for a user's home directory. ~linda would therefore be an abbreviation for the user linda's home directory. A solitary tilde character indicates the current user's home directory, meaning the pathname ~/copy1.m would reference the file copy1.m stored in the current user's home directory. Other special Unix-style pathname characters, such as . for the current directory and .. for the parent directory, should be removed from pathnames before they're used by any of the Foundation file-handling methods. An assortment of path utilities are available that you can use for this, and they're discussed later in this chapter.

You should try to avoid hard-coding pathnames into your programs. As you'll see in this chapter, methods and functions are available that enable you to obtain the pathname for the current directory, a user's home directory, and a directory that can be used for creating temporary files. You should avail yourself of these as much as possible. Foundation on Mac OS X has a function for obtaining a list of special directories, such as a user's Documents directory.

Table 16.1 summarizes some basic NSFileManager methods for working with files. In that table, *path*, *path1*, *path2*, *from*, and *to* are all NSString objects; *attr* is an NSDictionary object; and *handler* is a callback handler that you can provide to handle errors in your own way. If you specify nil for *handler*, the default action will be taken, which for methods that return a BOOL is to return YES if the operation succeeds and NO if it fails. We won't be getting into writing your own handler in this text.

---

1. The conventions of using slash to separate directories and a period to separate a filename from its extension do not necessarily have to be those adopted by the underlying file system.

Table 16.1   **Common** `NSFileManager` **File Methods**

Method	Description
`-(NSData *) contentsAtPath:` *`path`*	Reads data from a file
`-(NSData *) createFileAtPath:` *`path`* `contents: (NSData *)` *`data`* `attributes:` *`attr`*	Writes data to a file
`-(BOOL) removeFileAtPath:` *`path`* `handler:` *`handler`*	Removes a file
`-(BOOL) movePath:` *`from`* `toPath:` *`to`* `handler:` *`handler`*	Renames or moves a file (*to* cannot already exist)
`-(BOOL) copyPath:` *`from`* `toPath:` *`to`* `handler:` *`handler`*	Copies a file (*to* cannot already exist)
`-(BOOL) contentsEqualAtPath:` *`path1`* `andPath:` *`path2`*	Compares contents of two files
`-(BOOL) fileExistsAtPath:` *`path`*	Tests for file existence
`-(BOOL) isReadableFileAtPath:` *`path`*	Tests whether file exists and can be read
`-(BOOL) isWritableFileAtPath:` *`path`*	Tests whether file exists and can be written
`-(NSDictionary *) fileAttributesAtPath:` *`path`* `traverseLink: (BOOL)` *`flag`*	Gets attributes for file
`-(BOOL) changeFileAttributes:` *`attr`* `atPath:` *`path`*	Changes file attributes

Each of the file methods is invoked on an `NSFileManager` object that is created by sending a `defaultManager` message to the class, like so:

```
NSFileManager  *NSFm;
   ...
NSFm = [NSFileManager defaultManager];
```

For example, to delete a file called `todolist` from the current directory, you would first create the `NSFileManager` object as shown previously and then invoke the `removeFileAtPath:` method, like so:

```
[NSFm removeFileAtPath: @"todolist" handler: nil];
```

You can test the result that is returned to ensure that the file removal succeeds:

```
if ([NSFm removeFileAtPath: @"todolist" handler: nil] == NO) {
  NSLog (@"Couldn't remove file todolist");
  return 1;
}
```

The attributes dictionary enables you to specify, among other things, the permissions for a file you are creating or to obtain or change information for an existing file. For file creation, if you specify `nil` for this parameter, the default permissions are set for the file. The getAttributesForFile:traverseLink: method returns a dictionary containing the specified file's attributes. The traverseLink: parameter is YES or NO for symbolic links. If the file is a symbolic link and YES is specified, the attributes of the linked-to file are returned; if NO is specified, the attributes of the link itself are returned.

For preexisting files, the attributes dictionary includes information such as the file's owner, its size, its creation date, and so on. Each attribute in the dictionary can be extracted based on its key, all of which are defined in <Foundation/NSFileManager.h>. For example, NSFileSize is the key for a file's size.

Program 16.1 shows some basic operations with files. This example assumes you have a file called testfile in your current directory:

```
$ cat testfile
This is a test file with some data in it.
Here's another line of data.
And a third.
$
```

Program 16.1

```
// Basic file operations
// Assumes the existence of a file called "testfile"
// in the current working directory

#import <Foundation/NSObject.h>
#import <Foundation/NSString.h>
#import <Foundation/NSFileManager.h>
#import <Foundation/NSAutoreleasePool.h>
#import <Foundation/NSDictionary.h>

int main (int argc, char *argv[])
{
  NSAutoreleasePool *pool = [[NSAutoreleasePool alloc] init];
  NSString          *fName = @"testfile";
  NSFileManager     *NSFm;
  NSDictionary      *attr;

  // Need to create an instance of the file manager

  NSFm = [NSFileManager defaultManager];

  // Let's make sure our test file exists first

  if ([NSFm fileExistsAtPath: fName] == NO) {
        NSLog (@"File doesn't exist!\n");
        return 1;
  }
```

Program 16.1   **Continued**

```
// Now let's make a copy

if ([NSFm copyPath: fName toPath: @"newfile" handler: nil] == NO) {
    NSLog (@"File copy failed!\n");
    return 2;
}


// Let's test to see if the two files are identical

if ([NSFm contentsEqualAtPath: fName andPath: @"newfile"] == NO) {
    NSLog (@"Files are not equal!\n");
    return 3;
}


// Now let's rename the copy

if ([NSFm movePath: @"newfile" toPath: @"newfile2"
        handler: nil] == NO) {
    NSLog (@"File rename failed!\n");
    return 4;
}


// Get the size of newfile2

if ((attr = [NSFm fileAttributesAtPath: @"newfile2"
            traverseLink: NO]) == nil) {
    NSLog (@"Couldn't get file attributes!\n");
    return 5;
}

NSLog (@"File size is %i bytes\n",
    [[attr objectForKey: NSFileSize] intValue]);

// And finally, let's delete the original file

if ([NSFm removeFileAtPath: fName handler: nil] == NO) {
    NSLog (@"File removal failed!\n");
    return 6;
}

NSLog (@"All operations were successful!\n");

[pool release];
return 0;
}
```

Program 16.1   **Output**

```
2003-07-25 12:52:28.685 a.out[676] File size is 84 bytes
2003-07-25 12:52:28.687 a.out[676] All operations were successful!
$ cat newfile2
This is a test file with some data in it.
Here's another line of data.
And a third.
$
```

The program first tests whether `testfile` exists. If it does, it makes a copy of it and then tests the two files for equality. Experienced Unix users should note that you can't move or copy a file into a directory simply by specifying the destination directory for the `copyPath:toPath:` and `movePath:toPath:` methods; the filename within that directory must be explicitly specified.

The `movePath:toPath:` method can be used to move a file from one directory to another (it can also be used to move entire directories). If the two paths reference files in the same directory (as in our example), the effect is to simply rename the file. So, in Program 16.1, you use this method to rename the file `newfile` to `newfile2`.

As noted in Table 16.1, when performing copying, renaming, or moving operations, the destination file cannot already exist. If it does, the operation will fail.

The size of `newfile2` is determined by using the `fileAttributesAtPath:traverseLink:` method. You test to make sure a non-nil dictionary is returned and then use the `NSDictionary` method `objectForKey:` to get the file's size from the dictionary using the key `NSFileSize`. The integer value from the dictionary is then displayed.

Finally, the program uses the `removeFileAtPath:handler:` method to remove your original file `testfile`.

Each of the file operations is tested for success in Program 16.1. If any fails, an error is logged using `NSLog` and the program exits by returning a nonzero exit status. Each nonzero value, which by convention indicates program failure, is unique based on the type of error. If you are writing command-line tools, this is a useful technique because the return value can be tested by another program, such as from within a shell script.

Working with the `NSData` Class

When working with files, you frequently need to read data into a temporary storage area, often called a *buffer*. When collecting data for subsequent output to a file, a storage area is also often used. Foundation's `NSData` class provides an easy way to set up a buffer, read the contents of file into it, or write the contents of a buffer out to a file.

As you would expect, you can define either immutable (`NSData`) or mutable (`NSMutableData`) storage areas. We'll be introducing methods from this class in this chapter and in succeeding chapters as well.

Program 16.2 shows how easily you can read the contents of a file into a buffer in memory.

The program reads the contents of your file newfile2 and writes it to a new file called newfile3. In a sense, it implements a file copy operation, although not in as straightforward a fashion as the copyPath:toPath:handler: method.

Program 16.2

```
// Make a copy of a file

#import <Foundation/NSObject.h>
#import <Foundation/NSString.h>
#import <Foundation/NSFileManager.h>
#import <Foundation/NSAutoreleasePool.h>
#import <Foundation/NSData.h>

int main (int argc, char *argv[])
{
  NSAutoreleasePool *pool = [[NSAutoreleasePool alloc] init];
  NSFileManager     *NSFm;
  NSData            *fileData;

  NSFm = [NSFileManager defaultManager];


  // Read the file newfile2

  fileData = [NSFm contentsAtPath: @"newfile2"];

  if (fileData == nil) {
      NSLog (@"File read failed!\n");
      return 1;
  }

  // Write the data to newfile3

  if ([NSFm createFileAtPath: @"newfile3" contents: fileData
                attributes: nil] == NO) {
      NSLog (@"Couldn't create the copy!\n");
      return 2;
  }

  NSLog (@"File copy was successful!\n");

  [pool release];
  return 0;
}
```

Program 16.2   **Output**

```
2003-07-25 13:16:52.912 a.out[701] File copy was successful!
$ cat newfile3
This is a test file with some data in it.
Here's another line of data.
And a third.
```

The `NSData contentsAtPath:` method simply takes a pathname and reads the contents of the specified file into a storage area that it creates, returning the storage area object as the result or `nil` if the read fails (for example, if the file doesn't exist or can't be read by you).

The `createFileAtPath:contents:attributes:` method creates a file with the specified attributes (or uses the default if `nil` is supplied for the `attributes` argument). The contents of the specified `NSData` object are then written to the file. In our example, this data area contains the contents of the previously read file.

Working with Directories

Table 16.2 summarizes some of the methods provided by `NSFileManager` for working with directories. Many of these methods are the same as are used for ordinary files, as listed in Table 16.1.

Table 16.2   **Common `NSFileManager` Directory Methods**

Method	Description
`-(NSString *)` `currentDirectoryPath`	Gets the current directory
`-(BOOL)` `changeCurrentDirectoryPath: path`	Changes the current directory
`-(BOOL) copyPath: from toPath:` `to handler: handler`	Copies a directory structure; *to* cannot previously exist
`-(BOOL) createDirectoryAtPath:` `path attributes: attr`	Creates a new directory
`-(BOOL) fileExistsAtPath:` `path isDirectory: (BOOL *) flag`	Tests whether the file is a directory (YES/NO result is stored in flag)
`-(NSArray *)` `directoryContentsAtPath: path`	Lists the contents of the directory
`-(NSDirectoryEnumerator *)` `enumeratorAtPath: path`	Enumerates the contents of the directory
`-(BOOL) removeFileAtPath:` `path handler: handler`	Deletes an empty directory
`-(BOOL) movePath: from` `toPath: to handler: handler`	Renames or moves a directory; *to* cannot previously exist

Program 16.3 shows basic operations with directories.

Program 16.3

```
// Some basic directory operations

#import <Foundation/NSObject.h>
#import <Foundation/NSString.h>
#import <Foundation/NSFileManager.h>
#import <Foundation/NSAutoreleasePool.h>

int main (int argc, char *argv[])
{
  NSAutoreleasePool *pool = [[NSAutoreleasePool alloc] init];
  NSString          *dirName = @"testdir";
  NSString          *path;
  NSFileManager     *NSFm;

  // Need to create an instance of the file manager

  NSFm = [NSFileManager defaultManager];

  // Get current directory

  path = [NSFm currentDirectoryPath];
  NSLog (@"Current directory path is %@\n", path);

  // Create a new directory

  if ([NSFm createDirectoryAtPath: dirName attributes: nil] == NO) {
        NSLog (@"Couldn't create directory!\n");
        return 1;
  }

  // Rename the new directory

  if ([NSFm movePath: dirName toPath: @"newdir" handler: nil] == NO) {
        NSLog (@"Directory rename failed!\n");
        return 2;
  }

  // Change directory into the new directory

  if ([NSFm changeCurrentDirectoryPath: @"newdir"] == NO) {
        NSLog (@"Change directory failed!\n");
        return 3;
  }
```

Program 16.3   **Continued**

```
// Now get and display current working directory

path = [NSFm currentDirectoryPath];
NSLog (@"Current directory path is %@\n", path);

NSLog (@"All operations were successful!\n");

[pool release];
return 0;
}
```

Program 16.3   **Output**

```
2003-07-24 13:32:57.621 a.out[4539] Current directory path is
/Users/stevekochan/ch16
2003-07-24 13:32:57.660 a.out[4539] Current directory path is
/Users/stevekochan/ch16/newdir
2003-07-24 13:32:57.661 a.out[4539] All operations were successful!
```

Program 16.3 is relatively self-explanatory. The current directory path is first obtained for informative purposes. Next, a new directory called `testdir` is created in the current directory. The program then uses the `movePath:toPath:handler:` method to rename the new directory from `testdir` to `newdir`. Remember that this method can also be used to move an entire directory structure (that means including its contents) from one place in the file system to another.

After renaming the new directory, the program makes that new directory the current directory using the `changeCurrentDirectoryPath:` method. The current directory path is then displayed to verify that the change was successful.

Enumerating the Contents of a Directory

Sometimes you need to get a list of the contents of a directory. This enumeration process can be accomplished using either the `enumeratorAtPath:` or the `directoryContentsAtPath:` method. In the former case, each file in the specified directory is enumerated one at a time and, by default, if one of those files is a directory, its contents are also recursively enumerated. During this process you can dynamically prevent this recursion by sending a `skipDescendants` message to an enumeration object so that its contents will not be enumerated.

In the case of `directoryContentsAtPath:`, the contents of the specified directory are enumerated and the file list is returned in an array by the method. If any of the files contained in a directory is itself a directory, its contents are not recursively enumerated by this method.

Program 16.4 shows how you can use either method in your programs.

Program 16.4

```
// Enumerate the contents of a directory

#import <Foundation/NSString.h>
#import <Foundation/NSFileManager.h>
#import <Foundation/NSAutoreleasePool.h>
#import <Foundation/NSArray.h>

int main (int argc, char *argv[])
{
  NSAutoreleasePool     *pool = [[NSAutoreleasePool alloc] init];
  NSString              *path;
  NSFileManager         *NSFm;
  NSDirectoryEnumerator *dirEnum;
  NSArray               *dirArray;
  int                   i, n;

  // Need to create an instance of the file manager

  NSFm = [NSFileManager defaultManager];

  // Get current working directory path

  path = [NSFm currentDirectoryPath];

  // Enumerate the directory

  dirEnum = [NSFm enumeratorAtPath: path];

  printf ("Contents of %s:\n", [path cString]);

  while ((path = [dirEnum nextObject]) != nil)
        printf ("%s\n", [path cString]);

  // Another way to enumerate a directory
  dirArray = [NSFm directoryContentsAtPath:
                        [NSFm currentDirectoryPath]];
  printf ("\nContents using directoryContentsAtPath:\n");

  n = [dirArray count];

  for (i = 0; i < n; ++i)
        printf ("%s\n", [[dirArray objectAtIndex: i] cString]);

  [pool release];
  return 0;
}
```

Program 16.4   **Output**

```
Contents of /Users/stevekochan/mysrc/ch16:
a.out
dir1.m
dir2.m
file1.m
newdir
newdir/file1.m
newdir/output
path1.m
testfile

Contents using directoryContentsAtPath:
a.out
dir1.m
dir2.m
file1.m
newdir
path1.m
testfile
```

You can see from the output the difference between the two methods. The enumeratorAtPath: method lists the contents of the newdir directory, whereas directoryContentsAtPath: does not. If newdir had contained subdirectories, they too would have been enumerated by enumeratorAtPath:.

As noted, during execution of the while loop in Program 16.4, you could have prevented enumeration of any subdirectories by making the following change to the code:

```
while ((path = [dirEnum nextObject]) != nil) {
    printf ("%s\n", [path cString]);

    [NSFm fileExistsAtPath: path isDirectory: &flag];

    if (flag == YES)
        [dirEnum skipDescendents];
}
```

Here flag is a BOOL variable. The fileExistsAtPath: stores YES in flag if the specified path is a directory; otherwise, it stores NO.

Working with Paths: NSPathUtilities.h

NSPathUtilities.h includes functions and category extensions to NSString to enable you to manipulate pathnames. You should use these whenever possible to make your program more independent of the structure of the file system and locations of particular files and directories. Program 16.5 shows how to use several of the functions and methods provided by `NSPathUtilities.h`.

Program 16.5

```
// Some basic path operations

#import <Foundation/NSString.h>
#import <Foundation/NSArray.h>
#import <Foundation/NSFileManager.h>
#import <Foundation/NSAutoreleasePool.h>
#import <Foundation/NSPathUtilities.h>

int main (int argc, char *argv[])
{
  NSAutoreleasePool *pool = [[NSAutoreleasePool alloc] init];
  NSString          *fName = @"path.m";
  NSFileManager     *NSFm;
  NSString          *path, *tempdir, *extension, *homedir, *fullpath;
  NSString          *upath = @"~stevekochan/progs/../ch16/./path.m";
  NSArray           *components;
  int               i, n;

  NSFm = [NSFileManager defaultManager];

  // Get the temporary working directory

  tempdir = NSTemporaryDirectory ();

  printf ("Temporary Directory is %s\n", [tempdir cString]);

  // Extract the base directory from current directory

  path = [NSFm currentDirectoryPath];
  printf ("Base dir is %s\n", [[path lastPathComponent] cString]);

  // Create a full path to the file fName in current directory

  fullpath = [path stringByAppendingPathComponent: fName];
  printf ("fullpath to %s is %s\n", [fName cString], [fullpath cString]);

  // Get the file name extension

  extension = [fullpath pathExtension];
  printf ("extension for %s is %s\n", [fullpath cString],
      [extension cString]);
```

Program 16.5 **Continued**

```
// Get user's home directory

homedir = NSHomeDirectory ();
printf ("Your home directory is %s\n", [homedir cString]);

// Divide a path into its components

components = [homedir pathComponents];

n = [components count];

for (i = 0; i < n; ++i)
    printf ("  %s\n", [[components objectAtIndex: i] cString]);

// "Standardize" a path

printf ("%s => %s\n", [upath cString],
            [[upath stringByStandardizingPath] cString]);

[pool release];
return 0;
}
```

Program 16.5 **Output**

```
Temporary Directory is /tmp
Base dir is ch16
fullpath to path.m is /Users/stevekochan/mysrc/ch16/path.m
extension for /Users/stevekochan/mysrc/ch16/path.m is m
Your home directory is /Users/stevekochan
  /
  Users
  stevekochan
~stevekochan/progs/../ch16/./path.m => /Users/stevekochan/ch16/path.m
```

The function `NSTemporaryDirectory` returns the pathname of a directory on the system you can use for the creation of temporary files. If you create temporary files in this directory, be sure to remove them when you're done. Also, make sure that your file-names are unique, particularly if more than one instance of your application might be running at the same time (see exercise 5 at the end of this chapter). This can easily happen if more than one user logged on to your system is running the same application.

The `lastPathComponent` method extracts the last file in a path. This is useful when you have an absolute pathname and just want to get the base filename from it.

The `stringByAppendingPathComponent:` is useful for tacking on a filename to the end of a path. If the pathname specified as the receiver doesn't end in a slash, the method inserts one in the pathname to separate it from the appended filename. By combining the `currentDirectory` method with the method `stringByAppendingPathComponent:`, you can create a full pathname to a file in the current directory. That technique is shown in Program 16.5.

The `pathExtension` method gives the file extension for the provided pathname. In the example, the extension for the file `path.m` is m, which is returned by the method. If the file does not have an extension, the method simply returns an empty string.

The `NSHomeDirectory` function returns the home directory for the current user. You can get the home directory for any particular user by using the `NSHomeDirectoryForUser` function instead, supplying the user's name as the argument to the function.

The `pathComponents` method returns an array containing each of the components of the specified path. Program 16.5 sequences through each element of the returned array and displays each path component on a separate line of output.

Finally, sometimes pathnames contain tilde (~) characters, as we've previously discussed. The `FileManager` methods accept ~ as an abbreviation for the user's home directory or `~user` for a specified user's home directory. If your pathnames might contain tilde characters, you can resolve them by using the `stringByStandardizingPath` method. This method returns a path with these special characters eliminated, or standardized. You can also use the `stringByExpandingTildeInPath` method to expand just a tilde character if it appears in a pathname.

Table 16.3 summarizes many of the commonly used methods for working with paths. In this table, *components* is an `NSArray` object containing string objects for each component in a path, *path* is a string object specifying a path to a file, and *ext* is a string object indicating a path extension (for example, @`"mp4"`).

Table 16.3 **Common Path Utility Methods**

Method	Description
`+(NSString *)` `  pathWithComponents:` *components*	Constructs a valid path from elements in *components*
`-(NSArray *) pathComponents`	Deconstructs a path into its constituent components
`-(NSString *) lastPathComponent`	Extracts the last component in a path
`-(NSString *) pathExtension`	Extracts the extension from the last component in a path

`-(NSString *)`
`  stringByAppendingPathComponent:`
`  path`
	Adds *path* to the end of an existing path

Table 16.3 **Continued**

`-(NSString *)`
`  stringByAppendingPathExtension:`
`  ext`
	Adds the specified extension to the last component in the path

`-(NSString *)` `  stringByDeletingLastPathComponent`	Removes the last path component
`-(NSString *)` `  stringByDeletingPathExtension`	Removes the extension from the last path component
`-(NSString *)` `  stringByExpandingTildeInPath`	Expands any tildes in the path to the user's home directory (~) or a specified user's home directory (~user)
`-(NSString *)` `  stringByResolvingSymlinksInPath`	Attempts to resolve symbolic links in the path
`-(NSString *)` `  stringByStandardizingPath`	Standardizes a path by attempting to resolve ~, . (parent directory), . (current directory), and symbolic links

Table 16.4 presents the *functions* available to obtain information about a user, her home directory, and a directory for storing temporary files.

Table 16.4 **Common Path Utility Functions**

Function	Description
`NSString *NSUserName (void)`	Returns the current user's login name
`NSString *NSFullUserName (void)`	Returns the current user's full username
`NSString *NSHomeDirectory (void)`	Returns the path to the current user's home directory
`NSString *NSHomeDirectoryForUser` `(NSString *user)`	Returns the home directory for *user*
`NSString *NSTemporaryDirectory` `(void)`	Returns the path to a directory that can be used for creating a temporary file

You also might want to look at the Foundation function `NSSearchPathForDirectoriesInDomains`, which you can use to locate special directories on the system, such as the Application directory.

A Program to Copy Files and the `NSProcessInfo` Class

Program 16.6 illustrates a command-line tool to implement a simple file copy operation. Usage of this command is as follows:

```
copy from-file to-file
```

Unlike `NSFileManager`'s `copyPath:toPath:handler:` method, your command-line tool enables *to-file* to be a directory name. In that case, the file is copied into the *to-file* directory under the name *from-file*. Also unlike the method, if *to-file* already exists, you allow its contents to be overwritten. This is more in line with the standard Unix copy command `cp`.

You could get the filenames from the command line by using the `argc` and `argv` arguments to `main`. We discussed these arguments in Chapter 13, "Underlying C Language Features."

Instead of having to deal with C strings, which is what you have to do when you work with `argv`, you'll use a Foundation class called `NSProcessInfo`. `NSProcessInfo` contains methods that allow you to set and retrieve various types of information about your running application (that is, your *process*). These methods are summarized in Table 16.5.

Table 16.5 `NSProcessInfo` **Methods**

Method	Description
`+(NSProcessInfo *) processInfo`	Returns information about the current process
`-(NSArray *) arguments`	Returns the arguments to the current process as an array of `NSString` objects
`-(NSDictionary *) environment`	Returns a dictionary of variable/value pairs representing the current environment variables (such as PATH and HOME) and their values
`-(int) processIdentifier`	Returns the process identifier, which is a unique number assigned by the operating system to identify each running process
`-(NSString *) processName`	Returns the name of the current executing process
`-(NSString *) globallyUniqueString`	Returns a different unique string each time it is invoked. This could be used for generating unique temporary filenames (see exercise 5)
`-(NSString *) hostName`	Returns the name of the host system (returns `Steve-Kochans-Computer.local` on my Mac OS X system)
`-(unsigned int) operatingSystem`	Returns a number indicating the operating system (returns the constant `NSMACHOperatingSystem` on my Mac, where the possible return values are defined in `NSProcessInfo.h`)
`-(NSString *) operatingSystemName`	Returns the name of the operating system (returns the constant `NSMACHOperatingSystem` on my Mac, where the possible return values are defined in `NSProcessInfo.h`)
`-(NSString *) operatingSystemVersionString`	Returns the current version of the operating system (returns `Version 10.2.6 (Build 6L60)` on my Mac OS X system)
`-(void) setProcessName: (NSString *) name`	Sets the name of the current process to *name*. Should be used with caution because some assumptions can be made about the name of your process (for example, by the user default settings)

Program 16.6

```
// Implement a basic copy utility

#import <Foundation/NSString.h>
#import <Foundation/NSArray.h>
#import <Foundation/NSFileManager.h>
#import <Foundation/NSAutoreleasePool.h>
#import <Foundation/NSPathUtilities.h>
#import <Foundation/NSProcessInfo.h>

int main (int argc, char *argv[])
{
  NSAutoreleasePool *pool = [[NSAutoreleasePool alloc] init];
  NSFileManager     *NSFm;
  NSString          *source, *dest;
  BOOL              isDir;
  NSProcessInfo     *proc = [NSProcessInfo processInfo];
  NSArray           *args = [proc arguments];

  NSFm = [NSFileManager defaultManager];

  // Check for two arguments on the command line

  if ([args count] != 3) {
    printf ("Usage: %s src dest\n", [[proc processName] cString]);
    return 1;
  }

  source = [args objectAtIndex: 1];
  dest = [args objectAtIndex: 2];


  // Make sure the source file can be read

  if ([NSFm isReadableFileAtPath: source] == NO) {
      printf ("Can't read %s\n", [source cString]);
      return 2;
  }

  // See if the destination file is a directory
  // if it is, add the source to the end of the destination

  fileExists = [NSFm fileExistsAtPath: dest isDirectory: &isDir];

  if (fileExists == YES && isDir == YES)
      dest = [dest stringByAppendingPathComponent:
```

Program 16.6 **Continued**

```
                      [source lastPathComponent]];

  // Remove the destination file if it already exists

  [NSFm removeFileAtPath: dest handler: nil];

  // Okay, time to perform the copy

  if ([NSFm copyPath: source toPath: dest handler: nil] == NO) {
      printf ("Copy failed!\n");
      return 4;
  }

  printf ("Copy of %s to %s succeeeded!\n", [source cString],
      [dest cString]);

  [pool release];
  return 0;
}
```

Program 16.6 **Output**

```
$ ls -l          see what files we have
total 96
-rwxr-xr-x 1 stevekoc staff 19956 Jul 24 14:33 copy
-rw-r--r-- 1 stevekoc staff  1484 Jul 24 14:32 copy.m
-rw-r--r-- 1 stevekoc staff  1403 Jul 24 13:00 file1.m
drwxr-xr-x 2 stevekoc staff    68 Jul 24 14:40 newdir
-rw-r--r-- 1 stevekoc staff  1567 Jul 24 14:12 path1.m
-rw-r--r-- 1 stevekoc staff    84 Jul 24 13:22 testfile
$ copy           try with no args
Usage: copy from-file to-file
$ copy foo copy2
Can't read foo
$ copy copy.m backup.m
Copy of copy.m to backup.m succeeeded!
$ diff copy.m backup.m    compare the files
$ copy copy.m newdir      try copy into directory
Copy of copy.m to newdir/copy.m succeeeded!
$ ls -l newdir
total 8
-rw-r--r-- 1 stevekoc staff 1484 Jul 24 14:44 copy.m
$
```

NSProcessInfo's arguments method returns an array of string objects. The setup of the array is similar to the argv C array discussed in Chapter 13 (except that array was a C array containing C strings, as opposed to an array object containing string objects). Like argv, the first element of the array is the name of the process and the remaining elements contain the arguments typed on the command line.

You first check to ensure that two arguments were typed on the command line. This is done by testing the size of the array args that is returned from the arguments method. If this test succeeds, the program then extracts the source and destination filenames from the args array, assigning their values to source and dest, respectively.

The program next checks to ensure that the source file can be read, issuing an error message and exiting if it can't.

The statement

```
[NSFm fileExistsAtPath: dest isDirectory: &isDir];
```

checks the file specified by dest to see whether it is a directory. As you've seen previously, the answer—YES or NO—is stored in the variable isDir.

If dest is a directory, you want to append the last path component of the source filename to the end of the directory's name. You use the path utility method stringByAppendingPathComponent: to do this. So, if the value of source is the string ch16/copy1.m and the value of dest is /Users/stevekochan/progs and the latter is a directory, you change the value of dest to /Users/stevekochan/progs/copy1.m.

The copyPath:ToPath:handler: method doesn't allow files to be overwritten. Thus, to avoid an error, the program tries to remove the destination file first by using the removeFileAtPath:handler: method. It doesn't really matter whether this method succeeds because it will fail anyway if the destination file doesn't exist.

Upon reaching the end of the program, you can assume all went well and issue a message to that effect.

Basic File Operations: NSFileHandle

The methods provided by NSFileHandle enable you to work more closely with files. At the beginning of this chapter, we listed some of the things you can do with these methods.

In general you'll follow these three steps when working with a file:

1. Open the file and obtain an NSFileHandle object to reference the file in subsequent I/O operations.

2. Perform your I/O operations on the open file.

3. Close the file.

Table 16.6 summarizes some commonly used NSFileHandle methods. In this table *fh* is an NSFileHandle object, *data* is an NSData object, *path* is an NSString object, and *offset* is an unsigned long long.

Table 16.6 **Common** NSFileHandle **Methods**

Method	Description
+(NSFileHandle *) fileHandleForReadingAtPath: *path*	Opens a file for reading
+(NSFileHandle *) fileHandleForWritingAtPath: *path*	Opens a file for writing
+(NSFileHandle *) fileHandleForUpdatingAtPath: *path*	Opens a file for updating (reading and writing)
-(NSData *) availableData	Returns data available for reading from a device or channel
-(NSData *) readDataToEndOfFile	Reads the remaining data up to the end of the file (UINT_MAX) bytes max
-(NSData *) readDataOfLength: (unsigned int) *bytes*	Reads a specified number of *bytes* from the file
-(void) writeData: *data*	Writes *data* to the file
-(unsigned long long) offsetInFile	Obtains the current file offset
-(void) seekToFileOffset: *offset*	Sets the current file offset
-(void) seekToEndOfFile	Positions the current file offset at the end of the file
-(void) truncateFileAtOffset: *offset*	Sets the file size to *offset* bytes (pad if needed)
-(void) closeFile	Closes the file

Not shown here are methods for obtaining NSFileHandles for standard input, standard output, standard error, and the null device. These are of the form fileHandleWith*Device*, where *Device* can be StandardInput, StandardOutput, StandardError, or NullDevice.

Also not shown here are methods for reading and writing data in the background, that is, asynchronously.

You should note that the FileHandle class does not provide for the creation of files. That has to be done with FileManager methods, as we've already described. So, both fileHandleForWritingAtPath: and fileHandleForUpdatingAtPath: assume the file exists and return nil if it doesn't. In both cases, the file offset is set to the beginning of the file, so writing (or reading for update mode) begins at the start of the file. Also, if you're used to programming under Unix, you should note that opening a file for writing does not truncate the file. You have to do that yourself if that's your intention.

Program 16.7 opens the original testfile file you created at the start of this chapter, reads in its contents, and copies it to a file called testout.

Program 16.7

```
// Some basic file handle operations
// Assumes the existence of a file called "testfile"
// in the current working directory

#import <Foundation/NSObject.h>
#import <Foundation/NSString.h>
#import <Foundation/NSFileHandle.h>
#import <Foundation/NSFileManager.h>
#import <Foundation/NSAutoreleasePool.h>
#import <Foundation/NSData.h>

int main (int argc, char *argv[])
{
  NSAutoreleasePool *pool = [[NSAutoreleasePool alloc] init];
  NSFileHandle      *inFile, *outFile;
  NSData            *buffer;


  // Open the file testfile for reading

  inFile = [NSFileHandle fileHandleForReadingAtPath: @"testfile"];

  if (inFile == nil) {
      NSLog (@"Open of testfile for reading failed\n");
      return 1;
  }

  // Create the output file first if necessary

  [[NSFileManager defaultManager] createFileAtPath: @"testout"
      contents: nil attributes: nil];

  // Now open outfile for writing

  outFile = [NSFileHandle fileHandleForWritingAtPath: @"testout"];

  if (outFile == nil) {
      NSLog (@"Open of testout for writing failed\n");
      return 2;
  }

  // Truncate the output file since it may contain data

  [outFile truncateFileAtOffset: 0];
```

Program 16.7 **Continued**

```
// Read the data from inFile and write it to outFile

buffer = [inFile readDataToEndOfFile];

[outFile writeData: buffer];

// Close the two files

[inFile closeFile];
[outFile closeFile];

[pool release];
return 0;
}
```

Program 16.7 **Output**

```
$ cat testout
This is a test file with some data in it.
Here's another line of data.
And a third.
```

The method `readDataToEndOfFile:` reads up to `UINT_MAX` bytes of data at a time, which is defined in `<limits.h>` and equal to $FFFFFFFF_{16}$ on many systems. This will be large enough for any application you'll have to write. You can also break up the operation to perform smaller-sized reads and writes. You can even set up a loop to transfer a buffer full of bytes between the files at a time, using the `readDataOfLength:` method. Your buffer size might be 8,192 (8kb) or 131,072 (128kb) bytes, for example. A power of 2 is normally used because the underlying operating system typically performs its I/O operations in chunks of data of such sizes. You might want to experiment with different values on your system to see what works best.

If a read method reaches the end of the file without reading any data, it returns an empty `NSData` object (that is, a buffer with no bytes in it). You can apply the `length` method to the buffer and test for equality with zero to see whether any data remains to be read from the file.

If you open a file for updating, the file offset is set to the beginning of the file. You can change that offset by seeking within a file and then perform your read or write operations on the file. So, to seek to the 10th byte in a file whose handle is `databaseHandle`, you could write the following message expression:

```
[databaseHandle seekToFileOffset: 10];
```

Relative file positioning is done by obtaining the current file offset and then adding to or subtracting from it. So, to skip over the next 128 bytes in the file, you'd write the following:

```
[databaseHandle seekToFileOffet:
        [databaseHandle offsetInFile] + 128];
```

And to move back the equivalent of five integers in the file, you'd write this:

```
[databaseHandle seekToFileOffet:
        [databaseHandle offsetInFile] - 5 * sizeof (int)];
```

Program 16.8 appends the contents of one file to another. It does this by opening the second file for writing, seeking to the end of the file, and then writing the contents of the first file to the second.

Program 16.8
```
// Append the file "fileA" to the end of "fileB"

#import <Foundation/NSObject.h>
#import <Foundation/NSString.h>
#import <Foundation/NSFileHandle.h>
#import <Foundation/NSFileManager.h>
#import <Foundation/NSAutoreleasePool.h>
#import <Foundation/NSData.h>

int main (int argc, char *argv[])
{
  NSAutoreleasePool      *pool = [[NSAutoreleasePool alloc] init];
  NSFileHandle           *inFile, *outFile;
  NSData                 *buffer;


  // Open the file fileA for reading

  inFile = [NSFileHandle fileHandleForReadingAtPath: @"fileA"];

  if (inFile == nil) {
      NSLog (@"Open of fileA for reading failed\n");
      return 1;
  }

  // Open the file fileB for updating

  outFile = [NSFileHandle fileHandleForWritingAtPath: @"fileB"];
```

Program 16.8 **Continued**

```
if (outFile == nil) {
        NSLog (@"Open of fileB for writing failed\n");
        return 2;
}

// Seek to the end of outFile

[outFile seekToEndOfFile];

// Read inFile and write its contents to outFile

buffer = [inFile readDataToEndOfFile];
[outFile writeData: buffer];

// Close the two files

[inFile closeFile];
[outFile closeFile];

[pool release];
return 0;
}
```

You can assume that you have called your test program append. Here's a sample execution.

Program 16.8 **Output**

```
$ cat fileA      Display contents of first file
This line 1 in the first file.
This line 2 in the first file.
$ cat fileB      Display contents of second file
This is line 1 in the second file.
This is line 2 in the second file.
$ append         Run our append program
$ cat fileB      See if it worked
This is line 1 in the second file.
This is line 2 in the second file.
This is line 1 in the first file.
This is line 2 in the first file.
$
```

You can see from the output that the contents of the first file were successfully appended to the end of the second file. Incidentally, seekToEndOfFile returns the current file offset after the seek is performed. We chose to ignore that value; you can use that information to obtain the size of a file in your program if you need it.

Exercises

1. Modify the copy program developed in Program 16.6 so that it can accept more than one source file to be copied into a directory, like the standard Unix cp command. So, the command

   `$ copy copy1.m file1.m file2.m progs`

   should copy the three files copy1.m, file1.m, and file2.m into the directory progs. Be sure that when more than one source file is specified, the last argument is in fact an existing directory.

2. Write a command-line tool called myfind that takes two arguments. The first is a starting directory to begin the search, and the second is a filename to locate. So, the command line

   `$ myfind /Users proposal.doc`
   `/Users/stevekochan/MyDocuments/proposals/proposal.doc`
   `$`

   begins searching the file system from /Users to locate the file proposal.doc. Print either a full path to the file if it's found (as shown) or an appropriate message if it's not.

3. Write your own version of the standard Unix tools basename and dirname.

4. Using NSProcessInfo, write a program to display all the information returned by each of its getter methods.

5. Given the NSPathUtilities.h function NSTemporaryDirectory and the NSProcessInfo method globallyUniqueString described in this chapter, add a category called TempFiles to NSString and in it define a method called temporaryFileName that returns a different, unique filename every time it is invoked.

6. Modify Program 16.7 so that the file is read and written kBufSize bytes at a time, where kBufSize is defined at the beginning of your program. Be sure to test the program on large files (that is, files larger than kBufSize bytes).

7. Open a file, read its contents 128 bytes at a time, and write it to the terminal. Use FileHandle's fileHandleWithStandardOutput method to obtain a handle for the terminal's output.

17

Memory Management

WE HAVE FOCUSED ON THE TOPIC OF memory management throughout this book. You should understand by now when you are responsible for releasing objects and when you are not. Even though the examples in this book have all been very small, nevertheless we emphasized the importance of paying attention to memory management to teach good programming practice and to develop leak-free programs.

Depending on the type of application you're writing, judicious use of memory can be critical. For example, if you're writing an interactive drawing application that creates many objects during the execution of the program, if you're not careful, your program might continue to consume more and more memory resources as it runs. In such cases, it becomes your responsibility to intelligently manage those resources and free them when they're no longer needed. This means freeing resources during the program's execution rather than just waiting until the end.

In this chapter, you will learn about Foundation's memory allocation strategy in more detail. This involves a more thorough discussion of the autorelease pool and the idea of retaining objects. You will also learn about an object's reference count.

The Autorelease Pool

You are familiar with the autorelease pool from previous program examples in this second part of the book. When dealing with Foundation programs, you must set up this pool yourself to use the Foundation objects.[1] This pool is where the system keeps track of your objects for later release. The pool can be set up by your application with a call, like so:

```
NSAutoreleasePool *pool = [[NSAutoreleasePool alloc] init];
```

---

1. If you're writing Cocoa applications, the pool is automatically set up for you. But because you're just writing Foundation applications here, you need to set up the pool yourself.

Once the pool is set up, Foundation automatically adds certain arrays, strings, dictionaries, and other objects to this pool. When you're done using the pool, you can release the memory it uses with the `release` method:

```
[pool release];
```

The autorelease pool gets its name from the fact that any objects that have been marked as autorelease and therefore added to the pool are automatically released when the pool itself is released. In fact, you can have more than one autorelease pool in your program, and they can be nested as well.

Multiple Autorelease Pools

If your program generates a large number of temporary objects (which can easily happen when executing code inside a loop), you might need to create multiple autorelease pools in your program. For example, the code fragment

```
NSAutoreleasePool  *tempPool;
  ...
for (i = 0; i < n; ++i) {
  tempPool = [[NSAutoReleasePool alloc] init];
  // lots of work with temporary objects here
  [tempPool release];
}
```

illustrates how you could set up autorelease pools to release the temporary objects created by each iteration of the `for` loop.

You should note that the autorelease pool doesn't contain the actual objects themselves—only a reference to the objects that are to be released when the pool is released.

You can add an object to the current autorelease pool for later release by sending it an `autorelease` message:

```
[myFraction autorelease];
```

The system then adds `myFraction` to the autorelease pool for automatic release later. As you'll see, the `autorelease` method is useful for marking objects from inside a method for later disposal.

Reference Counting

When we talked about the basic Objective-C object class `Object`, we noted that memory is allocated with the `alloc` method and could subsequently be released with a `free` message. Unfortunately, it's not always that simple. An object you create can be referenced in several places by a running application; it also might be stored in an array or referenced by an instance variable someplace else, for example. You can't free up the memory used by an object until you are certain that everyone is done using that object.

Luckily, the Foundation framework provides an elegant solution for keeping track of the number of references to an object. It involves a fairly straightforward technique called *reference counting*. The concept is as follows: When an object is created, its reference count is set to 1. Each time you need to ensure that the object be kept around, you increment its reference count by 1 by sending it a retain message, like so:

```
[myFraction retain];
```

Some of the methods in the Foundation framework also increment this reference count, such as when an object is added to an array.

When you no longer need an object, you decrement its reference count by 1 by sending it a release message, like this:

```
[myFraction release];
```

When the reference count of an object reaches 0, the system knows that the object is no longer needed (because, in theory, it is no longer referenced), so it frees up (*deallocates*) its memory. This is done by sending the object a dealloc message.

Successful operation of this strategy requires diligence on the part of you, the programmer, to ensure that the reference count is appropriately incremented and decremented during program execution. Some of this, but not all, is handled by the system, as you'll see.

Let's take a look at reference counting in a little more detail. The retainCount message can be sent to an object to obtain its reference (or *retain*) count. You will normally never need to use this method, but it's useful here for illustrative purposes (see Program 17.1).

Program 17.1

```
// Introduction to reference counting

#import <Foundation/NSObject.h>
#import <Foundation/NSAutoreleasePool.h>
#import <Foundation/NSString.h>
#import <Foundation/NSArray.h>
#import <Foundation/NSValue.h>

int main (int argc, char *argv[])
{
    NSAutoreleasePool  *pool = [[NSAutoreleasePool alloc] init];
    NSNumber           *myInt = [NSNumber numberWithInt: 100];
    NSNumber           *myInt2;
    NSMutableArray     *myArr = [NSMutableArray array];

    printf ("myInt retain count = %x\n", [myInt retainCount]);

    [myArr addObject: myInt];
    printf ("after adding to array = %x\n", [myInt retainCount]);
```

Program 17.1 **Continued**

```
myInt2 = myInt;
printf ("after asssignment to myInt2 = %x\n",
                    [myInt retainCount]);

[myInt retain];
printf ("myInt after retain = %x\n", [myInt retainCount]);
printf ("myInt2 after retain = %x\n", [myInt2 retainCount]);

myInt release];
printf ("after release = %x\n", [myInt retainCount]);

[myArr removeObjectAtIndex: 0];
printf ("after removal from array = %x\n", [myInt retainCount]);

[pool release];
return 0;

}
```

Program 17.1 **Output**

```
myInt retain count = 1
after adding to array = 2
after asssignment to myInt2 = 2
myInt after retain = 3
myInt2 after retain = 3
after release = 2
after removal from array = 1
```

The NSNumber object myInt is set to the integer value 100, and the output shows it has an initial retain count of 1. Next, the object is added to the array myArr using the addObject: method. Note that its reference count then goes to 2. This is done automatically by the addObject: method; if you check your documentation for the addObject: method, you will see this fact described there. Adding an object to any type of collection increments its reference count. That means if you subsequently release the object you've added, it will still have a valid reference from within the array and won't be deallocated.

Next, you assign myInt to myInt2. Note that this doesn't increment the reference count—this could be potential trouble later. For example, if the reference count for myInt were decremented to 0 and its space released, myInt2 would have an invalid object reference (remember that the assignment of myInt to myInt2 doesn't copy the actual object, only the pointer in memory to where the object is located).

Because `myInt` now has another reference (through `myInt2`), you increment its reference count by sending it a `retain` message. This is done in the next line of Program 17.1. As you can see, after sending it the `retain` message, its reference count becomes 3. The first reference is the actual object itself, the second from the array, and the third from the assignment. Although storing the element in the array creates an automatic increase in the reference count, assigning it to another variable does not, so you must do that yourself. Notice from the output that both `myInt` and `myInt2` have a reference count of 3; that's because they both reference the same object in memory.

Let's assume you're done using the `myInt` object in your program. You can tell the system that by sending a `release` message to the object. As you can see, its reference count then goes from 3 back down to 2. Because it's not 0, the other references to the object (from the array and through `myInt2`) remain valid. The memory used by the object is not deallocated by the system as long as it has a nonzero reference count.

If you remove the first element from the array `myArr` using the `removeObjectAtIndex:` method, you'll note that the reference count for `myInt` is automatically decremented to 1. In general, removing an object from any collection has the side effect of decrementing its reference count. This implies that the following code sequence

```
myInt = [myArr ObjectAtIndex: 0];
    . . .
[myArr removeObjectAtIndex: 0]
    . . .
```

could lead to trouble. That's because, in this case, the object referenced by `myInt` can become invalid after the `removeObjectAtIndex:` method is invoked if its reference count is decremented to 0. The solution here, of course, is to retain `myInt` after it is retrieved from the array so that it won't matter what happens to its reference from other places.

Reference Counting and Strings

Program 17.2 shows how reference counting works for string objects.

Program 17.2

```
// Reference counting with string objects

#import <Foundation/NSObject.h>
#import <Foundation/NSAutoreleasePool.h>
#import <Foundation/NSString.h>
#import <Foundation/NSArray.h>

int main (int argc, char *argv[])
{
```

Program 17.2   **Continued**

```
NSAutoreleasePool *pool = [[NSAutoreleasePool alloc] init];
NSString          *myStr1 = @"Constant string";
NSString          *myStr2 = [NSString stringWithString:
                                    @"string 2"];
NSMutableString   *myStr3 = [NSMutableString stringWithString:
                                    @"string 3"];
NSMutableArray    *myArr = [NSMutableArray array];

printf ("Retain count: myStr1: %x, myStr2: %x, myStr3: %x\n",
        [myStr1 retainCount], [myStr2 retainCount],
        [myStr3 retainCount]);

[myArr addObject: myStr1];
[myArr addObject: myStr2];
[myArr addObject: myStr3];

printf ("Retain count: myStr1: %x, myStr2: %x, myStr3: %x\n",
        [myStr1 retainCount], [myStr2 retainCount],
        [myStr3 retainCount]);

[myStr1 retain];
[myStr2 retain];
[myStr3 retain];

printf ("Retain count: myStr1: %x, myStr2: %x, myStr3: %x\n",
        [myStr1 retainCount], [myStr2 retainCount],
        [myStr3 retainCount]);

// Bring the reference count of myStr2 and myStr3 back down to 2

[myStr2 release];
[myStr3 release];

[pool release];
return 0;
}
```

Program 17.2   **Output**

```
Retain count: myStr1: ffffffff, myStr2: 1, myStr3: 1
Retain count: myStr1: ffffffff, myStr2: 2, myStr3: 2
Retain count: myStr1: ffffffff, myStr2: 3, myStr3: 3
```

The NSString object myStr1 is assigned the NSConstantString @"Constant string". Space for constant strings is allocated differently in memory than other objects. They have no reference counting mechanism because they can never be released, which is why when the retainCount message is sent to myStr1, it returns a value of 0xffffffff. (This value is actually defined as the largest possible unsigned integer value, or UINT_MAX, in the standard header file <limits.h>.)

The variables myStr2 and myStr3 are set to strings made by copies of constant character strings. These strings do have reference counts, as verified by the output. These reference counts can be changed by adding these strings to an array or by sending them retain messages, as verified by the output from the last two printf calls. Both of these objects were added to the autorelease pool by Foundation's stringWithString: method when they were created. The array myArr was also added to the pool by Foundation's array method.

Before the autorelease pool itself is released, the objects myStr2 and myStr3 are each released. This brings their reference counts both down to 2. The release of the autorelease pool then decrements the reference counts of these two objects to 0, which causes them to be deallocated. How does that happen? When the autorelease pool is released, each of the objects in the pool gets a release message sent to it for each time it was sent an autorelease message. Because the strings objects myStr2 and myStr3 were added to the autorelease pool when they were created by the stringWithString: method, they each are sent a release message. That brings their reference counts down to 1. When an array in the autorelease pool is released, each of its elements also is released. Therefore, when myArr is released from the pool, each of its elements—which includes myStr2 and myStr3—is sent release messages. This brings their reference counts down to 0, which then causes them to be deallocated.

You have to be careful not to overrelease an object. In Program 17.2, if you were to bring the reference count of either myStr2 or mystr3 below 2 before the pool was released, the pool would contain a reference to an invalid object. Then, when the pool was released, the reference to the invalid object would most likely cause the program to terminate abnormally with a message similar to this:

```
./c: line 1: 1384 Segmentation fault    a.out
c retain2B: exited with status 139
```

Reference Counting and Instance Variables

You also have to pay attention to reference counts when you deal with instance variables. For example, recall the setName: method from your AddressCard class:

```
-(void) setName: (NSString *) theName
{
    [name release];
    name = [[NSString alloc] initWithString: theName];
}
```

Suppose we had defined `setName:` this way instead and did not have it take owner-ship of its name object:

```
-(void) setName: (NSString *) theName
{
  name = theName;
}
```

This version of the method takes a string representing the person's name and stores it in the name instance variable. It seems straightforward enough, but consider the follow-ing method call:

```
NSString  *newName;
   ...
[myCard setName: newName];
```

Suppose newName is a temporary storage space for the name of the person you want to add to the address card and that later you want to release it. What do you think would happen to the name instance variable in myCard? That's correct; its name field would no longer be valid because it would reference an object that had been destroyed. That's why your classes need to own their own member objects: You don't have to worry about those objects inadvertently being deallocated or modified.

The next few examples illustrate this point in more detail. Let's start by defining a new class called ClassA that has one instance variable: a string object called str. You'll just write setter and getter methods for this variable (see Program 17.3).

Program 17.3
***

```
// Introduction to reference counting

#import <Foundation/NSObject.h>
#import <Foundation/NSAutoreleasePool.h>
#import <Foundation/NSString.h>

@interface ClassA: NSObject
{
  NSString *str;
}

-(void) setStr: (NSString *) s;
-(NSString *) str;
@end

@implementation ClassA;
-(void) setStr: (NSString *) s
{
  str = s;
}
```

Program 17.3 **Continued**

```
-(NSString *) str
{
   return str;
}
@end

int main (int argc, char *argv[])
{
   NSAutoreleasePool *pool = [[NSAutoreleasePool alloc] init];
   NSString   *myStr = [NSString stringWithString: @"A string"];
   ClassA     *myA = [[ClassA alloc] init];

   printf ("myStr retain count: %x\n", [myStr retainCount]);

   [myA setStr: myStr];
   printf ("myStr retain count: %x\n", [myStr retainCount]);

   [myA release];
   [pool release];
   return 0;
}
```

Program 17.3 **Output**

```
myStr retain count: 1
myStr retain count: 1
```

The program simply allocates a ClassA object called myA and then invokes the setter method to set it to the NSString object specified by myStr. The reference count for myStr is 1 both before and after the setStr method is invoked, as you would expect because the method simply stores the value of its argument into its instance variable str. Once again, however, if the program were to release myStr after calling the setStr method, the value stored inside the str instance variable would become invalid because its reference count would be decremented to 0 and the memory space occupied by the object it references would be deallocated.

This does in fact happen in Progam 17.3 when the autorelease pool is released. Even though we didn't add it to that pool explicitly ourselves, when we created the string object myStr using the stringWithString: method, it was added to the autorelease pool by that method. When the pool was released, so was myStr. Any attempt to access it after the pool was released would therefore be invalid.

Program 17.4 makes a change to the setStr: method to retain the value of str. This protects you from someone else later releasing the object str references.

Program 17.4

```objc
// Retaining objects

#import <Foundation/NSObject.h>
#import <Foundation/NSAutoreleasePool.h>
#import <Foundation/NSString.h>
#import <Foundation/NSArray.h>

@interface ClassA: NSObject
{
  NSString *str;
}

-(void) setStr: (NSString *) s;
-(NSString *) str;
@end

@implementation ClassA;
-(void) setStr: (NSString *) s
{
  str = s;
  [str retain];
}

-(NSString *) str
{
  return str;
}
@end

int main (int argc, char *argv[])
{
  NSAutoreleasePool *pool = [[NSAutoreleasePool alloc] init];
  NSString   *myStr = [NSString stringWithString: @"A string"];
  ClassA    *myA = [[ClassA alloc] init];

  printf ("myStr retain count: %x\n", [myStr retainCount]);

  [myA setStr: myStr];
  printf ("myStr retain count: %x\n", [myStr retainCount]);

  [myStr release];
  printf ("myStr retain count: %x\n", [myStr retainCount]);

  [myA release];
  [pool release];
  return 0;
}
```

Program 17.4 **Output**

```
myStr retain count: 1
myStr retain count: 2
myStr retain count: 1
```

You see that the reference count for myStr is bumped to 2 after the setStr: method is invoked. So, this particular problem has been solved. Subsequently releasing myStr in the program makes its reference through the instance variable still valid because its reference count is still 1.

Because you allocated myA in the program using alloc, you are still responsible for releasing it yourself. Instead of having to worry about releasing it yourself, you could have added it to the autorelease pool by sending it an autorelease message:

```
[myA autorelease];
```

This can be done immediately after the object is allocated if you want. Remember, adding an object to the autorelease pool doesn't release it or invalidate it; it just marks it for later release. You can continue to use the object until it is deallocated, which happens when the pool is released if the reference count of the object becomes 0 at that time.

You are still left with some potential problems that you might have spotted. Your setStr: method does its job of retaining the string object it gets as its argument, but when does *that* string object get released? Also, what about the old value of the instance variable str that you are overwriting? Shouldn't you release its value to free up its memory? Program 17.5 provides a solution to this problem.

Program 17.5

```
// Introduction to reference counting

#import <Foundation/NSObject.h>
#import <Foundation/NSAutoreleasePool.h>
#import <Foundation/NSString.h>
#import <Foundation/NSArray.h>

@interface ClassA: NSObject
{
  NSString *str;
}

-(void) setStr: (NSString *) s;
-(NSString *) str;
-(void) dealloc;
@end

@implementation ClassA;
-(void) setStr: (NSString *) s
{
```

Program 17.5   **Continued**

```
  // free up old object since we're done with it
  [str autorelease];

  // retain argument in case someone else releases it
  str = [s retain];
}

-(NSString *) str
{
  return str;
}

-(void) dealloc {
  printf ("ClassA dealloc\n");
  [str release];
  [super dealloc];
}
@end

int main (int argc, char *argv[])
{
  NSAutoreleasePool *pool = [[NSAutoreleasePool alloc] init];
  NSString  *myStr = [NSString stringWithString: @"A string"];
  ClassA   *myA = [[ClassA alloc] init];

  printf ("myStr retain count: %x\n", [myStr retainCount]);
  [myA autorelease];

  [myA setStr: myStr];
  printf ("myStr retain count: %x\n", [myStr retainCount]);

  [pool release];
  return 0;
}
```

Program 17.5   **Output**

```
myStr retain count: 1
myStr retain count: 2
ClassA dealloc
```

The setStr: method first takes whatever is currently stored in the str instance variable and autoreleases it.[2] That is, it makes it available for later release. This is important if the method might be called many times throughout the execution of a program to set the same field to different values. Each time a new value is stored, the old value should be marked for release. After the old value is released, the new one is retained and stored in the `str` field. The message expression

```
str = [s retain];
```

takes advantage of the fact that the `retain` method returns its receiver.

The `dealloc` method is not new. You encountered it before in Chapter 15, "Numbers, Strings, and Collections," with your `AddressBook` and `AddressCard` classes. Overriding `dealloc` provides a tidy way for you to dispose of the last object referenced by your `str` instance variable when its memory is to be released (that is, when its reference count becomes 0). In such a case, the system calls the `dealloc` method, which is inherited from `NSObject` and which you normally won't want to override. In the case of objects you retain, allocate with `alloc` or copy (with one of the copy methods discussed in the next chapter) inside your methods, you might need to override `dealloc` so that you get a chance to free them up. The statements

```
[str release];
[super dealloc];
```

first release the `str` instance variable and then call the parent's `dealloc` method to finish the job.

The `printf` was placed inside the `dealloc` method to print a message when it is called. We did this just to verify that the `ClassA` object is deallocated properly when the autorelease pool is released.

You might have spotted one last pitfall with the setter method `setStr`. Take another look at Program 17.5. Suppose `myStr` were a mutable string instead of an immutable one, and further suppose that one or more characters in `myStr` were changed after invoking `setStr`. Changes to the string referenced by `myStr` would also affect the string referenced by the instance variable because they reference the same object. Reread that last sentence to make sure you understand that point. Also, realize that setting `myStr` to a completely new string object does not cause this problem. The problem occurs only if one or more characters of the string are modified in some way.

The solution to this particular problem is to make a new copy of the string inside the setter if you want to protect it and make it completely independent of the setter's argument. This is why you chose to make a copy of the `name` and `email` members in the `setName:` and `setEmail:` `AddressCard` methods in Chapter 15.

Back to the Autorelease Pool

Let's take a look at one last program example in this chapter to ensure that you really understand how reference counting, retaining, and releasing/autoreleasing objects work. Examine Program 17.6, which defines a dummy class called `Foo` with one instance variable and only inherited methods.

2. If the `str` variable is `nil`, that's not a problem. All instance variables are initialized to `nil` by the Objective-C runtime, and it's okay to send a message to `nil`.

Program 17.6

```objc
#import <Foundation/NSObject.h>
#import <Foundation/NSAutoreleasePool.h>

@interface Foo: NSObject
{
  int x;
}
@end

@implementation Foo;
@end

int main (int argc, char *argv[])
{
  NSAutoreleasePool *pool = [[NSAutoreleasePool alloc] init];
  Foo    *myFoo = [[Foo alloc] init];

  printf ("myFoo retain count = %x\n", [myFoo retainCount]);

  [pool release];
  printf ("after pool release = %x\n", [myFoo retainCount]);

  pool = [[NSAutoreleasePool alloc] init];
  [myFoo autorelease];
  printf ("after autorelease = %x\n", [myFoo retainCount]);

  [myFoo retain];
  printf ("after retain = %x\n", [myFoo retainCount]);

  [pool release];
  printf ("after second pool release = %x\n", [myFoo retainCount]);

  [myFoo release];
  return 0;
}
```

Program 17.6   **Output**

```
myFoo retain count = 1
after poolrelease = 1
after autorelease = 1
after retain = 2
after second pool release = 1
```

The program allocates a new Foo object and assigns it to the variable myFoo. Its initial retain count is 1, as you've already seen. This object is not a part of the autorelease pool yet, so releasing the pool does not invalidate the object. A new pool is then allocated and myFoo is added to the pool by sending it an autorelease message. Notice again that its reference count doesn't change because adding an object to the autorelease pool does not affect its reference count—it only marks it for later release.

Next, you send myFoo a retain message. This changes its reference count to 2. When you subsequently release the pool the second time, the reference count for myFoo is decremented by 1 because it was previously sent an autorelease message and therefore is sent a release message when the pool is released.

Because myFoo was retained before the pool was released, its reference count after decrementing is still greater than 0. Therefore, myFoo survives the pool release and is still a valid object. Of course, you must now release it yourself, which is what we do in Program 17.6 to properly clean up and avoid memory leaks.

Reread this explanation of the autorelease pool again if it still seems a little fuzzy to you. When you understand Program 17.6, you will have a thorough understanding of the autorelease pool and how it works.

Summary of Memory Management Rules

Let's summarize what you've learned about memory management in this chapter:

- Releasing an object can free up its memory, which can be a concern if you're creating many objects during the execution of a program. A good rule is to release objects you've created or retained when you're done with them.

- Sending a release message does not necessarily destroy an object. When an object's reference count is decremented to 0, the object is destroyed. The system does this by sending the dealloc message to the object to free its memory.

- The autorelease pool provides for the automatic release of objects when the pool itself is released. The system does this is by sending a release message to each object in the pool for each time it was autoreleased. Each object in the autorelease pool whose reference count goes down to 0 is sent a dealloc message to destroy the object.

- If you no longer need an object from within a method but need to return it, send it an autorelease message to mark it for later release. The autorelease message does not affect the reference count of the object. So, it enables the object to be used by the message sender but still be freed up later when the autorelease pool is released.

- When your application terminates, all the memory taken by your objects is released, whether they were in the autorelease pool.

- When you develop more sophisticated applications (such as Cocoa applications), autorelease pools can be created and destroyed during execution of the program (for Cocoa applications, that happens each time an event occurs). In such cases, if you want to ensure that your object survives automatic deallocation when the autorelease pool itself is released, you need to explicitly retain it. All objects that a have a reference count greater than the number of autorelease messages they have been sent will survive the release of the pool.

- If you directly create an object using an `alloc` or `copy` method (or with an `allocWithZone:`, `copyWithZone:`, or `mutableCopy` method), you are responsible for releasing it. For each time you `retain` an object, you should `release` or `autorelease` that object.

- You don't have to worry about releasing objects that are returned by methods other than those noted in the previous rule. It's not your responsibility; those objects should have been autoreleased by those methods. That's why you needed to create the autorelease pool in your program in the first place. Methods such as `stringWithString:` automatically add newly created string objects to the pool by sending them `autorelease` messages. If you don't have a pool set up, you get a message that you tried to autorelease an object without having a pool in place.

The memory management techniques described in this chapter will suffice for most applications. However, in more advanced cases, such as when writing multithreaded applications, you might need to do more. See Appendix E, "Resources," for more details.

Exercises

1. Write a program to test the effects of adding and removing entries in a dictionary on the reference count of the objects you add and remove.

2. What effect do you think the `NSArray`'s `replaceObjectAtIndex:withObject:` method will have on the reference count of the object that is replaced in the array? What effect will it have on the object placed into the array? Write a program to test it. Then consult your documentation on this method to verify your results.

3. Return to the `Fraction` class you worked with throughout Part I, "The Objective-C Language." For your convenience, it is listed in Appendix D, "Fraction and Address Book Examples." Modify that class to work under the Foundation framework. Then add messages as appropriate to the various `MathOps` category methods to add the fractions resulting from each operation to the autorelease pool. When that is done, can you write a statement like this:
   ```
   [[fractionA add: fractionB] print];
   ```
   without leaking memory? Explain your answer.

4. Return to your `AddressBook` and `AddressCard` examples from Chapter 15. Modify each `dealloc` method to print a message when the method is invoked. Then run some of the sample programs that use these classes to ensure that a `dealloc` message is sent to every `AddressBook` and `AddressCard` object you use in the program before reaching the end of `main`.

18

Copying Objects

THIS CHAPTER DISCUSSES SOME OF THE SUBTLETIES involved in copying objects. We will introduce the concept of shallow versus deep copying and how to make copies under the Foundation framework.

Chapter 8, "Inheritance," discussed what happens when you assign one object to another with a simple assignment statement, such as

```
origin = pt;
```

In that example, `origin` and `pt` are both `Point` objects, that we defined like this:

```
@interface Point: Object
{
    int x;
    int y;
};
    ...
@end
```

You will recall that the effect of the assignment is to simply copy the address of the object `pt` into `origin`. At the end of the assignment operation, both variables point to the same location in memory. Making changes to the instance variables with a message such as

```
[origin setX: 100 andY: 200];
```

changes the x, y coordinate of the `Point` object referenced by both `origin` and `pt` variables because they both reference the same object in memory.

The same applies to Foundation objects: Assigning one variable to another simply creates another reference to the object (but it does not increase the reference count as discussed in Chapter 17, "Memory Management"). So, if `dataArray` and `dataArray2` are both `NSMutableArray` objects, the statements

```
dataArray2 = dataArray;
[dataArray2 removeObjectAtIndex: 0];
```

remove the first element from the same array that is referenced by both variables.

The copy and mutableCopy Methods

The Foundation classes implement methods known as copy and mutableCopy, which you can use to create a copy of an object. This is done by implementing a method in conformance with the <NSCopying> protocol for making copies. If your class needs to distinguish between making mutable and immutable copies of an object, you need to implement a method according to the <NSMutableCopying> protocol as well. You learn how to do that later in this section.

Getting back to the copy methods for the Foundation classes, given the two NSMutableArray objects dataArray2 and dataArray as described in the previous section, the statement

```
dataArray2 = [dataArray mutableCopy];
```

creates a new copy of dataArray in memory, duplicating all its elements. Subsequently, executing the statement

```
[dataArray2 removeObjectAtIndex: 0];
```

removes the first element from dataArray2 but not from dataArray. This is illustrated in Program 18.1.

Program 18.1

```
#import <Foundation/NSObject.h>
#import <Foundation/NSArray.h>
#import <Foundation/NSString.h>
#import <Foundation/NSAutoreleasePool.h>

int main (int argc, char *argv[])
{
  NSAutoreleasePool *pool = [[NSAutoreleasePool alloc] init];
  NSMutableArray  *dataArray = [NSMutableArray arrayWithObjects:
    @"one", @"two", @"three", @"four", nil];
  NSMutableArray  *dataArray2;
  int        i, n;

  // simple assignment

  dataArray2 = dataArray;
  [dataArray2 removeObjectAtIndex: 0];

  printf ("dataArray: ");
  n= [dataArray count];
  for (i = 0; i < n; ++i)
       printf ("%s ", [[dataArray objectAtIndex: i] cString]);

  printf ("\ndataArray2: ");
  n= [dataArray2 count];
  for (i = 0; i < n; ++i)
       printf ("%s ", [[dataArray2 objectAtIndex: i] cString]);
```

Program 18.1   **Continued**

```
// try a Copy, then remove the first element from the copy

dataArray2 = [dataArray mutableCopy];
[dataArray2 removeObjectAtIndex: 0];

printf ("\ndataArray: ");
n = [dataArray count];
for (i = 0; i < n; ++i)
        printf ("%s ", [[dataArray objectAtIndex: i] cString]);

printf ("\ndataArray2: ");
n = [dataArray2 count];
for (i = 0; i < n; ++i)
        printf ("%s ", [[dataArray2 objectAtIndex: i] cString]);


printf ("\n");
[dataArray2 release];
[pool release];
return 0;
}
```

Program 18.1   **Output**

```
dataArray: two three four
dataArray2: two three four
dataArray: two three four
dataArray2: three four
```

The program defines the mutable array object `dataArray` and sets its elements to the string objects `@"one"`, `@"two"`, `@"three"`, and `@"four"`, respectively.

As we've discussed, the assignment

```
dataArray2 = dataArray;
```

simply creates another reference to the same array object in memory. When you remove the first object from `dataArray2` and subsequently print the elements from both array objects, it's no surprise that the first element (the string `@"one"`) is gone from both references.

Next, you create a mutable copy of `dataArray` and assign the resulting copy to `dataArray2`. This creates two distinct mutable arrays in memory, both containing three elements. Now, when you remove the first element from `dataArray2`, it has no effect on the contents of `dataArray`, as verified by the last two lines of the program's output.

Note that making a mutable copy of an object does not require that the object being copied be mutable. The same thing applies to immutable copies: You can make an immutable copy of a mutable object.

Also note when making a copy of an array that the retain count for each element in the array is automatically incremented by the copy operation. Therefore, if you make a copy of an array and subsequently release the original array, the copy still contains valid elements.

Because a copy of `dataArray` was made in the program using the `mutableCopy` method, you are responsible for releasing its memory. The rule that says you are responsible for releasing objects you create with one of the copy methods was covered at the end of the last chapter. This explains the inclusion of the line

```
[dataArray2 release];
```

toward the end of Program 18.1.

Shallow Versus Deep Copying

Program 18.1 fills the elements of `dataArray` with immutable strings (recall that constant string objects are immutable). In Program 18.2, you'll fill it with mutable strings instead so that you can change one of the strings in the array. Take a look at Program 18.2 and see whether you understand its output.

Program 18.2

```
#import <Foundation/NSObject.h>
#import <Foundation/NSArray.h>
#import <Foundation/NSString.h>
#import <Foundation/NSAutoreleasePool.h>

int main (int argc, char *argv[])
{
  NSAutoreleasePool *pool = [[NSAutoreleasePool alloc] init];
  NSMutableArray    *dataArray = [NSMutableArray arrayWithObjects:
        [NSMutableString stringWithString: @"one"],
        [NSMutableString stringWithString: @"two"],
        [NSMutableString stringWithString: @"three"],
        nil
  ];
  NSMutableArray    *dataArray2;
  NSMutableString   *mStr;
  int               i, n;

  printf ("dataArray: ");
  n = [dataArray count];
  for (i = 0; i < n; ++i)
        printf ("%s ", [[dataArray objectAtIndex: i] cString]);
```

Program 18.2 **Continued**

```
// make a copy, then change one of the strings

dataArray2 = [dataArray mutableCopy];

mStr = [dataArray objectAtIndex: 0];
[mStr appendString: @"ONE"];

printf ("\ndataArray: ");
n = [dataArray count];
for (i = 0; i < n; ++i)
        printf ("%s ", [[dataArray objectAtIndex: i] cString]);

printf ("\ndataArray2: ");
n = [dataArray2 count];
for (i = 0; i < n; ++i)
        printf ("%s ", [[dataArray2 objectAtIndex: i] cString]);


printf ("\n");
[dataArray2 release];
[pool release];
return 0;
}
```

Program 18.2 **Output**

```
dataArray:  one two three
dataArray:  oneONE two three
dataArray2: oneONE two three
```

You retrieved the first element of `dataArray2` with the following statement:

```
mStr = [dataArray2 objectAtIndex: 0];
```

Then you appended the string @`"ONE"` to it with this statement:

```
[mStr appendString: @"ONE"];
```

Notice the value of the first element of both the original array and its copy: They both were modified. Perhaps you can understand why the first element of `dataArray` was changed but not why its copy was as well. When you get an element from a collection, you get a new reference to that element, but not a new copy. So, when the `objectAtIndex:` method is invoked on `dataArray`, the returned object is pointing to the same object in memory as the first element in `dataArray`. Subsequently modifying the string object `mStr` has the side effect of also changing the first element of `dataArray`, as you can see from the output.

But what about the copy you made? Why is its first element changed as well? This has to do with the fact that copies by default are *shallow* copies. That means when the array was copied with the `mutableCopy` method, space was allocated for a new array object in memory and the individual elements were copied into the new array. But copying each element in the array from the original to new location meant just copying the reference from one element of the array to another. The net result was that the elements of both arrays referenced the same strings in memory. This is no different from the assignment of one object to another that we covered at the start of this chapter.

To make distinct copies of each element of the array, you need to perform what is known as a *deep* copy. This means making copies of the contents of each object in the array, not just copies of the references to the objects (and think about what that implies if an element of an array is itself an array object). But deep copies are not performed by default when you use the `copy` or `mutableCopy` methods with the Foundation classes. This is simply a fact that you should be aware of. In Chapter 19, "Archiving," we'll show you how to use the Foundation's archiving capabilities to create a deep copy of an object.

When you copy an array, a dictionary, or a set, for example, you get a new copy of those collections. However, you might need to make your own copies of individual elements if you want to make changes to one collection but not to its copy. For example, assuming you wanted to change the first element of `dataArray2` but not `dataArray` in Program 18.2, you could have made a new string (using a method such as `stringWithString:`) and stored it into the first location of `dataArray2`, as follows:

```
mStr = [NSMutableString stringWithString:
[dataArray2 objectAtIndex: 0]];
```

Then you could have made the changes to `mStr` and added it to the array using the `replaceObject:atIndex:withObject:` method as follows:

```
[mStr appendString @"ONE"];
[dataArray2 replaceObjectAtIndex: 0 withObject: mStr];
```

Hopefully you realize that even after replacing the object in the array, `mStr` and the first element of `dataArray2` refer to the same object in memory. That means subsequent changes to `mStr` in your program will also change the first element of the array. If that's not what you want, you can always release `mStr` and allocate a new instance because an object is automatically retained by the `replaceObject:atIndex:withObject:` method.

Implementing the `<NSCopying>` Protocol

If you try to use the `copy` method on one of your own classes—for example, on your address book as follows:

```
NewBook = [myBook mutableCopy];
```

you'll get an error message that looks something like this:

```
2003-07-28 12:53:29.224 a.out[2337] *** -[AddressBook copyWithZone:]:
  selector not recognized
2003-07-28 12:53:29.254 a.out[2337] *** Uncaught exception:
<NSInvalidArgumentException> *** -[AddressBook copyWithZone:]:
  selector not recognized
```

As noted, to implement copying with your own classes, you have to implement one or two methods according to the <NSCopying> protocol.

Copying Fractions

We're going to show how you can add a copy method to your Fraction class, which you used extensively in Part I, "The Objective-C Language." Note that the techniques we will describe here for copying strategies will work fine for your own classes. If those classes are subclasses of any of the Foundation classes, you might need to implement a more sophisticated copying strategy that we won't describe here. You'll have to account for the fact that the superclass might have already implemented its own copying strategy.

You'll recall that your Fraction class contains two integer instance variables called numerator and denominator. To make a copy of one of these objects, you need to allocate space for a new fraction and then simply copy the values of the two integers into the new fraction.

When you implement the <NSCopying> protocol, your class must implement the copyWithZone: method to respond to a copy message. (The copy message just sends a copyWithZone: message to your class with an argument of nil.) If you want to make a distinction between mutable and immutable copies, as we noted, you'll also need to implement the mutableCopyWithZone: method according to the <NSMutableCopying> protocol. If you implement both methods, copyWithZone: should return an immutable copy and mutableCopyWithZone: a mutable one. Making a mutable copy of an object does not require that the object being copied also be mutable (and vice versa); it's perfectly reasonable to want to make a mutable copy of an immutable object (consider a string object, for example).

Go back to your Fraction class, which is listed in Appendix D, "Fraction and Address Book Examples." That class was written with the root object Object, so you must make it suitable for use with Foundation.[1] To do this, in the interface file change the line

```
#import <objc/Object.h>
```

to

```
#import <Foundation/NSObject.h>
```

1. If you completed exercise 3 at the end of Chapter 17, you already have a Fraction class that works under Foundation.

Also, here's what the @interface directive should look like:

```
@interface Fraction: NSObject <NSCopying>
```

Fraction is a subclass of NSObject and conforms to the NSCopying protocol.

In the implementation file fraction.m add the following definition for your new method:

```
-(Fraction *) copyWithZone: (NSZone *) zone
{
   Fraction *newFract = [[Fraction allocWithZone: zone] init];

   [newFract setTo: numerator over: denominator];
   return newFract;
}
```

The zone argument has to do with different memory zones that you can allocate and work with in your program. You need to deal with them only if you're writing applications that allocate a lot of memory and you want to optimize the allocation by grouping them into these zones. You can take the value passed to copyWithZone: and hand it off to a memory allocation method called allocWithZone:. This method allocates memory in a specified zone.

After allocating a new Fraction object, you copy the receiver's numerator and denominator variables into it. The copyWithZone: method is supposed to return the new copy of the object, which is what you do in your method.

Program 18.3 tests your new method.

Program 18.3
```
// Copying fractions

#import "Fraction.h"
#import <Foundation/NSAutoreleasePool.h>


int main (int argc, char *argv[])
{
        NSAutoreleasePool *pool = [[NSAutoreleasePool alloc] init];
        Fraction *f1 = [[Fraction alloc] init];
        Fraction *f2;

        [f1 setTo: 2 over: 5];
        f2 = [f1 copy];

        [f2 setTo: 1 over: 3];

        [f1 print];
        printf ("\n");
        [f2 print];
        printf ("\n");
```

Program 18.3 **Continued**

```
    [f1 release];
    [f2 release];
    [pool release];
    return 0;
}
```

Program 18.3 **Output**

```
2/5
1/3
```

The program creates a Fraction object called f1 and sets it to 2/5. It then invokes the copy method to make a copy, which sends the copyWithZone: message to your object. That method makes a new Fraction, copies the values from f1 into it, and returns the result. Back in main, you assign that result to f2. Subsequently setting the value in f2 to the fraction 1/3 verifies that it had no effect on the original fraction f1. Change the line in the program that reads

```
f2 = [f1 copy];
```

to simply

```
f2 = f1;
```

and remove the release of f2 at the end of the program to see the different results you will obtain.

If your class might be subclassed, your copyWithZone: method will be inherited. In that case, the line in the method that reads

```
Fraction *newFract = [[Fraction allocWithZone: zone] init];
```

should be changed to read

```
Fraction *newFract = [[[self class] allocWithZone: zone] init];
```

That way, you'll allocate a new object from the class that is the receiver of the copy. (For example, if it has been subclassed to a class named NewFraction, you should be sure you allocate a new NewFraction object in the inherited method, instead of a Fraction object.)

If you are writing a copyWithZone: method for a class whose superclass also implements the <NSCopying> protocol, you should first call the copy method on the superclass to copy the inherited instance variables and then include your own code to copy whatever additional instance variables (if any) you might have added to the class.

It's up to you to decide whether you want to implement a shallow or deep copy in your class. Just document it for other users of your class so they know.

Copying Objects in Setter and Getter Methods

Whenever you implement a setter or getter method, you should think about what you're storing in the instance variables, what you're retrieving, and whether you need to protect these values. For example, consider when you set the name of one of your AddressCard objects using the setName: method:

```
[newCard setName: newName];
```

Assume that newName is a string object containing the name for your new card. Assume that inside the setter routine you simply assigned the parameter to the corresponding instance variable:

```
-(void) setName: (NSString *) theName
{
    name = theName;

}
```

Now, what do you think would happen if the program later changed some of the characters contained in newName in the program? Right, it would also unintentionally change the corresponding field in your address card because they would both reference the same string object.

As you have already seen, a safer approach is to make a copy of the object in the setter routine to prevent this inadvertent effect. We did this by using the alloc method to create a new string object and then initWithString: to set it to the value of the parameter provided to the method.

You can also write a version of the setName: method to use copy, like so:

```
-(void) setName: (NSString *) theName
{
    name = [theName copy];

}
```

Of course, to make this setter routine memory-management friendly, you should autorelease the old value first, like so:

```
-(void) setName: (NSString *) theName
{
    [name autorelease];
    name = [theName copy];
}
```

The same discussion about protecting the value of your instance variables applies to the getter routines, if you think about it for a moment. If you return an object, you must ensure that changes to the returned value will not affect the value of your instance variables. In such a case, you can make a copy of the instance variable and return that instead.

Getting back to the implementation of a `copy` method, if you are copying instance variables that contain immutable objects (for example, immutable string objects), you might not need to make a new copy of the object's contents. It might suffice to simply make a new reference to the object by retaining it. For example, when implementing a copy method for the `AddressCard` class, which contains `name` and `email` members, the following implementation for `copyWithZone:` would suffice:

```
-(AddresssCard *) copyWithZone: (NSZone *) zone
{
    AddressCard *newCard = [[AddressCard allocWithZone: zone] init];
    [newCard retainName: name andEmail: email];
    return newCard;
}


-(void) retainName: (NSString *) theName andEmail: (NSString *) theEmail
{
    name = [theName retain];
    email = [theEmail retain];
}
```

The `setName:andEmail:` method isn't used here to copy the instance variables over because that method makes new copies of its arguments, which would defeat the whole purpose of this exercise. Instead, you just retained the two variables using a new method called `retainName:andEmail:`. (You could have set the two instance variables in `newCard` directly in the `copyWithZone:` method, but it involves pointer operations, which we've been able to avoid up to this point. Of course, the pointer operations would be more efficient and would not expose the user of this class to a method [`retainName:andEmail:`] that was not intended for public consumption, so at some point you might need to learn how to do that—just not right now!)

Realize that you can get away with retaining the instance variables here (instead of making complete copies of them) because the owner of the copied card can't affect the name and email members of the original. You might want to think about that for a second to verify that's the case (hint: it has to do with the setter methods).

Exercises

1. Implement a `copy` method for the `AddressBook` class according to the `NSCopying` protocol. Would it make sense to also implement a `mutableCopy` method? Why or why not?

2. Modify the `Rectangle` and `Point` classes defined in Chapter 8 to run under Foundation. Then add a `copyWithZone:` method to both classes. Make sure that the `Rectangle` copies its `Point` member `origin` using the `Point`'s copy method. Does it make sense to implement both mutable and immutable copies for these classes? Explain.

3. Create an NSDictionary dictionary object and fill it with some key/object pairs. Then make both mutable and immutable copies. Are these deep copies or shallow copies that are made? Verify your answer.

4. Who is responsible for releasing the memory allocated for the new AddressCard in the copyWithZone: method as implemented in this chapter? Why?

19

Archiving

In OBJECTIVE-C TERMS, *ARCHIVING* IS THE PROCESS of saving one or more objects in a format so that they can later be restored. Often, this involves writing the object(s) to a file so it can subsequently be read back in. We will discuss two methods for archiving data in this chapter: *property lists* and *coding*.

Archiving with Property Lists

Applications on Mac OS X use lists (or *plists*) for storing things such as your default preferences, application settings, and configuration information, so it's useful to know how to create them and read them back in. Their use for archiving purposes, however, is limited because when creating a property list for a data structure, specific object classes are not retained, multiple references to the same object are not stored, and the mutability of an object is not preserved.

If your objects are NSString, NSDictionary, NSArray, or NSData objects, you can use the writeToFile: method implemented in these classes to write your data to a file. In the case of writing out a dictionary or an array, this method writes the data out in the format of a property list. On the Mac, the property list created is in a format known as XML by default, which is an HTML-like language.[1] On GNUStep systems, a different format for property lists, known as the *traditional, old-style,* or *ASCII* (depending upon whether you're speaking to GNU or Mac programmers) format is used by default.

Program 19.1 shows how the dictionary you created as a simple glossary in Chapter 15, "Numbers, Strings, and Collections," can be written to a file as a property list.

---

1. The Mac also supports binary serialized property lists through the NSPropertyListSerialization class, which we won't describe here.

Program 19.1

```
#import <Foundation/NSObject.h>
#import <Foundation/NSString.h>
#import <Foundation/NSDictionary.h>
#import <Foundation/NSAutoreleasePool.h>

int main (int argc, char *argv[])
{
  NSAutoreleasePool  *pool = [[NSAutoreleasePool alloc] init];
  NSDictionary *glossary =
   [NSDictionary
      dictionaryWithObjectsAndKeys:
        @"A class defined so other classes can inherit from it.",
        @"abstract class",
        @"To implement all the methods defined in a protocol",
        @"adopt",
        @"Storing an object for later use. ",
        @"archiving",
        nil
        ];

  if ([glossary writeToFile: @"glossary" atomically: YES] == NO)
     printf ("Save to file failed!\n");

  [pool release];
  return 0;
}
```

The writeToFile:atomically: message is sent to your dictionary object glossary, causing the dictionary to be written to the file glossary in the form of a property list. The atomically parameter is set to YES, meaning you want the write operation to be done to a temporary backup file first and once successful, the final data is to be moved to the specified file named glossary. This is a safeguard that protects the file from becoming corrupt if, for example, the system crashes in the middle of the write operation. In that case, the original glossary file (if it previously existed) isn't harmed.

If you look at the glossary file created by Program 19.1, it looks like this on the Mac:

```
<?xml version="1.0" encoding="UTF-8"?>
<!DOCTYPE plist PUBLIC "-//Apple Computer//DTD PLIST 1.0//EN"
          "http://www.apple.com/DTDs/PropertyList-1.0.dtd">
<plist version="1.0">
<dict>
    <key>abstract class</key>
    <string>A class defined so other classes can inherit from it.</string>
    <key>adopt</key>
```

```
    <string>To implement all the methods defined in a protocol</string>
    <key>archiving</key>
    <string>Storing an object for later use. </string>
</dict>
</plist>
```

As noted, under GNUStep, the property list is written in a traditional format by default. The `glossary` file looks like this:

```
{
  "abstract class" = "A class defined so other classes can inherit from it.";
  adopt = "To implement all the methods defined in a protocol";
  archiving = "Storing an object for later use. ";
}
```

GNUStep programs can generate XML-style property lists by changing the user default settings `GSMacOSXCompatible` or `NSWriteOldStylePropertyLists`. Look at the `NSUserDefaults` class and check your GNUStep documentation for more details. Mac users can create traditional or old-style property lists using the `dataFromPropertyList:format:errorDescription:` method from the `NSPropertyListSerialization` class and specifying `NSPropertyListOpenStepFormat` as the `format` parameter. The Mac and GNUStep systems can read property lists created in either format.

If you create a property list from a dictionary, the keys in the dictionary must all be `NSString` objects. The elements of an array or the values in a dictionary can be `NSString`, `NSArray`, `NSDictionary`, `NSData`, `NSDate`, or `NSNumber` objects.

To read a property list from a file into your program, you use the `dictionaryWithContentsOfFile:` or `arrayWithContentsOfFile:` method. To read back data, use the `dataWithContentsOfFile:` method, and to read back string objects, use the `stringWithContentsOfFile:` method. Program 19.2 reads back the glossary written in Program 19.1 and then prints it contents.

Program 19.2
```
#import <Foundation/NSObject.h>
#import <Foundation/NSString.h>
#import <Foundation/NSDictionary.h>
#import <Foundation/NSEnumerator.h>
#import <Foundation/NSAutoreleasePool.h>

int main (int argc, char *argv[])
{
  NSAutoreleasePool  *pool = [[NSAutoreleasePool alloc] init];
  NSDictionary *glossary;
  NSEnumerator *keyEnum;
  id      key;
```

Program 19.2 **Continued**

```
glossary = [NSDictionary dictionaryWithContentsOfFile: @"glossary"];

keyEnum = [glossary keyEnumerator];

while ( (key = [keyEnum nextObject]) != nil ) {
        printf ("%s: %s\n\n", [key cString],
        [[glossary objectForKey: key] cString]);
}

[pool release];
return 0;
}
```

Program 19.2 **Output**

```
archiving: Storing an object for later use.

abstract class: A class defined so other classes can inherit from it.

adopt: To implement all the methods defined in a protocol
```

Your property lists don't need to be created from an Objective-C program; the property list can come from any source. You can make your own property lists using a simple text editor or use the Property List Editor program located in the /Developer/ Applications directory on Mac OS X systems.

If you have a property list stored in an NSString object, you can convert it into its equivalent dictionary, string, array, or data object by sending it a propertyList message. For example, consider the following code sequence:

```
NSString *months = @"{ \
  \"january\" = 31; \"february\" = 28; \"march\" = 31; \
  \"april\" = 30; \"may\" = 31; \"june\" = 30; \"july\" = 31; \
  \"august\" = 31; "\september\" = 30; \"october\" = 31; \
  \"november\" = 30; \"december\" = 31; }";

daysOfMonthDict = [months propertyList];
```

(Recall that to continue a long character string over several lines, a backslash character must appear as the very last character on the line. Also, to include a double quotation mark in a string, it must be *escaped* by preceding it with a backslash character.)

This sequence takes the dictionary encoded as a traditional property list in the string object months and converts it to a dictionary object. To subsequently get the number of days in July, for example, you could then write the following:

```
[[daysOfMonthDict objectForKey: @"july"] intValue]
```

Obviously, this is a contrived example because there would be no advantage here of hard-coding a property list into your program. The dictionary could have been set up directly.

Property Lists and URLs

Incidentally, you can also write a property list to a URL and read one from a URL. For example, the statement

```
glossary = [NSDictionary dictionaryWithContentsOfURL:
    [NSURL URLWithString:
        @"http://www.kochan-wood.com/examples/glossary.pl"]];
```

creates a dictionary from the property list stored at the specified URL.

The `dictionaryWithContentsOfURL:` method is not currently implemented under GNUStep. Another way to read the property list from a Web site is to use the `stringWithContentsOfURL:` method to first read it into a string and then convert it to a property list using the `propertyList` method. The can be done with a statement like this:

```
glossary = [[NSString stringWithContentsOfURL:
    [NSURL URLWithString: @"http://www.kochan-wood.com/examples/glossary.pl"]
    ] propertyList];
```

Data can be written to a URL using the `writeToURL:atomically:` method. For more information about working with URLs, consult the documentation for the Foundation class `NSURL` and the header file `<Foundation/NSURL.h>`.

Archiving with NSArchiver

A more flexible approach allows for the saving of any types of objects to a file, not just strings, arrays, and dictionaries. Let's begin with the simple glossary created in Chapter 15. Program 19.3 shows how the glossary can be saved to a file on disk using the method `archiveRootObject:toFile:` from the `NSArchiver` class. To use this class, include the file

```
#import <Foundation/NSArchiver.h>
```

in your program.

Program 19.3

```
#import <Foundation/NSObject.h>
#import <Foundation/NSString.h>
#import <Foundation/NSDictionary.h>
#import <Foundation/NSArchiver.h>
#import <Foundation/NSAutoreleasePool.h>
```

Program 19.3   **Continued**

```
int main (int argc, char *argv[])
{
  NSAutoreleasePool *pool = [[NSAutoreleasePool alloc] init];
  NSDictionary *glossary =
   [NSDictionary dictionaryWithObjectsAndKeys:
     @"A class defined so other classes can inherit from it",
     @"abstract class",
     @"To implement all the methods defined in a protocol",
     @"adopt",
     @"Storing an object for later use",
     @"archiving",
     nil
   ];


  [NSArchiver archiveRootObject: glossary toFile: @"glossary.archive"];

  [pool release];
  return 0;
}
```

Program 19.3 does not produce any output at the terminal. However, the statement

```
  [NSArchiver archiveRootObject: glossary toFile: @"glossary.archive"];
```

writes the dictionary `glossary` to the file `glossary.archive`. Any pathname can be specified for the file. In this case, the file is written to the current directory.

The archive file created can later be read into an executing program by using `NSUnarchiver`'s `unArchiveObjectWithFile:` method, as is done in Program 19.4.

Program 19.4

```
#import <Foundation/NSObject.h>
#import <Foundation/NSString.h>
#import <Foundation/NSDictionary.h>
#import <Foundation/NSEnumerator.h>
#import <Foundation/NSArchiver.h>
#import <Foundation/NSAutoreleasePool.h>

int main (int argc, char *argv[])
{
  NSAutoreleasePool  *pool = [[NSAutoreleasePool alloc] init];
  NSDictionary *glossary;
  NSEnumerator *keyEnum;
  id      key;
```

Program 19.4 **Continued**

```
glossary = [NSUnarchiver unarchiveObjectWithFile:
                @"glossary.archive"];

keyEnum = [glossary keyEnumerator];

while ( (key = [keyEnum nextObject]) != nil ) {
      printf ("%s: %s\n\n", [key cString],
      [[glossary objectForKey: key] cString]);
}

[pool release];
return 0;
}
```

Program 19.4 **Output**

```
abstract class: A class defined so other classes can inherit from it.

adopt: To implement all the methods defined in a protocol

archiving: Storing an object for later use.
```

The statement

```
glossary = [NSUnarchiver unarchiveObjectWithFile:
                @"glossary.archive"];
```

causes the specified file to be opened and its contents to be read. This file must be the result of a previous archive operation. You can specify a full pathname for the file or a relative path name, as was done in the example.

After the glossary has been restored, the program simply enumerates its contents to verify that the restore was successful.

Writing Encoding and Decoding Methods

Basic Objective-C class types such as NSString, NSArray, NSDictionary, NSSet, NSDate, NSNumber, and NSData can be archived and restored in the manner just described. That includes nested objects as well, such as an array containing string or even other array objects.

This implies that you can't directly archive your AddressBook using this method because the Objective-C system doesn't know how to archive an AddressBook object. If you were to try to archive it by inserting a line such as

```
[NSArchiver archiveRootObject: myBook toFile: @"addrbook.arch"];
```

into your program, you'd get the following message displayed if you ran the program under Mac OS X:

```
2003-07-23 12:03:05.267 a.out[3516] *** -[AddressBook encodeWithCoder:]:
  selector not recognized
2003-07-23 12:03:05.268 a.out[3516] *** Uncaught exception:
<NSInvalidArgumentException> *** -[AddressBook encodeWithCoder:]:
selector not recognized
a.out: received signal: Trace/BPT trap
```

From the error messages, you can see that the system was looking for a method called encodeWithCoder: in the AddressBook class, but you never defined such a method.

To archive objects other than those listed, you have to tell the system how to archive, or *encode*, your objects and also how to unarchive, or *decode*, them. This is done by adding encodeWithCoder: and initWithCoder: methods to your class definitions according to the <NSCoding> protocol. For our address book example, you'd have to add these methods to both the AddressBook and AddressCard classes.

The encodeWithCoder: method is invoked each time the archiver wants to encode an object from the specified class, and the method tells it how to do so. In a similar manner, the initWithCoder: method is invoked each time an object from the specified class is to be decoded.

In general, the encoder method should specify how to archive each instance variable in the object you want to save. Luckily, you have help doing this. For the basic Objective-C classes described previously, you can use the encodeObject: method. On the other hand, for basic Objective-C data types (such as integers and floats), you must use a slightly more involved method called encodeValueOfObjCType:at:. The decoder method, initWithCoder:, works in reverse: You use decodeObject for decoding basic Objective-C classes and decodeValueOfObjCType:at: for the basic data types.

Program 19.5 adds the two encoding and decoding methods to both the AddressCard and AddressBook classes.

Program 19.5   Addresscard.h **Interface File**

```
#import <Foundation/NSObject.h>
#import <Foundation/NSString.h>
#import <Foundation/NSArchiver.h>

@interface AddressCard: NSObject <NSCoding, NSCopying>
{
  NSString   *name;
  NSString   *email;
}

-(void) setName: (NSString *) theName;
-(void) setEmail: (NSString *) theEmail;
-(void) setName: (NSString *) theName andEmail: (NSString *) theEmail;
```

Program 19.5   **Continued**

```
-(NSString *) name;
-(NSString *) email;

-(NSComparisonResult) compareNames: (id) element;

-(void) print;

// Additional methods for NSCopying protocol
-(AddressCard *) copyWithZone: (NSZone *) zone;
-(void) retainName: (NSString *) theName andEmail: (NSString *) theEmail;

@end
```

Here are the two new methods for your `AddressCard` class to be added to the implementation file:

```
-(void) encodeWithCoder: (NSCoder *) encoder
{
  [encoder encodeObject: name];
  [encoder encodeObject: email];
}

-(id) initWithCoder: (NSCoder *) decoder
{
  name = [[decoder decodeObject] retain];
  email = [[decoder decodeObject] retain];

  return self;
}
```

The encoding method `encodeWithCoder:` is passed an `NSCoder` object as its argument. For each object you want to encode, you send a message to this object. In the case of your address book, you have two instance variables called `name` and `email`. Because these are both `NSString` objects, you use the `encodeObject:` method to encode each of them in turn. These two instance variables are then added to the archive. Note that `encodeObject:` can be used for any object that has implemented a corresponding `encodeWithCoder:` method in its class.

The decoding process works in reverse. The argument passed to `initWithCoder:` is again an `NSCoder` object. You don't need to worry about this argument; just remember that it's the one that gets the messages for each object you want to extract from the archive.

Because you've stored two objects in the archive with the encoding method, when decoding you must extract them in the same order in which they were added. First, you use the `decodeObject` message to get your `name` decoded, followed by a second message to get the email. You retain both instance variables to ensure that they still exist and are valid after the unarchiving process is completed. Note that the decoding method is expected to return itself.

Similarly to your `AddressCard` class, you add encoding and decoding methods to your `AddressBook` class. The only line you need to change in your interface file is the `@interface` directive to declare that the `AddressBook` class now conforms to the `NSCoding` protocol. The change looks like this:

```
@interface AddressBook: NSObject <NSCoding, NSCopying>
```

Here are the method definitions for inclusion in the implementation file:

```
-(void) encodeWithCoder: (NSCoder *) encoder
{

  [encoder encodeObject: bookName];
  [encoder encodeObject: book];
}


-(id) initWithCoder: (NSCoder *) decoder
{
   bookName = [[decoder decodeObject] retain];
   book = [[decoder decodeObject] retain];

   return self;
}
```

The test program is shown next as Program 19.6.

Program 19.6 **Test Program**

```
#import "AddressBook.h"
#import <Foundation/NSAutoreleasePool.h>

int main (int argc, char *argv[])
{
  NSString   *aName = @"Julia Kochan";
  NSString   *aEmail = @"jewls337@axlc.com";
  NSString   *bName = @"Tony Iannino";
  NSString   *bEmail = @"tony.iannino@techfitness.com";
  NSString   *cName = @"Stephen Kochan";
  NSString   *cEmail = @"steve@kochan-wood.com";
  NSString   *dName = @"Jamie Baker";
  NSString   *dEmail = @"jbaker@kochan-wood.com";

  NSAutoreleasePool *pool = [[NSAutoreleasePool alloc] init];

  AddressCard *card1 = [[AddressCard alloc] init];
  AddressCard *card2 = [[AddressCard alloc] init];
  AddressCard *card3 = [[AddressCard alloc] init];
  AddressCard *card4 = [[AddressCard alloc] init];
```

Program 19.6   **Continued**

```
    AddressBook  *myBook = [AddressBook alloc];


    // First set up four address cards

    [card1 setName: aName andEmail: aEmail];
    [card2 setName: bName andEmail: bEmail];
    [card3 setName: cName andEmail: cEmail];
    [card4 setName: dName andEmail: dEmail];

    myBook = [myBook initWithName: @"Steve's Address Book"];

    // Add some cards to the address book

    [myBook addCard: card1];
    [myBook addCard: card2];
    [myBook addCard: card3];
    [myBook addCard: card4];

    [myBook sort];

    if ([NSArchiver archiveRootObject: myBook toFile: @"addrbook.arch"] == NO)
      printf ("archiving failed\n");

    [card1 release];
    [card2 release];
    [card3 release];
    [card4 release];
    [myBook release];

    [pool release];
    return 0;
}
```

This program creates the address book and then archives it to the file
addrbook.arch. In the process of creating the archive file, realize that the encoding
methods from *both* the AddressBook and AddressCard classes were invoked. You can
add some printf calls to these methods if you want proof.

Program 19.7 shows how you can read the archive into memory to set up the address
book from a file.

Program 19.7

```
#import "AddressBook.h"
#import <Foundation/NSAutoreleasePool.h>

int main (int argc, char *argv[])
{
  AddressBook        *myBook;
  NSAutoreleasePool   *pool = [[NSAutoreleasePool alloc] init];

  myBook = [NSUnarchiver unarchiveObjectWithFile: @"addrbook.arch"];

  [myBook list];

  [pool release];
  return 0;
}
```

Program 19.7 **Output**

```
======== Contents of: Steve's Address Book =========
Jamie Baker        jbaker@kochan-wood.com
Julia Kochan       jewls337@axlc.com
Stephen Kochan     steve@kochan-wood.com
Tony Iannino       tony.iannino@techfitness.com
====================================================
```

In the process of unarchiving the address book, the decoding methods added to your two classes were automatically invoked. Notice how easily you can read the address book back into the program.

Archiving Basic Objective-C Data Types

The encodeObject: method works for built-in classes and classes for which you write your encoding and decoding methods according to the NSCoding protocol. If your instance contains some basic data types, such as integers or floats, you'll need to know how to encode and decode them. Here's a simple definition for a class called Foo that contains three instance variables—one is an NSString, another is an int, and the third is a float. The class has one setter method, three getters, and two encoding/decoding methods to be used for archiving:

```
@interface Foo: NSObject <NSCoding>
{
  NSString *strVal;
  int      intVal;
  float    floatVal;
}
```

```
-(void) setAll: (NSString *) ss iVal: (int) ii fVal: (float) ff;
-(NSString *)    strVal;
-(int)           intVal;
-(float)         floatVal;
@end
```

The implementation file follows:

```
@implementation Foo;

-(void) setAll: (NSString *) ss iVal: (int) ii fVal: (float) ff
{
  strVal = ss;
  intVal = ii;
  floatVal = ff;
}


-(NSString *) strVal   { return strVal; }
-(int)        intVal   { return intVal; }
-(float)      floatVal { return floatVal; }

-(void) encodeWithCoder: (NSCoder *) encoder
{
    [encoder encodeObject: strVal];
    [encoder encodeValueOfObjCType: @encode(int) at: &intVal];
    [encoder encodeValueOfObjCType: @encode(float) at: &floatVal];
}


-(id) initWithCoder: (NSCoder *) decoder
{
    strVal = [[decoder decodeObject] retain];
    [decoder decodeValueOfObjCType: @encode(int) at: &intVal];
    [decoder decodeValueOfObjCType: @encode(float) at: &floatVal];

    return self;
}
@end
```

The encoding routine first encodes the string value `strVal` using the
`encodeObject` method you used before. Next, you need to encode your integer and
float fields. The method `encodeValueOfObjCType:at:` takes two arguments to
encode a basic Objective-C data type. The first is a special encoding obtained by applying the `@encode` directive to the data type name. Because `intVal` is an integer data
type, you write `@encode(int)` as the argument. The second argument is a *pointer* (as
you encountered with the `fileExistsAtPath:isDir:` method in Chapter 16,

"Working with Files") to the actual instance variable to be encoded and can be created by applying the address operator (&) to the variable.

The floating variable `floatVal` is encoded in a similar manner, by passing the arguments `@encode(float)` and `&floatVal` to the `encodeValueOfObjCType:at:` method.

When decoding a basic data type, you use the `decodeValueOfObjCType:at:` method, and the arguments are the same. In this case, the value decoded is stored at the memory address specified by the `at:` argument.

You don't retain basic data types. They aren't objects, so they can't be retained.

In Program 19.8, a `Foo` object is created, archived to a file, unarchived, and then displayed.

Program 19.8 **Test Program**

```
#import <Foundation/NSObject.h>
#import <Foundation/NSString.h>
#import <Foundation/NSArchiver.h>
#import <Foundation/NSAutoreleasePool.h>
#import "Foo.h"  // Definition for our Foo class

int main (int argc, char *argv[])
{
    NSAutoreleasePool *pool = [[NSAutoreleasePool alloc] init];
    Foo *myFoo1 = [[Foo alloc] init];
    Foo *myFoo2;

    [myFoo1 setAll: @"This is the string" iVal: 12345 fVal: 98.6];
    [NSArchiver archiveRootObject: myFoo1 toFile: @"foo.arch"];

    myFoo2 = [NSUnarchiver unarchiveObjectWithFile: @"foo.arch"];
    printf ("%s\n%i\n%g\n", [[myFoo2 strVal] cString],
                            [myFoo2 intVal], [myFoo2 floatVal]);
    [myFoo1 release];
    [pool release];
    return 0;
}
```

Program 19.8 **Output**

```
This is the string
12345
98.6
```

Keyed Archives[2]

We noted in the discussion of the decoder methods that the fields in an archive must be read back in precisely the same order in which they were written. This technique might suit you; however, if you are creating archives from programs that might be going through many revisions, you might reorder some of the instance variables in one of your class definitions, or perhaps even add or remove some. In that case, restoring a previously created archive would be next to impossible.

A *keyed* archive is one in which each field of the archive has a name. When you archive an object, you give it a name, or *key*. When you retrieve it from the archive, you retrieve it by the same key. In that manner, objects can be written to the archive and retrieved in any order. Further, if new instance variables are added or removed to a class, the decoding method can account for it—for example, by setting a default value to a key that does not exist in the archive (for instance, if the archive were created by a different version of the program).

Instead of importing the file <Foundation/NSArchiver.h> in your interface file, to work with keyed archives you need to import <Foundation/NSKeyedArchiver.h>.

Referring to the Foo class defined in the previous example, if you define a class that others will use, you don't really know whether they'll try to archive objects from your class using keyed archiving. To account for that, you can write your encoding and decoding methods to handle either keyed or unkeyed archives. This can be done by sending an allowsKeyedCoding message to the encoder sent to your encodeWithCoder: method. If the answer is YES, you should use keyed archiving; otherwise, archive your objects in the manner described in the previous section. The same thing applies to your decoder: First, test whether keyed archiving is in effect and if it is, decode your instance variables accordingly.

Program 19.9 shows the modified Foo class interface and implementation files to allow for keyed archiving.

Program 19.9   Foo **Interface File**

```
@interface Foo: NSObject <NSCoding>
{
  NSString *strVal;
  int     intVal;
  float   floatVal;
}

-(void) setAll: (NSString *) ss iVal: (int) ii fVal: (float) ff;

-(NSString *) strVal;
-(int) intVal;
-(float) floatVal;
@end
```

2. Note that as of this writing that keyed archiving is not supported under GNUStep.

The interface file hasn't changed from the previous example, but the implementation file has.

Program 19.9   Foo **Implementation File**

```objc
@implementation Foo;
-(void) setAll: (NSString *) ss iVal: (int) ii fVal: (float) ff
{
  strVal = ss;
  intVal = ii;
  floatVal = ff;
}


-(NSString *) strVal   { return strVal; }
-(int)        intVal   { return intVal; }
-(float)      floatVal { return floatVal; }


-(void) encodeWithCoder: (NSCoder *) encoder
{
    if ( [encoder allowsKeyedCoding] ) {
        [encoder encodeObject: strVal forKey: @"FoostrVal"];
        [encoder encodeInt: intVal forKey: @"FoointVal"];
        [encoder encodeFloat: floatVal forKey: @"FoofloatVal"];
    } else {
        [encoder encodeObject: strVal];
        [encoder encodeValueOfObjCType: @encode(int) at: &intVal];
        [encoder encodeValueOfObjCType: @encode(float) at: &floatVal];
    }
}


-(id) initWithCoder: (NSCoder *) decoder
{
    if ( [decoder allowsKeyedCoding] ) {
        strVal = [[decoder decodeObjectForKey: @"FoostrVal"] retain];
        intVal = [decoder decodeIntForKey: @"FoointVal"];
        floatVal = [decoder decodeFloatForKey: @"FoofloatVal"];
    } else {
        strVal = [[decoder decodeObject] retain];
        [decoder decodeValueOfObjCType: @encode(int) at: &intVal];
        [decoder decodeValueOfObjCType: @encode(float) at: &floatVal];
    }

  return self;
}
@end
```

After testing for keyed archiving, the three messages

```
[encoder encodeObject: strVal forKey: @"FoostrVal"];
[encoder encodeInt: intVal forKey: @"FoointVal"];
[encoder encodeFloat: floatVal forKey: @"FoofloatVal"];
```

archive the three instance variables from the object. The `encodeObject:forKey:` method encodes an object and stores it under the specified key for later retrieval using that key. The key names are arbitrary, so as long you use the same name to retrieve the data as when you unarchived it, you can specify any key you like. The only time a conflict might arise is if the same key is used for a subclass of an object being encoded. To prevent this from happening, you can insert the class name in front of the instance variable name when composing the key for the archive, as was done in Program 19.9.

You use the method `encodeInt:forKey:` instead of `encodeValueOfObjCType:at:`, which you need to use for unkeyed archives. Table 19.1 depicts the various encoding and decoding methods you can use for keyed archives.

The process of decoding keyed objects is straightforward: You use `decodeObject:forKey:` for Objective-C objects and the appropriate method from Table 19.1 for basic data types.

Table 19.1 **Encoding and Decoding Basic Data Types in Keyed Archives**

Encoder	Decoder
encodeBool:forKey:	decodeBool:forKey:
encodeInt:forKey:	decodeInt:forKey:
encodeInt32:forKey:	decodeInt32:forKey:
encodeInt64: forKey:	decodeInt64:forKey:
encodeFloat:forKey:	decodeFloat:forKey:
encodeDouble:forKey:	decodeDouble:forKey:

Some of the basic data types, such as `char`, `short`, `long`, and `long long`, are not listed in Table 19.1. You'll have to determine the size of your data object and use the appropriate routine. For example, a `short int` is normally 16 bits, an `int` and `long` are 32 bits, and a `long long` is 64 bits. (You can use the `sizeof` operator as described in Chapter 13, "Underlying C Language Features," to determine the size of any data type.) So, to archive a `short int`, store it in an `int` first and then archive it with `encodeInt:forKey:`. Reverse the process to get it back: Use `decodeInt:forKey:` and then assign it to your `short int` variable.

The test program and output from the keyed archiving example is shown in Program 19.9.

Program 19.9 **Test Program**

```
#import <Foundation/NSObject.h>
#import <Foundation/NSAutoreleasePool.h>
#import <Foundation/NSString.h>
#import <Foundation/NSKeyedArchiver.h>
#import <Foundation/NSCoder.h>


int main (int argc, char *argv[])
{
  NSAutoreleasePool *pool = [[NSAutoreleasePool alloc] init];
  Foo *myFoo1 = [[Foo alloc] init];
  Foo *myFoo2;

  // First set and archive myFoo1 to a file
  [myFoo1 setAll: @"This is the string" iVal: 12345 fVal: 98.6];
  [NSKeyedArchiver archiveRootObject: myFoo1 toFile: @"foo.karch"];

  // Now restore the archive into myFoo2
  myFoo2 = [NSKeyedUnarchiver unarchiveObjectWithFile:
                      @"foo.karch"];
  printf ("%s\n%i\n%g\n", [[myFoo2 strVal] cString],
          [myFoo2 intVal], [myFoo2 floatVal]);

  [myFoo1 release];
  [pool release];
  return 0;
}
```

Program 19.9 **Output**

```
This is the string
12345
98.6
```

Using NSData to Create Custom Archives

You might not want to write your object directly to a file using the
archiveRootObject:ToFile: method, as was done in the previous program examples. For example, perhaps you want to collect some or all of your objects and store
them in a single archive file. This can be done in Objective-C using the general data
stream object class called NSData, which we briefly visited in Chapter 16.

As mentioned in Chapter 16, an NSData object can be used to reserve an area of memory into which you can store data. Typical uses of this data area might be as temporary storage for data that will subsequently be written to a file or perhaps to hold the contents of a file read from the disk. The simplest way to create a mutable data area is with the data method:

```
dataArea = [NSMutableData data];          .
```

This creates an empty buffer space whose size expands as needed as the program executes.

As a simple example, let's assume you want to archive your address book and one of your Foo objects in the same file. Assume for this example that you've added keyed archiving methods to the AddressBook and AddressCard classes (see Program 19.10). If you haven't, or keyed archives aren't supported on your system, you can modify this example to work without keyed archives.

Program 19.10

```
#import <Foundation/NSObject.h>
#import <Foundation/NSAutoreleasePool.h>
#import <Foundation/NSString.h>
#import <Foundation/NSKeyedArchiver.h>
#import <Foundation/NSCoder.h>
#import <Foundation/NSData.h>
#import "AddressBook.h"
#import "Foo.h"


int main (int argc, char *argv[])
{
  NSAutoreleasePool *pool = [[NSAutoreleasePool alloc] init];
  Foo               *myFoo1 = [[Foo alloc] init];
  Foo               *myFoo2;
  NSMutableData     *dataArea;
  NSKeyedArchiver   *archiver;
  AddressBook       *myBook;

  // Insert code from Program 19.6 to create an Address Book
  // in myBook containing four address cards

  [myFoo1 setAll: @"This is the string" iVal: 12345 fVal: 98.6];

  // Set up a data area and connect it to an NSKeyedArchiver object
  dataArea = [NSMutableData data];

  archiver = [[NSKeyedArchiver alloc]
            initForWritingWithMutableData: dataArea];
```

Program 19.10   **Continued**

```
    // Now we can begin to archive objects
    [archiver encodeObject: myBook forKey: @"myaddrbook"];
    [archiver encodeObject: myFoo1 forKey: @"myfoo1"];
    [archiver finishEncoding];

    // Write the archived data are to a file
    if ( [dataArea writeToFile: @"myArchive" atomically: YES] == NO)
        printf ("Archiving failed!\n");

    [archiver release];

    [myFoo1 release];
    [pool release];
    return 0;
}
```

After allocating an NSKeyedArchiver object, the initForWritingWithMutableData: message is sent to specify the area in which to write the archived data; this is the NSMutabledata area dataArea you previously created. The NSKeyedArchiver object stored in archiver can now be sent encoding messages to archive objects in your program. In fact, all encoding messages up until it receives a finishEncoding message are archived and stored in the specified data area.

You have two objects to encode here—the first is your address book and the second is your Foo object. You can use encodeObject: for these objects because you have previously implemented encoder and decode methods for the AddressBook, AddressCard, and Foo classes. It's important that you understand that concept.

When you are done archiving your two objects, you send the archiver object the finishEncoding message. No more objects can be encoded after that point, and you need to send this message to complete the archiving process.

The area you set aside and named dataArea now contains your archived objects in a form you can write to a file. The message expression

```
[data writeToFile: @"myArchive" atomically: YES]
```

sends the writeToFile:atomically: message to your data stream to ask it to write its data to the specified file, which you named myArchive.

As you can see from the if statement, the writeToFile:atomically: method returns a BOOL value: YES if the write operation succeeds and NO if it fails (perhaps an invalid pathname for the file was specified or the file system is full).

Restoring the data from your archive file is simple—you just do things in reverse. First, you need to allocate a data area like before. Next, you need to read your archive file into the data area, and then you have to create an NSKeyedUnarchiver object and tell it to decode data from the specified area. You must invoke decode methods to extract and decode your archived objects. When you're all done, you send a finishDecoding message to the NSKeyedUnarchiver object.

This is all done in Program 19.11 that follows.

Program 19.11

```
#import <Foundation/NSObject.h>
#import <Foundation/NSAutoreleasePool.h>
#import <Foundation/NSString.h>
#import <Foundation/NSKeyedArchiver.h>
#import <Foundation/NSCoder.h>
#import <Foundation/NSData.h>
#import "AddressBook.h"
#import "Foo.h"

int main (int argc, char *argv[])
{
  NSAutoreleasePool *pool = [[NSAutoreleasePool alloc] init];
  NSData           *dataArea;
  NSKeyedUnarchiver *unarchiver;
  Foo              *myFoo1;
  AddressBook       *myBook;
  // Read in the archive and connect an
  // NSKeyedUnarchiver object to it

  dataArea = [NSData dataWithContentsOfFile: @"myArchive"];
  unarchiver = [[NSKeyedUnarchiver alloc]
                      initForReadingWithData: dataArea];

  // Decode the objects we previously stored in the archive
  myBook = [unarchiver decodeObjectForKey: @"myaddrbook"];
  myFoo1 = [unarchiver decodeObjectForKey: @"myfoo1"];

  [unarchiver finishDecoding];

  [unarchiver release];

  // Verify that the restore was successful
  [myBook list];
   printf ("%s\n%i\n%g\n", [[myFoo1 strVal] cString],
          [myFoo1 intVal], [myFoo1 floatVal]);

  [pool release];
  return 0;
}
```

Program 19.11   **Output**

```
======== Contents of: Steve's Address Book =========
Jamie Baker      jbaker@kochan-wood.com
Julia Kochan     jewls337@axlc.com
```

Program 19.11 **Continued**

```
Stephen Kochan      steve@kochan-wood.com
Tony Iannino        tony.iannino@techfitness.com
=======================================================

This is the string
12345
98.6
```

The output verifies that the address book and your `Foo` object were successfully restored from the archive file.

Using the Archiver to Copy Objects

In Program 19.2, you tried to make a copy of an array containing mutable string elements and saw how a shallow copy of the array was made. That is, the actual strings themselves were not copied, only the references to them.

You can use the Foundation's archiving capabilities to create a deep copy of an object. For example, Program 19.12 copies `dataArray` to `dataArray2` by archiving `dataArray` into a buffer and then unarchiving it, assigning the result to `dataArray2`. You don't need to use a file for this process; the archiving and unarchiving process can all take place in memory.

Program 19.12

```objc
#import <Foundation/NSObject.h>
#import <Foundation/NSAutoreleasePool.h>
#import <Foundation/NSString.h>
#import <Foundation/NSArchiver.h>
#import <Foundation/NSArray.h>

int main (int argc, char *argv[])
{
    NSAutoreleasePool *pool = [[NSAutoreleasePool alloc] init];
    NSData        *data;
    NSMutableArray  *dataArray = [NSMutableArray arrayWithObjects:
        [NSMutableString stringWithString: @"one"],
        [NSMutableString stringWithString: @"two"],
        [NSMutableString stringWithString: @"three"],
        nil
    ];

    NSMutableArray   *dataArray2;
    NSMutableString  *mStr;
    int              i, n;
```

Program 19.12   **Continued**

```
// Make a deep copy using the archiver

data = [NSArchiver archivedDataWithRootObject: dataArray];
dataArray2 = [NSUnarchiver unarchiveObjectWithData: data];

mStr = [dataArray2 objectAtIndex: 0];
[mStr appendString: @"ONE"];

printf ("\ndataArray: ");
for (i = 0; i < [dataArray count]; ++i)
    printf ("%s ", [[dataArray objectAtIndex: i] cString]);

printf ("\ndataArray2: ");
n = [dataArray2 count];
for (i = 0; i < n; ++i)
    printf ("%s ", [[dataArray2 objectAtIndex: i] cString]);

printf ("\n");
[pool release];
return 0;
}
```

Program 19.12   **Output**

```
dataArray: one two three
dataArray2: oneONE two three
```

The output verifies that changing the first element of dataArray2 had no effect on the first element of dataArray. That's because a new copy of the strings was made through the archiving/unarchiving process.

The copy operation in Program 19.12 is performed with the following two lines:

```
data = [NSArchiver archivedDataWithRootObject: dataArray];
dataArray2 = [NSUnarchiver unarchiveObjectWithData: data];
```

You can even avoid the intermediate assignment and perform the copy with a single statement like this:

```
dataArray2 = [NSUnarchiver unarchiveObjectWithData:
                [NSArchiver archivedDataWithRootObject: dataArray]];
```

This is a technique you might want to keep in mind next time you need to make a deep copy of an object or of an object that doesn't support the NSCopying protocol.

Exercises

1. In Chapter 15, Program 15.8 generated a table of prime numbers. Modify that program to write the resulting array as a property list to the file `primes.pl`. Then, examine the contents of the file.

2. Write a program to read in the property list created in exercise 1 and store the values in an array object. Print all the elements of the array to verify that the restore operation was successful.

3. The glossary in Appendix A has been stored online as a traditional property list at the URL `http://www.kochan-wood.com/examples/glossary.pl`. Write a program to read the glossary into a dictionary object and then display its contents.

4. Modify the program developed in exercise 3 to look up an entry in the glossary based on a term entered on the command line. So

   ```
   $ glossary object
   ```

   should display the meaning of "object" as defined in the glossary. Be sure to handle the cases where a term can't be found or if the term consists of more than one word, like this:

   ```
   $ glossary instance method
   ```

   This should look up the meaning of the term "instance method" in the glossary.

5. Write a program to read in an archived `AddressBook` and look up an entry based on a name supplied on the command line, like so:

   ```
   $ lookup gregory
   ```

Afterword

Now that you have learned how to write Objective-C programs and use the Foundation framework, it's time to start writing your own Objective-C applications. You can use Appendix B, "Objective-C Language Summary," to refresh your memory on the semantics of the language and for quick reference. You are also now well-prepared to read the "official" reference manual on Objective-C published by Apple Computer, Inc. It's listed in Appendix E, "Resources," and is available online for free. Some more advanced topics (such as distributed objects) are covered in detail in that text.

As you've seen, the Foundation framework provides a solid foundation for program development, so take advantage of its many classes and learn how to use them to your advantage. Skim through the header file descriptions in Appendix B and see whether you find anything intriguing.

Some features offered by the Foundation framework were not covered in the text, either due to their advanced nature or lack of space. These include ways to

- Register an object to be notified when a particular event on the system occurs. This is handled primarily by Foundation's `NSNotification` class.

- Communicate with objects in different processes on the same system or on different systems. This is handled primarily by Foundation's `NSConnection` class.

- Work with dates with Foundation's `NSDate` and `NSCalendarDate` classes.

- Work with rectangles, sizes, and Cartesian coordinates using the defined types `NSRect`, `NSSize`, and `NSPoint`, respectively.

- Set up a run loop to process input events using the `NSRunLoop` class. (You'll want to learn how to do that for developing interactive graphical applications, multi-threaded programs, or network I/O.)

- Set up a way to handle exceptions (that is, errors that occur in a running application). This is handled with Foundation's `NSException` class.

- Work with URLs to load and unload data, manage cookies, and so on. These are handled primarily through the `NSURL`, `NSURLHandle`, and `NSHTTPCookie` classes in Foundation.

- Write multithreaded applications. Multithreaded applications can be used to have one or more portions of an application executed in parallel to the rest of the application. The `NSThread` and `NSLock` classes (and several other classes) in Foundation are used to develop multithreaded Objective-C programs.

Refer to the resources in Appendix E for more information on these topics.

If you want to start writing applications using a graphical user interface (GUI), you should learn how to use the Application Kit framework, which is part of Cocoa on Mac OS X. Appendix E lists books you can read to gain this knowledge. On Mac OS X, you also should learn how to use the tools that will make your development time more productive, such as Project Builder (or Xcode if it's available on your system) and Interface Builder. GNUStep also offers a variety of development tools, as well as a GUI library, which you might want to learn how to use.

Good luck in your programming efforts!

Stephen Kochan
`steve@kochan-wood.com`

III

Appendixes

A

Glossary

THIS APPENDIX CONTAINS INFORMAL DEFINITIONS for many of the terms you will encounter. Some of these terms have to do directly with the Objective-C language itself, whereas others have their etymology from the discipline of object-oriented programming. In the latter case, the meaning of the term as it specifically applies to the Objective-C language is provided.

abstract class A class defined to make creating subclasses easier. Instances are created from the subclass, not of the abstract class. *See also* concrete subclass.

Application Kit A framework for developing an application's user interface, which includes objects such as menus, toolbars, pasteboards, and windows. Part of Cocoa and more commonly called AppKit.

archiving Translating the representation of an object's data into a format that can later be restored (unarchived).

array An ordered collection of values. Arrays can be defined as a basic Objective-C type and are implemented as objects under Foundation through the NSArray and NSMutableArray classes.

automatic variable A variable that is automatically allocated and released when a statement block is entered and exited. Automatic variables have scope that is limited to the block in which they are defined and have no default initial value. They are optionally preceded by the keyword auto.

autorelease pool An object defined in the Foundation framework that keeps track of objects that are to be released when the pool itself is released. Objects are added to the pool by sending them autorelease messages.

bitfield A structure containing one or more integer fields of a specified bit width. Bitfields can be accessed and manipulated the same way other structure members can.

category A set of methods grouped together under a specified name. Categories can modularize the method definitions for a class and can be used to add new methods to an existing class.

character string A null-terminated sequence of characters.

class A set of instance variables and methods that have access to those variables. After a class is defined, instances of the class (that is, objects) can be created.

class method A method (defined with a leading + sign) that is invoked on class objects. *See also* instance method.

class object An object that identifies a particular class. The class name can be used as the receiver of a message to invoke a class method. In other places, the `class` method can be invoked on the class to create a class object.

cluster An abstract class that groups a set of private concrete subclasses, providing a simplified interface to the user through the abstract class.

Cocoa A development environment on Mac OS X that comprises the Foundation and Application Kit frameworks.

collection A Foundation framework object that is an array, a dictionary, or a set used for grouping and manipulating related objects.

compile time The time during which the source code is analyzed and converted into a lower-level format known as object code.

composite class A class that is composed of objects from other classes; often it's used as an alternative to subclassing.

concrete subclass A subclass of an abstract class. Instances can be created from a concrete subclass.

conform A class conforms to a protocol if it adopts all the methods in the protocol, either directly through implementation or indirectly through inheritance.

constant character string A sequence of characters enclosed inside a pair of double quotation marks. If preceded by an @ character, a constant character string object, typically of type `NSConstantString`, is defined.

data encapsulation The notion that the data for an object is stored in its instance variables and is accessed only by the object's methods. This maintains the integrity of the data.

delegate An object directed to carry out an action by another object.

designated initializer The method that all other initialization methods in the class, or in subclasses (through messages to `super`), will invoke.

dictionary A collection of key/value pairs implemented under Foundation with the `NSDictionary` and `NSMutableDictionary` classes.

directive In Objective-C, a special construct that begins with an at sign (@). `@interface`, `@implementation`, `@end`, and `@class` are examples of directives.

Distributed Objects The capability of Foundation objects in one application to communicate with Foundation objects in another application, possibly running on another machine.

dynamic binding Determining the method to invoke with an object at runtime instead of at compile time.

dynamic typing   Determining the class to which an object belongs at run-time instead of at compile time. *See also* static typing.

encapsulation   *See* data encapsulation.

extern variable   *See* global variable.

factory method   *See* class method.

factory object   *See* class object.

formal protocol   A set of related methods grouped together under a name declared with the @protocol directive. Different classes (not necessarily related) can adopt a formal protocol by implementing (or inheriting) all its methods. *See also* informal protocol.

forwarding   The process of sending a message and its associated argument(s) to another method for execution.

Foundation framework   A collection of classes, functions, and protocols that form the foundation for application development, providing basic facilities such as memory management, file and URL access, archiving, and working with collections, and number and date objects.

framework   A collection of classes, functions, protocols, documentation, and header files and other resources that are all related. For example, the Cocoa framework is for developing interactive graphical applications under Mac OS X.

function   A block of statements identified by a name that can accept one or more arguments passed to it by value and can optionally return a value. Functions can be local (static) to the file in which they're defined or global, in which case they can be called from functions or methods defined in other files.

gcc   The name of the compiler developed by the Free Software Foundation (FSF). gcc supports many programming languages, including C, Objective-C, and C++. gcc is the standard compiler used on Mac OS X and under GNUStep for compiling Objective-C programs.

gdb   The standard debugging tool for programs compiled with gcc.

global variable   A variable defined outside any method or function that can be accessed by any method or function in the same source file or from other source files that declare the variable as extern.

GNUStep   The Free Software Foundation's implementation of OPENSTEP.

header file   A file that contains common definitions, macros, and variable declarations that is included into a program using either an #import or #include statement.

id   The generic object type that can hold a pointer to any type of object.

immutable object   An object whose value cannot be modified. Examples from the Foundation framework include NSString, NSDictionary, and NSArray objects. *See also* mutable object.

implementation section   The section of a class definition that contains the actual code (that is, implementation) for the methods declared in the corresponding interface section (or as specified by a protocol definition).

informal protocol   A logically related set of methods declared as a category, often as a category of the root class. Unlike formal protocols, all the methods in an informal protocol do not have to be implemented. *See also* formal protocol.

inheritance   The process of passing methods and instance variables from a class, starting with the root object down to subclasses.

instance   A concrete representation of a class. Instances are objects that are typically created by sending an `alloc` or `new` message to a class object.

instance method   A method that can be invoked by an instance of a class. *See also* class method.

instance variable   A variable declared in the interface section (or inherited from a parent) that is contained in every instance of the object. Instance methods have direct access to their instance variables.

Interface Builder   A tool under Mac OS X for building a graphical user interface for an application.

interface section   The section for declaring a class, its superclass, instance variables, and methods. For each method, the argument types and return type are also declared. *See also* implementation section.

internationalization   *See* localization.

isa   A special instance variable defined in the root object that all objects inherit. The `isa` variable is used to identify the class to which an object belongs at run-time.

link   The process of taking one or more object files and converting them into a program that can be executed.

LinuxSTEP   A version of GNUStep that runs on Linux systems.

local variable   A variable whose scope is limited to the block in which it is defined. Variables can be local to a method, function, or statement block.

localization   The process of making a program suitable for execution within a particular geographic region, typically by translating messages to the local language and handling things such as local time zones, currency symbols, date formats, and so on. Sometimes *localization* is used just to refer to the language translation and the term *internationalization* to the rest of the process.

message   The method and its associated arguments that are sent to an object (the receiver).

message expression   An expression enclosed in square brackets that specifies an object (the receiver) and the message to send to the object.

method   A procedure that belongs to a class and can be executed by sending a message to a class object or to instances from the class. *See also* class method and instance method.

mutable object   An object whose value can be changed. The Foundation framework supports mutable and immutable arrays, sets, strings, and dictionaries. *See also* immutable object.

NEXTSTEP   A development environment developed by NeXT Software for application development with Objective-C.

nil   An object of type `id`, which is used to represent an invalid object. Its value is defined as 0. nil can be sent messages.

notification   The process of sending a message to objects that have registered to be alerted (notified) when a specific event occurs.

NSObject   The root object under the Foundation framework.

null character   A character whose value is 0. A null character constant is denoted by `'\0'`.

null pointer   An invalid pointer value, normally defined as 0.

NXObject   The root object under NEXTSTEP.

object   A set of variables and associated methods. An object can be sent messages to cause one of its methods to be executed.

Object   The root object in Objective-C. *See also* `NSObject`.

object-oriented programming   A method of programming based on classes and objects and performing actions on those objects.

OPENSTEP   An Objective-C development environment based on NEXTSTEP and standardized by NeXT Software and Sun Microsystems, Inc.

parent class   A class from which another class inherits. Also referred to as the *super class*.

pointer   A value that references another object or data type. A pointer is implemented as the address of a particular object or value in memory. An instance of a class is a pointer to the location of the object's data in memory.

polymorphism   The capability of objects from different classes to accept the same message.

posing   The process of substituting one class for another.

preprocessor   A program that makes a first pass through the source code processing lines that begin with a #, which presumably contain special preprocessor statements. Common uses are for defining macros with `#define`, including

other source files with `#import` and `#include`, and conditionally including source lines with `#if`, `#ifdef`, and `#ifndef`.

procedural programming language   A language in which programs are defined by procedures and functions that operate on a set of data.

Project Builder   An application on Mac OS X for entering, building, running, and debugging programs.

property list   A representation of different types of objects in a standardized and portable format. Property lists are typically stored in either a "traditional" or XML format.

protocol   A list of methods that a class must implement to conform or adopt the protocol. Protocols provide a way to standardize an interface across classes. *See also* formal protocol and informal protocol.

receiver   The object to which a message is sent. The receiver can be referred to as `self` from inside the method that is invoked.

reference count   *See* retain count.

retain count   A count of the number of times an object is referenced. It's incremented by sending a `retain` message to the object and decremented by sending a `release` message to it.

root object   The topmost object in the inheritance hierarchy that has no parent.

runtime   The time when a program is executing; also the mechanism responsible for executing a program's instructions.

selector   The name used to select the method to execute for an object. Compiled selectors are of type `SEL` and can be generated using the `@selector` directive.

self   A variable used inside a method to refer to the receiver of the message.

set   An unordered collection of unique objects implemented under Foundation with the NSSet, NSMutableSet, and NSCountedSet classes.

statement   One or more expressions terminated by a semicolon.

statement block   One or more statements enclosed in a set of curly braces. Local variables can be declared within a statement block, and their scope is limited to that block.

static function   A function declared with the static keyword that can be called only by other functions or methods defined in the same source file.

static typing   Explicitly identifying the class to which an object belongs at compile time. *See also* dynamic typing.

static variable   A variable whose scope is limited to the block or module in which it is defined. Static variables have default initial values of 0 and retain their values through method or function invocations.

structure   An aggregate data type that can contain members of varying types. Structures can be assigned to other structures, passed as arguments to functions and methods, and returned by them as well.

subclass   Also known as a *child class*, a subclass inherits the methods and instance variables from its parent or superclass.

super   A keyword used in a method to refer to the parent class of the receiver.

super class   The parent class of a particular class. *See also* super.

Unicode character   A standard for representing characters from sets containing up to millions of characters. The NSString and NSMutableString classes work with strings containing Unicode characters.

union   An aggregate data type like a structure containing members that share the same storage area. Only one of those members can occupy the storage area at any point in time.

Xcode   A compiling and debugging tool for program development released with Mac OS X v. 10.3.

XML   Extensible Markup Language. The default format for property lists generated on Mac OS X.

zone   A designated area of memory for allocating data and objects. A program can work with multiple zones to more efficiently manage memory.

B

Objective-C Language Summary

THIS APPENDIX SUMMARIZES THE OBJECTIVE-C LANGUAGE in a format suitable for quick reference. It is not intended that this be a complete definition of the language, but rather a more informal description of its features. You should thoroughly read the material in this appendix after you have completed the text. Doing so will not only reinforce the material you have learned, but also provide you with a better global understanding of Objective-C.

This summary is based on the ANSI C99 (ISO/IEC 9899:1999) standard with Objective-C language extensions, which are not standardized. As of this writing, the latest version of the GNU gcc compiler is version 3.3, which does not fully conform to the ANSI C99 standard[1]

Extensions to the C language in the gcc compiler that are not part of the ANSI standard are not summarized here.[2]

Digraphs and Identifiers

Digraph Characters
The following special two-character sequences (*digraphs*) are equivalent to the listed single-character punctuators:

Digraph	Meaning	Digraph	Meaning
<:	[	%>	}
:>	]	%:	#
<%	{	%:%:	##

1. You can find out which version of the compiler you're running with the command gcc -v. You can also give the gcc command the -std=c99 option to get more support for C99 features than is offered by default.
2. You can get a description of the GNU extensions at http://www.gnu.org/software/gcc/onlinedocs.

Identifiers

An *identifier* in Objective-C consists of a sequence of letters (upper- or lowercase), universal character names (1.2.1), digits, or underscore characters. The first character of an identifier must be a letter, an underscore, or a universal character name. The first 31 characters of an identifier are guaranteed to be significant in an external name, and the first 63 characters are guaranteed to be significant for an internal identifier or macro name.

Universal Character Names

A universal character name is formed by the characters \u followed by four hexadecimal numbers or the characters \U followed by eight hexadecimal numbers. If the first character of an identifier is specified by a universal character, its value cannot be that of a digit character. Universal characters, when used in identifier names, can also not specify a character whose value is less than $A0_{16}$ (other than 24_{16}, 40_{16}, or 60_{16}) or a character in the range $D800_{16}$ through $DFFF_{16}$, inclusive.

Universal character names can be used in identifier names, character constants, and character strings.

Keywords

The identifiers listed here are keywords that have special meanings to the Objective-C compiler.

_Bool	enum	return
_Complex	extern	self
_Imaginary	float	short
auto	for	signed
break	goto	sizeof
bycopy	if	static
byref	in	struct
case	inline	super
char	inout	switch
const	int	typedef
continue	long	union
default	oneway	unsigned
do	out	void
double	register	volatile
else	restrict	while

Directives

Compiler directives begin with an @ sign and are used specifically for working with classes and objects. These are summarized in Table B.1.

Table B.1 **Compiler Directives**

Directive	Meaning	Example
@"*chars*"	A constant character string object of implementation-defined type (typically of class NXConstantString or NSConstantString) containing *chars* is defined.	NSString *url = @"http://www.kochan-wood.com";
@class *c1*, *c2*, ...	Declares *c1*, *c2*, ... as classes.	@class Point, Rectangle;
@defs (*class*)	Returns a list of the structure variables for *class*.	struct Fract { @defs(Fraction); } *fractPtr; fractPtr = (struct Fract *) [[Fraction alloc] init];
@encode (*type*)	String encoding for *type*.	@encode (int *)
@end	Ends an interface section, an implementation section, or a protocol section.	@end
@implementation	Begins an implementation section.	@implementation Fraction;
@interface	Begins an interface section.	@interface Fraction: Object <Copying>

@protocol (*protocol*)	Creates a Protocol object for a specified *protocol*.	if ([myObj conformsTo:
		@protocol(Copying)])
		{
		   ...
		}

@protocol *name*	Begins a protocol definition for *name*.	@protocol Copying

@selector (*method*)	SEL object for specified *method*.	if ([myObj respondsTo:
		@selector (allocF)])
		{
		   ...
		}

Predefined Identifiers

Table B.2 lists identifiers that have special meanings in Objective-C programs. Some are typedefs and macros defined in the header file <objc/objc.h>.

Table B.2 **Special Predefined Identifiers**

Identifier	Meaning
_cmd	A local variable automatically defined in a method that contains the selector for the method
__func__	A local character string variable automatically defined in a function or method containing the name of the function or method
BOOL	Boolean value, typically used with YES and NO
Class	Class object type
id	Generic object type
IMP	Pointer to a method returning the value of type id
nil	Null object
Nil	Null class object
NO	Defined as (BOOL) 0
NSObject	Root Foundation object defined in <Foundation/NSObject.h>
Object	Root object defined in <objc/object.h>
Protocol	Name of class for storing information about protocols
SEL	A compiled selector
self	A local variable automatically defined in a method that references the receiver of the message
super	The parent of the receiver of the message
YES	Defined as (BOOL) 1

Comments

There are two ways to insert comments into program. A comment can begin with the two characters //, in which case any characters that follow on the line are ignored by the compiler.

A comment can also begin with the two characters /* and end when the characters */ are encountered. Any characters can be included inside the comment, which can extend over multiple lines of the program. A comment can be used anywhere in the program where a blank space is allowed. Comments, however, cannot be nested, which means that the first */ characters encountered end the comment, no matter how many /* characters you use.

Constants

Integer Constants

An integer constant is a sequence of digits, optionally preceded by a plus or minus sign. If the first digit is 0, the integer is taken as an octal constant, in which case all digits that follow must be 0–7. If the first digit is 0 and is immediately followed by the letter x (or X), the integer is taken as a hexadecimal constant and the digits that follow can be in the range 0–9 or a–f (or A–F).

The suffix letter l or L can be added to the end of a decimal integer constant to make it a long int constant. If the value can't fit into a long int, it's treated as a long long int. If the suffix letter l or L is added to the end of an octal or a hexadecimal constant, it is taken as a long int if it can fit; if it can't fit there, it is taken as a long long int. Finally, if it can't fit in a long long int, it is taken as an unsigned long long int constant.

The suffix letters ll or LL can be added to the end of a decimal integer constant to make it a long long int. When added to the end of an octal or a hexadecimal constant, it is taken as a long long int first, and if it can't fit there, it is taken as an unsigned long long int constant.

The suffix u or U can be added to the end of an integer constant to make it unsigned. If the constant is too large to fit inside an unsigned int, it's taken as an unsigned long int. If it's too large for an unsigned long int, it's taken as an unsigned long long int.

Both an unsigned and long suffix can be added to an integer constant to make it an unsigned long int. If the constant is too large to fit in an unsigned long int, it's taken as an unsigned long long int.

Both an unsigned and a long-long suffix can be added to an integer constant to make it an unsigned long long int.

If an unsuffixed decimal integer constant is too large to fit into a signed int, it is treated a long int. If it's too large to fit into a long int, it's treated as a long long int.

If an unsuffixed octal or hexadecimal integer constant is too large to fit into a signed int, it is treated as an unsigned int. If it's too large to fit into an unsigned int, it's treated as a long int, and if it's too large to fit into a long int, it's treated as an unsigned long int. If it's too large for an unsigned long int, it's taken as a long long int. Finally, if it's too large to fit into a long long int, the constant is treated as an unsigned long long int.

Floating-point Constants

A floating-point constant consists of a sequence of decimal digits, a decimal point, and another sequence of decimal digits. A minus sign can precede the value to denote a negative value. In addition, either the sequence of digits before the decimal point or after the decimal point can be omitted, but not both.

If the floating-point constant is immediately followed by the letter e (or E) and an optionally signed integer, the constant is expressed in scientific notation. This integer (the *exponent*) represents the power of 10 by which the value preceding the letter e (the *mantissa*) is multiplied (for example, 1.5e-2 represents 1.5×10^{-2} or .015).

A *hexadecimal* floating constant consists of a leading 0x or 0X, followed by one or more decimal or hexadecimal digits, followed by a p or P, followed by an optionally signed binary exponent. For example, 0x3p10 represents the value 3×2^{10}.

Floating-point constants are treated as `double` precision values by the compiler. The suffix letter `f` or `F` can be added to specify a `float` constant instead of a `double` one, and the suffix letter `l` or `L` can be added to specify a `long double` constant.

Character Constants

A character enclosed within single quotation marks is a *character* constant. How the inclusion of more than one character inside the single quotation marks is handled is implementation-defined. A universal character can be used in a character constant to specify a character not included in the standard character set.

Escape Sequences

Special escape sequences are recognized and are introduced by the backslash character. These escape sequences are listed here:

Character	Meaning
\a	Audible alert
\b	Backspace
\f	Form feed
\n	Newline
\r	Carriage return
\t	Horizontal tab
\v	Vertical tab
\\	Backslash
\"	Double quote
\'	Single quote
\?	Question mark
\nnn	Octal character value
\unnnn	Universal character name
\Unnnnnnnn	Universal character name
\xnn	Hexadecimal character value

In the octal character case, from one to three octal digits can be specified. In the last three cases, hexadecimal digits are used.

Wide Character Constants

A *wide character constant* is written as `L'x'`. The type of such a constant is `wchar_t`, as defined in the standard header file `<stddef.h>`. Wide character constants provide a way to express a character from a character set that cannot be fully represented with the normal `char` type.

Character String Constants

A sequence of zero or more characters enclosed within double quotation marks represents a character string constant. Any valid character can be included in the string, including any of the escape characters listed previously. The compiler automatically inserts a null character (`'\0'`) at the end of the string.

Normally, the compiler produces a pointer to the first character in the string and the type is "pointer to `char`." However, when the string constant is used with the `sizeof` operator to initialize a character array, or with the `&` operator, the type of the string constant is "array of `char`."

Character string constants cannot be modified by the program.

Character String Concatenation

The preprocessor automatically concatenates adjacent character string constants together. The strings can be separated by zero or more whitespace characters. So, the three strings

```
"a" " character "
  "string"
```

are equivalent to the single string

```
"a character string"
```

after concatenation.

Multibyte Characters

Implementation-defined sequences of characters can be used to shift between different states in a character string so that multibyte characters can be included.

Wide Character String Constants

Character string constants from an extended character set are expressed using the format `L"..."`. The type of such a constant is "pointer to `wchar_t`," where `wchar_t` is defined in `<stddef.h>`.

Constant Character String Objects

A constant character string *object* can be created by placing an `@` character in front of a constant character string. The type of the object is implementation-defined and is typically `NXConstantString` or `NSConstantString`. Using such string objects in a program usually requires the use of a header file (such as `<NSString.h>`) that defines the particular constant string object class.

Enumeration Constants

An identifier that has been declared as a value for an enumerated type is taken as a constant of that particular type and is otherwise treated as type `int` by the compiler.

Data Types and Declarations

This section summarizes the basic data types, derived data types, enumerated data types, and `typedef`. Also summarized in this section is the format for declaring variables.

Declarations

When defining a particular structure, union, enumerated data type, or `typedef`, the compiler does not automatically reserve any storage. The definition merely tells the compiler about the particular data type and (optionally) associates a name with it. Such a definition can be made either inside or outside a function or method. In the former case, only the function or method knows of its existence; in the latter case, it is known throughout the remainder of the file.

After the definition has been made, variables can be declared to be of that particular data type. A variable that is declared to be of any data type will have storage reserved for it, unless it is an `extern` declaration, in which case it might or might not have storage allocated (see the section "Storage Classes and Scope").

The language also enables storage to be allocated at the same time that a particular structure, union, or enumerated data type is defined. This is done by simply listing the variables before the terminating semicolon of the definition.

Basic Data Types

The basic Objective-C data types are summarized in Table B.3. A variable can be declared to be of a particular basic data type using the following format:

```
type name = initial_value;
```

The assignment of an initial value to the variable is optional and is subject to the rules summarized in the section "Variables." More than one variable can be declared simultaneously using the following general format:

```
type name = initial_value, name = initial_value, .. ;
```

Before the type declaration, an optional storage class can also be specified, as summarized in the section "Variables." If a storage class is specified and the type of the variable is int, then int can be omitted. For example

```
static counter;
```

declares `counter` to be a `static int` variable.

Table B.3 **Summary of Basic Data Types**

Type	Meaning
int	Integer value; that is, a value that contains no decimal point; guaranteed to contain at least 16 bits of accuracy
short int	Integer value of reduced accuracy; takes half as much memory as an int on some machines; guaranteed to contain at least 16 bits of accuracy

Table B.3   **Continued**

Type	Meaning
long int	Integer value of extended accuracy; guaranteed to contain at least 32 bits of accuracy
long long int	Integer value of extra-extended accuracy; guaranteed to contain at least 64 bits of accuracy
unsigned int	Positive integer value; can store positive values up to twice as large as an int; guaranteed to contain at least 16 bits of accuracy
float	Floating-point value; that is, a value that can contain decimal places; guaranteed to contain at least six digits of precision
double	Extended accuracy floating-point value; guaranteed to contain at least 10 digits of precision
long double	Extra-extended accuracy floating-point value; guaranteed to contain at least 10 digits of precision
char	Single character value; on some systems, sign extension can occur when used in an expression
unsigned char	Same as char, except it ensures that sign extension will not occur as a result of integral promotion
signed char	Same as char, except it ensures that sign extension will occur as a result of integral promotion
_Bool	Boolean type; large enough to store the value 0 or 1
float _Complex	Complex number
double _Complex	Extended accuracy complex number
long double _Complex	Extra-extended accuracy complex number
void	No type; used to ensure that a function or method that does not return a value is not used as if it does return one, or to explicitly discard the results of an expression; also used as a generic pointer type (void *)

Note that the signed modifier can also be placed in front of the short int, int, long int, and long long int types. Because these types are signed by default anyway, this has no effect.

_Complex and _Imaginary data types enable complex and imaginary numbers to be declared and manipulated, with functions in the library for supporting arithmetic on these types. Normally, you should include the file <complex.h> in your program, which defines macros and declares functions for working with complex and imaginary numbers. For example, a double_Complex variable c1 can be declared and initialized to the value 5 + 10.5i with a statement such as follows:

```
double _Complex c1 = 5 + 10.5 * I;
```

Library routines such as creal and cimag can then be used to extract the real and imaginary parts of c1, respectively.

An implementation is not required to support types _Complex and _Imaginary, and it can optionally support one but not the other.

Derived Data Types

A *derived* data type is one that is built up from one or more of the basic data types. Derived data types are arrays, structures, unions, and pointers (which include objects). A function or method that returns a value of a specified type is also considered a derived data type. Each of these, with the exception of functions and methods, is summarized in the following paragraphs. Functions and methods are separately covered in the sections "Functions" and "Classes," respectively.

Arrays

Single-Dimensional Arrays

Arrays can be defined to contain any basic data type or any derived data type. Arrays of functions are not permitted (although arrays of function pointers are).

The declaration of an array has the following basic format:

```
type name[n]  = { initExpression, initExpression, .. };
```

The expression *n* determines the number of elements in the array name and can be omitted, provided a list of initial values is specified. In such a case, the size of the array is determined based on the number of initial values listed or on the largest index element referenced if designated initializers are used.

Each initial value must be a constant expression if a global array is defined. Fewer values can exist in the initialization list than there are elements in the array, but more cannot exist. If fewer values are specified, only that many elements of the array are initialized—the remaining elements are set to 0.

A special case of array initialization occurs in the case of character arrays, which can be initialized by a constant character string. For example

```
char today[] = "Monday";
```

declares `today` as an array of characters. This array is initialized to the characters `'M'`, `'o'`, `'n'`, `'d'`, `'a'`, `'y'`, and `'\0'`, respectively.

If you explicitly dimension the character array and don't leave room for the terminating null, the compiler doesn't place a null at the end of the array:

```
char today[6] = "Monday";
```

This declares `today` as an array of six characters and sets its elements to the characters `'M'`, `'o'`, `\&'n'`, `'d'`, `'a'`, and `'y'`, respectively.

By enclosing an element number in a pair of brackets, specific array elements can be initialized in any order. For example

```
int   x = 1233;
int   a[] = { [9] = x + 1, [2] = 3, [1] = 2, [0] = 1 };
```

defines a 10-element array called `a` (based on the highest index into the array) and initializes the last element to the value of `x + 1` (1234) and the first three elements to 1, 2, and 3, respectively.

Variable-Length Arrays

Inside a function, method, or block you can dimension an array using an expression containing variables. In that case, the size is calculated at runtime. For example, the function

```
int makeVals (int n)
{
  int valArray[n];
  ...
}
```

defines an automatic array called valArray with a size of n elements, where n is evaluated at runtime and can vary between function calls. Variable-length arrays cannot be initialized.

Multidimensional Arrays

The general format for declaring a multidimensional array follows:

```
type name[d1][d2]...[dn] = initializationList;
```

The array name is defined to contain d1 x d2 x...x dn elements of the specified type. For example

```
int three_d [5][2][20];
```

defines a three-dimensional array, three_d, containing 200 integers.

A particular element is referenced from a multidimensional array by enclosing the desired subscript for each dimension in its own set of brackets. For example, the statement

```
three_d [4][0][15] = 100;
```

stores 100 into the indicated element of the array three_d.

Multidimensional arrays can be initialized in the same manner as one-dimensional arrays. Nested pairs of braces can be used to control the assignment of values to the elements in the array.

The following declares matrix to be a two-dimensional array containing four rows and three columns:

```
int matrix[4][3] =
        { { 1, 2, 3 },
          { 4, 5, 6 },
          { 7, 8, 9 } };
```

Elements in the first row of matrix are set to the values 1, 2, and 3, respectively; in the second row they are set to 4, 5, and 6, respectively; and in the third row they are set to 7, 8, and 9, respectively. The elements in the fourth row are set to 0 because no values are specified for that row. The declaration

```
int matrix[4][3] =
    { 1, 2, 3, 4, 5, 6, 7, 8, 9 };
```

initializes `matrix` to the same values because the elements of a multidimensional array are initialized in *dimension order*—that is, from leftmost to rightmost dimension.

The declaration

```
int matrix[4][3] =
          { { 1 },
            { 4 },
            { 7 } };
```

sets the first element of the first row of `matrix` to 1, the first element of the second row to 4, and the first element of the third row to 7. All remaining elements are set to 0 by default.

Finally, the declaration

```
int matrix[4][3] = { [0][0] = 1, [1][1] = 5, [2][2] = 9 };
```

initializes the indicated elements of the matrix to the specified values.

Structures

General Format:

```
struct name
{
    memberDeclaration
    memberDeclaration
     ...
} variableList;
```

The structure *name* is defined to contain the members as specified by each *memberDeclaration*. Each such declaration consists of a type specification followed by a list of one or more member names.

Variables can be declared at the time that the structure is defined simply by listing them before the terminating semicolon, or they can subsequently be declared using the following format:

```
struct name variableList;
```

This format cannot be used if *name* is omitted when the structure is defined. In that case, all variables of that structure type must be declared with the definition.

The format for initializing a structure variable is similar to that for arrays. Its members can be initialized by enclosing the list of initial values in a pair of curly braces. Each value in the list must be a constant expression if a global structure is initialized.

The declaration

```
struct point
{
    float x;
    float y;
} start = {100.0, 200.0};
```

defines a structure called `point` and a `struct point` variable called `start` with initial values as specified. Specific members can be designated for initialization in any order with the notation

```
.member = value
```

in the initialization list, as in

```
struct point end = { .y = 500, .x = 200 };
```

The declaration

```
struct entry
{
  char *word;
  char *def;
} dictionary[1000] = {
  { "a",       "first letter of the alphabet" },
  { "aardvark", "a burrowing African mammal" },
  { "aback",   "to startle"          }
};
```

declares `dictionary` to contain 1,000 `entry` structures, with the first 3 elements initialized to the specified character string pointers. Using designated initializers, you could have also written it like this:

```
struct entry
{
  char *word;
  char *def;
} dictionary[1000] = {
  [0].word = "a",      [0].def = "first letter of the alphabet",
  [1].word = "aardvark", [1].def = "a burrowing African mammal",
  [2].word = "aback",   [2].def = "to startle"
};
```

or equivalently like this:

```
struct entry
{
  char *word;
  char *def;
} dictionary[1000] = {
  { {.word = "a",      .def = "first letter of the alphabet" },
    {.word = "aardvark", .def = "a burrowing African mammal"} ,
    {.word = "aback",   .def = "to startle"}
};
```

An automatic structure variable can be initialized to another structure of the same type like this:

```
struct date tomorrow = today;
```

This declares the date structure variable tomorrow and assigns to it the contents of the (previously declared) date structure variable today.

A *memberDeclaration* that has the format

```
type fieldName : n
```

defines a *field* that is *n* bits wide inside the structure, where *n* is an integer value. Fields can be packed from left to right on some machines and right to left on others. If *fieldName* is omitted, the specified number of bits is reserved but cannot be referenced. If *fieldName* is omitted and *n* is 0, the field that follows is aligned on the next storage *unit* boundary, where a *unit* is implementation-defined. The type of a field can be int, signed int, or unsigned int. It is implementation-defined whether an int field is treated as signed or unsigned. The address operator (&) cannot be applied to a field, and arrays of fields cannot be defined.

Unions

General Format:

```
union name
{
    memberDeclaration
    memberDeclaration
    ...
} variableList;
```

This defines a union called *name* with members as specified by each *memberDeclaration*. Each member of the union shares overlapping storage space, and the compiler ensures that enough space is reserved to contain the largest member of the union.

Variables can be declared at the time that the union is defined, or they can be subsequently declared using the notation

```
union name variableList;
```

provided the union was given a name when it was defined.

It is the programmer's responsibility to ensure that the value retrieved from a union is consistent with the last value stored inside the union. The first member of a union can be initialized by enclosing the initial value, which, in the case of a global union variable, must be a constant expression, inside a pair of curly braces:

```
union shared
{
    long long int l;
    long int    w[2];
} swap = { 0xffffffff };
```

A different member can be initialized instead by specifying the member name, as in

```
union shared swap2 = {.w[0] = 0x0, .w[1] = 0xffffffff};
```

This declares the union variable `swap` and sets the `l` member to hexadecimal `ffffffff`.

An automatic union variable can also be initialized to a union of the same type, as in

```
union shared swap2 = swap;
```

Pointers

The basic format for declaring a pointer variable is as follows:

```
type *name;
```

The identifier *name* is declared to be of type "pointer to *type*," which can be a basic data type or a derived data type. For example

```
int *ip;
```

declares `ip` to be a pointer to an `int`, and the declaration

```
struct entry *ep;
```

declares `ep` to be a pointer to an `entry` structure. If `Fraction` is defined as a class, the declaration

```
Fraction *myFract;
```

declares `myFract` to be an object of type `Fraction`—or more explicitly, `myFract` is used to hold a pointer to the object's data structure after an instance of the object is created as assigned to the variable.

Pointers that point to elements in an array are declared to point to the type of element contained in the array. For example, the previous declaration of `ip` would also be used to declare a pointer into an array of integers.

More advanced forms of pointer declarations are also permitted. For example, the declaration

```
char *tp[100];
```

declares `tp` to be an array of 100 character pointers, and the declaration

```
struct entry (*fnPtr) (int);
```

declares `fnPtr` to be a pointer to a function that returns an `entry` structure and takes a single `int` argument.

A pointer can be tested to see whether it's null by comparing it against a constant expression whose value is 0. The implementation can choose to internally represent a null pointer with a value other than 0. However, a comparison between such an internally represented null pointer and a constant value of 0 must prove equal.

The manner in which pointers are converted to integers and integers are converted to pointers is machine dependent, as is the size of the integer required to hold a pointer.

The type "pointer to void" is the generic pointer type. The language guarantees that a pointer of any type can be assigned to a void pointer and back again without changing its value.

The type `id` is a generic object pointer. Any object from any class can be assigned to an `id` variable, and vice versa.

Other than these two special cases, assignment of different pointer types is not permitted and typically results in a warning message from the compiler if attempted.

Enumerated Data Types

General Format:

```
enum name { enum_1, enum_2, .. } variableList;
```

The enumerated type *name* is defined with enumeration values *enum_1*, *enum_2*,…, each of which is an identifier or an identifier followed by an equals sign and a constant expression. *variableList* is an optional list of variables (with optional initial values) declared to be of type enum *name*.

The compiler assigns sequential integers to the enumeration identifiers starting at 0. If an identifier is followed by = and a constant expression, the value of that expression is assigned to the identifier. Subsequent identifiers are assigned values beginning with that constant expression plus one. Enumeration identifiers are treated as constant integer values by the compiler.

If you want to declare variables to be of a previously defined (and named) enumeration type, you can use the following construct:

```
enum name variableList;
```

A variable declared to be of a particular enumerated type can be assigned only a value of the same data type, although the compiler might not flag this as an error.

typedef

The `typedef` statement is used to assign a new name to a basic or derived data type. The `typedef` does not define a new type but simply a new name for an existing type. Therefore, variables declared to be of the newly named type are treated by the compiler exactly as if they were declared to be of the type associated with the new name.

In forming a `typedef` definition, proceed as though a normal variable declaration were being made. Then, place the new type name where the variable name would normally appear. Finally, in front of everything, place the keyword `typedef`.

As an example,

```
typedef struct
{
float x;
float y;
    } POINT;
```

associates the name `POINT` with a structure containing two floating-point members called `x` and `y`. Variables can subsequently be declared to be of type `POINT`, like so:

```
POINT origin = { 0.0, 0.0 };
```

Type Modifiers: `const`, `volatile`, and `restrict`

The keyword `const` can be placed before a type declaration to tell the compiler the value cannot be modified. So, the declaration

```
const int x5 = 100;
```

declares x5 to be a constant integer (that is, it won't be set to anything else during the program's execution). The compiler is not required to flag attempts to change the value of a `const` variable.

The `volatile` modifier explicitly tells the compiler that the value changes (usually dynamically). When a `volatile` variable is used in an expression, its value is accessed each place it appears.

To declare `port17` to be of type "volatile pointer to `char`," you would write this line:

```
char *volatile port17.
```

The `restrict` keyword can be used with pointers. It is a hint to the compiler for optimization (similar to the `register` keyword for variables). The `restrict` keyword specifies to the compiler that the pointer will be the only reference to a particular object—that is, it will not be referenced by any other pointer within the same scope. The lines

```
int * restrict intPtrA;
int * restrict intPtrB;
```

tell the compiler that, for the duration of the scope in which `intPtrA` and `intPtrB` are defined, they will never access the same value. Their use for pointing to integers (in an array, for example) is mutually exclusive.

Expressions

Variable names, function names, message expressions, array names, constants, function calls, array references, and structure and union references are all considered expressions. Applying a unary operator (where appropriate) to one of these expressions is also an expression, as is combining two or more of these expressions with a binary or ternary operator. Finally, an expression enclosed within parentheses is also an expression.

An expression of any type other than `void` that identifies a data object is called an *lvalue*. If it can be assigned a value, it is known as a *modifiable lvalue*.

Modifiable lvalue expressions are required in certain places. The expression on the left side of an assignment operator must be a modifiable lvalue. The unary address operator can be applied only to a modifiable `lvalue` or a function name. Finally, the increment and decrement operators can be applied only to modifiable lvalues.

Summary of Objective-C Operators

Table B.4 summarizes the various operators in the Objective-C language. These operators are listed in order of decreasing precedence, and operators grouped together have the same precedence.

As an example of how to use Table B.4, consider the following expression:

```
b | c & d * e
```

The multiplication operator has higher precedence than both the bitwise OR and bitwise AND operators because it appears above both of these in Table B.4. Similarly, the bitwise AND operator has higher precedence than the bitwise OR operator because the former appears above the latter in the table. Therefore, this expression would be evaluated as

```
b | ( c & ( d * e ) )
```

Now, consider the following expression:

```
b % c * d
```

Table B.4 **Summary of Objective-C Operators**

Operator	Description	Associativity
()	Function call	
[]	Array element reference or message expression	
->	Pointer to structure member reference	Left to right
.	Structure member reference	
-	Unary minus	
+	Unary plus	
++	Increment	
--	Decrement	
!	Logical negation	
~	Ones complement	Right to left
*	Pointer reference (indirection)	
&	Address	
sizeof	Size of an object	
(type)	Type cast (conversion)	
*	Multiplication	
/	Division	Left to right
%	Modulus	
+	Addition	Left to right
-	Subtraction	
<<	Left shift	Left to right
>>	Right shift	
<	Less than	
<=	Less than or equal to	Left to right
>	Greater than	
>=	Greater than or equal to	

Table B.4   **Continued**

Operator	Description	Associativity
==	Equality	Left to right
!=	Inequality	
&	Bitwise AND	Left to right
^	Bitwise XOR	Left to right
|	Bitwise OR	Left to right
&&	Logical AND	Left to right
||	Logical OR	Left to right
?:	Conditional	Right to left
= *= /= %= += -= &= ^= |= <<= >>=	Assignment operators	Right to left
,	Comma operator	Right to left

Because the modulus and multiplication operators appear in the same grouping in Table B.4, they have the same precedence. The associativity listed for these operators is left to right, indicating that the expression would be evaluated as follows:

```
( b % c ) * d
```

As another example, the expression

```
++a->b
```

would be evaluated as

```
++(a->b)
```

because the -> operator has higher precedence than the ++ operator.

Finally, because the assignment operators group from right to left, the statement

```
a = b = 0;
```

would be evaluated as

```
a = (b = 0);
```

which would have the net result of setting the values of a and b to 0. In the case of the expression

```
x[i] + ++i
```

it is not defined whether the compiler will evaluate the left side of the plus operator or the right side first. Here, the way that it's done affects the result because the value of i might be incremented before x[i] is evaluated.

Another case in which the order of evaluation is not defined is in the expression shown here:

```
x[i] = ++i
```

In this situation, it is not defined whether the value of i will be incremented before or after its value is used to index into x.

The order of evaluation of function and method arguments is also undefined. Therefore, in the function call

```
f (i, ++i);
```

or in the message expression

```
[myFract setTo: i over: ++i];
```

i might be incremented first, thereby causing the same value to be sent as the two arguments to the function or method.

The Objective-C language guarantees that the && and || operators will be evaluated from left to right. Furthermore, in the case of &&, it is guaranteed that the second operand will not be evaluated if the first is 0; in the case of ||, it is guaranteed that the second operand will not be evaluated if the first is nonzero. This fact is worth bearing in mind when forming expressions such as

```
if ( dataFlag || [myData checkData] )
   ...
```

because, in this case, checkData is invoked only if the value of dataFlag is 0. As another example, if the array object a is defined to contain n elements, the statement that begins

```
if (index >= 0 && index < n && ([a objectAtIndex: index] == 0))
   ...
```

references the element contained in the array only if index is a valid subscript into the array.

Constant Expressions

A *constant* expression is an expression in which each of the terms is a constant value. Constant expressions are required in the following situations:

1. As the value after a case in a switch statement
2. For specifying the size of an array
3. For assigning a value to an enumeration identifier
4. For specifying the bit field size in a structure definition
5. For assigning initial values to external or static variables
6. For specifying initial values to global variables
7. As the expression following the #if in a #if preprocessor statement

In the first four cases, the constant expression must consist of integer constants, character constants, enumeration constants, and sizeof expressions. The only operators that can be used are the arithmetic operators, bitwise operators, relational operators, conditional expression operator, and type cast operator.

In the fifth and sixth cases, in addition to the rules cited earlier, the address operator can be implicitly or explicitly used. However, it can be applied only to external or static variables or functions. So, for example, the expression

```
&x + 10
```

would be a valid constant expression, provided that x is an external or static variable. Furthermore, the expression

```
&a[10] - 5
```

is a valid constant expression if a is an external or static array. Finally, because &a[0] is equivalent to the expression a

```
a + sizeof (char) * 100
```

is also a valid constant expression.

For the last situation that requires a constant expression (after the #if), the rules are the same as for the first four cases, except the sizeof operator, enumeration constants, and the type cast operator cannot be used. However, the special defined operator is permitted (see the section "The #if Directive").

Arithmetic Operators

Given that

| a, b | are expressions of any basic data type except void; |
| i, j | are expressions of any integer data type; |

the expression

-a	negates the value of a;
+a	gives the value of a;
a + b	adds a with b;
a - b	subtracts b from a;
a * b	multiplies a by b;
a / b	divides a by b;
i % j	gives the remainder of i divided by j.

In each expression, the usual arithmetic conversions are performed on the operands (see the section "Conversion of Basic Data Types"). If a is unsigned, -a is calculated by first applying integral promotion to it, subtracting it from the largest value of the promoted type, and adding 1 to the result.

If two integral values are divided, the result is truncated. If either operand is negative, the direction of the truncation is not defined (that is, $-3 / 2$ can produce -1 on some machines and -2 on others); otherwise, truncation is always toward 0 ($3 / 2$ always produces 1). See the section "Basic Operations with Pointers" for a summary of arithmetic operations with pointers.

Logical Operators

Given that

a, b   are expressions of any basic data type except `void`, or are both pointers;

the expression

a && b   has the value 1 if both a and b are nonzero and 0 otherwise (and b is evaluated only if a is nonzero);

a || b   has the value 1 if either a or b is nonzero and 0 otherwise (and b is evaluated only if a is 0);

! a   has the value 1 if a is 0, and 0 otherwise.

The usual arithmetic conversions are applied to a and b (see the section "Conversion of Basic Data Types"). The type of the result in all cases is `int`.

Relational Operators

Given that

a, b   are expressions of any basic data type except `void`, or are both pointers;

the expression

a < b   has the value 1 if a is less than b, and 0 otherwise;

a <= b   has the value 1 if a is less than or equal to b, and 0 otherwise;

a > b   has the value 1 if a is greater than b, and 0 otherwise;

a >= b   has the value 1 if a is greater than or equal to b, and 0 otherwise;

a == b   has the value 1 if a is equal to b, and 0 otherwise;

a != b   has the value 1 if a is not equal to b, and 0 otherwise.

The usual arithmetic conversions are performed on a and b (see the section "Conversion of Basic Data Types"). The first four relational tests are meaningful for pointers only if they both point into the same array or to members of the same structure or union. The type of the result in each case is `int`.

Bitwise Operators

Given that

i, j, n   are expressions of any integer data type;

the expression

i & j   performs a bitwise AND of i and j;

i | j   performs a bitwise OR of i and j;

i ^ j   performs a bitwise XOR of i and j;

~i   takes the ones complement of i;

i << n   shifts i to the left n bits;

i >> n   shifts i to the right n bits.

The usual arithmetic conversions are performed on the operands, except with << and >>, in which case just integral promotion is performed on each operand (see the section "Conversion of Basic Data Types"). If the shift count is negative or is greater than or equal to the number of bits contained in the object being shifted, the result of the shift is undefined. On some machines, a right shift is arithmetic (sign fill) and on others logical (zero fill). The type of the result of a shift operation is that of the promoted left operand.

Increment and Decrement Operators

Given that

l	is a modifiable lvalue expression, whose type is not qualified as const;

the expression

++l	increments l and then uses its value as the value of the expression;
l++	uses l as the value of the expression and then increments l;
--l	decrements l and then uses its value as the value of the expression;
l--	uses l as the value of the expression and then decrements l.

The section "Basic Operations with Pointers" describes these operations on pointers.

Assignment Operators

Given that

l	is a modifiable lvalue expression, whose type is not qualified as const;
op	is any operator that can be used as an assignment operator (see Table B.4);
a	is an expression;

the expression

l = a	stores the value of a into l;
l op= a	applies op to l and a, storing the result into l.

In the first expression, if a is one of the basic data types (except void), it is converted to match the type of l. If l is a pointer, a must be a pointer to the same type as l, a void pointer, or the null pointer.

If l is a void pointer, a can be of any pointer type. The second expression is treated as if it were written l = l op (a), except l is evaluated only once (consider x[i++] += 10).

Conditional Operator

Given that

a, b, c	are expressions;

the expression

a ? b : c	has as its value b if a is nonzero, and c otherwise. Only expression b or c is evaluated.

Expressions b and c must be of the same data type. If they are not, but are both arithmetic data types, the usual arithmetic conversions are applied to make their types the same. If one is a pointer and the other is 0, the latter is taken as a null pointer of the same type as the former. If one is a pointer to void and the other is a pointer to another type, the latter is converted to be a pointer to void and is the resulting type.

Type Cast Operator

Given that

type	is the name of a basic data type, an enumerated data type (preceded by the keyword enum), or a typedef-defined type, or is a derived data type;
a	is an expression;

the expression

(*type*)	converts a to the specified type.

Note that the use of a parenthesized type in a method declaration or definition is not an example of the use of the type cast operator.

sizeof Operator

Given that

type	is as described previously;
a	is an expression;

the expression

sizeof (*type*)	has as its value the number of bytes needed to contain a value of the specified type;
sizeof a	has as its value the number of bytes required to hold the result of the evaluation of a.

If *type* is char, the result is defined to be 1. If a is the name of an array that has been dimensioned (either explicitly or implicitly through initialization) and is not a formal parameter or undimensioned extern array, sizeof a gives the number of bytes required to store the elements in a.

If a is the name of a class, sizeof (a) gives the size of the data structure needed to hold an instance of a.

The type of the integer produced by the sizeof operator is size_t, which is defined in the standard header file <stddef.h>.

If a is a variable length array, then the expression is evaluated at runtime; otherwise, it is evaluated at compile time and can be used in constant expressions (refer to the section "Constant Expressions").

Comma Operator

Given that

a, b	are expressions;

the expression

a, b	causes a to be evaluated and then b to be evaluated. The type and value of the expression are that of b.

Basic Operations with Arrays

Given that

a	is declared as an array of *n* elements;
i	is an expression of any integer data type;
v	is an expression;

the expression

a[0]	references the first element of a;
a[n - 1]	references the last element of a;
a[i]	references element number i of a;
a[i] = v	stores the value of v into a[i].

In each case, the type of the result is the type of the elements contained in a. See the section "Basic Operations with Pointers" for a summary of operations with pointers and arrays.

Basic Operations with Structures[3]

Given that

x	is a modifiable lvalue expression of type struct s;
y	is an expression of type struct s;
m	is the name of one of the members of the structure s;
obj	is any object;
M	is any method;
v	is an expression;

the expression

x	references the entire structure and is of type struct s;
y.m	references the member m of the structure y and is of the type declared for the member m;
x.m = v	assigns v to the member m of x and is of the type declared for the member m;

3. This also applies to unions.

x = y	assigns y to x and is of type struct s;
f (y)	calls the function f, passing contents of the structure y as the argument (inside f, the formal parameter must be declared to be of type struct s);
[obj M: y]	invokes the method M on the object obj, passing the contents of the structure y as the argument (inside the method, the parameter must be declared to be of type struct s);
return y;	returns the structure y (the return type declared for the function or method must be struct s)

Basic Operations with Pointers

Given that

x	is an lvalue expression of type t;
pt	is a modifiable lvalue expression of type "pointer to t";
v	is an expression;

the expression

&x	produces a pointer to x and has type "pointer to t";
pt = &x	sets pt pointing to x and has type "pointer to t";
pt = 0	assigns the null pointer to pt;
pt == 0	tests whether pt is null;
*pt	references the value pointed to by pt and has type t;
*pt = v	stores the value of v into the location pointed to by pt and has type t.

Pointers to Arrays

Given that

a	is an array of elements of type t;
pa1	is a modifiable lvalue expression of type "pointer to t" that points to an element in a;
pa2	is an lvalue expression of type "pointer to t" that points to an element in a, or to one past the last element in a;
v	is an expression;
n	is an integral expression;

the expression

a, &a, &a[0]	each produces a pointer to the first element;
&a[n]	produces a pointer to element number n of a and has type "pointer to t";
*pa1	references the element of a that pa1 points to and has type t;
*pa1 = v	stores the value of v into the element pointed to by pa1 and has type t;
++pa1	sets pa1 pointing to the next element of a, no matter which type of elements is contained in a, and has type "pointer to t";

`--pa1`	sets `pa1` pointing to the previous element of a, no matter which type of elements is contained in a, and has type "pointer to *t*";
`*++pa1`	increments `pa1` and then references the value in a that `pa1` points to and has type *t*;
`*pa1++`	references the value in a that `pa1` points to before incrementing `pa1` and has type *t*;
`pa1 + n`	produces a pointer that points n elements further into a than `pa1` and has type "pointer to *t*";
`pa1 - n`	produces a pointer to a that points n elements previous to that pointed to by `pa1` and has type "pointer to *t*";
`*(pa1 + n) = v`	stores the value of v into the element pointed to by `pa1 + n` and has type *t*;
`pa1 < pa2`	tests whether `pa1` is pointing to an earlier element in a than is `pa2` and has type `int` (any relational operators can be used to compare two pointers);
`pa2 - pa1`	produces the number of elements in a contained between the pointers `pa2` and `pa1` (assuming that `pa2` points to an element further in a than `pa1`) and has integer type;
`a + n`	produces a pointer to element number n of a, has type "pointer to *t*," and is in all ways equivalent to the expression `&a[n]`;
`*(a + n)`	references element number n of a, has type *t*, and is in all ways equivalent to the expression `a[n]`.

The actual type of the integer produced by subtracting two pointers is specified by `ptrdiff_t`, which is defined in the standard header file `<stddef.h>`.

Pointers to Structures

Given that

x	is an lvalue expression of type `struct s`;
ps	is a modifiable lvalue expression of type "pointer to `struct s`";
m	is the name of a member of the structure s and is of type *t*;
v	is an expression;

the expression

`&x`	produces a pointer to x and is of type "pointer to `struct s`";
`ps = &x`	sets ps pointing to x and is of type "pointer to `struct s`";
`ps->m`	references member m of the structure pointed to by ps and is of type *t*;
`(*ps).m`	also references this member and is in all ways equivalent to the expression `ps->m`;
`ps->m = v`	stores the value of v into the member m of the structure pointed to by ps and is of type *t*.

Compound Literals

A *compound literal* is a type name enclosed in parentheses followed by an initialization list. It creates an unnamed value of the specified type, which has scope limited to the block in which it is created, or global scope if defined outside of any block. In the latter case, the initializers must all be constant expressions.

As an example,

```
(struct point) {.x = 0, .y = 0}
```

is an expression that produces a structure of type `struct point` with the specified initial values. This can be assigned to another `struct point` structure, like so:

```
origin = (struct point) {.x = 0, .y = 0};
```

Or, it can be passed to a function or method expecting an argument of `struct point`, like so:

```
moveToPoint ((struct point) {.x = 0, .y = 0});
```

Types other than structures can be defined as well—for example, if `intPtr` is of type `int *`, the statement

```
intPtr = (int [100]) {[0] = 1, [50] = 50, [99] = 99 };
```

(which can appear anywhere in the program) sets `intptr` pointing to an array of 100 integers, whose 3 elements are initialized as specified.

If the size of the array is not specified, it is determined by the initializer list.

Conversion of Basic Data Types

The Objective-C language converts operands in arithmetic expressions in a predefined order, known as the *usual arithmetic conversions*:

1. If either operand is of type `long double`, the other is converted to `long double` and that is the type of the result.

2. If either operand is of type `double`, the other is converted to `double` and that is the type of the result.

3. If either operand is of type `float`, the other is converted to `float` and that is the type of the result.

4. If either operand is of type `_Bool`, `char`, `short int`, `int` bit field, or an enumerated data type, it is converted to `int`, if an `int` can fully represent its range of values; otherwise, it is converted to `unsigned int`. If both operands are of the same type, that is the type of the result.

5. If both operands are signed or both are unsigned, the smaller integer type is converted to the larger integer type and that is the type of the result.

6. If the unsigned operand is equal in size or larger than the signed operand, the signed operand is converted to the type of the unsigned operand and that is the type of the result.

7. If the signed operand can represent all the values in the unsigned operand, the latter is converted to the type of the former if it can fully represent its range of values, and that is the type of the result.

8. If this step is reached, both operands are converted to the unsigned type corresponding to the type of the signed type.

Step 4 is known more formally as *integral promotion*.

Conversion of operands is well behaved in most situations, although the following points should be noted:

1. Conversion of a `char` to an `int` can involve sign extension on some machines, unless the `char` is declared as `unsigned`.

2. Conversion of a signed integer to a longer integer results in extension of the sign to the left; conversion of an unsigned integer to a longer integer results in zero fill to the left.

3. Conversion of any value to a `_Bool` results in 0 if the value is zero and 1 otherwise.

4. Conversion of a longer integer to a shorter one results in truncation of the integer on the left.

5. Conversion of a floating-point value to an integer results in truncation of the decimal portion of the value. If the integer is not large enough to contain the converted floating-point value, the result is not defined, as is the result of converting a negative floating-point value to an unsigned integer.

6. Conversion of a longer floating-point value to a shorter one might or might not result in rounding before the truncation occurs.

Storage Classes and Scope

The term *storage class* refers to the manner in which memory is allocated by the compiler in the case of variables and to the scope of a particular function or method definition. Storage classes are `auto`, `static`, `extern`, and `register`. A storage class can be omitted in a declarartion and a default storage class will be assigned, as discussed next.

The term *scope* refers to the extent of the meaning of a particular identifier within a program. An identifier defined outside any function, method, or statement block (herein referred to as a *BLOCK*) can be referenced anywhere subsequent in the file. Identifiers defined within a BLOCK are local to that BLOCK and can locally redefine an identifier defined outside it. Label names are known throughout the BLOCK, as are formal parameter names. Labels, instance variables, structure and structure member names, union and union member names, and enumerated type names do not have to be distinct from each other or from variable, function, or method names. However, enumeration identifiers do have to be distinct from variable names and from other enumeration identifiers defined within the same scope. Class names have global scope and so must be distinct from other variables and type names with the same scope.

Functions

If a storage class is specified when a function is defined, it must be either `static` or `extern`. Functions that are declared `static` can be referenced only from within the same file that contains the function. Functions specified as `extern` (or that have no class specified) can be called by functions or methods from other files.

Variables

Table B.5 summarizes the various storage classes that can be used in declaring variables as well as their scopes and methods of initialization.

Table B.5   **Variables: Summary of Storage Classes, Scope, and Initialization.**

If storage class is	And variable is declared	Then it can be referenced	And be initialized with	Comments
`static`	Outside any BLOCK	Anywhere within the file	Constant expression only	Variables are initialized only once at the start of program execution; values are retained through BLOCKs; the default value is 0
	Inside a BLOCK	Within the BLOCK		
`extern`	Outside any BLOCK	Anywhere within the file	Constant expression only	Variable must be declared in at least one place without the `extern` keyword, or in one place using the keyword `extern` and assigned an initial value
	Inside a BLOCK	Within the BLOCK		
`auto`	Inside a BLOCK	Within the BLOCK	Any valid expression	Variable is initialized each time the BLOCK is entered; no default value
`register`	Inside a BLOCK	Within the BLOCK	Any valid expression	Assignment to `register` not guaranteed; varying restrictions on types of variables that can be declared; cannot take the address of a `register` variable; initialized each time BLOCK is entered; no default value
`omitted`	Outside any BLOCK	Anywhere within the file or by other files that contain appropriate declarations	Constant expressions only	This declaration can appear in only one place; the variable is initialized at the start of program execution; the default value is 0;
	Inside a BLOCK	(See `auto`)	(See `auto`)	it defaults to `auto`

Instance Variables

Instance variables can be accessed by any instance method defined for the class, either in the `interface` section that explicitly defines the variable or in categories created for the class. Inherited instance variables can also be accessed directly without any special declarations. Class methods do not have access to instance variables.

The special directives `@private`, `@protected`, and `@public` can be used to control the scope of an instance variable. After these directives appear, they remain in effect until the closing curly brace ending the declaration of the instance variables is encountered or until another of the three listed directives is used. For example

```
@interface  Point: Object
{
@private
   int internalID;
@protected
   float x;
   float y;
@public
   BOOL valid;
}
```

begins an interface declaration for a class called `Point` containing four instance variables. The `internalID` variable is `private`, the `x` and `y` variables are `protected` (the default), and the `valid` variable is public.

These directives are summarized in Table B.6.

Table B.6 **Scope of Instance Variables**

If variable is declared after this directive...	...then it can be referenced...	Comments
`@protected`	By instance methods in the class, instance methods in subclasses, and instance methods in category extensions to the class	This is the default.
`@private`	By instance methods in the class and instance methods in any category extensions to the class, but not by any subclasses	This restricts access to the class itself.
`@public`	By instance methods in the class, instance methods in subclasses, and instance methods in category extensions to the class; it can also be accessed from other functions or methods by applying the structure pointer indirection operator (->) to an instance of the class followed by the name of the instance variable (as in `myFract->numerator`)	This should not be used unless necessary; it defeats the notion of data encapsulation.

Functions

This section summarizes the syntax and operation of functions.

Function Definition

General Format:

```
returnType  name ( type1 param1, type2 param2, .. )
{
    variableDeclarations

    programStatement
    programStatement
    ...
    return expression;
}
```

The function called *name* is defined, which returns a value of type *returnType* and has formal parameters *param1*, *param2*, ... *param1* is declared to be of type *type1*, *param2* of type *type2*, and so on.

Local variables are typically declared at the beginning of the function, but that's not required. They can be declared anywhere, in which case their access is limited to statements appearing after their declaration in the function.

If the function does not return a value, *returnType* is specified as void.

If just void is specified inside the parentheses, the function takes no arguments. If .. is used as the last (or only) parameter in the list, the function takes a variable number of arguments, as in the following:

```
int printf (char *format, ...)
{
  ...
}
```

Declarations for single-dimensional array arguments do not have to specify the number of elements in the array. For multidimensional arrays, the size of each dimension except the first must be specified.

See the section "The return Statement" for a discussion of the return statement.

An older way of defining functions is still supported. The general format is

```
returnType  name (param1, param2, .. )
param_declarations
{
    variableDeclarations
    programStatement
    programStatement
    ...
    return expression;
}
```

Here, just the parameter names are listed inside the parentheses. If no arguments are expected, nothing appears between the left and right parentheses. The type of each parameter is declared outside the parentheses and before the opening curly brace of the function definition. For example

```
unsigned int rotate (value, n)
unsigned int value;
int n;
{
  ...
}
```

defines a function called `rotate` that takes two arguments called `value` and n. The first argument is an `unsigned int`, and the second is an `int`.

The keyword `inline` can be placed in front of a function definition as a hint to the compiler. Some compilers replace the function call with the actual code for the function itself, thus providing for faster execution. An example is shown here:

```
inline int min (int a, int b)
{
  return ( a < b ? a : b);
}
```

Function Call

General Format:

```
name ( arg1, arg2, .. )
```

The function called *name* is called and the values *arg1*, *arg2*, ... are passed as arguments to the function. If the function takes no arguments, just the open and closed parentheses are specified (as in `initialize ()`).

If you are calling a function that is defined after the call, or in another file, you should include a prototype declaration for the function, which has the following general format:

```
returnType name (type1 param1, type2 param2, .. );
```

This tells the compiler the function's return type, the number of arguments it takes, and the type of each argument. As an example, the line

```
long double power (double x, int n);
```

declares power to be a function that returns a `long double` and that takes two arguments—the first of which is a `double` and the second of which is an `int`. The argument names inside the parentheses are actually dummy names and can be omitted if desired, so

```
long double power (double, int);
```

works just as well.

If the compiler has previously encountered the function definition or a prototype declaration for the function, the type of each argument is automatically converted (where possible) to match the type expected by the function when the function is called.

If neither the function's definition nor a prototype declaration has been encountered, the compiler assumes the function returns a value of type int and automatically converts all float arguments to type double and performs integral promotion on any integer arguments as outlined in 5.17. Other function arguments are passed without conversion.

Functions that take a variable number of arguments must be declared as such. Otherwise, the compiler is at liberty to assume the function takes a fixed number of arguments based on the number actually used in the call.

If the function was defined with the old-style format (refer to the section "Function Definition"), a declaration for the function takes the following format:

```
returnType name ();
```

Arguments to such functions are converted, as described in the previous paragraph.

A function whose return type is declared as void causes the compiler to flag any calls to that function that try to make use of a returned value.

All arguments to a function are passed by value; therefore, their values cannot be changed by the function. If, however, a pointer is passed to a function, the function can change values referenced by the pointer, but it still cannot change the value of the pointer variable itself.

Function Pointers

A function name, without a following set of parentheses, produces a pointer to that function. The address operator can also be applied to a function name to produce a pointer to it.

If fp is a pointer to a function, the corresponding function can be called either by writing

```
fp ()
```

   or

```
(*fp) ()
```

If the function takes arguments, they can be listed inside the parentheses.

Classes

This section summarizes the syntax and semantics associated with classes.

Class Definition

A class definition consists of declaring the instance variables and methods in an interface section and defining the code for each method in an implementation section.

Interface Section

General Format:

```
@interface className : parentClass <protocol, …>
{
    instanceVariableDeclarations
}
 methodDeclaration
 methodDeclaration
   ...
@end
```

The class *className* is declared with the parent class *parentClass*. If *className* also adopts one or more formal protocols, the protocol names are listed inside a pair of angular brackets after *parentClass*. In that case, the corresponding implementation section must contain definitions for all such methods in the listed protocol(s).

If the colon and *parentClass* are omitted, a new root class is declared.

Instance Variable Declarations

The optional *instanceVariableDeclarations* section lists the type and name of each instance variable for the class. Each instance of *className* gets its own set of these variables, plus any variables inherited from *parentClass*. All such variables can be referenced directly by name either by instance methods defined in *className* or by any subclasses of *className*. If access has been restricted with a @private directive, subclasses cannot access the variables declared as such (refer to the section "Instance Variables").

Class methods do not have access to instance variables.

Method Declaration

General Format:

```
mType (returnType)  name₁ : (type1) param1 name₂ : (type2) param2, ...;
```

The method $name_1:name_2:..$ is declared, which returns a value of type *returnType* and has formal parameters *param1, param2, ... param1* is declared to be of type *type1, param2* is declared to be of type *type2*, and so on.

Any of the names after $name_1$ (meaning $name_2$, ...) can be omitted, in which case a colon is still used as a placeholder and becomes part of the method name (see the following example).

If *mType* is +, a class method is declared, but if *mType* is -, an instance method is declared.

If the declared method is inherited from a parent class, the parent's definition is overridden by the new definition. In such a case, the method from the parent class can still be accessed by sending a message to super.

Class methods are invoked when a corresponding message is sent to a class object, whereas instance methods are invoked when a corresponding message is sent to an instance of the class. Class methods and instance methods can have the same name.

The same method name can also be used by different classes. The capability of objects from different classes to respond to the same named method is known as *polymorphism*.

If the method does not return a value, `returnType` is void. If the function returns an id value, `returnType` can be omitted, although specifying id as the return type is better programming practice.

If , ... is used as the last (or only) parameter in the list, the method takes a variable number of arguments, as in

```
-(void) print: (NSSTRING *) format, ...
{
  ...
}
```

As an example of a class declaration, the interface declaration section

```
@interface Fraction: Object
{
  int numerator, denominator;
}
+(Fraction *) newFract;
-(void) setTo: (int) n : (int) d;
-(void) setNumerator: (int) n andDenominator: (int) d;
-(int)  numerator;
-(int)  denominator;
@end
```

declares a class called `Fraction` whose parent is `Object`. The `Fraction` class has two integer instance variables called `numerator` and `denominator`. It also has one class method called `newFract`, which returns a `Fraction` object. It has two instance methods called `setTo::` and `setNumerator:andDenominator:`, each of which takes two arguments and does not return a value. It also has two instance methods called `numerator` and `denominator` that take no arguments and return an int.

Implementation Section

General Format:

```
@implementation className;
 methodDefinition
 methodDefinition
   ...
@end
```

The class called `className` is defined. The parent class and instance variables are not typically redeclared in the implementation section (although they can be) because they have been previously declared in the interface section.

Unless the methods for a category are being implemented (see the section "Category Definition"), all the methods declared in the interface section must be defined in the implementation section. If one or more protocols were listed in the interface section, all the protocols' methods must be defined—either implicitly through inheritance or explicitly by definition in the implementation section.

Each *methodDefinition* contains the code that will be executed when the method is invoked.

Method Definition

General Format:

```
mType (returnType)  name₁ : (type1) param1 : name₂ (type2) param2, ...
{
    variableDeclarations

    programStatement
    programStatement
    ...
    return expression;
}
```

The method *name₁:name₂:...* is defined, which returns a value of type *returnType* and has formal parameters *param1, param2, ... param1* is declared to be of type *type1, param2* is declared to be of type *type2*, and so on. If *mType* is +, a class method is defined; if *mType* is –, an instance method is defined. This method declaration must be consistent with the corresponding method declaration from the interface section or from a previously defined protocol definition.

An instance method can reference the class's instance variables and any variables it has inherited directly by name. If a class method is being defined, it cannot reference any instance variables.

The identifier `self` can be used inside a method to reference the object on which the method was invoked—that is, the *receiver* of the message.

The identifier `super` can be used inside a method to reference the parent class of the object on which the method was invoked.

If *returnType* is not `void`, one or more `return` statements with expressions of type *returnType* must appear in the method definition. If *returnType* is `void`, use of a `return` statement is optional, and if used, it cannot contain a value to return.

As an example of a method definition

```
-(void) setNumerator: (int) n andDenominator: (int) d
{
    numerator = n;
    denominator = d;
}
```

defines a `setNumerator:andDenominator:` method in accordance with its declaration (refer to the section "Method Declaration"). The method sets its two instance variables to the supplied arguments and does not execute a return (although it could) because the method is declared to return no value.

Declarations for single-dimensional array arguments do not have to specify the number of elements in the array. For multidimensional arrays, the size of each dimension except the first must be specified.

Local variables can be declared inside a method and are typically declared at the start of the method definition. Automatic local variables are allocated when the method is invoked and deallocated when the method is exited.

See the section "The `return` Statement" for a discussion of the `return` statement.

Category Definition

General Format:

```
@interface className (categoryName) <protocol,…>
 methodDeclaration
 methodDeclaration
    . . .
@end
```

This defines the category *categoryName* for the class specified by *className* with the associated listed methods. If one or more protocols are listed, the category adopts the listed protocol(s).

The compiler must know about *className* through a previous `@interface` section declaration for the class.

You can define as many categories as you want in as many different source files as you want. The listed methods become part of the class and are inherited by subclasses.

Categories are uniquely defined by *className/categoryName* pairs. For example, in a given program there can be only one `NSArray` (`Private`) category. However, individual category names can be reused. So, a given program can include an `NSArray` (`Private`) category and an `NSString` (`Private`) category, and both categories will be distinct from each other.

You do not need to implement the methods defined in a category that you do not intend to use.

A category can only extend the definition of a class with additional methods, or it can override existing methods in the class. It cannot define any new instance variables for the class.

If more than one category declares a method with the same name for the same class, it is not defined which method will be executed when invoked.

As an example

```
#import "Complex.h"
@interface Complex (ComplexOps)
-(Complex *) abs;
-(Complex *) exp;
-(Complex *) log;
-(Complex *) sqrt;
@end
```

defines a category for the `Complex` class called `ComplexOps`, with four instance methods. Presumably, a corresponding implementation section appears somewhere that implements one or more of these methods:

```
#import "ComplexOps.h"
@implementation Complex (ComplexOps)
-(Complex *) abs
{
  ...
}
-(Complex *) exp
{
  ...
}
-(Complex *) log
{
  ...
}
-(Complex *) sqrt
{
  ...
}
@end
```

A category that defines methods meant for other subclasses to implement is known as an *informal* protocol or *abstract* category. Unlike formal protocols, the compiler does not perform any checks for conformance to an informal protocol. At runtime, an object might or might not test for conformance to an informal protocol on an individual method basis. For example, one method might be required at runtime, whereas another method in the same protocol might not.

Protocol Definition
General Format:

```
@protocol protocolName <protocol, ...>
   methodDeclaration
   methodDeclaration
 ...
 @end
```

The protocol called `protocolName` is defined with associated methods. If other protocols are listed, `protocolName` also adopts the listed protocols.

This definition is known as a formal protocol definition.

A class conforms to the `protocolName` protocol if it defines or inherits all the methods declared in the protocol plus all the methods of any other protocols that are listed. The compiler checks for conformance and generates a warning if a class does not

conform to a declared formal protocol. Objects might or might not be tested for conformance to a formal protocol at runtime.

Protocols are often not associated with any particular class but provide a way to
define a common interface that is shared among classes.

Special Type Modifiers

The method parameters and return type declared in protocols can use the type qualifiers
listed in Table B.7. These qualifiers are used for distributed object applications.

Table B.7   **Special Protocol Type Modifiers**

Qualifier	Meaning
in	The argument references an object whose value will be changed by the sender and sent (that is, copied) back to the receiver.
out	The argument references an object whose value will be changed by the receiver and sent back to the sender.
inout	The argument references an object whose value will be set by both the sender and the receiver and will be sent back and forth; this is the default.
oneway	It's used for return type declarations; typically (oneway void) it's used to specify that the invoker of this method does not have to wait for a return value—that is, the method can execute asynchronously.
bycopy	The argument or return value is to be copied.
byref	The argument or return value is passed by reference and not copied.

Object Declaration

General Format:

```
className *var1, *var2, ...;
```

This defines *var1*, *var2*, ... to be objects from the class *className*. Note that this
declares pointer variables and does not reserve space for the actual data contained in
each object. The declaration

```
Fraction *myFract;
```

defines myFract as a Fraction object or, technically, as a pointer to one. To allocate
the actual space for the data structure of a Fraction, the alloc or new method is typically invoked on the class, like so:

```
myFract = [Fraction alloc];
```

This causes enough space to be reserved for a Fraction object and a pointer to it to
be returned and assigned to myFract. The variable myFract is often referred to as an
object or as an *instance* of the Fraction class. As the alloc method in the root object
is defined, a newly allocated object has all its instance variables set to 0. However, that

does not mean the object has been properly initialized and an initialization method (like init) should be invoked on the object before it is used.

Because the myFract variable has been explicitly declared as an object from the Fraction class, the variable is said to be *statically* typed. The compiler can check the use of statically typed variables for consistency by consulting the class definition for proper use of methods and their arguments and return types.

id **Object Declaration**

General Format:

```
id <protocol,…> var1, var2, …;
```

This declares *var1*, *var2*, ... to be objects from an indeterminate class that conform to the protocol(s) listed in the angular brackets. The protocol list is optional.

Objects from any class can be assigned to id variables, and vice versa. If one or more protocols is listed, the compiler checks that methods used from the listed protocols on any of the declared variables are used in a consistent manner—that is, consistent with respect to argument and return types for the methods declared in the formal protocol.

For example, in the statements

```
id <MathOps> number;
  ...
result = [number add: number2];
```

the compiler checks whether the MathOps protocol defines an add: method. If it does, it then checks for consistency with respect to the argument and return types for that method. So, if the add: method takes an integer argument and you are passing it a Fraction object above, the compiler complains.

The system keeps track of the class to which each object belongs; therefore, at runtime it can determine the class of an object and then select the correct method to invoke. These two processes are known as *dynamic typing* and *dynamic binding*, respectively.

Message Expressions

Format 1:

```
[receiver  name₁: arg1 name₂: arg2, name₃: arg3 .. ]
```

The method $name_1:name_2:name_3$ ... from the class specified by *receiver* is invoked and the values *arg1*, *arg2*, ... are passed as arguments. This is called a *message expression*. The value of the expression is the value returned by the method, or void if the method is declared as such and returns no value. The type of the expression is that of the type declared for the method invoked.

Format 2:

```
[receiver name];
```

If a method takes no arguments, this format is used to invoked the method name from the class specified by receiver.

If `receiver` is an `id` type, the compiler looks among the declared classes for a definition or inherited definition of the specified method. If no such definition is found, the compiler issues a warning that the receiver might not respond to the specified message. It further assumes the method returns a value of type id and converts any float arguments to type double and performs integral promotion on any integer arguments as outlined earlier in the section "Conversion of Basic Data Types." Other method arguments are passed without conversion.

If *receiver* is a *class* object (which can be created by simply specifying the class name), the specified *class* method is invoked. Otherwise, *receiver* is an instance of a class and the corresponding instance method is invoked.

If *receiver* is a statically typed variable or expression, the compiler looks in the class definition for the method (or for any inherited methods) and converts any arguments (where possible) to match the expected arguments for the method. So, a method expecting a floating value that is passed an integer has that argument automatically converted when the method is invoked.

If *receiver* is a null object pointer—that is, `nil`—it can be sent messages. If the method associated with the message returns an object, the value of the message expression is `nil`. If the method does not return an object, the value of the expression is not defined.

If the same method is defined in more than one class (either by explicit definition or from inheritance), the compiler checks for consistency for argument and return types among the classes.

All arguments to a method are passed by value; therefore, their values cannot be changed by the method. If a pointer is passed to a method, the method can change values referenced by the pointer, but it still cannot change the value of the pointer itself.

Statements

A program statement is any valid expression (usually an assignment or a function call) that is immediately followed by a semicolon, or it is one of the special statements described in the following. A *label* can optionally precede any statement and consists of an identifier followed immediately by a colon (see the `goto` statement).

Compound Statements

Program statements contained within a pair of braces are known collectively as a *compound* statement or *block* and can appear anywhere in the program that a single statement is permitted. A block can have its own set of variable declarations, which override any similarly named variables defined outside the block. The scope of such local variables is the block in which they are defined.

The `break` Statement

General Format:

```
break;
```

Execution of a `break` statement from within a `for`, `while`, `do`, or `switch` statement causes execution of that statement to be immediately terminated. Execution continues with the statement that immediately follows the loop or `switch`.

The `continue` Statement

General Format:

```
continue;
```

Execution of the `continue` statement from within a loop causes any statements that follow the `continue` in the loop to be skipped. Execution of the loop otherwise continues as normal.

The `do` Statement

General Format:

```
do
 programStatement
while ( expression );
```

programStatement is executed as long as *expression* evaluates to nonzero. Note that, because *expression* is evaluated each time after the execution of *programStatement*, it is guaranteed that *programStatement* will be executed at least once.

The `for` Statement

General Format:

```
for ( expression_1; expression_2; expression_3 )
  programStatement
```

expression_1 is evaluated once when execution of the loop begins. Next, *expression_2* is evaluated. If its value is nonzero, *programStatement* is executed and then *expression_3* is evaluated. Execution of *programStatement* and the subsequent evaluation of *expression_3* continue as long as the value of *expression_2* is nonzero. Because *expression_2* is evaluated each time before *programStatement* is executed, *programStatement* might never be executed if the value of *expression_2* is 0 when the loop is first entered.

Variables local to the `for` loop can be declared in *expression_1*. The scope of such variables is the scope of the `for` loop. For example

```
for ( int i = 0; i < 100; ++i)
  . . .
```

declares the integer variable i and sets its initial value to 0 when the loop begins. The variable can be accessed by any statements inside the loop, but it is not accessible after the loop is terminated.

The goto Statement

General Format:

```
goto identifier;
```

Execution of the goto causes control to be sent directly to the statement labeled *identifier*. The labeled statement must be located in the same function or method as the goto.

The if Statement

Format 1:

```
if ( expression )
  programStatement
```

If the result of evaluating *expression* is nonzero, *programStatement* is executed; otherwise, it is skipped.

Format 2:

```
if ( expression )
  programStatement_1
else
  programStatement_2
```

If the value of *expression* is nonzero, *programStatement_1* is executed; otherwise, *programStatement_2* is executed. If *programStatement_2* is another if statement, an if-else if chain is affected, like so:

```
if ( expression_1 )
  programStatement_1
else if ( expression_2 )
  programStatement_2
  . . .
else
  programStatement_n
```

An else clause is always associated with the last if statement that does not contain an else. Braces can be used to change this association if necessary.

The null Statement

General Format:

```
;
```

Execution of a null statement has no effect and is used primarily to satisfy the requirement of a program statement in a for, do, or while loop. The following statement copies a character string pointed to by from to one pointed to by to:

```
while ( *to++ = *from++ )
    ;
```

In this statement, the null statement is used to satisfy the requirement that a program statement appear after the looping expression of the while.

The return Statement

Format 1:

```
return;
```

Execution of the return statement causes program execution to be immediately returned to the calling function or method. This format can be used only to return from a function or method that does not return a value.

If execution proceeds to the end of a function or method and a return statement is not encountered, it returns as if a return statement of this form had been executed. Therefore, in such a case, no value is returned.

Format 2:

```
return expression;
```

The value of *expression* is returned to the calling function or method. If the type of *expression* does not agree with the return type declared in the function or method declaration, its value is automatically converted to the declared type before it is returned.

The switch Statement

General Format:

```
switch ( expression )
{
  case constant_1:
    programStatement
    programStatement
      . . .
    break;
  case constant_2:
    programStatement
    programStatement
```

```
   ...
   break;
  ...
 case constant_n:
   programStatement
   programStatement
    ...
   break;
  default:
   programStatement
   programStatement
    ...
   break;
}
```

expression is evaluated and compared against the constant expression values
constant_1, *constant_2*, ..., *constant_n*. If the value of *expression* matches one
of these case values, the program statements that immediately follow are executed. If no
case value matches the value of *expression*, the `default` case, if included, is executed. If
the `default` case is not included, no statements contained in the `switch` are executed.

The result of the evaluation of *expression* must be of integral type and no two
cases can have the same value. Omitting the `break` statement from a particular case
causes execution to continue into the next case.

The `while` Statement

General Format:

```
while ( expression )
  programStatement
```

programStatement is executed as long as the value of *expression* is nonzero.
Because *expression* is evaluated each time before the execution of
programStatement, *programStatement* might never be executed.

The Preprocessor

The preprocessor analyzes the source file before the compiler proper sees the code. Here
is what the preprocessor does:

1. It replaces trigraph sequences by their equivalents (refer to the section
   "Compound Statements").

2. It joins any lines that end with a backslash character (\\) together into a single line.

3. It divides the program into a stream of tokens.

4. It removes comments, replacing them by a single space.

5. It processes preprocessor directives (see the section "Preprocessor Directives") and
   expands macros.

Trigraph Sequences

To handle non-ASCII character sets, the following three-character sequences (called *trigraphs*) are recognized and treated specially wherever they occur inside a program (as well as inside character strings):

Trigraph	Meaning	Trigraph	Meaning
??=	#	??/	\
??(	[	??'	^
??)	]	??!	|
??<	{	??-	~
??>	}		

Preprocessor Directives

All preprocessor directives begin with the character #, which must be the first nonwhitespace character on the line. The # can be optionally followed by one or more space or tab characters.

The #define Directive

Format 1:

```
#define name text
```

This defines the identifier name to the preprocessor and associates with it whatever *text* appears after the first blank space after *name* to the end of the line. Subsequent use of *name* in the program causes *text* to be substituted directly into the program at that point.

Format 2:

```
#define name(param_1, param_2, ..., param_n) text
```

The macro *name* is defined to take arguments as specified by *param_1*, *param_2*, ..., *param_n*, each of which is an identifier. Subsequent use of *name* in the program with an argument list causes *text* to be substituted directly into the program at that point, with the arguments of the macro call replacing all occurrences of the corresponding parameters inside *text*.

If the macro takes a variable number of arguments, three dots are used at the end of the argument list. The remaining arguments in the list are collectively referenced in the macro definition by the special identifier   VA ARGS__. As an example, the following defines a macro called myPrintf to take a variable number of arguments:

```
#define myPrintf(...)  printf ("DEBUG: " __VA_ARGS__);
```

Legitimate macro uses would include

```
myPrintf ("Hello world!\n");
```

as well as

```
myPrintf ("i = %i, j = %i\n", i, j);
```

If a definition requires more than one line, each line to be continued must be ended with a backslash character. After a name has been defined, it can be used anywhere in the file.

The # operator is permitted in #define directives that take arguments and is followed by the name of an argument to the macro. The preprocessor puts double quotation marks around the actual value passed to the macro when it's invoked. That is, it turns it into a character string. For example, the definition

```
#define printint(x) printf (# x " = %d\n", x)
```

with the call

```
printint (count);
```

is expanded by the preprocessor into

```
printf ("count" " = %i\n", count);
```

or, equivalently

```
printf ("count = %i\n", count);
```

The preprocessor puts a \ character in front of any " or \ characters when performing this stringizing operation. So, with the definition

```
#define str(x) # x
```

the call

```
str (The string "\t" contains a tab)
```

expands to the following:

```
"The string \"\\t\" contains a tab"
```

The ## operator is also allowed in #define directives that take arguments. It is preceded (or followed) by the name of an argument to the macro. The preprocessor takes the value passed when the macro is invoked and creates a single token from the argument to the macro and the token that follows (or precedes) it. For example, the macro definition

```
#define printx(n) printf ("%i\n", x ## n );
```

with the call

```
printx (5)
```

produces the following:

```
printf ("%i\n", x5);
```

The definition

```
#define printx(n) printf ("x" # n " = %i\n", x ## n );
```

with the call

```
printx(10)
```

produces

```
printf ("x10 = %i\n", x10);
```

after substitution and concatenation of the character strings.
Spaces are not required around the # and ## operators.

The #error Directive

General Format:

```
#error text
    . . .
```

The specified *text* is written as an error message by the preprocessor.

The #if Directive

Format 1:

```
#if constant_expression
    . . .
#endif
```

The value of *constant_expression* is evaluated. If the result is nonzero, all program lines up until the #endif directive are processed; otherwise, they are automatically skipped and are not processed by the preprocessor or the compiler.

Format 2:

```
#if constant_expression_1
    . . .
#elif constant_expression_2
    . . .
#elif constant_expression_n
    . . .
#else
    . . .
#endif
```

If *constant_expression_1* is nonzero, all program lines up until the #elif are processed and the remaining lines up to the #endif are skipped. Otherwise, if *constant_expression_2* is nonzero, all program lines up until the next #elif are processed and the remaining lines up to the #endif are skipped. If none of the constant expressions evaluates to nonzero, the lines after the #else (if included) are processed.

The special operator defined can be used as part of the constant expression, so

```
#if defined (DEBUG)
  ...
#endif
```

causes the code between the #if and #endif to be processed if the identifier DEBUG has been previously defined (see also #ifdef in the next section). The parentheses are not necessary around the identifier, so

```
#if defined DEBUG
```

works just as well.

The #ifdef Directive

General Format:

```
#ifdef identifier
  ...
#endif
```

If the value of *identifier* has been previously defined (either through a #define or with the -D command-line option when the program was compiled), all program lines up until the #endif are processed; otherwise, they are skipped. As with the #if directive, #elif and #else directives can be used with a #ifdef directive.

The #ifndef Directive

General Format:

```
#ifndef identifier
  ...
#endif
```

If the value of *identifier* has not been previously defined, all program lines up until the #endif are processed; otherwise, they are skipped. As with the #if directive, #elif and #else directives can be used with a #ifndef directive.

The #import Directive[4]
Format 1:

```
#import "fileName"
```

If the file specified by *fileName* has been previously included in the program, this statement is skipped. Otherwise, the preprocessor searches an implementation-defined directory or directories first for the file *fileName*. Typically, the same directory that contains the source file is searched first, and if the file is not found there, a sequence of implementation-defined standard places is searched. After it's found, the contents of the file are included in the program at the precise point that the #import directive appears. Preprocessor directives contained within the included file are analyzed; therefore, an included file can itself contain other #import or #include directives.

Format 2:

```
#import <fileName>
```

If the file has not been previously included, the preprocessor searches for the specified file only in the standard places. Specifically, the current source directory is omitted from the search. The action taken after the file is found is otherwise identical to that described previously.

In either format, a previously defined name can be supplied and expansion will occur. So, the following sequence works:

```
#define ROOTOBJECT   <objc/Object.h>
   ...
#import ROOTOBJECT
```

The #include Directive
This behaves the same way as #import except no check is made for previous inclusion of the specified header file.

The #line Directive
General Format:

```
#line constant "fileName"
```

This directive causes the compiler to treat subsequent lines in the program as if the name of the source file were *fileName* and as if the line number of all subsequent lines began at *constant*. If *fileName* is not specified, the filename specified by the last #line directive, or the name of the source file (if no filename was previously specified), is used.

The #line directive is primarily used to control the filename and line number that are displayed whenever an error message is issued by the compiler.

4. As noted in the text, on non-Mac systems, the gcc compiler issues a warning message advising against the use of this statement and recommending the use of #include instead.

The #pragma **Directive**

General Format:

```
#pragma text
```

This causes the preprocessor to perform some implementation-defined action. For example, under the pragma

```
#pragma loop_opt(on)
```

causes special loop optimization to be performed on a particular compiler. If this pragma is encountered by a compiler that doesn't recognize the loop_opt pragma, it is ignored.

The special keyword STDC is used after the #pragma for special meaning. Current supported switches that can follow a #pragma STDC are FP_CONTRACT, FENV_ACCESS, and CX_LIMITED_RANGE.

The #undef **Directive**

General Format:

```
#undef identifier
```

The specified *identifier* becomes undefined to the preprocessor. Subsequent #ifdef or #ifndef directives behave as if the identifier were never defined.

The # **Directive**

This is a null directive and is ignored by the preprocessor.

Predefined Identifiers

The following identifiers are defined by the preprocessor:

Identifier	Meaning
__LINE__	Current line number being compiled
__FILE__	Name of the current source file being compiled
__DATE__	Date the file is being compiled, in the format "*Mmm dd yyyy*"
__TIME__	Time the file is being compiled, in the format "*hh:mm:ss*"
__STDC__	Defined as 1 if the compiler conforms to the ANSI standard and 0 if not
__STDC_HOSTED__	Defined as 1 if the implementation is hosted and 0 if not
__STDC_VERSION__	Defined as 199901L

Root Object Methods and Categories

Table B.8 summarizes the instance and class methods defined for the root object Object.

Table B.8   **Root** Object **Methods**

Method Type	Methods
Creation and copying methods	+new; +free; -free; +alloc; -copy; +allocFromZone: (void *) *zone*; -copyFromZone: (void *) *zone*; -(void *) zone;
Initialization methods	+ initialize; - init;
Introspection	+ class; +superclass; +(const char *) name; -class; -superclass; -(const char *) name; -(BOOL) isKindOf: *classObject*; -(BOOL) isMemberOf: *classObject*; -(BOOL) isKindOfClassNamed: (const char *) *className*; -(BOOL) isMemberOfClassNamed: (const char *) *className*; +(BOOL) instancesRespondTo: (SEL) *selector*; -(BOOL) respondsTo: *selector*; - (BOOL) conformsTo: (Protocol *) *protocol*; +(BOOL) conformsTo: (Protocol *) *protocol*;
Identifying and comparing instances	-self; - (unsigned int) hash;-(BOOL) isEqual: *object*;
Information about methods	-(struct objc_method_description *) descriptionForMethod: (SEL) *selector*; +(struct objc_method_description *) descriptionForInstanceMethod: (SEL) *selector*; -(IMP) methodFor: (SEL) *selector*; +(IMP) instanceMethodFor: (SEL) *selector*;

Table B.8 **Root** Object **Methods**

Method Type	Methods
Performing methods and forwarding	-perform: (SEL) *selector*;-perform: (SEL) *selector* with: *object*; -perform: (SEL) *selector* with: *object1* with: *object2*; -performv: (SEL) *selector* : (marg_list) *args*; -forward: (SEL) *selector* : (marg_list) *args*;
Posing	+poseAs: *classObject*;
Enforcing intentions	-subclassResponsibility: (SEL) *selector*; -notImplemented: (SEL) *selector*;
Error handling	-doesNotRecognize: (SEL) *selector*; -error: (const char *) *format*, ...;
Debugging	-(void) printForDebugger: (void *) *stream*;
Archiving	-awake;-read: (void *) *stream*; -write: (void *) *stream*; +setVersion: (int) *version*; +(int) version;

Table B.9 lists the informal protocols that are defined for the root object Object.

Table B.9 **Informal** Object **Protocols**

Protocol	Methods
Archiving	-startArchiving: (void *) *stream*; -finishUnarchiving;
Dynamic loading	+finishLoading: (struct mach_header *) *header*; +startUnloading;

C

Foundation Framework Headers

FOLLOWING IS A LIST OF THE STANDARD FOUNDATION framework header files distributed with Mac OS X v 10.2. These files can be found in the directory /System/Library/Frameworks/Foundation.framework/headers. Those header files marked with an asterisk (★) are not part of the standard GNUStep release. Note that GNUStep has its own extensions to the Foundation with filenames that begin with GS. These are not listed in this table.

It's useful just to read the list to see the types of capabilities supported by Foundation. Remember, you don't want to reinvent the wheel. Therefore, whenever you want to design a new class, see if there's one that already exists that fits the bill. If not, see whether you can subclass or make a composite class from one of the Foundation classes. That's part of the power of object-oriented programming.

Consult the Resources in Appendix E, "Resources," to obtain more information about the Foundation framework.

Header File	Description
Foundation.h	Master file; includes most of the other files in the Foundation header file directory.
NSAppleEventDescriptor.h★	Defines the NSAppleEventDescriptor class for working with Apple event descriptors.
NSAppleEventManager.h★	Defines the NSAppleEventManager class for registering event handlers and dispatching events to them.
NSAppleScript.h★	Defines the NSAppleScript class for loading, compiling, and executing AppleScript scripts.
NSArchiver.h	Defines the NSArchiver and NSUnarchiver concrete subclasses of NSCoder for archiving (encoding) and unarchiving (decoding) objects.
NSArray.h	Defines the NSArray and NSMutableArray classes for working with array objects.

Header File	Description
NSAttributedString.h	Defines the NSAttributedString and NSMutableAttributedString classes for managing strings that have attributes associated with characters in the strings.
NSAutoreleasePool.h	Defines the NSAutoreleasePool class for creating and managing autorelease pools.
NSBundle.h	Defines the NSBundle class for working with application resources during program execution.
NSByteOrder.h	Contains functions for doing byte swapping.
NSCalendarDate.h	Defines the NSCalenderDate class (subclass of NSDate) for working with dates in years, months, days, hours, minutes, and seconds.
NSCharacterSet.h	Definesthe NSCharacterSet and NSMutableCharacterSet classes for creating and manipulating character sets.
NSClassDescription.h	Defines the abstract class NSClassDescription for getting and registering the description for a class.
NSCoder.h	Defines the abstract class NSCoder for encoding and decoding objects. The concrete subclasses are NSArchiver, NSUnarchiver, and NSPortCoder. On Mac implementations, NSKeyedArchiver and NSUnkeyedArchiver are also concrete subclasses.
NSCompatibility.h*	Just imports the NSCoder.h header file.
NSConnection.h	Defines the NSConnection class for working with distributed objects; that is, communication between objects in different processes on the same system or over a network.
NSData.h	Defines the NSData and NSMutableData classes for managing storage areas (buffers) in memory.
NSDate.h	Defines the NSDate class and NSTimeInterval type for working with dates internally expressed as seconds since a reference date.
NSDateFormatter.h	Defines the NSDateFormatter class for formatting dates; concrete subclass of NSFormatter.
NSDebug.h	Defines the NSAutoreleasePoolDebugging category for debugging the autorelease pool as well as variables that can be used to assist in debugging programs.
NSDecimal.h	Contains the NSDecimal type and functions for performing decimal arithmetic; see also NSDecimalNumber.h.
NSDecimalNumber.h	Defines the NSDecimalNumber subclass of NSNumber for performing decimal arithmetic with a precision of at least 38 decimal digits.

Header File	Description
NSDictionary.h	Defines the `NSDictionary` and `NSMutableDictionary` classes for working with dictionary objects.
NSDistantObject.h	Defines the `NSDistantObject` class, subclass of `NSProxy`, for working with distributed objects.
NSDistributedLock.h	Defines the `NSDistributedLock` class for implementing a locking mechanism for distributed objects.
NSDistributed NotificationCenter.h	Defines the `NSDistributedNotificationCenter` class (subclass of `NSNotificationCenter`) for sending and receiving notifications with distributed objects.
NSEnumerator.h	Defines the `NSEnumerator` class for creating enumerations of arrays, dictionaries, and sets.
NSError.h*	Defines the `NSError` class for creating custom error descriptions.
NSException.h	Defines the `NSException` class for the custom handling of exceptions (abnormal interruptions of a program's execution).
NSFileHandle.h	Defines the `NSFileHandle` class for performing I/O operations with files, devices, and sockets.
NSFileManager.h	Defines the `NSFileManager` class for working with the file system and performing operations such as creating, copying, renaming, and removing files and directories. Also defines `NSDirectoryEnumerator` (subclass of `NSEnumerator`) for enumerating the contents of a directory.
NSFormatter.h	Defines the abstract class `NSFormatter`.
NSGeometry.h	Defines the `NSPoint`, `NSSize`, and `NSRect` types for working with (x, y) coordinates, sizes, and rectangles; also contains functions for manipulating these types.
NSHFSFileTypes.h★	Defines the functions for working with HFS file types.
NSHTTPCookie.h★	Defines the `NSHTTPCookie` class for working with cookies.
NSHTTPCookieStorage.h★	Defines the `NSHTTPCookieStorage` class, also for working with cookies.
NSHashTable.h	Defines functions for working with a hash table (type `NSHashTable`).
NSHost.h	Defines the class `NSHost` for obtaining information about systems on the network.
NSInvocation.h	Defines the `NSInvocation` class for use in message forwarding.
NSJavaSetup.h*	Defines the variables and functions for loading and working with the Java virtual machine.

Header File	Description
NSKeyValueCoding.h	Defines informal protocols for NSKeyValueCoding, NSKeyValueCodingExtras, and NSKeyValueCodingException.
NSKeyedArchiver.h*	Defines the concrete classes NSKeyedArchiver and NSKeyedUnarchiver (subclasses of NSCoder) for archiving (encoding) and unarchiving (decoding) objects using keyed archives.
NSLock.h	Defines the NSLock class for locking data or code shared by multithreaded applications.
NSMapTable.h	Defines the NSMapTable type and functions for creating and working with map tables.
NSMethodSignature.h	Defines the NSMethodSignature class for finding out information about a method.
NSNetServices.h*	Defines the NSNetService and NSNetServiceBrowser classes for publishing and searching for services and domains.
NSNotification.h	Defines the NSNotification and NSNotificationCenter classes for registering and posting notifications.
NSNotificationQueue.h	Defines the NSNotificationQueue class for queuing and dequeuing notifications.
NSNull.h	Defines the NSNull class, with method null, for creating a null object (can be added to collections as a valid object).
NSNumberFormatter.h	Defines the NSNumberFormatter class, the concrete subclass of NSFormatter, for controlling how numbers appear when converted to their textual representations.
NSObjCRuntime.h	Contains various definitions (such as nil and YES) and function definitions (such as NSStringFromClass).
NSObject.h	Defines the root NSObject classes and associated methods that are inherited by all subclasses.
NSObjectScripting.h*	Defines the NSScripting category for the NSObject class for working with the scriptable properties of an object.
NSPathUtilities.h	Defines the functions and NSString methods for manipulating pathnames and obtaining usernames, the temporary directory, and home directory paths.
NSPort.h	Defines the NSPort abstract class and concrete subclasses NSMachPort, NSMessagePort, and NSSocketPort for local and remote message sending.
NSPortCoder.h	Defines the NSPortCoder (concrete subclass of NSCoder); used by the distributed objects system.

Header File	Description
NSPortMessage.h	Defines the NSPortMessage class used by the distributed objects system for sending and receiving low-level messages.
NSPortNameServer.h	Defines the NSPortNameServer class used by the distributed objects system for port registration.
NSProcessInfo.h	Defines the NSProcessInfo class for obtaining information about the running process, such as its name and arguments, as well as other information such as the name and version of the operating system.
NSPropertyList.h*	Defines the NSPropertyListSerialization class for converting NSData, NSString, NSArray, NSDictionary, NSDate, and NSNumber objects into property lists and back again.
NSProtocolChecker.h	Defines the NSProtocolChecker class to filter messages sent among distributed objects.
NSProxy.h	Defines the abstract class NSProxy for working with objects that fill in for other objects; its concrete subclass is NSDistantObject.
NSRange.h	Defines the NSRange type and functions for creating and working with ranges.
NSRunLoop.h	Defines the NSRunLoop class for processing input events (such as from the mouse, keyboard, and so on).
NSScanner.h	Defines the abstract class NSScanner for parsing number and string tokens from NSString objects.
NSScriptClassDescription.h* NSScriptCoercionHandler.h* NSScriptCommand.h* NSScriptCommandDescription.h* NSScriptExecutionContext.h* NSScriptKeyValueCoding.h* NSScriptObjectSpecifiers.h* NSScriptStandardSuiteCommands.h* NSScriptSuiteRegistry.h* NSScriptWhoseTests.h*	These are all Mac OS X header files for working with Apple Script scripts.
NSSerialization.h	Defines the NSSerializer and NSDeserializer classes. On Mac OS X this is an obsolete header file that is superceded by the NSPropertyListSerialization class.
NSSet.h	Defines the NSSet, NSMutableSet, and NSCountedSet classes for working with set objects.
NSSpellServer.h*	Defines the NSSpellServer class for registering a spell checker for use by other applications.

Header File	Description
NSString.h	Defines the NSString and NSMutableString classes for working with string objects.
NSTask.h	Defines the NSTask class for running and monitoring another program as a child process.
NSThread.h	Defines the NSThread class for controlling the threaded execution of a program.
NSTimeZone.h	Defines the NSTimeZone class for accessing and setting time zones.
NSTimer.h	Defines the NSTimer class for creating and setting a timer and specifying the message to be sent to an object when the timer expires.
NSUndoManager.h	Defines the NSUndoManager class for managing Undo and Redo operations in an application.
NSURL.h	Defines the NSURL class for defining and manipulating URLs as objects.
NSURLAuthenticationChallenge.h★ NSURLCache.h★ NSURLConnection.h★ NSURLCredential.h★ NSURLCredentialStorage.h★ NSURLDownload.h★ NSURLError.h★ NSURLProtectionSpace.h★ NSURLProtocol.h★ NSURLRequest.h★ NSURLResponse.h★	These are all Mac-specific header files for working with URLs.
NSURLHandle.h	Defines the NSURLHandle class for uploading and downloading data specified by an NSURL object.
NSUserDefaults.h	Defines the NSUserDefaults class for accessing and modifying default user settings for an application.
NSUtilities.h	Just includes some other header files.
NSValue.h	Defines the NSValue and NSNumber subclasses for creating and working with numbers as objects.
NSZone.h	Defines the functions for working with memory zones.

Fraction and Address Book Examples

Hᴇʀᴇ, ꜰᴏʀ ʏᴏᴜʀ ʀᴇꜰᴇʀᴇɴᴄᴇ ᴘᴜʀᴘᴏꜱᴇꜱ, are the complete interface and implementation files for the fractions you worked with extensively in Part I, "The Objective-C Language," and the address book example you worked with throughout Part II, "The Foundation Framework." This includes the definitions for the Fraction, AddressCard, and AddressBook classes. You should implement these classes on your system. Also, extend the class definitions to make them more practical and powerful (for example, see exercises 2–7 at the end of Chapter 15, "Numbers, Strings, and Collections"). This is an excellent way for you to learn the language and become familiar with building programs, working with classes and objects, and (in the case of the address book) working with the Foundation framework.

The source code in this appendix (as with all the examples in this book) is also available from http://www.kochan-wood.com.

Recall that the Fraction class uses Object as its root object, whereas the AddressBook and AddressCard classes are Foundation classes and thus have NSObject as their roots.

The Fraction Class

Fraction Class Interface File

```
#import <objc/Object.h>

// Define the Fraction class

@interface Fraction : Object
{
```

```
    int  numerator;
    int  denominator;
}

-(Fraction *) initWith: (int) n: (int) d;

-(void) setNumerator: (int) n;
-(void) setDenominator:  (int) d;
-(void) setTo: (int) n over: (int) d;

-(int) numerator;
-(int) denominator;

-(void) reduce;
-(double) convertToNum;
-(void print;
@end

// Define the MathOps category

@interface Fraction (MathOps)
-(Fraction *) add: (Fraction *) f;
-(Fraction *) mul: (Fraction *) f;
-(Fraction *) sub: (Fraction *) f;
-(Fraction *) div: (Fraction *) f;
@end
```

Fraction Class Implementation File

```
#import "Fraction.h"
#import <stdio.h>

@implementation Fraction;

-(Fraction *) initWith: (int) n: (int) d
{
     self = [super init];
     if (self)
          [self setTo: n over: d];

     return self;
}

-(void) setNumerator: (int) n
{
     numerator = n;
}
```

```objc
-(void) setDenominator: (int) d
{
     denominator = d;
}

-(int) numerator
{
     return numerator;
}

-(int) denominator
{
     return denominator;
}

-(double) convertToNum
{
     if (denominator != 0)
          return (double) numerator / denominator;
     else
          return 0.0;
}

-(void) setTo: (int) n over: (int) d
{
     numerator = n;
     denominator = d;
}

- (void) reduce
{
     int  u = numerator;
     int  v = denominator;
     int  temp;

     if (u < 0)
          u = -u;

     while (v != 0) {
          temp = u % v;
          u = v;
          v = temp;
     }

     numerator /= u;
     denominator /= u;
}
```

```
-(void) print
{
     printf (" %i/%i ", numerator, denominator);
}
@end


// MathOps category implementation

@implementation Fraction (MathOps);
-(Fraction *) add: (Fraction *) f
{
     // To add two fractions:
     // a/b + c/d = ((a*d) + (b*c)) / (b * d)

     Fraction *result = [[Fraction alloc] init];
     int    resultNum, resultDenom;

     resultNum = (numerator * [f denominator]) +
       (denominator * [f numerator]);
     resultDenom = denominator * [f denominator];

     [result setTo: resultNum over: resultDenom];
     [result reduce];

     return result;
}

-(Fraction *) sub: (Fraction *) f
{
     // To sub two fractions:
     // a/b - c/d = ((a*d) - (b*c)) / (b * d)

     Fraction *result = [[Fraction alloc] init];
     int    resultNum, resultDenom;

     resultNum = (numerator * [f denominator]) -
       (denominator * [f numerator]);
     resultDenom = denominator * [f denominator];

     [result setTo: resultNum over: resultDenom];
     [result reduce];

     return result;
}
```

```
-(Fraction *) mul: (Fraction *) f
{
        Fraction *result = [[Fraction alloc] init];

        [result setTo: numerator * [f numerator]
              over: denominator * [f denominator]];
        [result reduce];

        return result;
}

-(Fraction *) div: (Fraction *) f
{
        Fraction *result = [[Fraction alloc] init];

        [result setTo: numerator * [f denominator]
              over: denominator * [f numerator]];
        [result reduce];

        return result;
}
@end
```

The AddressBook and AddressCard Classes

AddressCard Interface File

```
#import <Foundation/NSObject.h>
#import <Foundation/NSString.h>
#import <Foundation/NSArchiver.h>

@interface AddressCard: NSObject <NSCoding, NSCopying>
{
     NSString *name;
     NSString *email;
}

-(AddressCard *) initWithName: (NSString *) theName
                   andEmail: (NSString *) theEmail;

-(void) setName: (NSString *) theName;
-(void) setEmail: (NSString *) theEmail;
-(void) setName: (NSString *) theName andEmail: (NSString *) theEmail;
-(void) retainName: (NSString *) theName andEmail: (NSString *) theEmail;
```

```
-(NSString *) name;
-(NSString *) email;

-(NSComparisonResult) compareNames: (id) element;
-(void) print;
@end
```

AddressBook Interface File

```
#import <Foundation/NSArray.h>
#import "AddressCard.h"

@interface AddressBook: NSObject <NSCopying, NSCoding>
{
    NSString        *bookName;
    NSMutableArray *book;
}

-(id) initWithName: (NSString *) name;
-(void) setName: (NSString *) theName;
-(void) setBook: (NSArray *) theBook;

-(NSString *) bookName;
-(NSMutableArray *) book;

-(void) addCard: (AddressCard *) theCard;
-(void) removeCard: (AddressCard *) theCard;

-(AddressCard *) lookup: (NSString *) theName;

-(int) entries;
-(void) list;
-(void) sort;

@end
```

AddressCard Implementation File

```
#import "AddressCard.h"

@implementation AddressCard;

-(id) initWithName: (NSString *) theName andEmail: (NSString *) theEmail
{
  self = [super init];
```

```
      [self setName: theName andEmail: theEmail];
      return self;
}

-(void) setName: (NSString *) theName
{
   [name autorelease];
   name = [theName copy];
}

-(void) setEmail: (NSString *) theEmail
{
   [email autorelease];
   email = [theEmail copy];
}

-(void) setName: (NSString *) theName andEmail: (NSString *) theEmail
{
   [self setName: theName];
   [self setEmail: theEmail];
}

-(NSString *) name
{
   return name;
}

-(NSString *) email
{
   return email;
}

-(NSComparisonResult) compareNames: (id) element
{
   return [name compare: [element name]];
}
-(void) dealloc
{
   [name release];
   [email release];
   [super dealloc];
}

-(void) print
{
```

```
      printf ("====================================\n");
      printf ("| |                               \n");
      printf ("| %-31s |                          \n", [name cString]);
      printf ("| %-31s |                          \n", [email cString]);
      printf ("| |                               \n");
      printf ("| |                               \n");
      printf ("| |                               \n");
      printf ("|              O O |               \n");
      printf ("====================================\n");
}

-(void) encodeWithCoder: (NSCoder *) encoder
{
   if ( [encoder allowsKeyedCoding] ) {
      [encoder encodeObject: name forKey: @"AddressBookname"];
      [encoder encodeObject: email forKey: @"AddressBookemail"];
   } else {
      [encoder encodeObject: name];
      [encoder encodeObject: email];
   }
}

-(id) initWithCoder: (NSCoder *) decoder
{
   if ( [decoder allowsKeyedCoding] ) {
      name = [[decoder decodeObjectForKey: @"AddressBookname"] retain];
      email = [[decoder decodeObjectForKey: @"AddressBookemail"] retain];
   } else {
      name = [[decoder decodeObject] retain];
      email = [[decoder decodeObject] retain];
}

      return self;
}

-(AddressCard *) copyWithZone: (NSZone *) zone
{
  AddressCard *newCard = [[AddressCard allocWithZone: zone] init];

  [newCard retainName: name andEmail: email];
  return newCard;
}

-(void) retainName: (NSString *) theName andEmail: (NSString *) theEmail
{
  name = [theName retain];
  email = [theEmail retain];
}
@end
```

AddressBook **Implementation File**

```
#import "AddressBook.h"

@implementation AddressBook;

// set up the AddressBook's name and to an empty book

-(id) initWithName: (NSString *) name
{
  self = [super init];
  if (self != nil) {
    bookName = [name copy];
    book = [[NSMutableArray alloc] init];
        // cleanup if the book doesn't initialize
        if (book == nil) {
           [self autorelease];
           self = nil;
        }
  }
  return self;
}
-(void) setName: (NSString *) theName
{
  [bookName autorelease];

  bookName = [theName copy];
}

-(void) setBook: (NSArray *) theBook
{

  [book autorelease];
  book = [[NSMutableArray alloc] initWithArray: theBook];
}

-(void) addCard: (AddressCard *) theCard
{
  [book addObject: theCard];
}

-(NSMutableArray *) book
{
  return [book [mutableCopy autorelease]];
}

-(NSString *) bookName
{
  return [bookName [mutableCopy autorelease]];
}
```

```
-(void) removeCard: (AddressCard *) theCard
{
  [book removeObjectIdenticalTo: theCard];
}

-(void) sort
{
  [book sortUsingSelector: @selector(compareNames:)];
}


// lookup address card by name - returns 1st exact match

-(AddressCard *) lookup: (NSString *) theName
{
  AddressCard *nextCard;

  int  i, elements;

  elements = [book count];

  for ( i = 0; i < elements; ++i) {
    nextCard = [book objectAtIndex: i];

    if ( [[nextCard name] caseInsensitiveCompare: theName]
         == NSOrderedSame )
      return nextCard;
  }

  return nil;
}

-(int) entries
{
  return [book count];
}

-(void) list
{
  int    i;
  AddressCard *theCard;

  int    elements = [book count];

  printf ("\n======== Contents of: %s =========\n", [bookName cString]);
  for ( i = 0; i < elements; ++i ) {
    theCard = [book objectAtIndex: i];
    printf ("%-20s %-32s\n", [[theCard name] cString],
        [[theCard email] cString]);
  }
```

```
  printf ("====================================================\n\n");
}

-(void) dealloc
{
  [bookName release];
  [book release];
  [super dealloc];
}

// Methods for NSCoding protocol

-(void) encodeWithCoder: (NSCoder *) encoder
{
  if ( [encoder allowsKeyedCoding] ) {
    [encoder encodeObject:bookName forKey: @"AddressBook bookName"];
    [encoder encodeObject:book forKey: @"AddressBook book"];
  } else {
    [encoder encodeObject: bookName];
    [encoder encodeObject: book];
  }
}

-(id) initWithCoder: (NSCoder *) decoder
{
  if ( [decoder allowsKeyedCoding] ) {
    bookName = [[decoder decodeObjectForKey:
          @"AddressBook bookName"] retain];
    book = [[decoder decodeObjectForKey: @"AddressBook book"] retain];
  } else {
    bookName = [[decoder decodeObject] retain];
    book = [[decoder decodeObject] retain];
  }

  return self;
}


// Method for NSCopying protocol

-(AddressBook *) copyWithZone: (NSZone *) zone
{
  AddressBook *newBook = [[self class] allocWithZone: zone];

  [newBook initWithName: bookName];
  [newBook setBook: book];

  return newBook;
}
@end
```

Resources

THIS APPENDIX CONTAINS A SELECTIVE LIST of resources you can turn to for more information. Some of the information might be on your system, online at a Web site, or available from a book. We've compiled resources for the C language, Objective-C, Foundation programming, GNUStep, and Cocoa. The list here will give you a good starting point to help you locate whatever it is you're looking for. If you can't find what you need, send me an email at steve@kochan_wood.com and I'll try to help you.

Answers to Exercises, Errata, and so on

You can visit the Web site www.kochan-wood.com to get answers to exercises and errata (of course, there isn't any!) for this book. You'll also find an up-to-date resource guide there as well.

The Objective-C Language

Books

- *The Objective-C Programming Language.* Apple Computer, Inc., 2002—This is the best reference available on the Objective-C language and is a good book for you to read after completing this one. It is available as a .pdf file for downloading at http://developer.apple.com/documentation/Cocoa/Conceptual/ObjectiveC/ObjC.pdf.

  It is also available online in HTML format at http://developer.apple.com/documentation/Cocoa/Conceptual/ObjectiveC/index.html.

  If you have a Mac OS X system, this book is also installed on your hard drive in /Developer/Documentation/Cocoa/ObjectiveC/ObjC.pdf as a .pdf document and in //Developer/Documentation/Cocoa/ObjectiveC/index.html as an HTML document. Under Panther, the repsective paths are /Developer/Documentation/Cocoa/Conceptual/ObjectiveC/ObjC.pdf and /Developer/Documentation/Cocoa/Conceptual/ObjectiveC/index.html.

- *Object-Oriented Programming: An Evolutionary Approach, Second Edition*. Brad Cox and Andy Novobilski. Addison-Wesley, 1991—This is the original book about Objective-C, coauthored by the Brad Cox, the designer of the language.
- *Objective-C Pocket Reference*. Andrew M. Duncan. O'Reilly Associates Inc., 2003—This is a terse reference for the Objective-C language.

Web Sites

- `http://developer.apple.com/documentation/Cocoa/ ObjectiveCLanguage-date.html`—The part of the Apple Web site devoted to the Objective-C language. Contains, among other things, online documentation, sample code, and technical notes.
- `http://www.dekorte.com/Objective-C/`—This is a Web site with many useful links.

The C Programming Language

Because C is the underlying programming language, you might want to study it in more depth. The language has been around for more than 25 years, so there's certainly no dearth of information on the subject.

Books

- *Programming in ANSI C, Revised Edition*. Stephen Kochan. Sams Publishing, 1994—This is the first book I wrote (way back when), revised several times along the way. This is a tutorial, but it covers in greater detail many of the language features that were lumped together in Chapter 13, "Underlying C Language Features."
- *The C Programming Language*. Brian W. Kernighan and Dennis M. Ritchie. Prentice Hall, Inc., 1988—This has always been the bible as far as a reference for the language goes. It was the first book ever written about C and was cowritten by Dennis Ritchie, who created the language.
- *C: A Reference Manual, Fifth Edition*. Samuel P. Harbison III and Guy L. Steele, Jr. Prentice Hall, 2002—Another excellent reference book for C programmers.

Web Sites

- `www.kochan-wood.com`—At this Web site you'll find a new online edition of the book *Topics in C Programming*, which I wrote with Patrick Wood as a follow-up to my *Programming in ANSI C* tutorial.

The Foundation Framework

Mac OS X users have excellent Framework documentation already installed on their hard drives in the folder `/Developer/Documentation/Cocoa/Reference/ Foundation/Reference/ObjC_classic`. You can get an Acrobat `.pdf` version there, as well as an HTML version (open the file `FoundationTOC.html`, or `index.html` under Panther, in that folder). The same documentation is available online at the following Web sites.

Web Sites

- `http://www.gnustep.org/resources/documentation/base/Base.html`— This contains documentation for the GNUStep Foundation framework.
- `http://developer.apple.com/documentation/Cocoa/Reference/ Foundation/ObjC_classic/index.html#//apple_ref/doc/uid/ 20001091`—This contains Apple's online Foundation reference in HTML.
- `http://developer.apple.com/documentation/Cocoa/Reference/ Foundation/ObjC_classic/Foundation.pdf`—This is Apple's Foundation framework reference in `.pdf` format.

Cocoa

If you are serious about application development under Mac OS X, you'll need to learn how to program with Cocoa. Many books are available on Cocoa, with new ones being published all the time. You can type in "Cocoa" in the amazon.com search window and see what pops up. The following are just a few of the books available.

Books

- *Cocoa Programming.* Scott Anguish, Erik M. Buck, and Donald A. Yacktman. Sams Publishing, 2002—This is an impressive book of more than 1,200 pages that covers almost every aspect of Cocoa programming.
- *Cocoa Programming for Mac OS X.* Aaron Hillegass. Addison-Wesley, 2003—This is an excellent introduction to Cocoa written in an easy-to-read style.
- *Cocoa in a Nutshell.* Michael Beam and James Duncan Davidson. O'Reilly & Associates, Inc., 2003—This is a good reference resource for the many different classes and methods that are part of the Cocoa development system.
- *Learning Cocoa with Objective-C, Second Edition.* James Duncan Davidson and Apple Computer, Inc. O'Reilly & Associates, Inc., 2002—This is an introductory book on Cocoa programming.

Web Sites

- `http://developer.apple.com/cocoa/`—Apple's main Web site for Cocoa developers includes documentation, sample code, technical notes, and a wealth of information.
- `http://www.cocoadevcentral.com`—/This is a Web site designed to help people learn how to program in Cocoa with Objective-C.
- `http://www.cocoadev.com/`—This is an open Web site that can be edited by

anyone. There's a lot of good information to be found here.

Compilers and Development Environments

Following is a list of Web sites where you can download (for free!) Objective-C compilers and development environments, as well as obtain online documentation.

gcc

- `http://gcc.gnu.org/`—gcc is the free compiler developed by the Free Software Foundation. It's also used by Apple on its Mac OS X systems. You can download an Objective-C compiler from this Web site.

MinGW

- `http://www.mingw.org`—If you want to get started writing Objective-C programs in a Windows environment, you can get a GNU gcc compiler from here. Also consider downloading MSYS as an easy-to-use shell environment in which to work.

CygWin

- `http://www.cygwin.com`—CygWin provides a Linux-style environment that runs under Windows. You should note that the compiler distributed with CygWin does not by default support Objective-C.

GNUStep

- `http://www.gnustep.org`—You can download the GNUStep development environment here, which will enable you to compile and run all the program examples in this book, as well as develop your own.
- `http://www.gnustep.org/resources/documentation/manual_toc.html`— Here you'll find an online Objective-C and GNUStep programming manual.

LinuxSTEP

- `http://www.linuxstep.org`—According to the Web site, "LinuxSTEP is a (sp.) operating environment that is based on the concepts and ideas established in NeXTSTEP, OpenStep, and Mac OS X." You can get what you need here to compile and run Objective-C programs under Linux.

Index

C

E

F

How can we make this index more useful? Email us at indexes@samspublishing.com

H

for loops, 74-85
execution order, 77
nested, 82-84
terminal input, 80-82
variants, 84-85
while loops, 85-89
lowercaseString method, 326
lvalues, expressions, 477

M

Mac OS X development environment, Cocoa, 1
machine dependency, 48
macros, 232-233
operator and, 234
operator and, 235
#define statments and, 232-233
Macintosh
classes, NSPropertyListSerialization class, 427
compiling and
Project Builder, 10-15
Terminal window, 8-10
Foundation framework documentation, 308
OS X system
Cocoa, 156
Interface Builder, 458
Project Builder, 459
plists
old-style format, 429
traditional format, 429
XML format, 427
programs, Property List Editor program, 430
main function, 298
argc argument and, 298
argv argument and, 298
managing files. *See* **file management**
managing memory. *See* **memory management**
mantissa, floating-point values, 49
map tables, NSMapTable.h header file, 518
matrixes, 250
elements, 250
two-dimensional arrays and, 250
memory
addresses
indirection operator, 292
pointers and, 291–292
allocating, 156-157
autorelease pool, 399-400
cells, 291
leaking, 142

pool, autorelease pool, 317-320
releasing, 333-335
uses, 291
zones, NSZone.h header file, 520
memory management, 399
message expressions, 458, 501-502
as function calls, 301
message forwarding, 189
delegate, 189
NSInvocation.h header file, 517
Object class and, 189
messages, 26, 458
class message, 185
message expressions, 458
NSPort.h header file, 518
NSProtocolChecker.h header file, 519
methods, 458
adding to classes, 152-164
alloc, 37, 318
arguments, 34
local variables, 136
multiple, 130-135
no name, 133
arrays, passing, 258-259
arrayWithCapacity:, 337
arrayWithObjects:, 337
as functions, 301
categories, defining, 213
choosing correct, 151
class method, 27, 33-35, 456
accessing variables, 197
allocF class method, 197-199
count class method, 197-199
setting variables, 197
compare, 319
conformTo method, protocols and, 221
convertToNum, 97-99
copy method, 416-418, 425
custom archiving, 444-448
declarations, 35, 495-496
decoding methods, writing, 433-438
definition, 35
class definition, 497-498
protocols and, 220
deleteCharactersInRange:, 332
designated initializer, 456
doesNotRecognize method, 186
encoding methods, writing, 433-438
factory methods, 27, 457
free, overriding, 169-171
getter methods, 424-425

How can we make this index more useful? Email us at indexes@samspublishing.com